D1595645

The Sacred Cauldron

THE SACRED CAULDRON

Psychotherapy as a Spiritual Practice

Lionel Corbett

 CHIRON PUBLICATIONS • WILMETTE, ILLINOIS

Book and cover design by Marianne Jankowski.
Printed in the United States of America.

Library of Congress Cataloging-in-Publication Data
Corbett, Lionel.
    The sacred cauldron : psychotherapy as a spiritual
practice / Lionel Corbett.
        p. cm.
    Includes bibliographical references and index.
    ISBN 978-1-888602-51-7 (alk. paper)
    1. Psychotherapy--Religious aspects. I. Title.
RC489.S676C665 2011
616.89'14--dc22

                                                2010053804

to Raechel and Laura

CONTENTS

PREFACE *xi*

INTRODUCTION
Psychotherapy as a Sacred Activity *1*

ONE
Psychotherapy as a Spiritual Practice *19*

TWO
The Expression of the Sacred in Psychotherapy *49*

THREE
Faith, Love, Forgiveness, and Hope in Psychotherapy *85*

FOUR
A Psychological Approach to Spiritual Development *115*

FIVE
Psychotherapy as Care of the Soul *155*

SIX
Psychodynamics and Spirituality *189*

SEVEN
Psychotherapy as a Form of Spiritual Direction *221*

EIGHT
The Nondual Perspective in Psychotherapy *235*

NINE
Suffering and the Discovery of Meaning in Psychotherapy   *261*

References   *295*

Index   *317*

It is only through the psyche that we can establish that God acts upon us.

—C. G. JUNG, *ANSWER TO JOB*

PREFACE

The sacred cauldron of the title refers to the many analogies between psychotherapy and hexagram number 50 of the *I Ching*, "The Caldron." This image is part of a paradigm that deals with "skinning the old and grasping or founding the new." The text tells us that the old grounds for grief are departing and that we are to grasp renewal (Karcher 2003, p. 350). Fittingly, since the present work leans heavily on Jung's religious writing, this is the hexagram that Jung describes in his foreword to Wilhelm's translation of the *I Ching*. The cauldron is a sacred container which signifies connection to the spiritual dimension and to our ancestors. In antiquity it was used ritually to submit a question to the gods, asking about the right moment to act. Psychologically, the cauldron symbolizes the act of examining our situation deeply, "slowly turning and examining things" (ibid., p. 357), a cooking process that releases transformative energy and renewal. The image of the cauldron also suggests a mandate or fate conferred by heaven "that is also a duty or responsibility" (ibid., p. 356). If we follow Dourley's (1981) suggestion that the psyche is sacramental because it reveals the numinosum, then the practice of psychotherapy is a spiritual practice for both participants.

Psychotherapy as a Sacred Activity

This book makes a case for the idea that psychotherapeutic work has a sacred dimension. I suggest that to view psychotherapy as a spiritual practice is in keeping with its place in our cultural history and with the nature of the work. This is not a new idea; Bion (1979) suggested that psychoanalysis—and I would include psychotherapy in general—is located at the intersection of two axes, the medical and the religious. The medical axis is by far the most common one in the psychotherapy literature, but to associate psychotherapy exclusively with natural science does not do justice to the spiritual dimension of the therapeutic process. The importance of the spiritual axis has been taken seriously only by a recent generation of therapists.

I offer this book in the service of what Maslow calls "resacralization" (1971, p. 284), the notion that we can see the person from a spiritual perspective as well as developmentally, genetically, behaviorally, and psychodynamically. To acknowledge that there is a divine element within us, or that each individual is an expression of the Absolute, has implications for our attitude toward psychotherapy.

Many psychotherapists, and many people undergoing therapy, would like to be able to incorporate a spiritual dimension into their therapeutic work, but they are limited by the belief that traditional religions are the only form of spirituality available to them. This attitude ties them to preconceived ideas about spirituality and unconsciously colludes with theological ideas about the form the individual's spirituality *ought* to take, rather than trying to discern the form it *actually* takes. The psychotherapist is quite likely to be working with one of the many people who have a personal sense of the sacred which cannot be contained within traditional religious institutions.[1] Even if the person in therapy does belong to an established religious tradition, it is not uncommon for the therapist to hear that what goes on in church or temple has little connection to the person's daily life. This complaint is to be expected; the therapist works with suffering people, and our spirituality is not only evoked but also challenged by periods of emotional stress, exactly the situations that bring people into psychotherapy. At these times of life, one is most open to new forms of spirituality.

My thesis is that, especially for the religiously unaffiliated, psychotherapy is a valuable resource for addressing the spiritual questions that are likely to emerge when we suffer. At these moments, I suggest that there is no need to speak of psychotherapy and spirituality as if they were radically separate disciplines, because the spirit manifests itself by means of the psyche, producing soulful experience. This kind of spirituality is grounded in the body and in daily life and may have little to do with institutional religion.

This book makes the now-commonplace distinction between religion as an institution or a social entity, with prescribed beliefs and practices, and spirituality in a broader sense. This may mean a subjective, personal relationship with the sacred, understood in an individual way, or it may simply acknowledge a transpersonal dimension beyond everyday reality and the personal self (Zinnbauer et al., 1997). The nature of this dimension may not be clear; the word *transpersonal* might refer to the divine in a traditional sense, or it may acknowledge the presence of spiritual forces at work beyond human understanding. In its widest sense, one's spirituality may simply be one's personal way of dealing with life's ultimate questions, or whatever is of the highest value to the individual, in which case it may not involve any conscious intention to connect with the sacred (for a discussion of the pros and cons of these approaches, see Pargament 1997). Spirituality may also imply a certain quality of awareness rather than a particular belief system, perhaps an appreciation for the complexity of life and the connections between all its aspects. In some spiritual traditions, the quality of one's attention is considered to indicate the level of one's spiritual attainment. Given all these meanings, spirituality by its nature is not something that can be defined in rigorous or restricted terms.

What is common to these disparate approaches is that the individual's spirituality is emotionally important and allows the person to find meaning, depth, significance, and purpose in life. However, because spirituality is such an individual matter, institutional religion may not encourage one to practice the spirituality that comes naturally, so that today many people find that their spirituality is private and quite distinct from organized religion. The discovery of such an individual spirituality is not uncommon during the process of psychotherapy. Sometimes this involves helping a person free himself or herself from early religious conditioning that has produced excessive guilt or shame, and sometimes it involves the discovery of a sense of the sacred that may have little to do with the way in which the sacred is traditionally defined.

Although some traditional religionists worry that psychotherapy might disinhibit people to the point where they will behave in a shameless or irresponsible manner, this does not seem to be a side effect of the therapeutic process. Neither does the discovery of a personal sense of the sacred mean that one is distracted from social involvement and social responsibility, leaving nothing but a retreat to the inner world, as certain critics of psychotherapy have claimed. A personal spirituality may involve the discovery of a private myth of meaning, but that does not necessarily imply social withdrawal; in fact, such a discovery could make a major difference to the way one behaves in the world. Nor is there concern that the psychotherapeutic emphasis on the development of a healthy sense of self will deny the spiritual importance of selflessness. Indeed, with a firm sense of self that is able to tolerate painful affects, one is more likely to be able temporarily to put oneself aside in the service of others. Similarly, although psychotherapy tends to promote a personal sense of agency, this does not preclude spiritual surrender. Again, a firm sense of self may allow this surrender to occur more easily.

Some therapists who wish to practice with a spiritual sensibility are committed to a theistic religious tradition, such as Judaism or Christianity, which involves belief in a Supreme Being (the theistic view of human nature and its psychotherapeutic implications are well described by Richards and Bergin 2005). Other therapists who believe that there is a spiritual dimension to the person find traditional theism to be untenable, and for them the word *God* is problematic because it has so much baggage attached to it (so has the word *spiritual,* but there seems to be no adequate alternative). Fortunately, it is not necessary to import preexisting theological or theistic notions into psychotherapy. For example, the therapist may simply adhere to some version of the Perennial Philosophy (Huxley 1945), the broad notion that there is a spiritual reality or ground that affects our lives and consciousness, that there is something of the Absolute in us, and that we may contact or have intuitive knowledge of that level of reality. With this attitude, there is no need to adhere to traditional theistic images of the divine as a celestial entity, creator, and moral lawgiver who has a plan for the salvation of humanity. The psychotherapist who does not belong to a specific tradition can also ignore theological arguments between the traditions. To the spiritually uncommitted psychologist these arguments seem to be largely human projections onto the unknown. We need to take traditional beliefs into account only when they are important to the person with whom we work therapeutically.

For some therapists, it is enough to know from personal experience that the psyche has its own intrinsically spiritual dimensions, which can produce or mediate experiences of the sacred. These experiences may or may not correspond to the ways in which traditional religions tell us that the sacred appears.[2] A life dilemma may be addressed by attending to these levels of the psyche as they appear, for instance, in dreams. At least in the Jungian tradition, psychotherapy is thought to take place within the larger field of consciousness of the transpersonal Self, which affects the outcome of the work. In that tradition, our psychology cannot be radically separated from our spirituality, because the human personality has an archetypal or spiritual foundation as well as its developmental and human aspects. Accordingly, the therapist may simultaneously work psychologically and spiritually.

The therapist may be uneasy about acknowledging a spiritual dimension to his or her work, especially if his or her professional training was limited to a materialistic or reductionist approach to the psyche, whether this was cognitive-behavioral, biological, or psychodynamic. Yet, to suggest that psychotherapy is a spiritual practice is hardly a new idea. For millennia, physical and psychological healing was the province of shamans, medicine men and women, priests and priestesses (Ellenberger 1970; Bromberg 1975; Koenig, McCullough and Larson 2001). Often these were individuals who for many years were forced to deal with a serious and often unusual illness, either physical or mental, which they finally were able to overcome (Eliade 1951). During this time, the future shaman would be preoccupied with a search for the meaning of his or her illness. He or she would usually be able to fulfill ordinary social obligations but would suffer from a feeling of extreme isolation and preoccupation with the illness. Sometimes the individual would go through this period alone, at other times accompanied by a mentor. Finally, and often unexpectedly, this involuntary "creative illness" would resolve, and the individual would develop insights into the nature of spiritual reality. His or her personality would be permanently transformed by the experience, which in retrospect was seen to be a prolonged spiritual crisis that acted as an initiation into a healing vocation. As a result of intense suffering, these individuals' spiritual and psychological evolution had been accelerated, and they had developed the capacity to help others—they had become "wounded healers" (Jung 1951b, par. 239). Their illness was considered to be a "divine gift" which they did not wish for and sometimes actively resisted but which was imposed upon them (Lukoff 1985). In other words, some illnesses or prolonged periods of emotional distress can function as developmental experiences that result in greatly increased psychological and spiritual well-being. It is often the case that contemporary psychotherapists have had to struggle with their own difficulties as a preparation for the ability to help others. In the process, they develop spiritually, whether or not this happens consciously.

Emotional difficulties, or a burdensome daily life, can seriously call into question our sense of life's meaning and purpose. Problems such as despair, emptiness, hopelessness, and lack of connection to others are commonly expressed in psychotherapy, where the spiritual dimension of these difficulties can be discussed if both participants are open to this topic (Josephson and Wiesner 2004). A developed spiritual life is of great benefit in dealing with such questions, which tacitly or explicitly are often present when we suffer. Whereas some people emerge from a life crisis with their basic religious beliefs intact or even strengthened, others are forced to radically reevaluate their beliefs because they have not been helpful. The psychotherapist constantly sees people in such crises, which make us feel vulnerable and painfully aware of our limitations. These times of life are likely to make us think about ultimate concerns, about whether life is worth living, whether life is meaningful, whether the universe is "a tale told by an idiot" or the result of a supernal intelligence. I find that such questions may arise at any point in psychotherapy; occasionally they emerge in the first session, although they are more likely to appear later in the process, when the person has discovered that it is safe to discuss them. Even if one takes an atheistic existentialist position that life has a tragic aspect and has no particular meaning except whatever we choose to give it, this too is an attitude that can legitimately be addressed within the context of psychotherapy. Here it is important to note that the therapeutic approach is not trying to compete with religious traditions; rather, psychotherapy offers either a complementary or an alternative approach to suffering when the established religious traditions do not prove sufficiently helpful. Pargament (1997) points out that a common complaint about churches and synagogues is that their religious services and educational programs are often irrelevant to the problems of daily life.

In spite of the fact that suffering raises spiritual questions, for most of its modern history psychotherapists have been cautious about talking about spirituality. In an attempt to remain scientifically respectable, until recent years the prevailing Zeitgeist within mainstream psychology and psychiatry has been materialistic, reductionist, and positivistic. Many psychologists tried to ignore spirituality, which was considered to be something of an embarrassment or too difficult to study empirically. However, in the last few decades, literature has appeared that describes the integration of psychotherapy and spirituality, which is finally becoming a respectable topic of research (Richards and Bergin 2005; Miller 1999).

While the psychotherapist may think of emotional difficulties purely in terms of the psychology of the individual, for many people in therapy they are also important spiritual crises, indicating the inextricable connection between one's psychological makeup and one's spirituality. At the same time as the psychotherapist works with such difficulties with his or her psychological armamentarium, it is important to be aware of the spiritual concerns raised by emotional problems, because the discovery of meaning in suffering is of enormous help (Wong and Fry 1998). Our current models of treatment, although valuable, are far from perfect. The results of treating emotional difficulties with psychodynamic psychotherapy are only moderately good (Roseborough 2006), and the effects of cognitive-behavioral or pharmacological approaches are also mixed. Using these latter approaches in the treatment of major depression, good results are achieved in only 65 percent of people who receive active treatment, while up to 45 percent of untreated patients improve (Walsh et al. 2002). Many people who initially benefit from treatment have a recurrence of their depression within the next three years (Fava, Rafanelli, Grandi, Conti and Belluardo 1998). This is not to mention the persistence of low-level distress, inadequate satisfaction with life, and the absence of positive emotions in many people who have been treated for emotional difficulties, all of which correlate with increased mortality and morbidity (Huppert and Whittington 2003). The average level of life satisfaction in the general population has not improved as a result of the introduction of psychotropic medications in the 1950s (Myers and Diener 1996).

The assumption that emotional distress is nothing more than a brain problem or the result of learned cognitive distortions is a subtle cultural promotion of materialism, which ignores the spiritual dimension of the personality and the spiritual questions raised by emotional difficulties. The discovery of a personal spirituality may make an important contribution in this area, and I hope to show that this discovery can be seamlessly incorporated into standard psychotherapy.

Increasingly, therapists are acknowledging the importance of health and happiness and the positive aspects of human experience (Seligman and Csikszentmihalyi 2000; Linley and Joseph 2004; Cloninger 2004), and surely this would include our spiritual lives. This focus promises to improve the quality of life and prevent the emotional distress that occurs when life seems empty and meaningless. It is increasingly recognized that an exclusive focus on psychopathology gives us a distorted view of the personality. In psychotherapy, positive feelings and personality attributes such as creativity, hope, wisdom, courage, and a spiritual life can no longer be taken for granted. Neither can they be dismissed as derivatives of "deeper" emotional dynamics, as some of the classical psychoanalysts suggested. A direct focus on positive emotions and those character traits that foster well-being improves happiness in daily life (Emmons and McCullough 2003) and reduces disability in people suffering from various emotional disorders (Seligman 2002; Fava, Rafanelli, Cazzaro, Conti and Grandi 1998; Fava et al. 2005). Similarly, a useful spirituality not only helps us cope with adversity, it fosters a sense of peace, tolerance, and kindness toward oneself and others. The operative word here is "useful," since a spirituality that is imposed on the individual by tradition or a hierarchy, especially when it is inimical to the individual's character structure, can only be a source of guilt and resentment. To be useful, one's spirituality has to be authentic, which means it has to arise organically from the depth of one's being; it cannot be imposed by a tradition when the teachings of the tradition do not match the personality of the individual. This problem may enter the psychotherapeutic process when it proves difficult for the individual to let go of his or her childhood religious conditioning, which happens because various religious traditions instill the notion that to deviate from their teaching is sinful and will be punished by God. Since the tradition has defined what is sinful, it offers the medicine for an illness that its own doctrines have created, causing untold suffering, for example, around sexuality. There are many spiritual square pegs trying to force themselves into traditional round holes.

Traditional Judeo-Christian believers may object that a personal rather than a collective spirituality is merely subjectively constructed and not the result of divine revelation. However, who is to say from whence our subjectivity arises? What is the origin of our sense of meaning and purpose in life? A spirituality that seems on the surface to be a personal construction may actually arise from the soul's deepest intimation of connection to the sacred. However it arises, such a personal spirituality is often more helpful than a set of imposed beliefs. The therapist can foster this development by encouraging the persons with whom he or she works to value their inner lives. Increasing consciousness and self-awareness, often induced by the kind of suffering that is the daily fare of psychotherapy, foster the development of a relationship to the transpersonal dimension.

There are universal accounts of mystical experiences that allow us to infer the existence of a transcendent reality. These accounts of contact with the sacred do not prove its existence to the satisfaction of the skeptic, but the "God hypothesis" is a reasonable approach to these phenomena. They are so consistent across time and geography that they must be taken into account by the student of human psychology. As a discipline, psychology cannot avoid attention to sacred experiences, although the psychologist cannot prove that they are experiences of a transpersonal dimension. In any case, this book takes the position that sacred experience appears to the individual in the way that any other experience appears, as something given. It may have a sensory quality, or it may simply feel like a sense of presence. What matters in the therapeutic setting is that the individual takes the experience to be one of the sacred. The psychotherapist is interested in the subjective experience of the person with whom he or she works. To reiterate, we do not need to commit ourselves to the God-image of traditional theism. Furthermore, when we take the unconscious into account, no theological statement can be taken at face value; the doctrine, dogma, and liturgy to which we are attracted can have implications that tell us something about the psychology of the individual believer.

In this book, it will be obvious that I do not subscribe to notions that consciousness or the psyche can be entirely reduced to the workings of the brain (Chalmers 1996; Kandel, Schwartz and Jessell 2008). Within mainstream psychiatry and psychology, there is still a strong current of materialistic reductionism that tries to attribute the cause of all human experience to brain mechanisms.

Much of our academic culture still insists that only that which can be grounded in material explanation is absolutely real. A strictly materialist viewpoint is particularly common among people with a scientific education, which sometimes makes them embarrassed to admit that they have a spiritual life, as if it were something shameful. Yet, to believe that human beings are nothing more than a biological accident in an indifferent, purely material universe may be emotionally unsettling, even for those with a robust constitution. For most people in this situation whose lives have become difficult, the sense that there is nothing to rely on except a combination of luck and human resources predisposes them to depression, anxiety, loneliness, or despair. These emotions ravage the body and mind. Even violence in such a situation becomes understandable because life has no particular value and one's rage at life may be displaced onto other human beings. Given this situation, it is no accident that antidepressants and tranquillizers of all kinds are so popular.

Such an individual may enter psychotherapy, at which time it is often a shock to the committed materialist to consciously experience the spiritual dimension in the form of a mystical experience, a powerful dream, or a synchronistic event that defies rational, materialistic explanation. I describe some of these types of events in chapter 2. Suffice it to say here that such an experience can be healing, which is why Jung writes that "the approach to the numinous [the experience of divinity] is the real therapy" (1973–1975, vol. 1, p. 377). Often, people can see no way out of materialism until they have such an experience, because today no one has any use for arguments from authority. While there are no logical proofs of the existence of a spiritual realm, a direct experience of the sacred or the holy *is* convincing to the one who experiences it. Even though the experience is not absolute proof of the existence of this realm, such experience acts to moisten a dry soul and has important psychological benefits, such that recognizing and affirming the value of sacred experience is an important part of psychotherapeutic practice. This attitude would not satisfy a psychologist committed to a positivistic, strictly empirical approach to reality nor would it convince a traditional psychoanalyst who is convinced that religion is merely defensive. Nevertheless,

I am committed to the idea that spiritual experience gives us an intimation of a real dimension of reality, albeit awareness that is filtered through our own minds and limitations. As well as the evidence of our own experience, discoveries such as nonlocality and the uncertainty principle in quantum physics undermine a purely rational, materialistic metaphysics.[3] Yet such is the hold of materialism in the academy that only now, after years of being marginalized, is the unconscious making a comeback in academic circles—but only because it is now established that the brain contains circuits that operate unconsciously to influence behavior. The fact that it has become possible to correlate certain psychodynamic principles to studies of brain function has caused some excitement, as if the profession needed this discovery to confirm the existence of the unconscious or to revitalize our interest in it (Mancia 2006).[4] From a neurobiological point of view, the unconscious is simply an evolutionary development in the human brain that helps the organism survive by allowing very rapid reactions to environmental challenges, without the necessity for consciousness which would react more slowly. The main value of consciousness is to increase our repertoire of possible responses to a problem, especially when the problem is a novel one that is not part of our innate pattern of responses. In this purely brain-based model of human behavior, emotions evolved to increase or decrease the probability of certain behaviors (Rolls 2005). Because emotions seize the attention of consciousness, they allow unconscious processes to modulate conscious behavior in response to an environmental challenge. Thus, if we are angry about an event, we are likely to deal with it assertively; if we are afraid, we are likely to be careful, and so on. Contrast this approach to the unconscious and to emotions with that of Jung, for whom consciousness is one of the great natural mysteries. For him, the unconscious means the unknown; it has spiritual dimensions, and emotions are an experience of spirit in the body.

Even among schools of psychotherapy that once based themselves on empirical, evidence-based science, it is increasingly recognized that the spiritual dimension of the person must be taken into account (Tan and Johnson 2002; D'Souza and Rodrigo 2004). There are now attempts to enhance cognitive-behavioral psychotherapy by helping people develop spiritually, using an approach that applies interventions based on the principles of psychobiology (Cloninger 2004). At the other end of the psychotherapeutic spectrum, a purely depth psychological approach to spirituality prefers to let the transpersonal psyche speak for itself. In the Jungian tradition this means paying close attention to dreams, to synchronistic events, and to numinous experiences.

Mainstream Judaism and Christianity focus much more on worship services, ritual practices, scripture reading, and moral behavior than they do on an examination of the inner life by means of dreams and the imagination, which have become the province of depth psychology. Among contemporary monotheistic traditions, the lack of attention to the psyche contributes to the attraction many Westerners have toward Eastern meditative approaches, which are complex methods of studying consciousness. These methods are based on a very different worldview than that found in the West. They tend to deal with consciousness itself as experienced in meditation, rather than paying attention to the contents of consciousness as they arise in the form of symptoms, emotional problems, relationships, and dream imagery.

In the Jungian model of the psyche, human consciousness is permeated with and structured by spiritual elements (Corbett 1996; Corbett 2007). Therefore, by attending to our psychology, depth psychology can provide a specifically Western form of yoga, a way of connecting with the divine. However, the spontaneous imagery produced by the psyche may or may not take a specifically Christian form, which may account for some of the traditional wariness of spontaneous mystical experience found in that tradition. The established churches are not entirely comfortable with the possibility of an immediate experience of the sacred, since the experience may contradict received doctrine.

The contemporary disregard for spontaneous manifestations of the psyche is also, in part, the result of the adoption by medieval Christian thinkers of the thinking of Aristotle, who believed that we do not have direct contact with the spiritual realm. Rather, we experience reality through the five senses and by means of reason. The Enlightenment followed by the scientific revolution further denied the existence of a nonmaterial world. A rational, scientific worldview gradually overtook theological explanations of reality, and religions have been fighting a rearguard action ever since— witness the current debates about evolution.

For all these reasons, contemporary mainstream Christianity tends to stress worship and faith rather than inner work such as attention to dreams. Yet early Christianity clearly saw dreams as messages from the spiritual realm—for example, a dream of Joseph reported in the Gospel of Matthew warned him to escape from Herod, and another dream told him that Jesus was conceived of the Holy Spirit. Today, however, especially the fundamentalist tradition prefers to rely on an examination of the Bible rather than an examination of one's dreams. However there is nothing unchristian about dream work if one accepts the ancient idea of "dreams sent by God" as a form of revelation (Sanford 1951).

Because our Western religious traditions neglect the psyche, it is not surprising that so many people turn to a depth psychological approach to the inner life. In the Jungian tradition, experiences of the unconscious are considered to be important spiritual indicators. Rather than locating the divine in some transcendent realm, Jung locates it deeply within our own subjectivity, as an inner experience at least mediated by, or possibly even identical with, transpersonal levels of the psyche. Working within this paradigm, individuals who pay attention to material from the unconscious, especially its transpersonal levels, are working spiritually. Since the psyche is a medium for the experience of the divine, as Dourley (1981) points out, the psyche is sacramental. To me this means that to work psychotherapeutically with the individual's dreams and complexes is to work with sacred text. The individual's life story is a sacred story.

I realize that to think of psychotherapy in this way will be troubling to those who wish to keep this discipline separate from spirituality. However, I believe that the tradition of depth psychology, now more than a century old, is mature enough to contain a spiritual attitude. To add a spiritual dimension to psychotherapy is a logical outgrowth of our experiences of the transpersonal levels of the psyche that occur in psychotherapeutic work. By focusing on this aspect of the work, I am not advocating a new religion, but a spiritual attitude articulated with a psychological language.

Even though some truths are eternal, they can be spoken of in new ways. New approaches to the spiritual dimension regularly appear within human history, and they always carry the risk of insisting that the new way is the only way. The psychotherapist guards against the danger of such inflation by letting the psyche speak for itself, by following its lead and not imposing any kind of preconceived dogmas onto our practice. The only assumption we make is that there is a spiritual dimension of the psyche which shows up in psychotherapeutic work. This attitude seems to be a reasonable development of the psychotherapeutic endeavor, and development is essential to prevent stagnation. Unless we allow the field to evolve organically, we will remain caught between the need for an institutional container for the work, for the purposes of training and professionalism, and the risk that, like all institutions, the container will eventually become rigid and harmful to the spirit of the work. This happens when the institution becomes preoccupied with the details of its regulation rather than with the soulful qualities of its practitioners.

It is obvious that our religious traditions contain a great deal of spiritual wisdom, and each of them contributes to our understanding of human spirituality. The problem for any new approach to spirituality is to discern which aspects of the traditional approaches are still relevant. The traditions all claim to have the final truth, and they would claim that their approach has been developed and refined over a long period of time, whereas a psychological approach to spirituality is too new to rely on. However, the reality is that our Western religious traditions mainly deal with the conscious mind and conscious behavior. They simply are not equipped to deal with the unconscious, which is a new discovery in historical terms. Our spiritual forbears who developed our religious traditions were not aware of the existence of the unconscious in the sense that we understand it. If it is true that spiritual experience is mediated by means of the unconscious, a fact that has been recognized at least since William James, a depth psychological approach to spirituality is logical. Neither were the founders of our religious traditions aware of quantum reality, and psychologists have barely touched the implications of that discovery for our understanding of the psyche.

One of Jung's major contributions is to point out the reality of the psyche as a domain in its own right. I suggest that the psyche and the spiritual dimension of reality are not two different things, just as some of the Eastern religious traditions see consciousness or transcendent mind as an ultimate, irreducible principle of reality. This approach seems appealing because the alternative is that the psyche and spiritual reality are different dimensions of reality but with a consistent relationship to each other, in which case we run into the problem of explaining how they interact with each other.

Since I believe that psychology and spirituality are different approaches to the same reality, there is no need to synthesize them, so I do not use terms such as *psycho-spiritual* or *spiritual psychology*, which are attempts to join the two fields at the level of language. There is no need reconcile or unite that which is already a whole. The distinction between psychology and spirituality is as arbitrary as a line on a map dividing two countries.

This book recommends an approach to spirituality based largely on experience rather than received teachings. Our spirituality then has a chance to breathe and evolve and is not confined to rigid forms of expression. Of course it is possible that we will misinterpret spiritual experiences, but all our religious traditions are based on some form of interpretation. The psychotherapist who accepts Jung's notion that the psyche has an innate religious function assumes that revelation continues, that the divine manifests itself by means of the psyche, and that there are transpersonal elements active within the therapy room. The psychotherapist who is aware of this presence listens with a different sensibility and sees the situation with different eyes, because the material that emerges has both psychological and spiritual value.

A NOTE ON TERMINOLOGY

Throughout this book, to avoid using the words *patient* or *client* I use the term *person* as a shorthand way of referring to the person in psychotherapy. I also take the position that there is no difference between psyche and soul, so that to explore the psyche is a form of soul work.

I use terms such as *the unconscious, spiritual essence,* and *Self* for the sake of convenience and because they are conventional. I do not use these words to imply some kind of entity, as if they are God-terms in psychological dress, or as a disguised way of importing traditional theism into psychotherapy. I use this language in order to talk about what the therapist experiences. Similarly, although I speak of the sacred as if it were somehow a separate dimension, I do so only for the sake of clarity. If we have eyes to see it, the sacred is not separate from the everyday world.

NOTES

1. In various polls, about 90 percent of Americans say they believe in the existence of God or a universal spirit. See www.religioustolerance.org/godpoll.htm. Religion overall remains a potent social force in the United States, although much less so in Europe. Overall, membership in mainline Catholic and Protestant denominations is declining, but adherence to Baptist, evangelical, and Eastern religions is increasing.

2. I'm assuming here that no matter what we think we know about the divine, or what we have been told by theologians committed to particular traditions, any list of qualities such as God as one or God as love is only meaningful when we personally experience the divine in these ways. Meister Eckhart prayed "God save me from God" because he wanted to avoid preconceived ideas of God. For him, God is not only presence but absence; not only being but nothing; not only ground but abyss, and so on. Neither is there any need to refer to the divine by any particular name.

3. In classical physics, particles influence each other because they are affected by information traveling between them. This information must travel at a speed that cannot be faster than the speed of light. Also, for classical physics, a cause must always happen before its effects, so reality is local. Quantum physics describes a nonlocal level of reality in which quantum connected particles change instantaneously, apparently with no time for information to travel between them, unless that information travels faster than the speed of light. At the level of quantum reality the universe seems to be an undivided whole. The uncertainty principle in quantum physics states that it is impossible to simultaneously measure both the exact position and the exact momentum of a particle. This means that classical determinism—the notion that the future can be predicted based on past conditions—is untenable at this level of reality.

4. In 1996 a group of Italian neurophysiologists discovered "mirror neurons," a group of nerve cells whose activity correlates with the experience of empathy for other people. These neurons fire when the individual is observing someone performing a particular action, as if one is looking into a mirror watching oneself performing the actions (Gallese et al.1996). This is obviously a very important brain system for social behavior, because it correlates with our ability to understand other people empathically.

Psychotherapy as a Spiritual Practice

The attitude of the psychotherapist is infinitely more important than the theories and methods of psychotherapy.

—C. G. JUNG, "PSYCHOTHERAPISTS OR THE CLERGY,"

CW II, PAR. 537

Spiritual questions may arise during psychotherapy because suffering, loss, trauma, and substance abuse tend to make us examine and question our beliefs (Fallot and Heckman 2005). Suffering and other existential problems raise questions that cannot be solved by the methods of empirical psychology; these problems take the therapist beyond the textbooks and make us respond out of who we are. Confronted with suffering all day, it is helpful if the therapist has thought about this problem in its larger spiritual context. We might think of suffering as the result of karma, as a divine mystery, or as plain bad luck, part of the tragic side of life. Whatever our attitude to suffering, when we try to make sense of it in this larger context we slip beyond the technical aspects of psychotherapy into spirituality. The therapist's response to suffering is inevitably colored by his or her metaphysical commitments, so it is important that the therapist is conscious of them. There are metaphysical assumptions behind our personal theory of therapy, our view of the person, our view of the good life, the nature of good and evil, and

19

our notion of psychological health. Whether we view psychological problems in terms of brain chemistry, learned behavior, developmental dynamics, sin, or emotional conflict, our spirituality is implicit in our attitude to these questions (Albee 2000).[1]

Many people cope with life-threatening situations using a religious form of coping. During a personal crisis, it is common to hear people declare that the situation has some spiritual value or meaning. Then, because of a spiritual appraisal of the situation, what would otherwise be unbearable becomes meaningful. Traditional believers may use off-the-shelf religious explanations for tragedy, such as the notion that the painful event happened as a test of faith or for some larger purpose. These attempts at reframing may be deeply satisfying. For many people in psychotherapy, however, traditional explanations of suffering are inadequate. What we have been told to believe by an institutional religion may not be helpful when suffering erupts. Under stress, many people lose or at least question their faith; in the presence of serious illness, this may even become a risk factor for death (Albaugh 2003; Oxman, Freeman and Manheimer 1995). Thus a new approach is necessary, especially since we know from empirical research that a positive spiritual attitude tends to have a beneficial effect on health and happiness (Koenig, McCullough and Larson 2001) and helps one to cope with adversity, just as adversity may deepen one's spirituality.

Spirituality becomes particularly important when we suffer because it helps us to cope and find some significance in what we are going through. In the broadest sense of the word, everyone has a spirituality of some kind, although not necessarily belief in a traditional image of God. Essentially, our spirituality is our personal myth, our way of understanding the nature of things. Our spirituality is reflected in our values, in the ways we pursue significance, and sometimes in a sense that there is an unseen, subtle realm of existence that orders our lives. We express our spirituality in our relationship to that level, in our sense of mystery, in our aesthetic sense, and in our attitude to death. Our spirituality also involves knowing ourselves as deeply as possible. In some spiritual traditions the quality of the individual's attention is considered to be an indicator of his or her level of spiritual attainment. Needless to say, all of these factors are intimately connected to our character structure and to the ways in which we maintain the cohesion of the personality and deal with fragmentation anxiety.

The boundary between organized religion and spirituality is fuzzy, but typically we use the term *spirituality* to mean an individual or private sense of the sacred, rather than an institutional approach that adheres to particular doctrine and dogma, a defined system of theology, prescribed rituals, and so on. In these postmodern times, there is a general mistrust of claims of universal truth. We are skeptical of religious authorities who have lost their moral authority. Some of us no longer believe in absolute standards of morality and behavior. Many of us are interested in finding our own truth rather than being told what the Truth is, and psychotherapy is one avenue for exploring this issue.

It is sometimes countered that a personal spirituality divorced from a religious institution can become too idiosyncratic or even dangerous, not accountable to the community, too self-centered, and a way of avoiding the difficult aspects of consistent spiritual practice. However, institutional religion is a mixed blessing; in its positive aspects, it satisfies what seems to be an intrinsic human need for connection to something more or to a transcendent level of reality. Religions respond to profound questions of meaning and to our sense of finitude and mortality. However, it is also true that many people have become alienated from institutionalized religion because they see it as divisive, too aligned with politics, often intolerant, sometimes justifying violence, and often not particularly spiritual. The sexual and financial scandals that regularly emerge among the clergy do nothing to convince the skeptics that religion is effective in changing behavior. Religion is legitimately criticized on the grounds that it causes wars, marginalizes people, and in some sectors promotes homophobia, racism, and the religious inferiority of women. Ironically, although our religions traditionally offered solutions to life's existential dilemmas, they now create these dilemmas for many people. Individuals who see religion in this light often feel that they have no institutional way of channeling their own spiritual sensibility, which for them becomes a personal pursuit.

If we acknowledge the presence of a spiritual reality operating in our lives, there are no problems that are purely psychological or purely spiritual; all difficult life situations are a mixture of both. Problems such as alienation, isolation, chronic pain, a sense that life is empty, or the inability to relate to others or to fulfill one's potential are simultaneously spiritual and psychological problems. Our spirituality is revealed by our attitude to these existential difficulties and our suffering. The therapist may see extreme examples of this combination, for example, in the case of a severely depressed person who believes he is being punished by God for a peccadillo committed earlier in his life. As I will discuss in chapter 2, the psychodynamic origins of such a punitive God-image can often be understood in terms of early relationships and may become grist for the therapeutic mill. In such a situation, the spiritual and psychological dimensions of that person's life are inextricably linked in his mind.

When people are asked to articulate their spiritual beliefs, they often repeat elements of doctrine and dogma that have been internalized from parents, Sunday school lessons, and sacred texts. These beliefs are often mainly cognitive, without much emotional content, part of our personal narrative. It is axiomatic, however, that the sacred cannot be captured by this kind of conceptual thought. Our real spirituality is often based on a subtle body sense, an indefinable feeling or a sense of presence whose exact content is not clear. We may be unable to articulate, or we may be unconscious of, our authentic spirituality and our connection to the transcendent level that lies beyond thought.

Spiritual experience is an emotional experience, and emotion is embodied. Although the monotheistic traditions have largely downplayed the importance of the body, we often feel a spiritual presence in the form of body energy.[2] It sometimes happens during the course of psychotherapy that the therapist senses this subtle presence as a kind of somatic insight or bodily knowing. Often this is a shared experience, when each person feels the same sensation as the two bodies resonate with each other. This resonance may occur whether we are talking about psychological or spiritual material. Limbic system resonance goes on all the time between people (Lewis, Amini and Lannon 2000), and in the course of important relationships our autonomic nervous systems and body postures tend to coordinate. Facial expression, body posture, and tone of voice are all important and so subtle that they are often registered only unconsciously. The discernment of the other person's spirituality is often mediated by this level of the somatic unconscious and a somatic level of empathy, which is facilitated if the therapist maintains a body posture of receptivity and an awareness of any muscular tensions or other sensations that might emerge as the conversation goes on.

Sometimes, the individual's real spirituality is a deeply held secret. It may not be articulated in therapy even when it is present, but it may be operating behind the scenes. The therapist often encounters a type of spirituality that is not centered on a personal God. It may occur in relationships, in creativity, through dreams, the body, in service to others, or in the natural world. Unfortunately, many people repress their spirituality when it does not coincide with what they have been told to expect. Whatever form one's spirituality takes, the notion that the universe is meaningful and we can rely on a larger intelligence may be helpful in difficult life situations. For the psychotherapist, such inner knowing, or the memory of a personal experience of the sacred, is helpful in allowing us to be with a person's suffering without being overwhelmed. This ability does not airily assume that the suffering is somehow "good" for the person. On the contrary, we feel his or her suffering deeply. In these situations, as Jung puts it, "soul must work on soul" (1928a, par. 544). A spiritual orientation helps the therapist tolerate being with someone in great pain, and to do so becomes a spirituality of presence in its own right.

When sitting with a suffering person, the therapist's metaphysical commitments affect what he or she believes about the problem. Some therapists will assume that the individual's suffering is the result of random misfortune, while others will feel that the pain is part of this individual's destiny and must be the way it is because there is a larger intelligence at work. That type of acceptance is a form of transcendence, but not transcendence in the sense of otherworldly avoidance.

The healing potential of suffering can be realized in the setting of a containing therapeutic relationship. The therapeutic container is essential, especially when the person with whom we work has lost faith in life. Even when the therapist believes that a transpersonal process is going on, to look for meaning in the midst of a painful life situation is very demanding for both people. The search for meaning is in stark contrast with approaches that simply try to get rid of symptoms as expediently as possible. Perhaps here it is worth remembering that our traditional role models, such as Moses, Jesus, Mohammed, and the Buddha, all had to go through great difficulties before they finally found a clear sense of direction. They did so individually, often swimming against the tide of the mainstream, guided by their own spiritual sense rather than by following an established line of belief.

All religious traditions offer some response to the problem of suffering and try to offer a way of helping people find meaning in the face of suffering. Many empirical studies have shown that a spiritual attitude to suffering may help people to cope with it (Jenkins and Pargament 1988). Religion allows traditional believers to reframe or reappraise their situation by saying things like "this situation is a test of my faith" or "it is intended to strengthen me; it is part of God's plan," and so on. For some Christians, to suffer is to participate in the suffering of Jesus, or it is a challenge to grow spiritually. These kinds of appraisals can be helpful, and they act as a buffer when we are in distress. However, religious appraisals can be a mixed blessing. Some religious explanations for suffering see it as punishment for sin, thus adding guilt to the suffering. Usually, such appraisal correlates with the introjection of harsh, judgmental parents. Certain religious beliefs, such as the conviction of personal sinfulness, add to the individual's stress level. In such a case, the therapeutic task is to soften a harsh superego projected onto a punitive God-image, as in "I must have done something to deserve this." The psychotherapeutic transformation of character traits and longstanding, deeply held beliefs, values, and self-image may lead to a concomitant transformation of the individual's spirituality. The person in therapy realizes that he has been projecting parental imagoes onto his image of the divine and is able to withdraw these projections. However, characterological rigidity, which is often accompanied by rigid theological beliefs, may not yield to our best efforts. I saw an extreme example of this attitude in the case of a woman who was so convinced that her cancer was a divine punishment that she refused all medical treatment and allowed herself to die.

Fortunately, therapists do not need to restrict themselves to a specific traditional response to the problem of suffering. One can find a response to suffering within psychotherapy itself, in various ways. Sometimes the relationship with the therapist is enough to sustain the person during a painful period of life. Having an empathic witness to one's suffering is sometimes enough to help one cope with it. The therapist may join with the person in the pursuit of personal meaning by attending to material emerging from the unconscious, which is an important source of spiritual experience. As Jung pointed out, the psyche has an intrinsic religious function which may produce imagery that is independent of established religious traditions (1944, par. 14). Meaning can arise from direct contact with transpersonal levels of the psyche, as an experience of the sacred, which is described in chapter 4. This happens in the form of dreams, synchronistic events, and visions that allow us to see that there is an intelligence guiding the process.

Everyday psychological problems, if looked into deeply enough, are found to have profound spiritual implications. The sacred is nested in the ordinary. For example, one might find that someone who consistently overworks does so as a way of distracting himself from a fear of death or because he finds life essentially pointless—these are spiritual as well as psychological problems. A woman tells me she has been fear-driven all her life. Her mother was extremely anxious, and as a child both parents gave her the message that the world is a dangerous place, so she did not feel protected. The fact that she was sexually abused as a child confirmed her worst fears. At the same time as she is so fearful, she is a devout Christian and believes she is cared for by a loving God. The spiritual problem embedded in the personal material is the problem of understanding how she can feel so afraid while also feeling protected by God. Another woman, because of a strict religious upbringing and harsh internal objects, feels that she must be self-sacrificing to the point of exhaustion and is not allowed any joy of her own. She believes that if she does anything for herself, she is selfish. Virtue is connected only to privation. She fears that if she does not sacrifice herself, or if she gives to herself, she will be condemned to spend eternity in a painful state. This kind of material shows the seamless interaction between developmental difficulties and a person's spirituality. When we address this type of spiritual belief in psychotherapy in the light of the individual's psychology, the work opens into spiritual practice.

People need to feel safe to be able to talk about spiritual beliefs in therapy because these beliefs feel private, and people are afraid they will be shamed by a skeptical therapist. Spiritual material will not emerge if the person senses that the therapist is not open to it. Sometimes people feel it is inappropriate to mention spiritual beliefs in therapy, but they may give clues about their beliefs that the therapist can attend to or ignore; the person may say "I prayed for this" or "I deserve to be punished" or "it's all happening for a reason" or "it's in the hands of God." The therapist can use this type of remark as an opening to discuss spiritual material—for example, by asking, "What does being in God's hands mean to you?" If there is no such opening, one might simply ask what helps the person during times of crisis, or whether he or she has any spiritual beliefs. Sometimes it is a relief for people to discuss this topic, for example, when a person believes that his or her difficulties are a punishment for sin. In such situations the person's spirituality has been colored by a harsh superego, and softening the inner critic will affect the person's belief system.

Spirituality now appears with increasing frequency in the psychotherapy literature (Sperry and Shafranske 2005; Cornett 1998; Peteet 1994). Various measures of religiosity, religious commitment, and the spiritual effects of psychotherapy have appeared (Richards and Bergin 2005, pp. 232–49), although it should be noted that these measures tend to be biased in favor of a theistic approach to spirituality. This development is not surprising; one cannot deal with themes such as sexuality, death, and aging without including the broader perspective of a particular worldview, which is frequently connected to one's spirituality. Even therapists who are not personally interested in spirituality recognize that it may be important to ask about the person's religious beliefs, since these are aspects of the whole person. It is worth trying to understand the core beliefs of the person's tradition and scriptures, for various reasons. These beliefs may contribute strongly to moral conflicts, such as those about abortion or marriage, and they may add to the person's shame or guilt. The individual's belief system tells us something about his or her intrapsychic structures, because what we believe about reality often reflects our internal world.

Some practitioners make a formal spiritual assessment part of their initial interview; they believe they need to elicit this information since it may not emerge spontaneously.[3] They ask direct questions such as: "Do you have religious beliefs that help you in a crisis?" "What gives your life meaning?" "Do you believe in a supreme being?" "What are you grateful for?" "Are you part of a religious community that supports you?" It is especially important to ask whether spirituality is important to the person if he or she says something like "I've lost all faith in God," which may indicate a depression. The therapist could also ask about the God-image that was taught in Sunday school compared to the way in which the individual actually experiences the divine—there is often a great discrepancy between these two images. The therapist could ask how the person prays, what the response seems to be, and how the person knows the communication is from God. One can ask whether the person believes that a certain situation is the will of God, what God's intention seems to be, or what is the person's idea of God's involvement in the situation. Does the person think that God is angry with him or her? Are there fantasies that God is testing the person? The response to these questions gives the therapist some indication of the person's level of spiritual maturity.

Some practitioners are afraid that this kind of formal spiritual assessment is too personal. Although it is sometimes a relief for people to talk about their spiritual beliefs, it is also true that some people are more uncomfortable discussing the way in which they pray than they are discussing their sexuality. If the person denies having any spiritual life, one could ask about the way in which he or she appreciates beauty or finds some larger sense of meaning in life. One could ask about peak experiences or feelings of awe.

Although it may be useful to take a "spiritual history," it is often too clumsy to ask these questions in a formal way during an initial evaluation for psychotherapy. A checklist of questions tends to make people feel they are taking an exam or being pathologized. I prefer to get a sense of the person's spirituality gradually as it unfolds in the course of the therapeutic conversation over time, especially as it applies to the psychological issue at hand. I don't believe that one can quickly put into words one's deeply felt spirituality, so the checklist type of assessment may produce shallow responses rather than truly meaningful ones. But there is no doubt that the person's spirituality may be at work behind the scenes, for good or ill. For example, the person may feel that her relationship to God is a major support, or the conviction of sinfulness may be adding to her depression. The person may believe that his suffering is karmic, which may lead to a fatalistic attitude. Understanding the person's spirituality helps us understand his or her worldview and may also give the therapist some insight into the person's character structure.

Psychotherapy as a discipline cannot directly answer controversial questions about the existence of God or the nature of ultimate reality, but these questions may arise in the course of therapy. By paying attention to them, people may develop their own responses. The therapist may be concerned that he or she is not a spiritual authority; I don't believe there is such a thing, if by authority we mean someone who has a final answer to these questions. Ideally, a creative response arises out of direct spiritual experience, the individual's inner knowing, or out of the unconscious, which is a deeper source of wisdom than the ego.

What does the therapist do to help someone committed to a traditional religion who complains that he or she has lost faith, or that life just seems empty? This can be a very painful experience for someone who has spent his or her life within a particular tradition. The person may say: "I've prayed, meditated, asked for help, but I'm still in great pain. I don't understand what this illness is all about, or what it means, or why it's happening to me, or what I'm supposed to learn from it. I'm asking God but I'm getting no answers." In a situation of severe illness or chronic pain, people may feel abandoned or betrayed by God. They may feel isolated, helpless, and that life is meaningless. Sometimes relationships with others are the only lifeline, but even then it may be hard to find people who understand what the person is going through. The suffering person gets tired of well-meaning advice, often useless, that is given because the listener cannot tolerate feeling helpless and cannot deal with the despair induced by projective identification with the suffering person. The sufferer often feels resentment or anger at not being understood, and this may further alienate the person. No one can really know what it is like to live with chronic pain and illness without having been there. The therapist can imagine it empathically, or we may only be able to do so based on our own experience of pain, which is usually not chronic. Disease makes the body a problem and a burden rather than a place of joy and rest. The body cannot be trusted; it becomes alien and threatening, destroying itself. It may become impossible to plan one's life, because the body is unpredictable and unreliable, so one's activities become increasingly restricted, and one is increasingly confined. How can one maintain faith in a benevolent providence in such circumstances?

Chronic pain and illness are not only incapacitating in their own right, they are demoralizing. They impair our usual coping mechanisms such as connection to others, the ability to hope for a better future, and the sense that one has some control of one's life and that life is meaningful. Chronic pain that cannot be relieved can have devastating effects on the personality. It can lead to despair, bitterness, and self-absorption. Pain is profoundly isolating, not least because it is the most real thing in the world for the sufferer but it cannot be felt by others.[4] Chronic pain can take the meaning and joy out of life and make the future unimaginable. It is very important, if nothing else can be done, to be able to be with someone in such a state without abandoning the person emotionally, without judgment, without advice, without avoidance—just as a witness, a companion, or a selfobject. Sometimes the only thing that gives the sufferer some relief is to feel understood. To be present in these roles is a spiritual practice for the therapist, because doing so demands faith.

These states of body and mind approach the limits of human endurance; they are severe existential crises. The problem is that if one despairs and gives up, a hopeless state of mind has a reciprocally harmful effect on the immune system and can worsen the underlying disease state. But the empirical research shows that if one can maintain meaningful relationships and attachments to others during a chronic illness, its course is likely to be more favorable, while isolation and hopelessness foster a worse prognosis. Social isolation and pessimism are known to increase the progression of cancer. Spirituality and religious affiliation have been shown to benefit resilience to disease (Sperry and Shafranske 2005, pp. 11–12; Griffith and Griffith 2002, pp. 266–68), probably by modulating the emotional and physiological responses to illness, although the exact mechanism of this link is not clear.

When they suffer, some people in the Christian tradition are helped by apologists such as C. S. Lewis (1940), who argues that pain is a wake-up call from God. For him, pain is a necessary signal to make us remember that we are finite, and we must look beyond the physical world. However, this attitude does not take into account the fact that many people who suffer terribly are already spiritually awake, and indeed these arguments did not help Lewis some years later when his wife lay dying of cancer. Then it felt to him as if God was a torturer, alternately raising and crushing his hope. This is the kind of reaction to suffering that may lead to a radical reevaluation of one's God-image. Often, such disillusionment occurs because prayer seems to have been ineffectual. At one time, prayer was considered to be an important healing modality, but technological medicine gradually eliminated prayer in favor of scientific approaches. In recent years there have been renewed claims about the health value of intercessory prayer, but it remains controversial and is probably impossible to study rigorously.

Some people enter therapy because of what Griffith and Griffith (2002) describe as an unspeakable dilemma, a situation in which the person is faced with a forced choice between two equally distressing options with no possibility of escape. At the same time, the person cannot talk to those involved in the situation, so that the person has to hide their distress. For example, a person has an abusive boss but is afraid of being fired if she speaks about it. Or one is forced to work in a family business that one dislikes. Or a boy feels forced by his father to play sports which he hates. Or one is in a situation of impossible love that no one knows about. These dilemmas may produce somatization—bodily symptoms of distress such as pain that is not due to organic disease.

In such situations, the person's spiritual beliefs may arise during therapy, and the therapist can explore whether these beliefs play a part in the person's attitude toward his or her situation. For example, the person may feel that he is being tested by God, or there may be some other coherent spiritual story that gives meaning to the situation, sustains the person, and gives hope. It may be important to discuss any moments of happiness, and what provides them. There may be aspects of the sufferer's life for which he or she is grateful. The person's spiritual community may be helpful or judgmental. There may be shame about illnesses such as AIDS because of religious belief. Beliefs such as life after death may be comforting.

Often, however, the individual's beliefs about life, death, and the meaning of suffering—personal mythology—are not explored in psychotherapy, even though they have a major influence on the person's behavior and attitude to life. People sometimes withhold such information from the therapist because they discern subtle cues that it will be unwelcome. As usual in therapy, these cues can be entirely unconscious. Some of this counterresistance occurs because few therapists feel trained to deal with spiritual issues. Psychologists as a group are not particularly religious people; many of them see religion as incompatible with scientific naturalism and empiricism. Some psychologists believe that religions place too much emphasis on faith and not enough on questioning received authority. Consequently, the atmosphere of many academic departments militates against religious belief, which many psychologists associate with assertions preached from the pulpit that people are expected to believe without evidence. Even though positivism is not as academically respectable as it used to be, many psychologists still adhere to a positivistic model of science which argues that for a statement to be regarded as factual, it has to be verified by sensory experience. On these grounds, they believe that statements about God are meaningless. Psychotherapists of this persuasion confine their practice to the realm of what is empirically refutable, measurable, and objective and only consider religious issues to be important if they seem to be relevant to the person's emotional difficulties. Some of them see spiritual beliefs as purely defensive.

It is common to find psychotherapists who are avowed atheists. Whereas the overwhelming majority of Americans believe in God (95 percent in a 1993 Gallup poll), about 21 percent of psychiatrists and 28 percent of clinical psychologists consider themselves to be atheists. Many of these atheists have had psychoanalytic training (Bronheim 1998, p. 20), and they explain spirituality in terms of psychodynamics. Traditional behaviorists regard spirituality as nothing more than learned behavior. The early behaviorists were committed to naturalism, the doctrine that there is no need to postulate any spiritual or supernatural explanation for the universe and its processes. Of those contemporary psychologists who do have an interest in spirituality, 51 percent prefer alternative spirituality to organized religion (Shafranske and Malony 1990).

In spite of the incidence of atheism or agnosticism among psychotherapists, spiritual issues are common in the practice of psychotherapy. According to one study, one in six people in psychotherapy present religious or spiritual issues, and 29 percent of psychotherapists agree that these issues are important in the treatment of at least some of their clients (Bergin and Jensen 1990). However, professional training in psychotherapy has a secular framework, and many therapists feel ill-equipped to work in the area of spirituality. Nevertheless, whether conscious or not, most therapists have some metaphysical assumptions about the nature of ultimate reality and the presence or absence of a spiritual dimension. These beliefs may be unexamined and may be the residue of the therapist's own development, childhood religious background, and characterological factors. It is inevitable that they will influence the therapist's responses to serious existential dilemmas.

Many psychotherapists are themselves experiencing a kind of spiritual hunger, of the same type as the people with whom they work. Psychotherapists also want some sense of purpose, meaning, and fulfillment. This suggests a reservoir of spiritual interest among therapists although many of them are indifferent to organized religion, the obvious exception being pastoral psychotherapists. At the extreme, atheistic therapists see organized religion as magical thinking, superstition, and dogmatism, only useful to emotionally immature people. These therapists see "God-talk" as defensive, a form of resistance, and they see Judeo-Christian beliefs as nothing but a reflection of psychological needs. Some therapists suffer from painful childhood experiences in parochial schools which left a residue of anger toward established religion. As children, many of these therapists were hurt by clergy or religious teachers, or they are still struggling with their own ambivalence toward religious

PSYCHOTHERAPY AS A SPIRITUAL PRACTICE

parents or early indoctrination. If the therapist has left the religious tradition of childhood, he may be struggling with guilt. The therapist must then beware of projecting his own doubts onto the other person. Skepticism about the other's beliefs may be based on the therapist's personal conflict about spiritual material. These factors in the therapist may produce uncomfortable countertransference reactions to spiritual issues that require self-reflective work on the part of the therapist.

Even when they are religious believers, many contemporary psychotherapists compartmentalize their spirituality and their professional practice because they consider themselves to be "practitioner-scientists." It is difficult for them to embrace a spiritual approach to psychotherapy if their model of science is based on the need to replicate data and refute hypotheses. A brief digression into an alternative philosophy of therapy is therefore necessary. To the positivist or materialistic critique, the spiritually oriented therapist can respond that spirituality involves subjective experience, passion, love, trust, feelings both joyful and painful, and a sense of mystery and beauty in life that lead to a kind of inner knowing. These are intangibles that make us human but are not necessarily amenable to quantitative methods of study borrowed from the physical sciences. Spirituality must include thought, but it is more than a set of ideas, and in the end the sacred cannot be captured in the net of concepts. As Barth pointed out, our knowledge of God is not like other types of knowledge (in Bromiley 1979). The sense of the presence of the divine is the type of subjective knowledge that is impossible to verify by any public means. The therapist is concerned with the meaning of this knowledge to the person, rather than the philosophical question of whether such knowledge can be logically or empirically justified.

Spiritually oriented therapists acknowledge that there is more to human beings than brains, learned experiences, intrapsychic conflicts, and the like. We feel that human beings are expressions of a transpersonal dimension of reality. We would like to take this level into account in our psychotherapeutic work, although psychology and science in general cannot tell us its nature. Neither can these disciplines help us understand the meaning of our existence. Although for many people traditional religious doctrine has been irrevocably undermined by science, science cannot prove or disprove the existence of a spiritual realm. From the time of the Renaissance, science has been separated from religion, a distinction that was necessary to free inquiry. Today, science supplies many of the answers that used to be asked of religion, and there is a pervasive sense that Western culture has been steadily losing its sense of the sacred, especially since the Enlightenment. Many people believe that we are at the end of the Christian period of civilization. (There are many historical reviews of the way in which this came about; see, for example, Smith 1995, pp. 27–33.) It used to be said, in an oversimplified way, that religion works by faith while science works by reason and evidence and that these approaches conflict with each other (Lindberg and Numbers 1986). This is now understood to be too rigid a distinction because science has its own faith claims, its own doctrines and dogmas, and its own metaphysical assumptions, such as materialism, while theology and faith also use reason, although reason alone does not account for our sense of the sacred.[5] It has also been argued that science and spirituality deal with two different domains, although in fact they both deal with the natural world; they just do so in different ways.

It would be wise to ignore the fundamentalists on both sides of the science and religion debate. We have reached a point where science and spirituality can be seen to be complementary, sometimes addressing different issues and sometimes the same issues from different perspectives. They do not need to be seen as hostile to each other. This realization is one reason that spirituality is now emerging within psychological discourse.

Karl Jaspers suggests that the ideal therapist combines both a profound existential faith with a skeptical scientific attitude (1963, p. 808). I would combine faith and skepticism by pointing out that although there is a transcendent dimension to our existence, which allows faith, the traditional theological response to this dimension is constructed by human beings, which invites skepticism about the degree to which we can know it. The therapist cannot decide on the reality or falsity of religious beliefs from within the discipline of psychology. For the therapist, what matters is the meaning of a religious belief to the person and the effects of belief on the person's life. We can explore religion in the person's life as if it were any other aspect of the way the person functions in the world. It may be useful to help people articulate religious beliefs in therapy because religious beliefs are a personal mythology that people live by, and they can be helpful or destructive. People like Dr. Martin Luther King Jr. and Mohandas Gandhi were able to foster powerful social change because of their religious convictions.

Some research suggests that patient-therapist similarity with regard to religious values is one of the predictors of a successful outcome of therapy (Kelly and Strupp 1992), although in such a case both may have the same blind spots about the problematic aspects of a particular tradition. On the other hand, there are occasions on which the therapist's spiritual commitments are so different than those of another person that they may not be suited to work together. Ideally, the therapist can make allowances for this difference even if he or she has an entirely different worldview. If the therapist has an empathic and nonjudgmental stance, he or she does not need to share the person's spiritual beliefs to be helpful in understanding the influence of these beliefs on the person's life situation. One can learn about these beliefs as part of the therapy. However, if the therapist is very skeptical about religion, this attitude may color her responses and make it hard to respect and empathize with the person's worldview. Spero believes that it matters whether the therapist thinks that God is actually real, psychologically real, or only metaphorically real (1984, p. 76; Spero 1985; Spero 1990). Most people will be able to sense what their therapist really believes in this area because her attitude will be communicated nonverbally when spiritual issues are raised.

The therapist who has a spiritual commitment may find his beliefs challenged by expressions of atheism on the part of the person with whom he is working. However, one can usually understand such feelings when the person is reacting to the difficulties of the human condition or the state of the world.[6] Sometimes atheism is the result of serious philosophical inquiry, but at times it results from personal tragedies or major disappointments in the person's life that seem to exclude the possibility of a God. Sometimes the therapist discovers that the person's "atheism" is really a repudiation of the Judeo-Christian God-image, and the person actually has a different kind of spirituality.

THE ISSUE OF VALUES

The therapist's values are always present, and it is almost inevitable that they will tend to influence the process of psychotherapy, tacitly if not overtly (Tjelveit 1986). Typical mental health professionals have values such as the following: the importance of self-knowledge, good self-esteem, relatedness, genuineness, personal responsibility, commitment, the ability to do fulfilling work, the ability to express feelings, and the ability to forgive when possible.[7] Every therapist has a personal list of behaviors that they like and don't like, and this list is based on values that may unconsciously affect their responses. It is difficult to be sure of the origin of these values; Gordon (1973) suggests that some of them are intrinsic to the psyche. In this category she lists: creativity and imagination, the need to discover a true and authentically experienced self, concern for loved persons and guilt if one hurts or betrays them, a search for meaning, integration, relationships beyond the self, the experience of wonder and awe, and humor. Whether or not there are innate values, it does seem that some values are based in the therapist's character structure and developmental history, while others are a function of theoretical orientation.

There is no consensus about which values are most able to alleviate human suffering. Therapists of all persuasions argue that their values promote mental health and so may be used to guide therapy (Bergin 1995). For instance, Kleinians stress the importance of reparation for damage done to early objects and the value of struggling with hatred, hoping that love and gratitude will emerge victorious. Adlerians value creative relationships with social reality, cooperation with others, and the search for significance. Jungians value consciousness of the shadow, relationship to the transpersonal Self, and the process of individuation or the fullest possible development of the potentials of the personality. As Bergin points out, few contemporary therapists believe in the kind of ethical relativism that characterized the early founders of the profession (Bergin, Payne and Richards 1996).[8]

Our values are cloaked in the form of professional codes of behavior and ethics, not to mention our diagnostic categories and language. Just to say that someone needs "treatment" for a "disorder" is to imply certain values about what is healthy. The skeptic sees psychotherapy as a way of inducing people to conform to the changes of which we approve or, at the extreme, sees psychotherapy as a way of promoting social norms, disguised as a "treatment plan." Part of the problem occurs when the therapist unconsciously promotes social values that are harmful to certain people. Do we encourage adaptation to society even if doing so is antithetical to the individuation process of the person with whom we work? Are we agents of social change or of social stability? Do the values of the psychotherapist merely reflect current political ideology? What is the relationship between our political values and our theories of psychotherapy? Writers such as deMause (2002) and Samuels (2001) have convincingly demonstrated the relationship between one's inner world and one's political beliefs, and the therapist is not immune to this connection.

Most therapists do not want their personal values to interfere with their therapeutic practice and do not want to prescribe values or moral standards, but the therapist's feelings about important issues such as abortion will inevitably be present and cannot be fully concealed. In fact, they may be even more potent if we communicate them indirectly rather than directly and clearly. Therapists who are committed to a particular religious tradition may believe in moral absolutes that they consider essential for the welfare of those with whom they work. But while the major theistic religious traditions agree on many values, they also differ in some important areas, and there are no psychological grounds for deciding which of the competing belief systems is correct. Nevertheless, many theistically oriented therapists believe that without the moral values of the world's monotheistic traditions there would be no basis for healthy self-regulation of behavior (Bergin and Payne 1991). This is a very dubious proposition. Atheistic ethical humanists may behave impeccably for reasons that have nothing to do with theistic beliefs. In certain situations the moral judgment of an atheist and a religious believer may be identical, just as the therapeutic couple may have very different spiritual beliefs but no difficulty agreeing on a moral issue that may arise. Apart from our superego development and societal conditioning, there is some (inconclusive) evidence that morality is encoded in the brain by evolution, a universal moral grammar within the brain that allows us to decide ethical dilemmas (Hauser 2006).⁹ This process may not be accessible to conscious reflection—it may correspond to Jung's notion that the psyche has an intrinsic moral function, not dependent on the internalization of societal and family values as described by Freud.

Some therapists, committed to a particular tradition, believe it is ethical to promote specific religious values in therapy (Peteet 2004), but many therapists feel that as long as the person's values are reasonably healthy, growth promoting, and not hurtful to others, they should be respected without reference to any particular religion. Within these limits, one can encourage self-determination and accept the fact that some of the person's values can be highly personal rather than collective.

Ideally, one's values and one's self-structures are consistent with each other, although we often see people struggling with a socially acquired value system that is incompatible with their personality. For example, competitiveness and acquisitiveness are encouraged by the culture, and it takes an independent turn of mind to decide that one will live differently. The development of an authentic personality at times requires that one swim against the tide of the culture. However, it may be difficult to encourage personal values when the therapist is working with a person who has values that the therapist considers to be unhealthy or dangerous. In such a case, perhaps the most one can do is respectfully suggest what one considers to be healthy values and explore the psychodynamic underpinnings of destructive values (Bergin 1991; Richards and Bergin 2005).

Not only are we concerned with the degree to which the therapist might deliberately try to influence the person, we are also concerned with the possibility that the person might unconsciously identify with the therapist's values. Perhaps, like any identification, this is unobjectionable if it is a temporary stepping-stone in therapy. But what if the person asks directly about the therapist's values? Does the therapist only admit his or her own values after first exploring those of the person? What happens when a woman is in turmoil about whether to have an abortion, and the therapist has strong feelings about this issue, on either side of the debate? Or the problem might be the need for a blood transfusion for a Jehovah's

Witness. A Muslim woman may struggle with competing Islamic and American societal values. The therapist has to be conscious of countertransference in the presence of a belief that radically opposes the therapist's values, for example, when the person believes that homosexuality is a sin but the therapist believes it is morally neutral, simply a part of one's genetic endowment.

An example of the clash of religious and psychological values might occur when a religious therapist works with a person who is unable to leave an unhappy marriage while having an extramarital affair. Apart from the traditional religious connotations of this situation, the therapist working with a purely psychodynamic approach to marriage recognizes that many of the reasons we marry are unconscious. We marry people who embody some characteristics of a problematic parent, or someone who is just the opposite type of person. We project parental imagoes onto the partner and struggle with a new edition of the same pathology with which we struggled as a child. We bring our selfobject needs and our internal object relations to bear in the marriage, so that we bring both a conscious and unconscious set of expectations to the relationship. The Jungians would also point out the projection of the anima or the animus onto the partner, and the attraction of different psychological types. Therefore, given the complexity of marital relationships, it is not surprising that friction occurs, that people outgrow the dynamics that initially brought them together, and that the couple may simply develop in incompatible directions. But even if the therapist understands all that, the therapist who adheres to traditional religious and social values may subtly or not so subtly imply that the couple should stay together at all costs. The idea of the dissolution of a marriage may produce countertransference anxiety in the therapist which may enter into interventions.

In such situations, does the therapist mention one's beliefs, or do we confine ourselves to entering the person's inner world empathically? We could argue that the therapist's task is only to try to clarify the psychological underpinning of the problem for the person and let the decision emerge organically. This is a position many therapists adopt, because they feel that moral issues are personal decisions and not the province of psychotherapy. However, this argument sidesteps the moral issue in favor of a technical approach to the question, whereas at times the person urgently needs to discuss the morality of a situation he or she is in. The therapist's refusal to do so may lead to a disruption of the self-selfobject tie, at least when an idealizing transference is uppermost, because the person feels that the therapist lacks the courage to commit himself or herself about the very reason the person came into therapy. One cannot deal with intrapsychic or relational material in a way that ignores real-life dilemmas. In these situations, Richards and Bergin (2005) have suggested what they call an "explicit minimizing" approach; the therapist minimizes the chance of imposing values on the person while being explicit about her values at the appropriate time. My own preference is to explore the person's values, including their unconscious and developmental underpinnings if they can be discerned, discuss where the therapist differs, and look at the effects of this difference on the therapeutic relationship. Whether we like it or not, London suggests, psychotherapists are not neutral technicians but intrinsically moral agents. He believes that therapists are a "secular priesthood" (1985, p. 156), which may seem like an extreme view to therapists with a secular orientation.

The therapeutic couple may have conflicting values particularly when the two people have very different worldviews. One person may have an existentialist bent and assume that life has no particular meaning, so that we have to *give* it meaning, while the other person may feel that life is intrinsically meaningful and we have to *discover* its inherent meaning. When there is such a difference, do we just try to understand the person's beliefs, even if they seem unhealthy to us, or do we try to influence the person in the direction of our own beliefs? We do not have to agree with or value the person's beliefs in order to empathize with the person, and it would be a blunder to criticize values and beliefs that the therapist does not share. It is preferable to explore these beliefs, and the effects that the difference of opinion has on the relationship, as grist for the therapeutic mill. The therapist can be conscious of whether his attitude to the other person's beliefs is affecting the kinds of interventions he makes.

As an extreme example of a clash of values, what are we to make of "Christian counseling" in the form proposed by writers such as Adams (1973)? He attacks most forms of psychotherapy because he believes that people are basically sinful and therapy tends to condone irresponsible behavior or sexual promiscuity. Adams believes that therapy is not helpful unless it emphasizes dependence on God rather than self-reliance. For him, the solution to psychological problems is repentance, confession, and belief in Jesus. Most therapists offer a very different approach to psychological problems than that proposed by Adams, and this difference may contribute to the fact that many people who hold fundamentalist religious beliefs deeply distrust psychotherapy. They fear that the therapist will try to undermine their beliefs or reduce them to the "merely psychological," implying that they are not real. Some fundamentalists literally see psychotherapy as the work of the devil, put here to lead people astray. One can take an empathic approach to fundamentalism (without being patronizing or judgmental) if we remember that fundamentalists are often people who need external structure. They prefer certainty, clear dogma, and an emphasis on rules and regulations. The fundamentalist needs a system of thought that acts as a container for anxiety in a threatening world. They pay a price, however, since some Christian fundamentalists live in constant shame or guilt about their anger, which they believe they are not supposed to feel. Belief in a clear set of rules of behavior buttresses the individual's sense of self and reduces anxiety but does not necessarily change or develop personality structures.

Working with a fundamentalist Christian, the therapist must bear in mind that many Christians have been raised to believe that human beings are alienated from God because of sin, and we are in need of redemption that we cannot attain by our own efforts. For example, Bobgan and Bobgan say that suffering is due to our separation from God because of our sinful condition and because of the presence of sin in the world after the fall (1987, p. 207). For these authors, Jesus is the only way to reestablish a relationship with God, there is only one path to redemption, and psychotherapy is potentially destructive because the gate is narrow (ibid., p. 225). This attitude may produce severe guilt and fear. To be told that suffering is the result of sin may lead to the sense that the sufferer has been abandoned by God, or that he or she is being punished for sin, which adds to the individual's burden. To many therapists, the notion that suffering is a "test of faith" looks like an anthropomorphic projection onto the divine, but to many fundamentalists this is felt to be factual. Such belief is particularly problematic if the person has a masochistic character structure, so that he or she is willing to suffer for some perceived greater good (Glickhauf-Hughes and Wells 1991). With such a person the therapist has to remember that part of the Christian story involves the theme that what seems to be intense suffering and defeat is actually a form of victory, suggesting a degree of isomorphism between character structure and religious doctrine.

Psychotherapy is particularly threatening to Christian fundamentalists because it offers its own brand of salvation (in the original sense of the word, meaning to be healed) which is not dependent on belief in Jesus. Psychotherapy is a way of developing internal structure, which means that one would rely less on a set of externally imposed values. While psychotherapy requires us to acknowledge our own shadow material and try to integrate it, fundamentalists often try to split off and project the shadow by seeing it as the work of the devil, or by viewing others as sinful and unredeemed. These splitting and projective defenses are important in maintaining a precarious sense of self, and so resist interpretation. The attraction of Christian fundamentalists toward the book of Revelation, with its imagery of avenging angels, blood, and destruction, suggests tremendous rage at unbelievers, perhaps because they stimulate the true believer's unconscious doubts about his faith. One sees in this book little of the compassion and love that Jesus taught. Jung suggested that the writer of Revelation was struggling with powerful negative feelings, which then "burst upon consciousness in the form of revelation" (1954b, par. 438).

For the fundamentalist darkness must be overcome, while for the psychotherapist darkness must be explored, understood, and made conscious. For the Christian fundamentalist the path to salvation and redemption is to accept Jesus; for the psychotherapist the path is through understanding our symptoms and changing self-structures and pathogenic beliefs. Yet this too is a statement of faith, no less than the fundamentalist's faith; the therapist has faith in the psyche, or in the truth of the personality, or in the value of relationship. We have faith in the benefit of understanding the psychological origin of evil behavior and its function within the psychology of the individual, because we believe that by doing so evil can sometimes be transformed.

The tension between the psychotherapeutic and the fundamentalist approaches raises the problem of the clash of values that arise whenever religious beliefs seem negative to the therapist, or when religious doctrine is used as a way of rationalizing psychopathology or prejudice. Contemporary examples of this process include biblically justified homophobia or the notion that men are the divinely appointed leaders of the family and women should submit to them. The biblical injunction that tells women to "submit to your husbands" (Eph. 5) may be used to rationalize misogyny or even sadomasochistic character structures. If one grows up with constant criticism and abuse, leading to the conviction that one is bad, it is easy to believe the preacher's insistence that all human beings are basically sinful (Rom. 5:12).

When a religious belief is very strong, it organizes a person's life experience and radically influences his or her self-image. In the case of what sounds like spiritually motivated asceticism, it may be difficult to discern the line between self-denial and masochism. The therapist will try to examine beliefs that lead to alienation and despair or those that are dangerous. It is difficult to know how the therapist should respond when the person believes that God has told him to do something violent, such as bomb an abortion clinic. We risk losing the person if we are not empathic with the psychodynamic origin of such extreme beliefs, which we would try to interpret and contain within the therapy, but we also have a duty to warn those who may be in danger. Whatever we say when a person proposes action that is abhorrent to the therapist, no matter how tactful we try to be, the person will often be able to detect how we actually feel. For the therapist to be deceptive is counterproductive in the long run, while to say nothing may imply that we agree with the action. Fortunately, most of the people who are prepared to be violent in the service of their beliefs are outside of mainstream religion. Sometimes, such an extremist does not really understand the theology of his own tradition, or misinterprets it, so consultation with a minister may be useful, although there is always the risk that the clergyman will reinforce the belief.

It is essential to be empathic with the function of particular beliefs in the mind of the individual, especially in the case of hateful, destructive, and violent beliefs. When these beliefs are used to prevent fragmentation anxiety and maintain self-esteem, they are manifestations of deeply ingrained character pathology. Their emotional and developmental underpinnings have to be understood before such beliefs can be challenged directly. Usually this does not happen early in therapy; if dangerous beliefs are approached too early, it is likely to make the person defensive about them, so they are best approached in a gingerly manner when a level of trust has been established. But eventually there comes a time when religious beliefs can be part of the therapy, and this is particularly useful when a belief has remained unspoken, so the person hardly realizes what he believes because it has remained just a vague feeling.

It is common for therapists in specific religious traditions to combine consciously the roles of therapist and spiritual director. When dealing with problems of suffering and meaning, a secular therapist may occasionally find herself in the role of a spiritual teacher, concomitant with her psychotherapeutic work. This may not be a role that the secular therapist consciously chooses and she may not feel particularly qualified for it, but the material that emerges in psychotherapy may force it upon the therapist. At times, a conscious wish to teach spiritual material emerges within a therapist as a sense of vocation, an inner calling that is confirmed simply because students start to appear. Sometimes the transpersonal Self initiates one into the role of teacher by a process of internal awakening. However, one has to be ruthlessly honest about one's motivation to teach; to be self-important or interested in power is totally incompatible with authentic spirituality. The role of the spiritual teacher is fraught with potential dangers which have become painfully obvious in the last few decades. (For a discussion of the vicissitudes of spiritual apprenticeship, see Bogart 1997.) Spiritual abuse can be devastating to a person who has been traumatized by an unscrupulous teacher or a narcissistic therapist. It is therefore important to understand the psychodynamics of idealization that are involved, which are discussed in chapter 6.

The problem is exacerbated when the spiritual teacher or therapist is narcissistically invested in a system of practice. The dangerous indicators of this kind of narcissism in a spiritual teacher are claims of being very special, contempt for other traditions, or the use of spirituality to acquire wealth or manipulate others. The possibility of abusing the person arises from the misuse of power, using the person for one's own needs, projecting onto the person one's own values or doubt, or controlling or dominating the person, overriding the person's feelings. This is one of the risks of all hierarchical organizations that claim special (divine) authority, just as it is a risk of being overly invested in a particular system of psychotherapy.

TALKING ABOUT SPIRITUAL EXPERIENCES

Psychotherapists subtly train the people with whom they work to talk about some things more than others, depending on the material to which the therapist pays particular attention. The therapist's theoretical orientation then dissuades a person from talking about material that the therapist does not consider to be important. While many therapists are willing to talk about spirituality if the person opens up the discussion, some feel that it is not their province and avoid discussing the subject when it arises. The person may then be afraid that their spirituality will be dealt with reductively or dismissed as defensive. For example, some therapists subscribe to the contemporary belief that the sacred is not really sui generis, something objectively existing, but is merely a social or linguistic construct. If the person senses that the therapist has this kind of attitude, he or she is not likely to reveal very private spiritual experiences. But a relationship with the divine is as important as any other type of relationship—it is just harder to describe because it has unique characteristics. The relationship is often nonverbal. The presence of the divine is often a vague, felt sense in the body, a feeling of warmth or light or peace or an inner knowing that cannot always be put into words.

If we ignore the person's spirituality, we collude with the idea that the person is not supposed to mention spirituality in therapy. If the person has a sense of a transcendent reality, it is important to understand in what way that affects them. When the person overtly rejects any spiritual belief, it is useful to articulate this attitude because the reasons for the rejection of organized religion may be important in that they tell us something about the quality of early identifications and group affiliation needs. The person's relationship to traditional beliefs may be intimately entwined with the person's psychodynamics, object relations, and the attitudes to religion in their family of origin. It is worth knowing, for example, that there are differences between the effects of early religious training in people of different religious backgrounds. Jews tend to be very subject to family pressures and guilt about intermarriage, while Catholics tend to be angry about control by religious authorities and are assailed by doubt about doctrine. According to Lovinger (1984), Protestants tend to be guilty about *acting* on selfish feelings, while Catholics may feel guilty about *having* selfish feelings.

THE ISSUE OF FREEDOM AND DETERMINISM IN RELATION TO PSYCHOTHERAPY

The question of whether we have free will, or to what extent our behavior is determined, is a complex philosophical problem, and neither side of the argument is totally provable. The relevance of this debate to psychotherapy arises when behavior that is controlled by unconscious factors feels wrong, shameful, or contravenes religious standards. The theistic religious traditions assume that we have free will and define sinful behavior as (usually deliberately) behaving in a way that contravenes the will of God. The depth psychological position assumes that at least some of this behavior may be motivated by unconscious factors that preclude choice; an example is compulsive sexuality driven by painful internal emptiness.

One of the traditional goals of psychotherapy is to free the person from pathological internal constraints on their capacity to make choices. Typical constraints are internalized prohibitions on sexuality or pleasure in general or any unconscious organizing principle or complex that limits healthy, reasonable self-expression. The desire to increase personal freedom is a value that we bring to the practice of psychotherapy, and this value may conflict with the individual's religious training. A person may apply collective standards of right and wrong to their behavior, but the therapist may feel that, within common-sense limits, behavior does not have to conform to collective opinion or the opinion of a religious hierarchy. This tension becomes relevant when a person is struggling with an issue such as divorce or abortion, in which case the therapist has to decide to what extent the choices that are made are motivated by an emotional disorder or made freely. In situations of moral conflict, the therapist may not feel that the person is making a choice that is free of pathological influences. A person's religious tradition may see certain behavior as deliberately willful whereas the therapist sees it as driven by unconscious psychological factors.

However we think of the issue of freedom of choice, it is clear that we can have the subjective experience of choosing what we do, and this is a reasonable therapeutic outcome. Becoming aware of unconscious complexes and relational configurations and reworking them within the therapeutic relationship lessens their hold on us. Our therapeutic task is to help the person at least feel *as if* the person is free to choose, so that we can be reasonably self-assertive while balancing our own needs with the needs of others, in a way that is fulfilling and socially reasonable. Freedom also means that our spirituality is not rigidly governed by unconscious factors. Therapy with these outcomes is of profound spiritual as well as psychological value.

NOTES

1. For example, classical behaviorism typically assumes determinism rather than free will, assumes that the self is constituted by learned behaviors and has no room for the soul. Cognitive models look for underlying schemas that produce dysphoric affects; a schema is an organized set of reactions and experiences that form a relatively cohesive and persistent body of knowledge affecting perception and behavior. This is a way of describing what Jungian psychology refers to as the human shell of a complex. In the Jungian tradition, a complex also has an archetypal or spiritual core, which is not acknowledged by classical behaviorism.

2. According to Lizelle Reymond (1972), the Indian spiritual teacher Sri Anirvan said that all spiritual experience is felt as sensations in the body.

3. There are several instruments for assessing a spiritual history, for example, Anandarajah and Hight (2001).

4. On the problem of pain, see Good (1992) and Scarry (1985).

5. For a review of the post-positivistic philosophy of science, see Jones (1996).

6. Religion is commonly accused of causing violence—religious wars, witch trials, and the Inquisition are typically cited. However, as Bruce Chilton points out, atheistic regimes such as the Third Reich, the Bolshevik revolution, and Maoist Communism have been far more destructive. Furthermore, there has been no "flowering of pacifism" since the Enlightenment. I recommend Chilton's (2008) critique of contemporary naïve atheism and McGrath's (2007) demonstration of Dawkins's dogmatic, fundamentalist approach to atheism.

7. The results of a national survey of the values of mental health professionals are found in Jensen and Bergin (1988).

8. Ethical relativism is the notion that there are no universally valid moral principles, all of which are a matter of what the culture or the individual believes to be right. Some of the early behaviorists believed in ethical hedonism, the notion that the highest good for the individual is that which allows the most pleasure and the least pain.

9. The notion of innate morality is debatable; for a counter view, see Prinz (2007).

The Expression of the Sacred in Psychotherapy

This chapter describes some of the ways in which an experience of the sacred or the holy might be reported in psychotherapy, and points out various factors that may affect the psychotherapist's response to such experience.[1] I assume that the experience of the sacred is an experience of something real; the skeptical or atheistic therapist will maintain that these experiences are merely *believed* by the individual to be experiences of the sacred.[2] Yet all therapists would agree that psychotherapy is very concerned with the individual's relationships, and for many people the experience of relationship with the divine is of great importance.

The term *sacred experience* is extremely broad; it covers a spectrum that includes everything from a sense of presence to reports of the union of the soul with God or unmistakable revelations of the divine. The common factor is a sense of contact with a larger consciousness. This experience can vary in intensity and may feel positive, uncanny, or terrifying. Stark (1965) has provided a list of types of spiritual experience, which I have adapted below with some modifications. These are common to people of all religious traditions.

A sense of reverence or holiness may occur during occasions such as a baptism or marriage, a birth or death, or just watching a dramatic sunset. An experience of heightened consciousness may occur, such that the subject feels a sudden sense of the presence of God, a feeling that the divine is very close, directly in the room rather than present in a general sense everywhere. This sense of presence is important and common to the mystics of all traditions, all of whom describe a concomitant sense of uplift and peace, sometimes even joy or bliss. Some people have a fairly continuous sense of a background spiritual presence guiding and sustaining their lives, or a sense of mutual affection or friendship with the divine, or a feeling of constant spiritual guidance. At times it may feel as if one has been given a personal message about divine intentions, which may occur in the form of visions or voices that give information about the future or a warning that one is in danger. This "something there" experience may also produce a sense of the presence of evil.

A sense of mutuality may occur in which it feels as if the divine specifically acknowledges the presence of the human. This may produce a feeling of gratitude or a sense of being "saved." This may happen during a period of crisis and may feel like a miraculous intervention, for example, when illness is healed or one is rescued from physical danger. This type of experience may also be felt as divine punishment when misfortune occurs or as if one is being tempted to sin.

Among charismatic Christian groups, phenomena such as spiritual healing or the state of being "slain by the spirit" (in which the subject loses motor control and falls to the floor) still frequently occur. These ecstatic experiences are said to be the result of being "touched by the Holy Spirit," which produces shaking, screaming, and/or the ability to speak in tongues. When assessing such an experience, the therapist has to take into account what is normal for the group to which the individual belongs, remembering at the same time that group norms may be pathological, as we see in mass suicides or murderous attacks on people with other beliefs by members of a cult. The ecstatic form of sacred experience may feel erotic; there is a long tradition that combines religious ecstasy with sexual arousal.

The negative form of this type of experience is a horrifying encounter with the devil or the feeling of being possessed by the devil—a common problem in the Middle Ages and rare but not unknown today. States of "possession" by an evil force are still reported and may be presented to the psychotherapist.[3] The anthropologist Vivian Garrison (1977) describes the story of Maria, a 39-year-old Puerto Rican woman. While sitting at her bench in a factory in New York City, she suddenly began to scream and tear her clothes off. She then tried to throw herself through a window. When restrained, she fell to the floor unconscious with her body twitching. Because she declared herself to be possessed, a wide variety of interpretations were invoked, ranging from malingering to hysteria to paranoid schizophrenia. In her own subculture, such experience is said by the *espiritista* (practitioner of a spirit medium religion) to be the result of possession by spirits sent against her by witchcraft. This type of *ataque de nervios* is a culturally approved mechanism for coping with stress, which traditional psychiatry sees as a hysterical or dissociative defense against anger and anxiety. The problem was triggered by the illness and death of her husband combined with other family problems and sexual difficulties. Whether one takes such experiences of possession at face value or reduces them to some form of psychopathology depends on one's metaphysical commitment. Garrison notes that, within their own subculture, spirit mediums themselves do not all agree about the existence or the exact nature of the spirits. For some of these practitioners, the spirits are no more concrete than the psychoanalyst's belief in the id, ego, and superego, all of which are reified concepts. She cautions that it is an ethnocentric oversimplification to consider the spirit medium religion magical while psychotherapy is more scientific or to equate belief in possession with categories from our psychiatric nomenclature.

For some Jungians, "spirit possession" means that one is temporarily overwhelmed by an autonomous complex which controls behavior. Because the individual's emotional life influences the atmosphere and behavior of those around him, von Franz pointed out that the complex is not simply intrapsychic; she describes it as "free-floating" in the surrounding environment (1986, p. 282). This implies that the experience of a complex can feel like that of an autonomous spirit, in which case one is in some sense "haunted" by one's complexes.

Many types of paranormal experience may be heard in therapy.[4] These include psi phenomena such as extrasensory perception, clairvoyance, or telepathy, precognitive dreams, psychic healing, near-death experiences, and encounters with a deceased person, typically a close relative or friend. Such an encounter may happen as a sense of presence in the waking state or as a dream. When one dreams of a dead person, the therapist may understand the figure in various ways. It can be seen as the personification of some quality of the dreamer, as a defensive way of dealing with grief, or as a visit from the soul of the deceased person. These dreams are often reported to have a particular quality about them which feels rather different than ordinary dreams. The experience of a figure that no one else sees includes children's experiences of imaginary playmates that are totally real and very important to the child. The therapist's reaction to these experiences depends on whether he or she accepts the existence of a spiritual dimension of reality that may interact with our consensual reality.

Parapsychological phenomena cannot readily be explained by current science, so that materialistic scientists decry them as the result of human self-deception or manipulation. I believe there is simply too much evidence to dismiss them all as unreal (Radin 1997; Cardeña, Lynn and Krippner 2000). I mention this here because the therapist's skepticism may prevent a person reporting such an event even when it is emotionally significant. In a neglected paper, Jerome Frank describes various parapsychological abilities of the therapist, such as clairvoyance, telepathy, and what he called "healing power" (1982, p. 7). More research is needed in this area because it is clear that psychic phenomena occur in psychotherapy, sometimes involving an extrasensory communication between the therapeutic couple. (Perhaps a mechanism such as telepathy contributes to phenomena such as empathy and projective identification.)

Should a paranormal experience be reported, what matters is the emotional importance of the experience to the subject. It is potentially hurtful if the experience is ignored or dismissed as illusory. The therapist's task is to explore its meaning to the individual. If the therapist's belief system allows for the existence of paranormal events, he or she may affirm the validity of the person's experience if it seems credible. A skeptical therapist may simply maintain a respectful interest, including the event in the therapeutic discourse with an open mind about its reality.

Paranormal experiences usually occur during periods of distress or intense need, and they may be very powerful for the subject. For some people they are interesting, for others they are frightening; in fragile people they may stimulate paranoid anxieties. It may then be necessary to normalize the experience, perhaps putting it in perspective by pointing out that these events are fairly common and there is a good deal of research tending to confirm their reality, even though we do not understand their mechanism. Therefore, they need not make one inflated, overstimulated, or afraid. (I'm assuming throughout this discussion that the person is not psychotic. Many psychotic people report experiences such as voices and visions that are profoundly important to them, but these individuals are not taken seriously because they are too disorganized. See Wapnick 1969.)

Parapsychological events confirm our sense of a deep level of connection between people. They challenge the assumptions of classical physics about the nature of reality and make us realize that there are dimensions of reality and of human nature that are not accessible to everyday consciousness. These experiences reinforce our skepticism about materialism and make it highly unlikely that consciousness is only a product of the brain.

NUMINOUS EXPERIENCE IN PSYCHOTHERAPY

In 1917, in *The Idea of the Holy*, Rudolph Otto, a Lutheran theologian, suggested that the truly distinctive feature of religious experience is a particular quality that he described as numinous. Examples from the Bible are Moses hearing God's voice emerging from a burning bush that is not consumed by the flames, or Saul on the road to Damascus hearing the voice of Jesus asking, "Why do you persecute me?" Otto believed that such experiences are an irreducible experience of the holy, or of the *mysterium tremendum et fascinans*, a mystery that is tremendous and fascinating. They are dreadful, uncanny, awesome, and mysterious. Beyond words, they penetrate to the core of our being, and we are unable to understand what has happened in terms of everyday reality. In the face of such power, the subject experiences "creature consciousness," the sense that one is in the presence of that which is transcendent. At the same time, we are attracted to numinous experience because it offers the promise of love and grace beyond our understanding. We are transported or intoxicated in a moment of ecstasy and may feel blessed, healed, or a sense of atonement. At other times the experience is uncanny, horrifying, or terrifying.

Various writers have described the characteristic phenomenology of mystical experience. William James (1958) outlined four qualities: the experience is ineffable—it cannot be put into ordinary language; it is noetic—it provides information or knowledge that seems to carry its own authority; the experience is transient, often lasting only a few minutes and rarely more than half an hour; and it happens of its own accord, not as a result of our own effort. During the experience, the subject is passive; his or her own will is in abeyance. Sometimes the experience has no distinct content, just a feeling of love, compassion, or merger with the totality, when the ego seems to fuse with the world, producing a sense of wholeness, ecstasy, or aliveness. Maslow (1970) noticed that self-actualizing people commonly report such events, which he called peak experiences.

It is important to note that experiences of this type are not confined to saints, mystics, or characters in the Bible. They occur to ordinary people, in a variety of modalities, and they may be reported in psychotherapy. Numinous experience may occur in dreams, visions, in the natural world, in the body, in the form of psychopathology, through the use of entheogens (psychedelic agents), and in various other forms which may feel positive or negative to the subject (Corbett, 2006).[5] Positive experiences are those such as that of a woman whose car spun out of control on an icy road. As she helplessly hurtled toward a tree at high speed, convinced she was about to die, she heard a voice say, "It's not your time yet; let go." A typical near-death experience followed. She survived the crash and regained consciousness with the conviction that she had a reason to live and with radically changed values.

Numinous experiences often occur during times of great personal turmoil. A woman in conflict and pain about a forbidden love affair was praying for guidance in church when suddenly "time stood still; a golden light flooded everywhere, and I felt connected to the whole universe. I felt permeated by indescribable love, and I was outside of time and space. My conflict fell away; I knew for certain that nothing was wrong." Eigen, who is one of an increasing number of spiritually oriented psychotherapists, reports a typical numinous experience that took place on a bus during a period of emotional agony in his twenties.

> I doubled over into my pain and focused on it with blind intensity. As I sat there in this wretched state, I was amazed when the pain turned to redness, then blackness (a kind of blanking out), then light, as if a vagina in my soul opened, and there was radiant light. The pain did not vanish, but my attention was held by the light. I felt amazed, uplifted, stunned into awareness of wider existence . . . above all was reverence, respect . . . It was an unforgettable moment. Life can never be quite the same after such experiences. (1995, p. 386)

Numinous experiences may have the emotional quality that Otto and James describe, even though their content is not related to traditional Judeo-Christian imagery. The numinosum may occur in a dream such as the following:

> I was surrounded by a fine mist. I sensed a presence, as if someone was coming toward me. The mist opened to reveal a gigantic blue eye, about three feet across. I felt penetrated by its gaze as I stood there in awe and fascination. The contours of the eye became red, orange, and gold. The eye came closer, until I was aware only of the round iris, which became square, then round, then square again, continuing to change in this way. The eye now seemed like a huge window or door, beyond which I could see a world of light, and into which I could now enter. I was excited by this landscape, yet also frightened by the sense of infinity, boundlessness, and eternity I saw. The

light beyond the door was unlike any light I have ever seen; it
was silvery and cold, but also warm, soft, and colorless. I felt as
though I was falling into it.

The eye is an ancient symbol of the all-seeing divine. The dreamer
felt that she had been seen by the eye of God, here acting as a por-
tal or window into the transpersonal realm.

The following is a typical example of a frightening numinous
dream:

> I am suddenly aware of a huge figure standing by the side of
> my bed. The figure is obviously alive, although gray in color, as
> if carved out of stone. To my horror and terror I see that it has
> one head but three faces. One face looks down at me, while the
> other two faces emerge from the sides of its head. I'm afraid
> the figure is evil; all I can think of to do is to bless it, and it
> vanishes as soon as I do so.

It would not be helpful to dismiss this dream as a meaningless
nightmare or, for some religious believers, as demonic. Such dreams
are of profound importance. To understand such material, a Jungian approach is helpful. Jung points out that the unconscious may
produce numinous imagery from any mythic tradition, not necessarily the religion in which the subject was raised. In antiquity,
deities with three heads or three faces were not uncommon.[6] The
figure in this dream seems to be a representation of the mythological Hermes-Mercury, a pre-Christian divinity often represented as
a trinity. He was the god who guided souls to the underworld and
acted as a messenger between gods and mortals. Hermes is the god
of "betwixt and between," the archetype of transition between different phases of life. With the advent of Christianity, pagan gods
such as Hermes were ignored or suppressed, but the psychological
processes they represent have not disappeared. Today we refer to
them as the archetypal or spiritual processes of the unconscious,
which still appear in this kind of dream imagery.

In Jungian psychology, in order to put this dream in its larger
historical and cultural context, the dream can also be amplified by
the use of alchemical imagery. The alchemists spoke of Mercury in

two ways; on the surface they were referring to metallic quicksilver, but they also used the word *Mercury* to describe the elusive spirit concealed in matter, or the soul of matter, and also as a way of talking about the process by which matter and spirit are transformed into each other. Mercury was therefore an apt metaphor for the slippery quality of the unconscious, which is impossible to grasp, or for the mysterious transformations involved in the individuation process.

Jung pointed out that the alchemists were expressing themes and imagery that had been repressed by the Church. For example, medieval alchemists took very seriously the notion that matter is ensouled, rather than thinking of matter as inert and inferior to spirit. Alchemy therefore represented a kind of underground compensation for the psychological processes that were being ignored by the larger culture of the time. According to Jung, the alchemical attempt to make gold was actually a disguised search for spiritual gold, or the Self. In the process the alchemists were forced to confront the dark forces of the unconscious which they projected onto the material operations of the laboratory. The traditional Christian image of God is only light, but Jung pointed out that this attitude ignores the dark side of the Self, the side of the spirit that either causes or colludes with the presence of evil and suffering, as we see in the case of the biblical Job. Jung therefore suggests that the alchemical Mercury is an ambivalent figure; as well as having a transformative side, he represents the unacknowledged "dark chthonic" half of the divine (1948b, par. 271). The dreamer is forced to face this fact and to realize that this apparition probably heralds the beginning of a new phase of life. In the case of the dream above, the tyhree-faced apparition presaged the onset of a serious illness.

Most schools of psychotherapy do not treat dreams as spiritually important. In the Jungian tradition, however, the transpersonal Self is the maker of dreams, and they therefore do not simply originate from personal levels of the mind. This attitude would be considered nonsense by biologically oriented psychologists who subscribe to purely neurological explanations for dreams. Some regard dreams as the result of the brain's attempt to clear its circuits of meaningless information picked up during the day, as ways of unlearning or forgetting (Crick and Mitchison 1983; 1986). Others suggest that dreams originate as the frontal lobes try to make sense of a bombardment of random data from the brain stem (McCarley and Hobson 1977). Or, dreams evolved so that we could process information during sleep that would not have been possible during the day because this data had to be separated from locomotion and during sleep motor neurons are inhibited (Winson 1990). I mention these neurophysiologic theories of dreaming to indicate the yawning gap between the spiritually oriented approach to psychotherapy and a materialistic approach. But most contemporary Christians also ignore the spiritual importance of dreams, even though the early Christian Church and most other spiritual traditions have viewed dreams as an important means of contact with the divine (Sanford 1951; Kelsey 1974).

Many writers point out that we cannot experience the divine without some kind of medium. For some, the sacred is experienced by means of the natural world. Respect for nature as a manifestation of the divine is found in all traditions. The Benedictine monk Bede Griffiths, for instance, remembers the awe he experienced as a boy during an evening walk, listening to birds and seeing hawthorn blossoms. "I felt inclined to kneel on the ground, as though I had been standing in the presence of an angel; and I hardly dared to look on the face of the sky, because it seemed as though it was but a veil before the face of God" (1977, p. 27). He experienced "an overwhelming emotion in the presence of nature . . . It began to have a kind of sacramental character for me" (ibid., p. 28). But there has also been a tendency in the Judeo-Christian tradition to interpret Genesis 1:28, a command to subdue the earth, as if the earth were not sacred in its own right. Traditional believers want to remove themselves from the worship of nature (pantheism), and so at most will admit only that the divine is present in nature (panentheism), in which case nature is a vehicle for the experience of a God who transcends nature. It is common for people to experience moments of intense spiritual awareness while in the wilderness, although some conservative writers on mysticism deny that such experiences are authentic experiences of the divine itself, which they believe is detached from nature (Zaehner 1961).

For some people, the body acts as a medium of connection to the sacred. It may be a surprise to people if the therapist takes the stance of affirming the spiritual importance of the body, because some of our religious traditions still have a prejudice against it. The respectful treatment of the body found in the graves of our early hominid ancestors is evidence that they had a religious attitude, but later theology viewed the body as a kind of prison of the soul, even as something sinful. These attitudes are fading, but therapists still see people who are ashamed of their bodies and their sexuality.[7] It is difficult to deal with this shame by reason alone. Enlightened Christian spiritual directors point out that the body is the temple of the spirit and that to devalue the body is to devalue the creation and the notion of the incarnation. But these commonsense arguments may have no effect on deeply ingrained shame that will not yield to good advice. The psychotherapeutic treatment of shame takes time, and improvement occurs when the person feels safe enough to be able to express shameful feelings and memories which are accepted and treated respectfully by the therapist rather than judged. When successful, this process is a form of redemption of the body.

Another important type of numinous experience, described by the mystics of all traditions, is one of unity or union with the divine, in which there is no sense of a separate self, no distinction between oneself and others or between oneself and the world. Stace describes this as "the apprehension of an ultimate, non-sensuous unity in all things, a oneness or a One to which neither the senses nor reason can penetrate" (1960, pp. 14–15). During the experience, perception is very clear and wide open, but there is no sense of a separate perceiver who is having the experience. The nature of the experience is identified when one retrospectively remembers it. In the Eastern religious traditions, these experiences are described as unity with the divine, but the Christian tradition prefers to call them experience of union rather than unity, in order to preserve a distinction between the human and the divine.

During the twentieth century, some theologians would not accept the notion that depth psychology could be describing the transcendent level of reality. There was concern that to speak of religious experience as psychological, or as a product of the psyche, implied that this was not the experience of an objective reality outside the psyche. Jung's assertion that the unconscious either mediates or may even be the source of religious experience caused theologians to accuse him of psychologism, as if he was suggesting that the psyche itself is the divine ground (Goldbrunner 1966, pp. 171–72). In response to such charges, Jung pointed out that the psyche is real, so that to suggest that numinous experiences arise within the psyche is not to deny their reality (1940, par. 2). We cannot explain their origin or say what they are. They are simply empirical facts. Because they occur in the psyche, they are the legitimate province of the psychologist, who can study them without making metaphysical assertions about their source. Whatever might exist beyond the psyche is not part of the discipline of psychology. Jung never fully committed himself to the idea that what we call God is actually *produced* by the unconscious—he usually said that we cannot empirically distinguish between God and the experience of the unconscious. In any case, for Jung, the very notion of the unconscious is only something we posit, a way of talking about what is unknown to us.

By the end of the twentieth century, many academic theologians and philosophers of religion had turned toward conceptual thought, while others no longer attempted to justify their religious faith logically but in terms of their experience of divine love (Morris 1994). For theologians like Karl Barth, theology was an attempt to understand faith, rather than an attempt to prove the existence of God logically. While ministers of religion focused on prayer, preaching, morality, and Bible study, depth psychologists concentrated on symbolic or numinous experience of the sacred. Such appeals to experience tend to challenge institutionalized concepts of divinity because spontaneous sacred experience may not be in accord with received doctrine. People who belong to an established church but who have no personal experience of the numinosum must either borrow from, or go along with, whatever the church has to offer. They run the risk of becoming complacent, relying on dogma, and thereby ignoring their individual spirituality. At the same time, as Jung points out, dogma—such as the notions of the trinity or the virgin birth—is not invented intellectually but is itself an archetypal product of the psyche that probably originated long ago in the form of dreams and visions. We can therefore study dogma and myth for their psychological and symbolic, if not literal, truth. For example, there is something very important in the mythic idea of the divine child (the baby Jesus or Buddha), an image that expresses the possibility of renewal and spiritual potential. The notion that the divine incarnates itself in the human, and that this process is painful for the ego, is a powerful aspect of the Christian myth. A psychological approach to these stories reveals what may be essential elements of meaning within religious traditions.

If an established religious tradition provides living contact with the sacred, there is no pressing need for a depth psychological approach to spirituality. However, for many people traditional symbols no longer mediate the sacred because they have little emotional resonance. Traditional religious rituals have also become ineffective for many people because they are too stereotyped and repetitive. Rituals are based on dogma, doctrine, and a mythology to which the individual may not subscribe. Therefore, not only is traditional ritual not conducive to spontaneous religious experience, Jung suggested it may be a substitute for direct experience of the sacred (1940, par. 75).

A numinous experience may feel important only to the individual, or it may be relevant to an entire community. One may be given a new revelation that may be orthodox or heterodox, in which case it may challenge the prevailing theology. Accordingly, religious institutions tend to view new revelations with suspicion. Neumann pointed out that the encounter of the ego with the transpersonal level of the psyche not only produces numinous experience but is inherently "revolutionary and heretical," striving to "dissolve the traditional forms of religion and worship" (1968, p. 386). An authentic numinous experience is always new, and so could be antidogmatic. This seems contrary to Katz's suggestion that mystical experience is defined in advance by the mystic's sociocultural beliefs, conditioning, and preexisting concept of God (1978, p. 34). However, it may be that mystics committed to an institutional religion do not report experiences that do not fit with their tradition.

If one's spiritual instinct remains unsatisfied by traditional religious forms, one has to satisfy this instinct in a personal way. One way of doing so is to pay attention to spontaneously arising numinous experience, which awakens a primordial religious sensibility and generates true faith. People in this position can no longer look to an outside authority. They are the bearers of a new spirituality that seems to be emerging which stresses direct experience of the transpersonal psyche. Should such a person be engaged in psychotherapy, the therapist can assist in this process. Assistance may be necessary because those in this position lose the protection of the organized church, and they are exposed to material from the unconscious that may be difficult to assimilate—the traditional "perils of the soul."

The experience of the numinosum cannot be taught or transmitted by tradition or education; its occurrence may be fostered by spiritual practice or it may occur spontaneously. One is either open to it or not. Certain atmospheres can evoke a sense of the numinous, especially places of natural beauty or power, structures such as Stonehenge, or a great cathedral. Art may also do so—hence the icons found in several traditions. Music is another such stimulus, which is why it is prominent in many forms of worship.

It is important for the therapist to ask about the quality of the atmosphere surrounding a numinous experience—whether it was one of love and joy or one of sadness and darkness. The concern of traditional believers has been whether numinous experience was of God or just something that arose from within one's own mind. If the experience seems negative, some traditional religionists would insist that it must arise either from Satan or from personal psychodynamics and thus cannot be an authentic experience of the sacred. However, if the experience meets criteria such as those described by Otto and James, the therapist may still consider it an experience of the sacred even if it is negative. It would then be considered to be an experience of what Jung calls the dark side of the Self.

Direct awareness of the sacred feels different than thinking about it or imagining it. As Alston points out, numinous experiences seem to be presented to our consciousness in the same way as the ordinary objects of sense perception (1991, p. 14). Because numinous experiences have the same quality as any other perception, they do not feel like purely internal experiences that we retrospectively explain as experience of the divine. Even when the experience does not have any of the usual sensory qualities that we associate with ordinary objects, such as colors or sounds, they produce a distinct sense of something objective presenting itself to us. Accordingly, when people try to describe numinous encounters, they say things such as: "It began to dawn on me that I was not alone in the room. Someone else was there . . . I neither saw him nor heard him . . . I had no doubt about it." Or, "the room was filled by a Presence . . . I was overwhelmingly possessed by Someone who was not myself" (Beardsworth 1997, cited in Alston 1991, p. 17). Alston goes on to point out that in such cases it is reasonable to assume that something may be present that is not detectable by our five senses but nonetheless occurs as mystical perception. This something is taken by the subject to be an awareness of the divine. If one is open to the possibility that these are real phenomena, one has to deal with the content of the experience as one would any other source of sensory information.

It is not always clear through which sensory channel numinous experience arises. Corbin suggests that we have a psychospiritual perceptual ability that is not dependent on the five senses; through this may appear what he calls the imaginal world (quoted in Bloom 1996). This world is suprasensory; it is neither the world of the senses nor the intellect, but it is just as real. According to Corbin, in Sufism the heart is the organ that achieves knowledge of God and perceives the divine mysteries (1969, p. 221). Obviously this is not the physical heart; the Sufis are describing a subtle organ or spiritual center that may correspond to the heart chakra of the Eastern religious traditions. It is important that access to the imaginal world depended on a process of initiation by spiritual adepts who followed a rigorous spiritual discipline.

The experience of the numinosum may not be dramatic. The Bible describes the story of Elijah, who is exhausted after competing with the prophets of Baal to demonstrate the superiority of his God (1 Kings 19). He hides in a cave in the wilderness to escape King Ahab's resentment and vengeance and wants to die to end his suffering. In response, God first sends a strong wind, then an earthquake, then a fire, each of which Elijah ignores. He only responds when he hears God as a "still small voice," which must have had a particularly numinous quality.

Synchronistic events are an important variety of numinous experience.[8] *Synchronicity* was Jung's term for an experience in which

an event in the physical world corresponds in a meaningful way
to the psychological state of the subject, even though there is no
causal connection between the subject's mental state and the outer
event. In some way that we do not understand, the outer event and
the inner experience correspond to each other, linked by a common meaning. To be considered synchronistic, the event need not
be precisely simultaneous but should be closely related in time.
For example, one dreams of a friend one has not seen or thought
of for years, only to receive a letter from him the next day. Obviously, dreaming about the friend did not cause the letter to arrive,
and the letter did not cause the dream to occur, but the two events
are meaningfully connected. (A possible explanation here is a tele-
pathic communication between the two people.) The committed
materialist will dismiss such events as nothing more than random
coincidences with no deeper significance, since there is no rational
explanation for them. However, if one admits the possibility of an
order or pattern operating behind the scenes that permeates our
reality, synchronistic events are not to be dismissed so lightly. They
imply a realm of reality that is outside of time and space as we
understand them.

Jung believed that synchronistic events occur because psyche
and matter are continuous with each other; they are two aspects
of an undivided level of reality. At this level of the *unus mundus* or
one world, the psyche and material events that seem to be separate
from it are actually part of a deep level of unity. As the example of
the dream and letter shows, the same meaning, or the same archetypal pattern, expresses itself both physically and psychologically.[9]
It looks as if the surface appearance of separateness actually belongs to a continuous underlying fabric. Our ordinary concepts of
time, space, and causality do not apply at this level of reality, where
qualities that we usually think of as opposites, such as inner and
outer or matter and spirit, are part of a continuum. Synchronistic
events feel numinous because a deeper level of order has revealed
itself, in which the psyche and the material world shade into each
other.

Our traditional view of separate objects and our commonsense
ideas of space, time, and cause and effect have been superseded
by developments in quantum physics, which describes a unitary

level of reality in terms of nonlocality and acausality. The fact that the consciousness of the physicist cannot be separated from the physical effects observed in his experiment seems to demonstrate that there is an unseen connection between consciousness and matter. Unfortunately, the full implications of this phenomenon, which implies an undivided psychophysical field, have not yet been incorporated into our daily psychotherapeutic practice, probably because it is difficult to imagine how to do so. Some of these implications are discussed in chapter 8.

Synchronistic events are emotionally powerful, and they make us aware of the connection between the ego and the archetypal or spiritual dimension of our lives, a contact that produces a sense of "depth and fullness of meaning that was unthinkable before" (Jung 1954a, par. 405). One is amazed, one sees new meaning, one feels a part of a larger whole, and it is as if one has experienced grace or a blessing.

If it is true that reality is undivided, every important event in physical reality is correlated with some aspect of our psyche, but we do not perceive the connection when the psychological content is unconscious—what Jung calls an "unconscious synchronicity" (1973–1975, vol. 2, p. 495). The existence of this phenomenon is impossible to prove, so it acts as a personal myth for therapists who believe it, and it influences their attitude in the therapy room because it implies that what happens to the person in some way "belongs" to him or her. Or one could say that a synchronicity is a way of meeting the unconscious in the form of an outer event.

The interpretation of the meaning of a synchronistic event is sometimes difficult, especially when it is not obviously related to the individual's personality or life situation. Synchronistic events— often of a negative kind—are fairly common in the lives of schizophrenic people, who tend to interpret them in terms of their delusional system.[10] Even in normal individuals, we may wonder if the meaning that emerges is truly a priori, given to us (which Jung believed), or whether we merely project our personal meaning onto the situation. In either case, to understand the experience it is helpful to look at the event symbolically, as if it were a dream. Sometimes the outer event compensates for a one-sided conscious attitude in the same way that a dream makes us pay attention to what we are ignoring. Such compensation is possible because, in contrast to the ego, whose knowledge of reality is very limited, Jung believed that the transpersonal unconscious has "absolute knowledge" (1952b, par. 931).

It seems impossible to know whether the psyche generates numinous experience, in which case what we call God is actually a manifestation of the transpersonal psyche, or whether the psyche is simply the essential medium for the experience of a divinity that is beyond the psyche. Whichever is the case, for the spiritually oriented psychotherapist, the psyche is a means of connection to the sacred. We cannot make a sharp distinction between the psyche's human and transpersonal levels, or between one's personal psychodynamics and one's archetypal core. This approach makes the experience of the sacred immediate and internal, in contrast to the more transcendent God-images of traditional monotheism. Jung's approach therefore caused considerable controversy with theologians such as Buber, who prefer to think of the divine as radically independent of the psyche.[11] For Buber, Jung reduces divinity to something "merely psychological" and therefore not transcendent, whereas for Buber the divine is an "absolute Other," beyond the psyche, and radically independent of the human being (1952, p. 68).

As I noted earlier, in response to such theologians, Jung pointed out that to say that an experience originates in the psyche is *not* to say the experience is unreal, because the psyche itself is real, and it is an empirical fact that the divine mystery chooses to manifest itself by means of the psyche (1952a, par. 1503). For many Jungians, the Other is actually the transpersonal level of the psyche, with which the ego is in dialog. One can understand why this attitude would cause considerable controversy, since it implies that the monotheistic traditions might originate intrapsychically.[12] However, for the therapist, to approach the sacred in terms of subjective experience avoids the problem of deciding which of the competing metaphysical claims of traditional religions is correct. The claim that the divine manifests itself by means of the psyche does not exclude the possibility of a transcendent level of divinity—it simply means that that level is not the province of psychology. In any case, the distinction between transcendence and immanence is only relevant at the level of the ego; at the absolute level is it meaningless.

The psychological approach has other advantages; no elaborate theology (which only the specialists understand) is necessary. Faith arises out of the naturally occurring experience of the numinosum and is not demanded by a hierarchy.

Jung's working assumption is that the divine operates in the psyche as the transpersonal Self, which is both the totality and the organizing principle of the psyche (1944, par. 44). The Self is an a priori spiritual director that guides the development of the personality toward wholeness. Jung acknowledges that we cannot know to what extent the Self corresponds to a transcendent divinity, although personally he takes the existence of God for granted (1973–1975; p. xi). He admits that "in all decisive matters I . . . was alone with God" (1961, p. 48), so accusations that he was an atheist are unreasonable. I believe he would have liked to have stated categorically that the source of the Self was God, but he felt he could not do so as a psychologist, yet he is in no doubt that the Self is a spiritual principle. In practice, the importance of this idea is that the Self is not wholly transcendent, but in dialog with the ego in dreams and other manifestations of the unconscious. (One could think of the Self as what Whitehead referred to as the divine initiative that works in every creature. He was speaking philosophically and not psychologically, but the idea is comparable.)[13]

Various writers make the point that the experience of the numinosum feels intensely real, so that, as Jung notes, the experience produces "a peculiar alteration of consciousness" (1940, par. 6). A powerful numinous experience is often enough to convince the individual of the existence of a spiritual level of reality. Nevertheless, for the relentlessly materialist therapist, it is not difficult to reduce this kind of experience to residual primary narcissism, a regressive, infantile experience of merger with mother or a return to intrauterine bliss. I prefer Hunt's (1995) suggestion that, in contrast to thinking of numinous experiences as regressive, they should be thought of as an emergent cognitive capacity, a separate line of development of higher mental abilities. Only the therapist's personal metaphysical commitment will decide how he or she understands such an experience. The skeptic will point out that the spiritually oriented therapist is biased in favor of a spiritual interpretation of the experience, which is intrinsically not repeatable, not amenable to experimental verification or replication, and not in keeping with materialistic scientific attitudes. A useful rejoinder is to point out that all researchers have implicit biases that color their interpretation of their data, which does not necessarily invalidate their conclusions. Many scientists do not accept a purely naturalistic or materialistic view of reality (Griffin 2000), and there is no reason that the therapist should be bound by this worldview. Many real phenomena are not subject to experimental replication; they require a different method of approach. To say that a numinous experience is an experience of the divine is an inference, but a reasonable one for those who accept the reality of a transcendent dimension. To borrow Alston's metaphor, it would be like inferring that the presence of a contrail in the sky means that a jet plane has passed by. This argument would not convince the die-hard materialist, who would suggest that the individual is simply labeling an emotionally powerful experience as an experience of the divine, based on preconceived metaphysical assumptions or background beliefs. However, our skeptic would then have to explain how the subject can distinguish other types of emotionally powerful experiences that he or she does *not* label as experiences of the sacred. The skeptic might further object that, unlike ordinary sense perception, there is no possibility of independent verification of the nature of numinous experience. However, many subjective experiences cannot be confirmed by an external observer, and this objection does not prove that there is nothing real causing the experience.

For those of us who accept that numinous experiences are experiences of the sacred dimension, the problem becomes one of integrating the experience into the larger context of our lives. When a numinous experience happens to a person who is committed to a particular tradition, he or she tends to place the experience in the context of that tradition's theology, doctrines, and dogmas. The therapist will try to relate the experience to the person's overall psychology, to his or her developmental history, individuation process, and emotional life. We also try to discern the implications of the experience for the future course of the personality. If the therapist has had a personal numinous experience, it is easier to grasp the quality of the other person's experience. The therapist's memory of a personal encounter with the numinosum helps him or her to act as a container for a great deal of emotional pain that might otherwise be unbearable.

Here I should add an important caveat. If an experience of the numinosum is truly an experience of the divine, obviously we only experience it in small measure, since our organs of experience have built-in limitations. For example, to experience the divine as love is only to say what effect it has on us, what it is like to have such an experience. Although such an experience may give us a taste of the divine, obviously the part cannot encompass the whole. A metaphor may help: if we imagine white light refracted through a prism, the relationship of photons or light waves to the molecular structure of glass might be a crude analogy to the passage of the numinosum through the human being. An interaction occurs, and the prism—the body-mind—affects the way we perceive the light.

Since many people in therapy are undergoing personal crises, it is important to note that numinous experiences are more likely to occur when the subject is under serious stress, especially when the person feels he or she is at the limits of his or her ability to handle a situation. Often they occur when the individual gives up in despair and feels completely inadequate. Sometimes this is accompanied by a conscious decision to "let go," what is traditionally referred to as "dying to the self," while at other times the experience simply erupts into daily life with no warning.[14]

It is important to add here that in the mainstream psychological literature, numinous or mystical experiences are considered to be anomalous (Cardeña, Lynn and Krippner 2000). Perhaps this is because in the recent past mainstream psychiatry and psychology have associated religious experiences with psychopathology (Larson et al. 1986), although there is actually little relationship between them (Berenbaum, Kerns and Raghavan 2000, p. 32). In fact, as a rule, numinous experiences produce positive life changes and psychological benefit (Wulff 2000); they do not produce major disruption in the individual's life. The exception occurs when a numinous experience triggers a psychosis. It is not clear to what extent this is due to the fragility of the subject's ego combined with the misunderstanding and lack of support of friends and family. Perhaps a psychosis is more likely if the individual's experience is derided and dismissed.

There is in fact a positive correlation between various measures of well-being and self-reports of relationship with a divine being such as God or Christ (Pollner 1989). People who report mystical experiences tend to score lower on scales of psychopathology and higher on indicators of psychological well-being than control groups (Caird 1987; Hood 1974; Spanos and Moretti 1998). Near-death experiences, for example, usually produce beneficial long-term effects such as a greater appreciation for life and reduced death anxiety (van Lommel, van Wees, Meyers and Elfferich 2001; Greyson 2000). However, distress may occur if the experience radically contradicts the subject's belief system (Greyson 1997) or if the subject is ridiculed when he or she tells others of the experience. A numinous vision or sensation of unusual energy may produce enough emotional distress to disrupt the subject's emotional and social equilibrium, especially if the environment is not supportive. Grof and Grof (1989) refer to this type of experience as a "spiritual emergency." Like any type of numinous experience, these crises may occur spontaneously or they may be induced by severe stress or by spiritual practices such as meditation. They happen when the ego is flooded with material from the unconscious that is too much to contain because of its affective intensity.

The most helpful attitude to numinous experience is for the therapist to be curious and interested while exploring the details of the experience and affirming its importance. If the person is not sure of the nature of the experience, the therapist may point out that it was, or may have been, an experience of the numinosum, depending on how certain the therapist is based on the person's description. Even people who are reasonably normal may develop an unrealistic or even paranoid interpretation of the experience if they are not given a helpful explanation of its nature. The therapist can subject a numinous experience to a process of discernment, in which we try to sort out the human from the truly transpersonal level. Needless to say, the therapist will instinctively be aware of any evidence of psychosis, dissociative disorder, or hysteria, but this assessment can be complicated by the fact that disturbed people may have authentic numinous experiences.

If the individual describes numinous experiences, voices, or visions, one has to differentiate these experiences from psychosis. How does the therapist respond if the person says he hears God's voice but cannot exactly say how? Some individuals occasionally hear voices but have no other signs of psychosis, in which case it would be an untoward reduction to assume that such voices are invariably pathological and should not be taken seriously. An extremely intelligent physician with no evidence of mental illness or serious emotional instability told me that she was occasionally visited at night by an invisible spiritual energy or being that would make love to her. She felt this as a physically real sensation. In this type of situation, assuming that the therapist's metaphysical commitments are similar to those of the person—here, for example, that both share a belief in the subtle body—the therapist can take the experience at face value and try to make sense of it in the context of the subject's life. One can inquire where the experience seems to come from, what its effects are, whether it is helpful or hurtful to the subject or to others, what the subject thinks would be an appropriate response to the experience, and so on. Normal responses to these questions have to do with enhancing one's spirituality, self-understanding, improved relationships, or constructive action of some sort (Barnhouse 1986). Psychotic responses would be idiosyncratic, bizarre, or obviously delusional.

It is a prejudice of materialistic scientific thinking to dismiss all numinous experience as illusory if not frankly insane, but in fact these experiences not uncommonly occur to healthy people. Nevertheless, great difficulty arises when a genuinely numinous experience arises in the context of preexisting severe psychopathology. Emotionally fragile people do experience the divine. In fact, if the barrier between consciousness and the unconscious is overly permeable, as it is in psychotic or borderline states, it may be that transpersonal experiences are more likely to erupt than they would when that barrier is firm. The problem is that the psychotic person who describes a numinous experience is not likely to be taken seriously because of his or her disorganization, thought process disorder, affective incongruity, perceptual changes, and other evidence of impaired reality testing. The emotionally healthy person is able to contain the emotional intensity of a numinous experience and relate to it, rather than being overwhelmed by it. There is an enormous difference between saying "I had a vision of Jesus" and developing the delusional idea that "I am Jesus." In the former case, ordinary ego functioning is preserved; in the latter case, the reality ego is lost (Wapnick 1969). Nevertheless, it may be helpful to address the religious imagery that appears during a psychosis (Bradford 1985), because it may be possible to integrate the spiritually important aspects of the psychosis during the recovery period (Lukoff 1985; 1988).

A particular problem arises when the therapist is not familiar with the individual's culture, so that ideas that are normal in a particular society may be mistakenly thought to be delusional. Greenberg and Witztum (1991) suggest various criteria that distinguish a psychotic episode from religious beliefs that are normal within the individual's religious community. These authors point out that psychotic episodes are more intense than normative religious experiences for that community, and the rest of the community recognizes the experiences as abnormal. These episodes are terrifying, the individual is highly preoccupied with them, they are associated with deterioration in social skills and personal hygiene, and they involve special messages from religious figures.

When the individual is clearly not psychotic, he or she may need affirmation and support for the subjective reality of a numinous experience. Sometimes a numinous experience induces a fear of insanity in a healthy person, in which case the therapist can reassure the person that numinous experiences are well known and not signs of abnormality. The individual often asks questions such as, Did my mind play tricks? Did that really happen? Was that real? Am I losing control? Explanation and reassurance are then necessary, and here the therapist's own belief system will color his or her approach to the experience. The person will often detect any disbelief on the part of the therapist. If the therapist is not convinced of the objective reality of numinous experience, the best he or she can do is to be respectful and treat the experience as one would a dream that has symbolic, subjective importance to the individual. In this area, because of professional ignorance or prejudice, there remains a risk that normal people who experience a powerful numinous experience might be thought to be mentally ill.

It is important to ask for the individual's associations to the experience, since the meaning of the experience often emerges as it is discussed. In this way, what may be a frightening episode is gradually normalized and put into a larger perspective. It often takes some time before one can put the experience into the context of the individual's life, but one usually finds that numinous experience addresses an important life issue or an important complex, often in a way that is transformative (Corbett 1996; Hastings 1983). There is little risk that the individual may become self-important as a result of the experience, because the emotional power of numinous experience usually produces awe and humility rather than grandiosity.

Much of the response to an anomalous or numinous experience depends on the individual's cultural background and personal belief system. Targ, Schlitz, and Irwin (2000) report the case of a deeply religious Mexican woman who had a dream in which her husband was hit by a bus. Soon after this precognitive dream her husband was killed in exactly this way. She was stricken by grief and guilt because she believed that her "bad thoughts" had caused this tragedy. This kind of personal interpretation of an event is partly culture-bound and partly the result of individual psychodynamics. However, precognitive dreams of this type are well known and can be seen as a type of synchronicity. In the case of such a prophetic dream, one can reassure the person that synchronistic events are acausal; the dream does not cause the event it forecasts, but the dream and the event are linked by a common meaning.

Grof and Grof (1989) make a useful distinction between spiritual emergence and spiritual emergency. Both are the result of the eruption of transpersonal levels of consciousness into the empirical personality, but a spiritual emergence is a manageable form of numinous experience that produces the unfolding of spiritual potential without adversely affecting the individual's capacity to function in consensual reality. Typical examples are transient out-of-body experiences, the spontaneous arising of kundalini energy, a near-death experience, a sudden, powerful insight into the nature of reality, or a momentary sense of connection with all things.[15] These experiences can lead to improved well-being, or, if they do not fit into the individual's belief system, they are quickly repressed or dismissed as unimportant. In cases where the subject is not sure of the nature of the experience, the therapist's capacity to recognize its true nature may tip the balance between rejecting the experience and valuing it.

A spiritual emergency is a severe emotional crisis, which may be induced by prolonged meditation or other spiritual practices or may occur spontaneously. A numinous experience that is emotionally unmanageable for the individual or one that is intense and prolonged can produce a state of mind that looks like a psychosis because it disrupts the individual's ability to function.

Various writers such as Agosin (1992) and Perry (1974) have suggested that psychosis is an attempt at self-healing. Perry believed that the prepsychotic personality of the individual was the real problem. The psychosis is the psyche's way of trying to heal restricted emotional development and is a form of spiritual awakening. For Perry, a psychosis is a developmental crisis, the psyche's way of dissolving old states of being and dismantling old personality structures. During the episode, archetypal imagery of the type found in myth emerges in an attempt to reorganize the personality. Unfortunately, the journey is typically misunderstood and pathologized, so instead of being seen for what it is, the process is medicated and not allowed to complete itself.

Lukoff (1985) has suggested that good prognostic indicators help to distinguish between psychopathology and spiritual emergency with psychotic features. These indicators are good previous functioning, acute onset during a period of less than three months, stressful precipitants, and a positive, exploratory attitude. These are also the criteria used by traditional psychiatrists to define an acute, stress-induced psychosis, a condition that commonly resolves without treatment. The clinician's assessment therefore depends on his or her personal belief system.

The therapeutic response to a spiritual emergency partly depends on the capacity of the individual to contain the emotional intensity of the experience without fragmentation. If this ability is strong, the subject may only need reassurance, understanding, and a supportive environment that allows the process to express itself. If possible, the individual should be surrounded by family and friends who are given an explanation of what is happening. One has to help ground the individual in any way possible, often using expressive modalities such as art, dance, or writing. Should all this fail and the individual or others around him become physically endangered, hospitalization may be necessary. Often these experiences are time-limited, but they may be terrifying. In a traditional psychiatric hospital, they are usually understood to be a form of brief psychosis and they are treated with antipsychotic medication. Authors such as Perry believe that these medications abort the natural history of the process. Whether one sees such an experience as a spiritual emergency, a form of mental illness, or both at the same time, is a matter of the lens through which one views the episode.

Sometimes people say that they have never had a numinous experience, yet they may admit they have been deeply moved by nature, by creative work, by the birth of a child, or other situations that produce profound peace, fullness, joy, love, awe, mystery, acceptance, aliveness, gratitude, or a sense of the rightness of things. All these are typical descriptions of the numinosum. It is important for the therapist to remember that the religious instinct can express itself in many ways, for example, in our need for relationship, sexuality, or beauty. It may appear in a pathological form as a craving or addiction; the use of substances such as alcohol or marijuana can be thought of as an attempt at ecstatic merger with the totality. As a culture, we are beginning to rethink our conventional ways of speaking about the sacred, but so strong is our cultural conditioning around the meaning of the word "God" that we seem to need permission to acknowledge that we are experiencing the sacred in our own ways.

Although rarely spoken of by contemporary ministers of religion, numinous experiences are in fact fairly widespread. In 1975, Greeley asked 1,468 Americans whether they had ever felt close to a powerful spiritual force "that seemed to lift you out of yourself" (p. 140). Thirty-five percent reported that they had felt such a force at some time of their life. Twelve percent said they had felt it several times, and five percent felt it often. In a British survey at about the same time, similar figures were obtained, and the survey was repeated in the United States in the 1990s (Wulff 2000; Hardy 1979). According to one study, 4.5 percent of people bring mystical experiences into therapy (Allman, DeLa Roche, Elkins and Weathers 1992). Given the discrepancy between the numbers of people who report numinous experiences and the number that are actually reported to therapists, it seems possible that some people are reluctant to talk to their therapist about such experience. It is not easy to talk about one's experience of the sacred because it feels very private and people are often shy about discussing it.

Much mainstream religion stresses belief rather than direct experience of the sacred, but experiences are far more important than beliefs. Some beliefs, such as the idea of heaven, may be nothing more than defensive ideas that the ego needs in order to support itself or to deal with death anxiety. Such beliefs are soothing and difficult to change. Other beliefs, such as the divine as a trinity, may have no basis in personal experience and are simply formulas that people have grown up with and take for granted. Beliefs such as the notion of the divine as a benevolent heavenly Father may crumble under painful circumstances. Still other beliefs, such as ideas about what God "wants" from us or how we are to "please" God, sound like the anthropomorphic projection of human needs onto the divine, as though the divine needs something from us—an idea that is hardly consistent with the notion of divine perfection. We can be fairly sure that whatever similar concepts human beings have made up about the divine are also likely to be projections, since the divine is not amenable to conceptual thought. Accordingly, in psychotherapy, one can explore the emotional need for, and the developmental origin of, beliefs that have no basis in experience, without fear that one is undermining some essential truth. On the contrary, we may then find that we liberate an authentic image of the divine from imposed doctrine that was obscuring it.

In all cases of spiritual experience, discernment traditionally includes assessing the fruits of the experience. Psychotherapy is an ideal setting for this discernment, because an in-depth understanding of the subject's psychology helps us see the meaning of the experience and its relevance to the person's individuation process. Numinous experience often addresses a particular complex that has been a major issue in the person's therapy. For example, numinous experience tends to dissolve narcissistic structures such as grandiosity, since the experience often leads to humility, greater self-awareness, more compassion for others, a deeper capacity for love and relationship, increased wisdom, and similar benefits. It is not unusual for a numinous experience to suggest a vocation or a developmental step for the individual.

Properly understood, numinous experiences are helpful but temporary affirmations, supports, pointers, or stepping stones. They may indicate a goal, but they are not the goal itself. Inflation results if the ego becomes overly attached to the experience and overidentifies with it rather than relating to it in gratitude and then letting it go. One becomes inflated if one takes the experience to mean that one is particularly special. When the experience is used for such narcissistic enhancement, the therapist can sense that it is being used defensively, to support a fragile sense of self.

Numinous or mystical experiences can be explained in various ways. Some people believe they are reducible to brain phenomena—recently a "God module" was discovered in the brain.[16] If numinous experiences indeed have a neurological correlate, this can be understood in two ways. Either they are produced by the brain itself, and so they are not really experiences of the sacred, or the brain is specifically designed to allow us to experience the sacred and the God module is the necessary organ. It has been suggested that ineffable, mystical experiences arise in the right brain because this side specializes in emotional, synthetic, and holistic responses, whereas the left brain is linguistic, analytic, rational, and logical. In 1963, the neurosurgeon Penfield reported that mild electrical stimulation of the right temporal lobes could produce vague, unknown voices (in Schott 1993). In 1976, Jaynes (1990) suggested that thousands of years ago these voices were common, since at that time the two hemispheres operated relatively independently of each other. In times of crisis, when the left brain could not think of a solution, the right brain's ability to solve the problem would be experienced as the voice of a god. Jaynes suggested that, as consciousness and language developed, the right temporal lobe became quieter and more inhibited, but we retain a vestigial neurological ability to experience mystical experiences, oracular consciousness, and the like.[17]

As well as such neurological explanations, various authors attempt to reduce the experience of the holy to psychodynamic factors. Pruyser (1976) quotes Goodenough's *The Psychology of Religious Experiences*, which suggests that one could think of the *tremendum* aspect of numinous experience as simply the experience of the dynamic unconscious, the id, a source of terror that we sense in ourselves. Religion is then a way of domesticating the unconscious externally, while repression does it internally. In contrast to such reductive explanations, Jung believed that numinous experience is an experience of the Self.[18]

Within mainstream psychiatry, mysticism was pathologized for a long time. In 1976, a monograph by the Group for the Advancement of Psychiatry (GAP) considered mysticism to be a narcissistic regression, a defensive response to overwhelming demands and disappointments in the outer world or the result of an attempt to deal with feelings of being a rejected outsider (GAP 1976, pp. 804–6). The GAP suggested that reports of mystical union with the divine actually represent union with an estranged parental figure. The organization's monograph reported a mystical experience that became the focus of treatment. A woman in her early thirties was in therapy because of unresolved struggles with her parents and guilt over a brother's psychosis. After two years, she experienced a period of ecstasy, a sense of union with the universe, heightened awareness transcending time and space, and an increased sense of meaning and purpose in her life. Her mood could have been referred to as either ecstatic or euphoric depending on whether one wants to use spiritual or psychiatric language. Although it took some time to integrate the experience, she gained from it the conviction that she was a worthwhile person and not the intrinsically evil person, "rotten to the core," that her mother had convinced her she was. Because of her unusual mood, the authors initially considered the possibility that she was suffering from hysteria, mania, or schizophrenia. However, they rejected these diagnoses because in many respects her functioning was "more integrating than disintegrating," and they recognized that her experience was akin to those described by the mystics "who found a new life through them." Nevertheless, for these writers, mystical phenomena are "forms of behavior intermediate between normality and frank psychosis" (ibid., p. 731). The GAP monograph concedes that mystics employ rigorous spiritual disciplines while they maintain ordinary social relationships, whereas schizophrenics are overwhelmed and taken by surprise by their experiences and cannot maintain contact with consensual reality. In fact, the GAP attitude perpetuates a long-standing psychoanalytic prejudice that has only recently begun to fade; although it is true that mystical experience can be disruptive and may be the reason people enter psychotherapy (Nobel 1987), mystics are often capable and socially well adjusted people. Indeed, it may be that mystical experience represents an advanced stage of human consciousness, even the harbinger of an evolutionary advance. Fortunately, contemporary psychoanalysts are considerably more favorably disposed to mystical experience than were their predecessors—so much so, that Eigen is able to write that "there are moments when psychoanalysis is a form of prayer . . . Analytic workers may be touched by intimations of something sacred in the work" (1998, p. 11).

The psychotherapist can study numinous experiences as an outsider, or even as an atheist. Or, one can view them from the inside, as a subject, in which case one is not objective and may not be taken seriously by academic researchers. Nevertheless, one can be grounded in one's own experience and still work with some kind of interpretive approach, using a paradigm that includes both personal experience and systematic study. The interpretation of numinous experience, however, always remains an issue for the therapist; just to recognize an event as numinous is itself an interpretation. Often the experience speaks for itself and requires no interpretation. However, the therapist may be skeptical that an event is an authentic experience of the sacred because of the well-known problems of illusion, hallucination, self-deception, or retrospective falsification. In the individual case, this is always a matter of judgment.

When working with a traditional Christian believer, it is important to remember that the Church has been suspicious of numinous experiences because throughout history various false messiahs and claims of individual revelation have proved to be wrong, although sometimes they are only "wrong" in that they disagree with a particular Church teaching. For example, Barry and Connolly believe that "not all spiritual experiences are from the Lord"

(1982, p. 103). They suggest that moments of harmony and tranquility, for instance, may distract the person from focusing on Jesus.[19] According to these authors, only "touchstone" experience of God may be trusted, and all others should be compared with it. They quote St. Paul's statement (Gal. 5:22–23) that the fruits of the spirit are positive qualities such as love, joy, peace and so on, implying that negative or painful experiences are not those of the spirit. For contemplative psychology, however, there is no requirement that a numinous experience should take a traditional form, and since the Self has a dark side the experience may be subjectively felt as positive or negative.

It is important to add the caveat that to find the sacred in the ordinary is as important as dramatic numinous experiences—perhaps more so. With a spiritual sensibility, one can see any creature or any object that inspires awe, a sense of beauty, mystery, grace, or terror as an expression of the divine. With this vision, we can resacralize or reenchant the world.

THE IMPORTANCE OF COMMUNITY

In typical discussions of mystical experience, the importance of community is not usually held to be as important as subjective experience. However, participation with others in a shared vision of reality is powerful and important. Part of this is due to the experience of twinship (Kohut 1984), the feeling that one is not alone, that one is like other people. As a part of a community, one feels safe and supported, especially if one also feels chosen or saved, the special child of an omnipotent deity, in contrast to those who are not so blessed. Of course, there is a shadow side to belonging to a community of believers. Individual autonomy may be discouraged, and the price of protection by the group is submission to a hierarchy. The group tries to preserve itself at all cost, so individuals become less important than the group. Outsiders are suspect, even to the point of paranoia. Tribalism breeds exclusion and enmity, sometimes to the extent that others are less than human, so that even the killing of members of other groups may be divinely sanctioned.

It may be difficult for individuals interested in a personal spirituality to find a group of like-minded people. It may then be necessary for the therapist to point out that individuation may require that the individual not be a part of an organized system of thought. Ideally, we need spiritual communities that are designed to support each member in the discovery of his or her personal spirituality.

NOTES

1. Strictly speaking, the word *holy* refers to that which the divine itself has revealed, whereas to call something sacred is a human attribution; it means that human beings venerate a thing or place or experience. Thus, a fundamentalist Christian might say that the Bible is holy but the sacred books of the East, or Native American ritual items, are sacred only to people who revere them. In this text, I will use the terms *holy* and *sacred* interchangeably, since I'm interested in subjective experience.

2. For a discussion of the epistemological issues involved in the perception of the divine, I recommend Alston (1991).

3. It is noteworthy that, as Anthony Stevens points out, the notion of possession and its treatment by exorcism is the "rhizome from which dynamic psychiatry and analysis have sprouted" (1993, p. 110). Barbara Hannah's (2011) lectures on the animus provide in-depth discussion of a well-documented case of medieval possession.

4. For a discussion of paranormal events in psychotherapy, see Mintz (1983).

5. For a more detailed discussion of numinous experience, see Corbett (1996; 2007).

6. Examples include the Celtic god Cernunnos, the Hellenistic Egyptian deity Serapis, and the Greek god Hermes. According to Jung, the triadic character is an attribute of gods of the underworld (1948b, par. 270). See also Miller (2005).

7. The traditional Christian prejudice against sexuality may be the result of the belief that Jesus was not married and did not express his sexuality, so that human sexuality is an unredeemed aspect of our nature and therefore is problematic.

8. For a discussion of synchronicity, see Aziz (1990).

9. *Unus mundus* is a medieval term for the notion that the world is a unity. At the present state of our knowledge, the notion of the *unus mundus* is a hypothesis—some would say a metaphysical one, even though Jung said he eschewed metaphysics. Similarly, Jung's notion that the same transcendental meaning could manifest itself both intrapsychically and in the outer world also smacks of metaphysics (1952, par. 915). It is important to note however that the notion of a transcendent ground that expresses itself both

psychologically and physically gets us past the notion that Jung's psychology is purely intrapsychic. Synchronicity links psyche and the material world.

10. For an example of a delusional interpretation of a synchronistic event, see von Franz (1980, pp. 196–97).

11. For a discussion of this controversy, see Dourley (1994) and Stephens (2001).

12. Not to mention the fact that each monotheistic tradition claims that its revelation is the final one or the only correct one, so that its community is privileged, whereas for the spiritually oriented therapist, revelation is continuous and no one experience of the numinosum is more valid than any other. For many Jungian therapists, traditional monotheistic God-images are expressions of particular aspects of the Self. Thus, the notion that God is one is an attempt to express the underlying unity of the Self, although it is clear that the Self or the unconscious has many centers of interest and cannot be thought of as an entity or as one as a mathematical number in the ordinary sense. Seen in this light, there is no need for the competition between the monotheistic traditions.

13. For a comparison of Jung and Whitehead, see Smith (1995, p. 160ff.).

14. Most religious conversion occurs gradually, as noted in 1897 in a now classical account by Edwin Starbuck. He found that conversion experiences in adolescents were typically preceded by a sense of sin and confusion that was resolved through the conversion experience. Modern research has confirmed this. Ullman (1989), for instance, found that most converts were searching for meaning before their conversion. Many of them had experienced severe childhood deprivation and a difficult father, which predisposed them to a powerfully important relationship with the guru, rabbi, or priest leading the group to which they were converted.

15. A kundalini experience is one in which a feeling of tingling, heat, or other sensation rises up the spine, often accompanied by tremors or other involuntary movements, followed by complex visual phenomena. Traditionally it is thought to be due to the rising of a latent form of spiritual energy that usually lies dormant at the base of the spine, but which may rise up as a result of spiritual practice. People who spontaneously experience this arising in an unprepared way are often diagnosed as psychotic or hysterical. See Sanella (1987).

16. Researchers at the University of California San Diego have discovered a region of the brain that, when stimulated, creates effects that are interpreted as mystical or spiritual experiences. This "God module" is now thought to be the seat of religious belief (Ramachandran et al. 1997). It has been suggested that this area of the brain evolved to produce religions in order to reduce conflict and reinforce social stability and kinship.

17. For a review of other neurological explanations of mystical experience, see Wulff (2000).

18. Jung asserts that "consciousness experiences this supraordinate totality [the Self] as something numinous, as a *tremendum* or *fascinosum*" (1959, par. 874). It is arguable that if the Self is the totality of consciousness, the ego cannot be conscious of the Self, since the ego is only a fragment, which could not grasp the whole. Yet the Self is the source of numinous experience. This kind of paradox is inevitable and insoluble.

19. They also cite the example of St. Ignatius of Loyola, who often saw a beautiful image that comforted him a great deal. When kneeling before a crucifix, he saw the image again without its usual beautiful color, "with a strong affirmation of his will he knew very clearly that it came from the demon" (Barry and Connolly 1982, p. 103). Note that he has to exert his will, based on his preconceived ideas, to discount the experience.

Faith, Love, Forgiveness, and Hope in Psychotherapy

FAITH

Although faith is traditionally thought of in its theological dimension, it is also of considerable psychological importance in the lives of many people. Without faith, many people would collapse emotionally—for them, faith is more important than reliance on reason alone, in spite of many attempts to insist on the primacy of reason. Faith is not only a source of strength but also of religious violence. Faith is also important to the psychotherapist because faith in the process of therapy is demanded of both participants. The psychodynamic underpinnings of faith, and whatever might undermine it, are therefore very relevant to the therapist.

Faith is common to people of all religious traditions and so links people in a way that transcends doctrinal differences. Yet faith is difficult to define neatly because it is inextricably connected with trust and hope. Some attempts at definition describe capacities that develop because of faith, rather than being descriptions of the nature of faith itself. Panikkar (1979) points out that faith is a container for one's beliefs rather than a particular intellectual content, so faith is different from belief in specific religious ideas, which are only a vehicle for the expression of faith. Faith is sometimes described as belief in a spiritual dimension in the absence of incontrovertible evidence of its existence; this makes for a rather weak definition, as what constitutes evidence is open to discussion. For the scientific naturalist who believes that matter is the only reality, evidence means data that is empirically testable—but this definition insists that the objective, scientific approach to reality is the only meaningful one and so discounts the importance of human subjectivity. Especially if one has directly experienced a transcendent level of reality, explanations of faith in terms of evolutionary biology seem trivial. In contrast, for many people, faith means their felt sense that the universe is intelligible, the sense that there exists a deep ground to which one can respond and surrender, and the sense that one is supported by that ground. We do not really understand why some people have faith in a spiritual dimension and others do not. It seems that some of us are grasped by something that feels very real, as if we are being drawn to a deeper and deeper understanding or truth, what Tillich called "ultimate concern."

Perhaps the closest we have to a psychological explanation of faith has to do with the development of trust and hope in early childhood. Erikson believes that our childhood sense of hope, based on parenting that is reliable enough for the child to develop basic trust, is eventually transformed into mature faith. Influenced by Erikson, Fowler suggests that basic trust is an early stage of faith, which goes on to mature in tandem with chronological age, culminating in universalizing faith in which one embraces the world as one's community and becomes selfless. As Fowler puts it, faith "involves an alignment of the will, a resting of the heart, in accordance with a vision of transcendent value and power, one's ultimate concern . . . an orientation of the total person, giving purpose and goal to one's hopes and strivings, thoughts and actions" (1981, p. 14).

Since it is common for therapists and the people with whom they work to experience periods of doubt and uncertainty during the process of psychotherapy, it is important that we have faith in the therapeutic process. The ability of both participants to stay with a difficult situation when there is no obvious reason to hope for improvement is an act of faith. To trust a therapist and to trust that the relationship will evolve in the necessary way are both acts of faith. Just as people profess faith in different religious systems, so faith allows therapists of different orientations to feel that their approach will ultimately be of value if they persevere. Confidence in the process of therapy is particularly important during times when the therapist cannot say exactly what is happening. If the therapist has been through such periods in his or her personal therapy, he or she has developed faith in the process, and the person senses this.

Practitioners with a spiritual sensibility recognize and have faith in a transcendent presence in the therapy room. Jung refers to this presence as the transpersonal Self, which he regards as synonymous with the (unknowable) totality of the psyche. To have faith that we can trust the psyche means to realize that it is a real domain in its own right and that its images are meaningful and relevant. We find an analogous idea to Jung's notion of the Self in the work of Bion, for whom the inner world arises from what he calls "Ultimate Reality" or "O," which

> stands for the absolute truth in and of any object; it is assumed that this cannot be known by any human being; it can be known about, its presence can be recognized and felt, but it cannot be known. It is possible to be at one with it. That it exists is an essential postulate of science but it cannot be scientifically discovered. No psycho-analytic discovery is possible without recognition of its existence. (1979, p. 30)

One aspect of what Bion is referring to here is the sense of something mysterious or uncanny that sometimes seems to be a part of the therapeutic field. We can sense this dimension but we cannot perceive it with our ordinary sense organs. We feel a dynamic agency in the room that is not controlled by our own will, as Jung puts it (1940, par. 6). Bion urges the therapist to search for the "O" of the session or the "O" of the person, his or her essence or "true self," even as we recognize that we cannot attain it. We open ourselves in the faith that we will meet "O." Since we "cannot know 'O,' one must be it" (1979, p. 27). That is to say, there is a difference between just knowing and actually being who we are. In the pursuit of "O," faith operates just as it does in traditional religion; faith in this presence grants the courage to struggle with the painful emotions that afflict both participants in psychotherapy. Otherwise, if

we try to cling to what we know, to what theory tells us, there will
be no new understanding, no true contact, and no mystery.

According to Bion, "O" can only be apprehended when there
is no memory, desire, knowledge, or understanding, because these
impede being by attempting to change reality instead of accepting
it. Such radical openness to the unknown is an act of faith which
takes the therapist beyond his or her knowledge and technique.
Ideally, according to Bion, the therapist's attitude to the work is an
act of faith, which he regards as essential (1979, pp. 41–54). (Bion's
attitude is reminiscent of Krishnamurti's stress on the importance
of choice-less attention to what-is, discussed further in chapter 8.)
Bion says that the religious mystics have probably come closest to
the experience of "O." Milton referred to it as the formless infinite,
and Huxley called it the divine ground of being. For Plato it was
the level of Ideal Forms, while for Kant it was the noumenal level
of reality. "O" is the gap in our knowledge, the emptiness from
which all existence comes. Bion realized that to some people this
state may appear terrifying, chaotic, and annihilating, but for Bion,
faith is that very quality which enables us to face and work with
catastrophe. Faith allows us to relinquish control at times and accept the way things are.

Eigen writes about the importance of attending to the emotional truth of a situation. He points out that we adjust ourselves
to what truth discloses; we cannot control where truth will lead; we
have to "relate to truth with faith" (1999, p. 32). Eigen implies,
correctly I believe, that we have an innate impulse to understand
the truth of our lives. This search is an implicit or tacit assumption
within most schools of dynamic psychotherapy, although therapists with a postmodern outlook may feel that such truth is purely
a personal narrative and is not absolute. In contrast, my personal
therapeutic myth—which may sound old-fashioned to the dedi-
cated post-modernist—tells me that each personality has its own
objective truth, and this discovery has a helpful effect.

LOVE IN THE THERAPEUTIC RELATIONSHIP

Religious traditions often stress the transformative power of love.

Since the therapist is interested in anything that contributes to transformation, it is worth considering the role of love in psychotherapy, where love often arises. If it is true, as St. Paul says, that love "bears all things" and "endures all things" (1 Cor. 13:7), then such a powerful force must be important to the spiritually oriented therapist. Our task is to understand something of its vicissitudes and discern its psychological and spiritual relevance to the individual and the therapeutic process.

There have been many attempts to define love, but none are satisfactory, partly because the word seems to have so many meanings. We use the same word for experiences that are both personal and transpersonal.[1] Explanations for the existence of love range from the neurological to the behavioral and psychoanalytic (e.g., Sternberg and Barnes 1988; Sternberg and Weis 2006; Lewis, Amini and Lannon 2000). Fromm, for example, defines the essence of human love as a type of correct giving that does not create indebtedness (1956, p. 36). He is probably trying to get at the bridging function of love, which prevents isolation and encourages participation and service to others. But such behavior seems to be the result of love, rather than love itself, and such a definition would not account for experiences such as the following:

> One day, I was sweeping the stairs . . . when suddenly I was overcome, overwhelmed, saturated . . . with a sense of a most sublime and living *love*. It not only affected me, but seemed to bring everything around me to *life*. The brush in my hand, my dustpan, the stairs, seemed to come alive with love. I seemed no longer me, with my petty troubles and trials, but part of this infinite power of love, so utterly and overwhelmingly wonderful that one knew at once what the saints had grasped. It could only have been a minute or two, yet for that brief particle of time it seemed eternity. (Cohen and Phipps 1979, p. 70)

We could not possibly say what possessed this person if she were to describe this numinous experience in the therapy room. Whatever it was, it was not simply a product of her developmental history. It would be reductive to explain it entirely in terms of psychodynamic theory, as a repeat of feelings she first experienced in relation to her early objects. Indeed, to attempt such an explanation would be to risk trivializing her experience. Her account reveals one of love's paradoxes: although love is an experience of the transpersonal dimension, at the same time it feels intensely personal.

The nature of love is a mystery, so that Krishnamurti is surely correct when he says that we can only say what love is not. He points out that love is not desire, pleasure, possessiveness, lust, dependency, the pain of absence, or any of the other feelings that may be mistaken for love or associated with it, which are all concerns of the ego. It is fashionable to say that there are various kinds of love, so that erotic love is different than spiritual love or *agape*, which is in turn different from loving friendship, and so on. I suggest that when one can describe love in specific terms, one is not talking about that mysterious form of transpersonal love that eludes all definition—the love that Dante said "moves the sun and other stars." That is why Jung wrote that love is primitive, primeval, and "more spiritual than anything we can describe. . . . It is an eternal secret" (1973–1975, p. 298). The psychotherapist may be able to see what gets in the way of love and describe some of the conditions necessary for it to flourish, but none of that is to explain its nature. As Jung points out, in antiquity Eros was understood to be a god that could not be comprehended or represented. There is no adequate language to express transpersonal love, which is, in Jung's words, "a *kosmogonos*, a creator and father-mother of all higher consciousness" (1961, p. 353).[2] According to Jung, we are the victims and the instruments of cosmogonic love, which is something superior to the individual. He suggests that because love is an undivided whole, we cannot grasp its nature, since we are a part rather than a whole. We are at love's mercy; we may assent to it or rebel against it, but we are always caught up by it and enclosed within it, dependent on it and sustained by it. Love is our light and our darkness, whose end we cannot see. We should "name the unknown by the more unknown . . . that is, by the name of God" (ibid., p. 354). Love can be a bridge to the experience of the divine, but at the same time, love has a dangerous aspect that can be destructive, so that like any spiritual process, love must be tempered by as much insight, consciousness, and differentiation as possible. That is, for the sake of balance love needs to be coupled with a degree of Logos.

Whether love will appear is beyond our control; the best we can do is allow the conditions for it to arise, and when it does so the most we can do is pay careful attention to it and wait to see its demands. If we cannot say what love is, we know some of the things it can do and we recognize the presence of love by its effects. Walter Hilton, a fourteenth-century English priest, said it well when he said that "Love worketh wisely and softly in a soul where he will, for he slayeth mightily ire and envy and all passions of angriness and melancholy in it, and bringeth into the soul virtues of patience and mildness, peaceability and amity" (cited in Cohen and Phipps 1979, p. 60). For the therapist, these virtues are important when we feel ambivalence, hatred, or rage toward the person with whom we are working—which happens to all of us at times—yet because of love, we are able to at least try to be therapeutic rather than retaliate. Winnicott (1947) emphasized the importance or inevitability of hatred, which sometimes has to occur before love can be tolerated. Psychotherapeutic theory tells us how to behave in such circumstances, but in spite of our knowledge of technique, at the level of the heart only love is powerful enough to contain our destructive feelings. When these arise, the therapist's capacity for love becomes a conscious concern, because the inability to love is a painful problem when working with people who seem distinctly unlovable. Even under ordinary circumstances, the burden of human suffering—the sheer amount and intensity of need—often seem to overwhelm the therapist's capacity for love.

One could make a good case for the idea that although love is not sufficient by itself, it is an essential ingredient of the process of effective psychotherapy.[3] The field of depth psychotherapy began with Freud's discovery that major change in the patient's psyche requires love. He described this in terms of erotic love within the transference, but this is only one aspect of a larger process. It is an important event when love occurs within psychotherapy, but to describe this love only in terms of a repeat within the transference of early object relations or as the projection of the anima or animus or as an attempt at reparation for damage to our early objects is not the whole story (Racker 1968). These intellectual constructs do not do it justice. To reduce love to an intrapsychic phenomenon is to ignore the reality of the other person. We would be better to think of love as an autonomous, transpersonal experience. When it arises in the therapy room, it is best to recognize it as a divine guest; one then has to be a proper host to it.

Falling in love with the therapist (or with anyone else) leads to a repeat of early relational dynamics with their attendant needs, yearnings, and frustrations. Romantic love, or love within the transference, can therefore stimulate the process of individuation, because when we love we invariably run into problems that are important raw material for the individuation journey. We meet our shadow, jealousy, loneliness, the desire to possess the other, qualities about ourselves and the loved one that we would like to change, and so on. Consequently, the psychoanalytic literature has a rather jaundiced view of love and tends to focus on its sexual dynamics and its pathology rather than its positive aspects (Rubin 2004; Kernberg 1995). Classical psychoanalysts are largely skeptical about the healing power of love, although there have been important exceptions such as Fromm, who stressed the importance of love in psychotherapy, and Ferenczi, who believed that "the patient is ill because he has not been loved" (cited in Thompson 1943, p. 64), so that love is indispensable to the healing process. Ferenczi makes the important point that the therapist cannot just decide to love; it has to emerge spontaneously (1926; 1995). Influenced by Ferenczi, Suttie declared that one-sided love cannot be curative, and "the physician's love heals the patient" (1935, p. 212).

Until recently, few writers would acknowledge that therapists often love their patients, but this possibility is gradually creeping into the literature. Natterson (1996) suggests that psychotherapy is a "mutually loving process" in which the therapist's capacity to subordinate his or her own subjectivity fosters the actualization of love and the development of the patient's self. Shaw (2003) differentiates "analytic love" from romantic, sexual, and countertransference love yet at the same time points out that the search for love and for the sense of being lovable is at the heart of psychoanalysis and in fact motivates both participants, not just the analysand. It is hardly necessary to add that the presence of love in the therapy room does not preclude standard psychotherapeutic technique, maintenance of a frame, and responsible behavior.

To acknowledge that love in the therapy room is a transpersonal process makes that love sacred. Clinicians have been shy to describe it this way, preferring to use clinical terms, thereby contributing to an artificial sequestering of psychotherapy and spirituality. At the same time, it is important to acknowledge that love alone will not be sufficient to help many of the people with whom we work. We also need a firm foundation in the technical aspects of psychotherapy, as well as the realization that the therapist is not the source of love, but only its vehicle of expression.

In general, falling in love has a mixed reputation, and romantic love is often unfavorably contrasted with other, more enduring or serious kinds of love. Shideler has a trenchant description of the wide range of attitudes toward romantic love:

> The event is described as ridiculous, sublime, a transitory episode appropriate only for adolescents, a form of temporary insanity, the sole justification for living at any age, normative, normal, abnormal, pathological, and good clean healthy fun. No doubt it is all these things. (1962, p. 29)

The sudden experience of love, an involuntary fall in the true sense of the word, can be radically transformative. When we are "in" love, we are awakened to the transpersonal love that is within us and around us, so that everything looks a little different, more whole. It is often said that this happens because the lover is temporarily living in a world of illusion, idealization, and projection, a temporary perceptual aberration or near madness. But perhaps love removes the blinders produced by mundane reality, and the lover is actually seeing the world the way it really is—alive with love. Perhaps our ordinary loveless state of mind is the true illusion, and love is one of our sources of authentic transcendence. On the mundane or egoic level, the one we love is then a pointer to the love of God, or, as the nondual spiritual traditions would have it, at the absolute level he or she is an expression of the divine, and we have experienced that. In other words, I suggest that being in love is a state of mind that more closely reflects reality than does our ordinary consciousness. That may be why Plato recognized that love gives us an opening into knowledge of the spiritual world.

The notion that the experience of romantic love is an experience of the divine was termed "romantic theology" by Charles Williams (1990), who described it from a specifically Christian perspective.[4] An important aspect of the story of Jesus is that love always leads to some form of crucifixion. One can read the Gospel story as a metaphor for the way in which love becomes pinned down on the cross of material reality. Yet the fact that love often seems to fails us or fails to endure does not necessarily mean it was merely an illusory phenomenon from the start. Like all spiritually important states of mind, authentic love can be eroded by the demands of the ego, by narcissistic issues, by the repetition of unconscious pathogenic early object relations, or by very immature selfobject needs. These factors act as barriers to love, and their amelioration in psychotherapy helps spiritual as well as psychological development.

In psychotherapy, one has to bear in mind the relationship between power and love. In a letter, Jung suggests that even wanting to help a patient may not be legitimate if it is motivated by power. Helping can be an encroachment on the will of others, so according to Jung: "Your attitude ought to be that of one who offers an opportunity that can be taken or rejected. Otherwise you are most likely to get into trouble" (1973–1975, p. 83). We see this kind of encroachment most clearly among religionists who think they know what is right for other people's souls. It is easy to mistreat someone in the name of religion, insisting one is acting out of love but with a complete lack of empathy. We see a similar kind of impingement when the therapist has a "treatment plan" or a therapeutic "goal" that is based either on an ego-driven assumption that the therapist can understand the proper destiny of the individual or on a particular theoretical notion of mental health. The imposition of a treatment plan may require the use of power and submission to the therapist's agenda, which may repeat a childhood scenario. A more respectful approach is to follow where the soul wants to lead by being receptive to the quality of the unfolding therapeutic relationship, which is guided by the Self rather than by the ego.

FORGIVENESS IN PSYCHOTHERAPY

Forgiveness is a traditional spiritual virtue whose psychological (McCullough, Pargament and Thoreson 2000; Worthington 1998) and philosophical (Downie 1965; Horsbrugh 1974; Lewis 1980) importance is increasingly recognized. In addition to its spiritual implications, forgiveness or the lack thereof has important effects on physical and emotional health. However, forgiveness is a good example of the ways in which powerful psychological obstacles may make it difficult or impossible to implement a spiritual teaching. Anger and bitterness are understandable human reactions to being hurt, and these feelings are particularly difficult to let go of when they fuel our ability to resist abuse or injustice and allow us to cope with a situation rather than collapsing. Rage helps us to maintain self-esteem in the face of humiliation, and when rage becomes chronic it turns into hatred. To hate the perpetrator is a way of preventing feelings of helplessness and weakness, because hatred energizes the personality, thus becoming addictive and difficult to deal with. Our outrage at being violated is a powerful way of communicating to the offender that we have been hurt, and it attracts support from family and friends, although persistent rage at the perpetrator tends to have an alienating effect eventually and makes the establishment of new relationships more difficult. If we remain angry and bitter for a long period of time, the stress of chronic overarousal contributes to heart disease, impaired immune status, and other maladies (Diamond 1982). Not only does forgiveness improve physical health, forgiveness allows peace of mind and a sense of self-efficacy.

One way of thinking about forgiveness is to imagine that an offense has caused an interpersonal debt and that in order to forgive one has to cancel the debt, give up the need or the right to retaliate, let go of resentment at or contempt for the perpetrator, and not bear a continuous grudge (Baumeister, Exline and Sommer 1998). This issue arises in psychotherapy when we work with memories of abuse by parents with whom the individual is still angry or during the course of therapy with couples. A person with a harsh superego may find it difficult to forgive himself or herself for a personal failing, leading to self-punishment, diminished self-respect, depression, or sometimes the defense mechanism of undoing, the unconscious attempt to erase something one has done to try to expiate one's guilt. Some religious rituals and some volunteer work and public service involve this mechanism.

One may make the decision to forgive an offender and then try to forgive but be unable to do so because anger and resentment persist. This causes particular problems when the victim of an offense is committed to a tradition such as Christianity, which stresses forgiveness—"as the Lord has forgiven you, so you also must forgive" (Col. 3:13)—in which case the inability to forgive may lead to shame or guilt which further burden the individual long after the original injury. Not only this, the Christian has been told (Mat. 6:14–15) that if a person does not forgive others, his or her own wrongdoings will not be forgiven by God, a teaching that places a huge emotional burden on sincere believers. To try to forgive because one is told to be forgiving by a scripture may lead to denial of one's anger and hurt.

Psychotherapy with an aggrieved person means that the therapist has to walk a fine line; to forgive prematurely would produce an artificial denial of grief and rage at being hurt, which must be explored and worked through before forgiveness can be authentic. The therapist may need to point out that forgiveness is usually a gradual process. One may wish to forgive completely, but in practice forgiveness is sometimes tentative, incomplete, or conditional on no further injury being inflicted. When the victim feels humiliated or devalued by the offense, the damage to the victim's self-esteem must be repaired before forgiveness is even attempted. Furthermore, the current situation may be one of a recurrent pattern of abuse that may go back to childhood. In such a case, a new offense taps into a reservoir of resentment that has never been expressed, and the victim may find himself or herself feeling what seems to be irrational rage at the perpetrator.

Even if the individual would like to forgive, a variety of conscious or unconscious factors prevent forgiveness, such as the following:

- The wish to remain in the role of victim, which gives one leverage and may lead to financial or other benefits, such as a sense of moral superiority.

- The presence of continuous suffering or grief over a major loss caused by the offender.

- Persistent shame at being abused or offended, because one's sense of self-worth has been damaged.

- The insistence that justice is more important than forgiveness and mercy. This attitude is often more afunction of character structure than logic.

- The concern that forgiveness will be seen as a sign of weakness.

- The concern that forgiveness will be equated with condoning the injury.

- The concern that forgiveness shows lack of self-respect or excessive vulnerability.

- The attempt to forgive prematurely, before the injury has healed. This is often a form of denial.

- The fear that forgiveness will lead to further abuse.

- The inability to be empathic with the perpetrator or to see any mitigating circumstances, so that the victim cannot understand why the offense occurred.

- The persistent need to get the abuser to realize how badly one was hurt.

- The persistent need to force the abuser to acknowledge guilt and take responsibility.

- The persistent need for some kind of reparation from the abuser.

- Persistent narcissistic rage at the abuser, often with fantasies of revenge or retaliation.

- Abuse or betrayal that has reawakened a similar childhood dynamic.
- The absence of signs of repentance and apology from the abuser.
- The projection of the victim's own character difficulties onto the perpetrator.

Forgiveness is fostered by the realization that one's wounded sense of self is in fact a wound to an image we have of ourselves, that what has been hurt is the way we like to think of ourselves, and this is a socially and psychologically conditioned narrative. To the extent that we do not forgive, we are often holding onto this image in an attempt to strengthen or sustain it, sometimes because an aggrieved sense of moral superiority over the offender makes one feel better about oneself. This realization allows a change of consciousness—or perhaps a change of consciousness allows this change to occur; it is difficult to say which comes first, or if they arise together. In any case, if we remember that our deepest level of identity is not this image, forgiveness becomes easier. When we see that only our self-image has been hurt, we are more likely to remember that our spiritual essence, whether we call it witness consciousness, the Self, the Buddha nature, Christ-consciousness, Purusha, the Atman, or the divine within, remains inviolable. To bear this in mind while struggling with the issue of forgiveness takes us to an interface of psychotherapy and spiritual practice. For the therapist, working through rage and hurt usually takes precedence over discussions about our spiritual essence, so that the timing of a discussion about image-rather-than-essence requires tact and sensitivity to the person's state of mind. If one has been offended, one may know cognitively that it is "only" one's image of oneself that is hurting, but to see this reality may not stop the pain. Severe emotional turmoil or major characterological problems make it fruitless to point out that the spiritual essence of the individual is not his or her body, mind, or personality. It is hard to translate the *knowledge* that this is so into an *experience* of this truth.

Certain types of character pathology make forgiveness more

difficult. A narcissistic character structure acts as a serious obstacle to forgiveness because it precludes empathy for the perpetrator and prevents the humility that forgiveness demands. When the perpetrator is a narcissistic character, it is often too shameful to acknowledge wrongdoing. The narcissist's need to maintain self-esteem, deflect blame, and avoid shame is more important than maintaining a relationship with the victim. Masochistic character pathology may make the victim deny the gravity of the abuse and even defend the perpetrator. In such a case, the therapist may have to help the person acknowledge the severity of the abuse and the interpersonal dynamics involved before the issue of forgiveness is even on the therapeutic horizon. Conversely, some paranoid individuals are so sensitive to interpersonal slight that they perceive injury where none was intended. Psychopaths are notoriously unforgiving, as are obsessionals with a harsh superego. There are many people who are able to forgive others but not themselves. In all these situations, it is useful to remember that, for the therapist, forgiveness or the lack thereof is a psychological problem and not a moral issue in the way it is for the theologian or philosopher. It is pointless for the therapist to talk about the importance of *agape* with an angry borderline patient who has just received a further injury to an already fragile sense of self.

Current work in this area (McCullough, Worthington and Rachal 1997) suggests that the degree of sincerity of apology one receives affects the likelihood of being forgiven. In fact, some people withhold forgiveness unless the wrongdoer is obviously repentant, although others insist that forgiveness is a state of mind of the victim and has nothing to do with the behavior of the wrongdoer. Nevertheless, conciliatory behavior and attempts at reparation on the part of the abuser improve the likelihood of forgiveness, just as a reasonable attitude on the part of the victim is more likely to lead to repentance on the part of the perpetrator. When considering hurtful or abusive behavior, it helps if one can empathically imagine oneself in the position of the perpetrator and understand why he or she behaved in a hurtful way. One might even be able to imagine oneself behaving in a similar way under certain circumstances, which tends to ameliorate one's sense of outrage at being hurt. However, preoccupation with one's suffering or the need to hold on to a sense of grievance to bolster self-esteem make it difficult to take into account the motives of the perpetrator.

The problem for the therapist arises with a countertransference response in which the therapist overidentifies with the victim's hurt. It is difficult to encourage forgiveness in another if the therapist has trouble forgiving his or her own abusers. The therapist's personal need to forgive may arise in the context of a negative transference in which the therapist is the target of rage, hatred, or envy.

It is sometimes important for the therapist to point out that forgiveness is not the same as reconciliation. To forgive does not mean that we condone the perpetrator's behavior or that the offense is unimportant. Neither does the fact that one has forgiven the perpetrator mean that one has to stay in relationship with him or her or that one will be able to trust the perpetrator in the future. For example, an abused wife may forgive her husband because she understands that he had been abused as a child, but she still may decide to divorce him. Sexual predators were usually sexually abused in their own childhoods, and while this does not excuse their behavior or preclude legal consequences, it allows a degree of understanding. As Holmgren (1993) points out, one may forgive the abuser as a person but not include him in any kind of close relationship; one can forgive but not forget. Forgiveness is therefore not the same as pardoning; the offender may still have to pay a legal penalty for an offense. In the end, it is not up to the therapist to decide that a person "should" forgive an offense; some people take the position that they will never do so. Whatever one's decision, there is sometimes an element of grace involved; forgiveness may happen spontaneously, for no obvious reason.

In its larger cultural context, the issue of forgiveness has important implications for the question of whether there are some offenses against humanity that are unforgivable. If we really understood all the social, archetypal, and developmental factors that produced a character such as Hitler, Saddam Hussein, or a run-of-the-mill cold-blooded murderer, and given the notion of individual destiny, could such a person ever be truly forgiven? (To reiterate: to forgive does not mean to pardon and does not preclude legal penalties.) In spite of our outrage and abhorrence toward such people, it is arguable that the answer eventually must be affirmative, for several reasons. First because we recognize that such individuals are in the grip of emotional forces that they cannot control. As well, if we treat such a person in an inhumane manner, we become something like him and we tend to perpetuate his pathology. In the final analysis, we must remember that even these people are expressions of the Self.

Wounding to the ego or our sense of self can be a bridge to spiritual development, for example, when grief or pain leads to authentic spiritual surrender. Some authors see psychological and spiritual growth as different lines of development which sometimes intersect and sometimes are distinct. I suggest that the need to forgive illustrates the fact that there is often no difference between one's spirituality and one's psychology. At these times, working on one's emotional life becomes a spiritual practice in its own right.

In this context, we have to be careful about what Welwood (2002) called "spiritual bypassing." This means that one uses spiritual teachings and techniques to avoid psychological difficulties and everyday problems of living. For example, a person may live in a monastery that requires chastity as part of the tradition's spiritual practice, but the unconscious reason he is there is to avoid or contain a sexual problem. Another person will not allow anger because it is "unchristian," but in reality he stresses forgiveness mainly because he has a fear of his own rage. Nonattachment may conceal emotional withdrawal and lack of the capacity for intimacy, while "letting go" or forgiveness may be a disguise for masochistic submission. Some religious people are intolerant of their own neediness or selfishness, which they interpret as moral or spiritual failures. To deny these feelings, they become compulsive helpers of other people. They rationalize their self-sacrifice as a spiritual obligation, often to the extent that they ignore their own legitimate needs. For others, spiritual practice is used narcissistically to enhance the sense of self, to allow one to feel superior to those who do not practice. In other words, the spiritual search has unconscious motivations, and our spirituality may actually be a disguised container for our emotional difficulties. In therapy, this situation can be dealt with the way we deal with any other defensive operation: tactfully and sensitively, not too early or too bluntly. The therapist has to wait until the self-selfobject tie is secure enough to address the defense.

HOPE IN PSYCHOTHERAPY

The spiritual and psychological importance of hope can hardly be overstated. The world's theistic traditions all emphasize its importance, since the capacity to hope is so closely connected to faith in the divine. Nevertheless, although religious traditions recommend hope unreservedly, for the psychotherapist the situation is more complex because hope and hopelessness are intimately connected to the psychodynamics of the person. For the therapist to simply recommend hope might ignore these dynamics, which must be understood if talk of hope is to be of any help.

It is common for the psychotherapist to be confronted with a person who has completely given up hope. When working with a person in despair, it is difficult for the therapist to know how to respond. To try to instill hope in such a person may be grossly unempathic, making the person feel that the therapist does not really understand how bad things are. Attempts at encouragement may lead to the sense that the therapist cannot tolerate being with the person, which makes his or her situation worse. Yet whatever his or her conscious attitude, the fact that the person has come to therapy implies that hope is not dead. To clarify this dilemma it is worth discussing the nature of hope, although it is difficult to give an account of hope that would satisfy all practitioners.

Part of the complication is that our affective state radically affects our capacity to hope, and we do not have an agreed-upon approach to affect.[5] Nevertheless, most therapists would agree that a degree of hope seems to be an aspect of a normal mood and a healthy sense of self, while hopelessness is a common feature of depression and a collapsing sense of self. We often see hopelessness combined with painful internal emptiness.

Hope implies the future; it is a state of mind that allows one to search for something that is missing, accompanied by the sense that one might find it. Hope allows us to tolerate uncertainty without collapsing. At the conscious level, hope arises from an evaluation or appraisal of reality that is linked to our intentions and to our wishing and willing, part of a spectrum that includes longing and expectation. Another source of hope lies in the unconscious, where it results from a repository of early developmental experiences in which help arrived when we needed it. Consequently we do not decide to hope; hope may emerge into consciousness, apparently an act of grace, whereupon we either assent to it or we do not. Total loss of hope gives rise to despair, which could be thought of as the anticipation that loss, failure, and defeat are certain, combined with no capacity for accepting help when it is offered. Hope is not always positive, since one may hope for death, for example. Paradoxically, hopelessness can stimulate rage that motivates action, which may revitalize a depleted sense of self.

For the psychotherapist, the important questions are the effects of hope and hopelessness in therapy and the issue of why some people are able to cope with severe stress while remaining hopeful and others cannot. This issue is important because we know that the capacity to maintain hope is one of the positive variables in dangerous situations. Persistent hopelessness and despair are associated with a poor prognosis in people with malignancies. Hope has been shown to increase survival in wars, concentration camps, natural disasters, and among people with severe handicaps (Jacoby 1993).[6] Frankl (2006) reported a higher incidence of death among concentration camp victims whose liberation was expected but delayed just long enough to destroy their hope. In the last messages of the inmates of Nazi concentration camps, a number of people spoke of being surprised to find hope in themselves during their final days (Gollwitzer 1956). Frank (1963) pointed out that when the North Koreans manipulated American prisoners' appraisal of their situation, the effect on their hope was devastating. Clearly, factors such as hope are very important in such situations. Hopelessness—the sense that we have no control over our destiny—is very debilitating.

Anthropologists describe tribal cultures in which people die soon after being condemned by a medicine man and expelled from the community—the so-called "voodoo death," which may be due to terror and hopelessness (Cannon 1932). In contrast, many phy-

sicians know of cases of terminal patients who survive while waiting for an important family event such as a wedding, after which
they quickly die. Kübler-Ross points out that no matter what stage
the patient is at in the dying process, hope is the one thing that is
present in all of them (1969, p. 122). Susan Bach (1966) finds hope
in the paintings of terminally ill children.

In spite of its apparently positive effects, in the literature on
hope one can detect two distinct trends. On the one hand, hope
is praised as inspiring, energizing, able to keep people alive in difficult situations, and indispensable for our well-being. St. Paul eu-
logized faith, hope, and love. Aquinas believed that faith, hope,
and charity were supernatural "infused" virtues that direct us to
the divine. Hope is central to Christian eschatology because of the
divine promise of a better future. Bloch says that "Where there is
hope there is religion" (as cited in Meissner 1987, p. 174). Even
Marxist theoreticians believed in hope, albeit purely human hope
that is creative and not utopian but directed toward transformation
of the world for the better and aiming at the liberation of people
from alienation. However, writers with an existentialist bent point
out that hope can also be impractical, illusory, and false, even destructive, when it prevents our focusing on the present. Hope may
distract us from our responsibilities and pave the way for disappointment. Albert Camus describes the absurd hero Sisyphus,
doomed for eternity to roll a rock up a hill only to have it roll down
again. For Camus, Sisyphus is greater than his fate because even
though he is conscious that he has no hope of succeeding, he is
not desperate. Camus wants us to face the hopelessness of finitude
rather than accept the irrational leap of faith of the religious. Kast
however suggests not only that Sisyphus's behavior reveals a hidden hope, but also that Sisyphus is the "paramount hero of the ego"
(1991, p. 142). For her, although the French existentialists warned
against the dangers of false hope, Camus's attitude is one-sided
because Sisyphus's landscape is solitary, without relationship, not
to mention the fact that life can be very meaningful even as we roll
our boulders up our personal hills. Sisyphus's task was a punishment for the crime of trying to cheat death, so the myth may refer
more to the absurdity of this particular task than to the absurdity
of life itself.

The Greeks sometimes condemned hope as an illusion and a curse, because destiny was determined and unchangeable. For Aeschylus, hope is "the food of exiles" and "a never-fruiting flower" (as cited in Zieger 1946, p. 41). Some of the nineteenth-century poets also disapproved of hope: Shelley wrote, "Worse than despair, worse than the bitterness of death, is hope" (as cited in Reading 2004, p. 176). Nietzsche said that "Hope is the worst of all evils, for it prolongs the torment of man" (1878, p. 45). Emily Dickinson wrote, enigmatically, "Hope is the thing with feathers / That perches in the soul, / And sings the tune without the words, / And never stops at all" (1976, p. 116).

Most contemporary psychotherapists emphasize the healing benefits of hope and try to evoke it in the people with whom they work (Yahine and Miller 2006). Historically, psychoanalysts have given hope the same mixed reviews as the poets and philosophers, although on balance contemporary psychoanalysts seem to be in favor of it. For some psychoanalytic writers, everything depends on the presence or absence of hope. All our activities presuppose the hope of attaining an end. If hope is killed, whatever we do becomes senseless. Meissner sees hope as "the principle that directs the process of psychological growth toward increasing inner stability and more adequate interaction and integration with real objects" (1987, p. 187). Hope makes it possible for a child to relinquish the gratifications of its present level of development and reach out for new developmental possibilities. Hope is also an aspect of our capacity to emerge from and integrate loss and disappointment; it is restitutive (Rochlin 1965).

Some of the early psychoanalysts (Shand 1920) believed that hope increases the activity of desire and aids us in resisting misfortune and painful emotions. However, for other classical Freudians, following Freud himself, hope is often linked to illusion and fantasy; it is considered to be regressive, derived from primary process and magical thinking. (Perhaps this is true when the person comes to therapy with the idea that the therapist can magically fix whatever ails him.) Among some later ego psychologists, hope was thought to have the function of helping the ego's integrative function. They believed that the hope that our plans will be successful is the essential dynamic source of the ego's integrative capacity.

Hope makes it possible for the ego to make an effort in the service of rational behavior (French 1952).

William Alanson White (1916) believed that hope and fear produce a dialectic that underlies all human development. George Engel (1962) said that hope is derived from confidence and may even replace confidence when one is uncertain of one's abilities. Fromm (1968) thought that hope was an essential quality of life, and Menninger (1959) believed that whereas optimism and pessimism may be unrealistic and self-centered, hope represents the workings of the life instinct against the tendencies of the death instinct. Winnicott (1971b) distinguished between the hope of the true self and that of the false self; the hope of the true self may produce acting out to try to assert itself, while the hope of the false self is characterized by compliance. Winnicott (1955) also suggested that the self defends itself against environmental failure by generating an unconscious assumption about reality—what we might now call an unconscious pathogenic belief. This assumption can later stimulate the conscious hope for an experience in which the original relational failure can be unfrozen and worked through successfully. Bollas (1989) suggested that this frozen material is stored in a kind of "internal reference library" in which early pathogenic experiences remain relatively unchanged and untransformed, in the hope that some day they can be relived in the presence of a more transforming object. Casement (1985) pointed out that the patient unconsciously searches or hopes for what is needed to meet his or her unconscious needs, and it is important that the therapist be attuned to those moments when the patient approaches his or her unconscious hope.

Horney believed that the common factor in all neurosis is that the person has lost hope (1945, p. 178). She thought that lack of hope was based on not being accepted as a person and on the despair of ever becoming whole. For Horney (1942), lack of hope is the cause and essence of illness; emotional illness is equivalent to lack of hope. A hopeful attitude in the patient provides an incentive for improvement, and this forms the keystone of the curative process. She believed that without hope the necessary change of attitude is an almost impossible therapeutic task. Hope is the indispensable factor that must be present in the three constituents of therapy: the patient, the therapist, and the medium. The therapist must be hopeful about his or her own development and feel hopeful for the patient. If the therapist loses hope, cure becomes impossible because lack of hope is contagious—it is harmful if the therapist loses hope and the patient realizes that this has happened. Horney therefore regarded hope as a precondition for the therapeutic contract—the patient must believe that he can change. Recognition of hope in the patient and the combating of loss of hope are important allies in dealing with neurosis. In *Our Inner Conflicts* (1945), she describes analysis as a dynamic process that mediates between hope and lack of hope. The patient is paralyzed by lack of hope and the analyst must recognize and combat this.

Erikson is also on the side of hope, which he believed is "both the earliest and the most indispensable virtue inherent in the state of being alive . . . if life is to be sustained, hope must remain, even where confidence is wounded, trust impaired" (1964, p. 115). Erikson thought that hope guides the ego in its development. He believed that hope is a fundamental human quality that arises from early experiences with a trustworthy and responsive mother. Basic trust in the world develops early in life when the child's caretakers are reasonably reliable in meeting the child's needs and help arrives when it is needed. The child then develops the confidence that things will work out well most of the time. The baby's needs and desires are then blessed, and hope is instilled by the baby's experience of the world. Lynch (1965) also believed that hope is fundamental for human health, even for life, and the recovery of hope is one of the principle aims of psychotherapy. Not only does the patient enter therapy hoping to be helped, but therapists hope to be able to help. Frank (1968) believed that modern psychiatric thinking has restored hope to a position of respectability. He pointed out that restoration of morale and hope in a demoralized individual is very important, and this outcome is common to all forms of psychotherapy (Frank 1974). Some contemporary psychotherapists have preferred to focus on what is hoped for rather than on hope itself and suggest that the therapist must help the patient to get rid of impossible or unrealistic hopes and grieve their loss (Betz 1968).

Very relevant to the process of psychotherapy is Marcel's (1962) idea that hope is always associated with communion. The presence of another person is often crucial for the development of hope. Many psychoanalytic self psychologists believe that people who have completely given up hope that their selfobject needs will ever be met would never enter therapy. These theorists point out that the therapist's actual or perceived selfobject failure allows access to the person's childhood selfobject failures, at which time one can address the person's unconscious hope for an adequate selfobject response. As the self-selfobject tie deepens, and pathogenic material is worked on, hope seems to arise spontaneously even though we do not specifically focus on it.

A brief vignette illustrates the relevance of hope to the therapeutic situation. A man showed me a poem he had written that contained complex mythic imagery. I had the immediate feeling that he wanted me to comment on the imagery and talk about its meaning, so after some internal resistance I made some suggestions about the poem's content. To my surprise and bewilderment, he was hurt and disappointed by my reaction. I had completely misinterpreted the meaning of his offering me the poem, and I had in fact retraumatized him. As we worked on this disruption in our connection, he told me that he had hoped for an entirely different reaction from me. He did not want my suggestions about the meaning of his poetry; what he wanted was my pride and joy at him and his work (for that moment they were not separate) which would express my unconditional love for him. With some difficulty he told me that he had held alive the hope for such a response since childhood but was ashamed of it. After acknowledging and discussing how my failure had hurt him, I told him that the hope for unconditional acceptance was surely every child's birthright. The fact that it had stayed alive in him was an important sign of psychological health, since if this hope had died he would be in bad shape psychologically. My disappointing reaction was typical of his parents' reaction to his wish to be unconditionally accepted and loved—a hope that he had not been conscious of in childhood, because it would have had little chance of being met by his family. Obviously, my responsiveness in our work so far had reactivated this primal hope and allowed it to become conscious. I had become entangled unconsciously in my own material—I felt I had been put on the spot, tested, as if there was a demand for an instant, intelligent comment. This countertransference reaction prevented me from empathically grasping what he needed.

Ornstein (1991) describes an important dilemma of the person in psychotherapy. He or she consciously or unconsciously brings to the therapy the hope that his or her selfobject needs will be met but is also afraid that they will again be rejected—the "dread to repeat," which may lead to a rejection of hope because it would be too painful for this to be crushed again. The person is hoping for a particular quality of responsiveness that was never forthcoming in childhood, which led to disastrous consequences as this hope was recurrently dashed. When this hope reemerges in therapy and is not met with sufficient interest or attunement, the early trauma is reactivated, leading to a defensive reaction. For some people, hopelessness is at least known and is a reliable state of mind, whereas to agree to the restoration of hope is to take the risk of being hurt again. Unfortunately, however, the refusal to acknowledge any hope in therapy can act as a serious resistance. Whatever the reason for hopelessness, faced with a person who constantly repudiates any hope that arises, the therapist can also lose hope that the work will be of value.

When hopelessness becomes chronic, it becomes part of the person's self-representation and tends to keep the person out of touch with positive aspects of the self. The masochistic person may feel that to express hope rather than suffering will cause the therapist to abandon her. Some chronic depressive and borderline people destroy any sense of hope in the therapy, and the therapist has to contain their total lack of hope and the helplessness that this engenders in the therapist. The therapist's own hopelessness may be induced by projective identification because of a combination of the therapist's depressive dynamics and the person's material. Hopelessness may also be iatrogenic, the result of the therapist relentlessly using a technique that the person experiences as useless and unhelpful.

Paradoxically, acknowledgment of a sense of hopelessness in the room may benefit the therapy and enable the person to reconnect with his or her frozen hope. This intervention is helpful when it is experienced as a validation of the patient's ability to evoke a human response in regard to a sequestered area of the personality that the person had believed could not be shared. The patient then feels that his or her profound sense of isolation can be shared and understood by another. Such containment of hopelessness, without rejecting the patient and without the therapist being overwhelmed by the patient's distress, allows the patient to recognize and discuss the problem.

When treating a hopeless person, Ogden (1979) suggests that the therapist must contain the person's despair but at the same time not want to end the treatment. The therapist has to live with the feeling that he or she is working in a hopeless therapy, which is what the patient believes. In practice this is difficult and draining for the therapist, who can only preconsciously hold the possibility of hope for the person until he or she feels connected and safe enough to hope and has the opportunity to try again. Boris (1976) suggested that in such situations the therapist must invoke his or her own hope and reconnect with past periods of despair that he or she has survived. Boris distinguishes hope from desire. For him, desire is what one wants to happen, while hope is what we believe ought to happen. He suggests that desire demands instant gratification, a real object and real fulfillment, whereas hope lies within the realm of pure potential and loses its meaning once its object is attained. Boris suggests that hope arises from a set of preconceived, phylogenetically derived ideals that we compare with present experience. Hope is then a deep structure in the psyche, an a priori or archetypal process in the Jungian sense.

For one to be open to hope one must have had childhood experiences that resulted in a sense of mastery of one's environment and adequate responsiveness from one's selfobjects. Presumably, hope arises when a distressed child has had enough experiences of being held and soothed, or loved and valued. Such helpful experiences allow one to develop the sense that when one is distressed, things may improve for the better, which is why, under stress, people may soothe themselves with words, songs, and memories from childhood.

Needless to say, the hope for an all-comforting, all-powerful therapist who can make everything better is unrealistic. Mitchell refers to this kind of hope for an omnipotent, magical solution to one's problems as "hope in the paranoid-schizoid position" (1993, p. 212), in contrast to hope in the depressive position that entails courage and longing for an all-too-human, irreplaceable object that is outside of one's control. Presumably this means that some hope is adaptive and has the developmental foundations that allow it to be realistic, while other hope does not, leading to false hope. That is, only some types of hope are anchored in reality.

I believe that some of the differences of opinion about the value of hope occur because these authors are not all speaking about the same state of mind. Some are confusing hope with optimism, which may be naïve, egocentric, or unrealistic. Or hope is confused with expectation, which is more specific than hope, which has a quality of openness. Mature hope involves the tolerance of a degree of suffering and ambivalence, since our private hope may clash with the hopes of others, whereas narcissistically motivated hope is self-centered and used to buttress a fragmenting self. Mature hope does not deny reality and is based on a reasonable appraisal of a situation. As Lynch says: "There is nothing as strong as hope when it knows how to limit itself" (as cited in Meissner 1987, p. 182). Because we must limit ourselves to the realm of the possible, the problem for the therapist is to distinguish between hope that is realistic and hope that is merely a fantasy or a way of dealing with anxiety about the future. But Allan Watts (1964) reminded us that we should not too quickly dismiss wishful thinking, which is an aspect of the creative imagination.

It would probably be impossible to achieve anything without the hope that a goal could be reached. To hope effectively, we must interweave the reality of the present situation with a potential reality that we can imagine. As Bachelard pointed out, imagination is "the true source of psychic production. Psychically, we are created by our reverie" (1938, pp. 110–11). Here, Jung makes a useful distinction between daydreaming, in which we consciously invent imagery in our minds, and paying attention to the spontaneous flow of images that emerges out of the unconscious, images that have a life of their own and are not directed by the ego (1970, p. 192). This kind of creative imagination, which can stimulate us to act, is important to humanity, because without it we are prisoners of our present situation and we are more likely to become hopeless. Of course, we still have to deal with feasibility and implementation, but without the ability to imagine, we are stuck.

The relevance of this discussion of the imagination to psychotherapy is obvious. In many depressive states of mind, the imagination is either paralyzed or chronically and unrealistically pessimistic. In such a case only the therapist can imagine that the patient may recover, but here the therapist treads perilously close to having a personal agenda for the person, albeit a benign one. The therapist's hope for the person may be unrealistic, perhaps based on his or her faith in a particular philosophy of therapy, which is sometimes imposed on the person as a way of warding off the therapist's despair. Given this caveat, when dealing with a patient in despair, the unspoken, implicit fantasy that the therapist holds for the other's recovery seems to be helpful. It may only help the therapist, but that enables the therapist to stay with a despairing individual. If it is true that projective identification works in both directions, the therapist's hopeful fantasy may activate a corresponding sector in the patient and thus open up a new possibility. Perhaps hope and expectation are developmental necessities that move the personality forward. Even though expectation is not directly causal, there sometimes seems to be a mysterious relationship between expectation and what actually happens. This may sound like a form of magical thinking, but it seems to be true that events in the world often reflect our psychological state.

When life is unbearable because nothing can reasonably be hoped for and nothing in the person's situation can be expected to change, would it be helpful for the therapist to try to change the person's interpretation of such a situation, what Boris calls "the experience of what one experiences" (1976, p. 147)? Would doing so make life more tolerable, even if it means using a defensive operation such as denial? If the therapist cannot tolerate despair, and the therapy does not appear to be helping, the therapist might, for instance, suggest that the person focus on other areas of life that are reasonably satisfying. Alternatively, assuming that a truly hopeless life situation is being discussed, is it reasonable for the therapist to suggest a spiritual approach, or would this overstep the boundaries of therapy? Desperate life situations such as terminal illness were once the province of religions, which offer comfort and hope in such situations, if only hope for a future life. But when the person finds traditional religion unhelpful, he or she may still need spiritual help and may turn to the therapist for this purpose. Here, attitudes among therapists vary from the insistence that the person face reality as it is to the notion that overall emotional maturity includes spiritual development, which then becomes a legitimate therapeutic concern and often occurs naturally as therapy progresses.

NOTES

1. The Greeks distinguished between *epithemia*, desire in the sense of sensuality, the need for contact, holding, and touch, *philia*, love or friendship of the kind that fills one with joy, and *eros*, which has more sexual connotations, often involving ecstasy, suffering, and a need for merger at a soulful level. *Agape* is more detached, and to the Greeks meant the love of a god for a human being, which was not necessarily nonsexual, although its meaning has gradually changed to indicate a spiritualized kind of love.

2. *Kosmogonos* refers to that principle which created the universe.

3. Here I do not distinguish love from compassion, which, as Lewin (1996) has pointed out, is a core value that animates psychotherapy.

4. Williams identified love with Jesus Christ; for him, romantic theology was a Christology.

5. There are evolutionary approaches to affect, psychophysiological approaches, psychodynamic views, cognitive and motivational theories of affect. Most researchers agree that emotion is a signaling device that evolved so that the baby can evoke the necessary response from its caregivers. Emotion is part of one's attempt to deal with one's environment and is related to the meaning we attribute to events.

6. "The miserable hath no other medicine, but only hope" (Shakespeare, *Measure for Measure,* act 3, scene 1).

CHAPTER 4

A Psychological Approach to Spiritual Development

This chapter discusses various ways in which psychotherapy fosters spiritual development. Needless to say, the psychological and the traditional approaches to spiritual development are not mutually exclusive, and they may enhance each other. Traditionally, spiritual practices try to "tune" human consciousness so that it becomes increasingly transparent to transcendent levels of reality. This may be achieved, for instance, by meditation practice in which the practitioner's capacity for attention is increasingly refined. The meditator is then able to experience pure consciousness without concern for the meaning of the thoughts and feelings that inevitably arise. At first sight the psychological approach seems radically different, since the therapist is particularly interested in their meaning. On the surface, this seems to imply that meditation only affects processes of consciousness such as attention, while depth psychology concentrates on the contents of consciousness, but that would be to oversimplify the difference.

Meditation has psychological benefits (Murphy and Donovan 1994). As Rubin (1996) has pointed out, psychotherapeutic work is itself a form of meditation, and meditation fosters psychotherapeutic practice by improving the therapist's capacity for evenly hovering attention. As we work on the contents of consciousness in therapy, affect tolerance and self-understanding improve. Gradually, we identify less with these contents and our capacity for attention and surrender increase. Because the psyche is a vehicle for the experience of the numinosum, and the personality is profoundly affected by archetypal processes, the conscious development of the personality becomes a spiritual journey in its own right.

As we saw in chapter 2, the psychological approach to spirituality values and builds on individual experiences of the sacred that may have little or no connection to traditional images of the divine. These experiences arise from the depths of the soul. They are autonomous, and they are often intimately connected to the psychology of the subject and not necessarily related to any preexisting theology, doctrine, or dogma. In this model, the divine is not personified in any specific form, and we focus on those aspects of the sacred that we can experience rather than on its transcendent aspects. Spiritual development proceeds as we gradually integrate the effects of these experiences, which simultaneously expand the ego's awareness and place it in a larger perspective in relation to the Self.

There are several lines of psychological development, each with its own set of functions, so that one domain of the mind may be mature while others may remain immature. Here, I assume that spiritual development can be considered a developmental line in its own right, with its own specific crises analogous to those that occur during emotional, social, and cognitive development. Even though all of these developmental lines are occurring concomitantly, and they mutually interpenetrate, spiritual growth is not entirely synonymous with psychological growth. One can be emotionally stable and well adjusted to society without much spiritual development, while many spiritually developed people are not particularly stable psychologically.

May (1992) has provided a valuable description of some of the psychological correlates of spiritual maturation, which I mention here since they may be seen among people in psychotherapy. These phenomena are worth recognizing because they may be part of a spiritual process and not necessarily the result of the transference or related to other lines of development. Nevertheless, the therapist will notice how similar the following developments are to people in psychotherapy, whether or not the therapy is specifically spiritually oriented.

When an interest in spirituality begins, the person's environment may or may not be supportive. Some family members and friends will affirm the process, while others may dislike or be suspicious of the change that is happening. Family and friends of the individual may fear they will lose the person because of his or her change in values and attachments. Because of an increasing sense of connection to the divine, an increase in self-assurance may occur, with less need for the affirmation of others. This may be enough to disturb the individual's relationships with family and friends, who may sense a degree of withdrawal and accuse the individual of spiritual escapism.

An example of the problem of conflict between a former lifestyle and a new religious lifestyle and beliefs was given by Spero (1987), who describes a sixteen-year-old girl from a reform Jewish family who became religiously orthodox. She began to spend many hours studying Jewish texts, avoided her friends, and became sullen at meals because they were not sufficiently kosher. This led to her referral to a psychoanalyst, who discovered no emotional disorder. Her therapy dealt with the impact of her religious transformation on her identity and her relationships. Conversely, the loss of one's religious tradition, perhaps as part of the search for a personal spirituality, may engender considerable grief. Barra and colleagues reported the case of a student who gave up the religious tradition of her childhood only to experience alienation, fear, anxiety, anger, hopelessness, grief, and suicidal ideation (Barra et al. 1993). This type of loss may occur when a person marries into a different religious background or moves to an area that has no other members of his or her religious denomination.

When spiritual development begins, anger may surface due to the resurgence of painful childhood memories of religious school and family attitudes to religion. Frustration in the individual's prayer life is common. Evangelistic enthusiasm may emerge, which may be expressed in a way that challenges or irritates others. The individual may lose interest in activities that had been important to him or her. Long-held assumptions about life may be challenged or discarded, which may have a disconcerting effect on the individual's self-confidence and a sense that the person's identity is changing. The therapist may be called on to support the person during a period of reevaluation of his or her values or a period of not knowing, in part by clarifying the fact that these are aspects of an important developmental process.

May (1992) warns about the dangers of the use of spirituality to avoid responsibility, for example by using meditation as an escape. Another danger is that of "spiritual narcissism," the use of one's spirituality to increase self-importance—a holier-than-thou attitude or subtle feelings of pride at one's humility. Some of what looks like spiritual practice is actually employed for the purpose of enhancing the ego.

It is useful for the therapist to be aware of the traditionally recognized stages of spiritual development. When we notice them during psychotherapy, it helps to understand the process that is occurring so that we do not interpret it as some kind of pathology. This is an area in which the therapist can draw on the accumulated wisdom of millennia of spiritual tradition. The caveat here is that all stage theories can only be applied in a very general sense. For example, while it is true that mature faith often occurs in later life, this is by no means always the case. The stages of spiritual development are cyclical and not linear; we may go through the same process many times, at different levels.

Spiritual development may begin as a person gradually develops a spiritual longing; we realize there is something more within us, something more that we need besides our usual lives, a deeper source of meaning even when life seems to be proceeding well on the surface. The usual distractions no longer fully satisfy us. We cannot produce this longing; it comes upon us autonomously. Sometimes such an awakening seems to happen for no apparent reason, or it may be triggered by a numinous experience that makes us aware of spiritual reality, or a serious life crisis requires a transcendent perspective. These experiences may be seen as a call from the transpersonal Self. One may turn away from the initial call, whereupon we may be pursued again and again by the Self, or we may never be called again. Orthodox believers tell me that demonic forces may try to oppose spiritual awakening, but I see this opposition as the result of psychodynamic factors within the personality. Resistance to spiritual awakening is based on anxiety about its implications. We have to give up our existing image of ourselves and face some hard truths. A sacrifice of time, money, and energy may be necessary. It may be difficult to accept that the hegemony of the ego is over. It may be difficult to let go if one suffers from fragmentation anxiety or if status and success have been used to buttress a fragile sense of self. It is difficult to be responsive to the promptings of the Self if one is preoccupied with survival.

If one accepts the call, one has to develop a relationship with it. There follows what was traditionally referred to as "purgation," meaning the necessity to face the shadow or problematic personality traits such as self-importance, possessiveness, greed, fear, and envy. It is helpful to gently explore these difficulties with compassion for oneself or for the person with whom one is working therapeutically. Painful feelings are not obstacles to spiritual development but signposts that indicate where we need to work; they are the doorways into the soul's deeper places. After the awakening, the period of purgation is often experienced as a period of darkness; at times one feels one does not have the strength to go on. This stage may last for years, during which the person may be in therapy. At these periods, one reevaluates one's values and beliefs and may either recommit to a religious tradition or leave it entirely.

Gradually, our emotional lives are governed less by past resentments and hurts, we stop responding automatically, and there is less need to defend a fragile sense of self. We become more sensitive to suffering and often to the environment. This stage may lead to the realization that the image we had of ourselves is not our real identity. We have developed a "false self" to satisfy the family and the culture—we had to pretend to be someone we were not, in order to survive. Perhaps because of early family and social conditioning we thought we had to become rich and famous. Eventually we no longer work hard to sustain the image of who we thought we were.

Even when we would like to connect consciously with the Self, we may know no better than to make do with images of the divine that we have carried with us from childhood religious education. Occasionally these images are useful, but often our personal development has outstripped them. Here is where we must depend on our own experience of the numinous, our own intuition about the sacred, the testimony of experienced spiritual teachers we feel we can trust or spiritual writings with which we feel an affinity.

The next stage, traditionally known as "illumination," produces a revolution in consciousness. Here, a light dawns, and a sense of presence is felt more often. One sees one's complexes, one's lack of love, one's narcissism, one's shadow with more clarity. There is more silence and calm. This stage is referred to as illuminative because one senses the presence of a spiritual light or revelation which is often received through the practice of contemplation, a turning of the mind to God with no particular content. The divine is revealed through a process of understanding and insight. One may find oneself unexpectedly speaking words of wisdom, and one may be taught directly by means of a numinous experience. We begin to apprehend the reality we have been seeking when we see everything as a manifestation of the divine, and we have more experiences of divine companionship and love. In this stage, we can accept the apparent disharmonies of life with some equanimity, and we feel that we stand on the edge of another plane of being. This is a relatively passive stage, in which we become more and more receptive, and our longing for the presence of the divine becomes a preoccupation.

Often during the course of this process, a "dark night of the soul" occurs.[1] This term was originally used by St. John of the Cross, a sixteenth-century Carmelite monk, to describe a spiritual crisis. He used specifically Christian language, but the psychological process he describes is relevant to people of all traditions. "Dark Night of the Soul" is the title of both a poem and a commentary on the poem that describes various stages of St. John's spiritual journey. During a dark night there is no hope, no sense of presence, a feeling of being alone or of failure. The ego suffers, but one still has to carry out one's everyday duties. We are often able to help others but not ourselves. The dark night is a painful period in which, ideally, the ego surrenders, allowing change that transforms how we think about ourselves and our relationship to God. In the Christian mystical tradition, the individual finds that prayer becomes very difficult and unrewarding, as if one has been abandoned by God. One derives no pleasure or consolation in traditional prayer and practices. This period is difficult but is traditionally believed to be a blessing in disguise, a severe test of faith in which the individual is trained to grow from vocal and mental prayer to a deeper contemplative prayer that takes the individual beyond conceptual thought. The purpose seems to be to move us away from personal concerns into a closer sense of communion with the divine. This period is said to result in a spiritual purification of the soul that is only experienced by people advanced in the spiritual life, during which one is very aware of one's imperfections in relation to the divine. One's will is purified, resulting in the love of God and a view of reality as full of divine presence.

Needless to say, these states of mind are not confined to people in the Christian tradition, and they can be described without the use of specifically Christian imagery. They occur to all of us in the form of existentially painful periods that produce a crisis of faith in life. Just as the Christian mystic sees such a period as divinely ordained for the purposes of spiritual development, the therapist can see such a period as an experience stimulated by the Self, necessary for the individuation process of the individual. If the therapist understands that this is an archetypal or transpersonal process, the situation will not be understood simply as a depression in the clinical sense of that word. The distinction is important but not absolute, because one cannot radically separate one's psychology from one's spirituality. In the following description, I deliberately draw the distinction rather sharply for the sake of clarity. In practice these states overlap and mingle, and one can use binocular vision to see both processes going on at the same time. A sad mood is part of the picture of a dark night, but sadness understood as the result of a spiritual crisis is not something to be "treated" in the clinical sense.

In a typical depression, the individual's state of mind is primarily characterized by feelings such as abandonment, loss, inadequacy, self-loathing, personal badness, hopelessness, unworthiness, pessimism, anger, emptiness, and so on. A depression is usually triggered by losses, by relationship or occupational failures, by a serious life dilemma or by unresolved grief that is demanding our attention. If those are the main features of the situation, with no possibility of opening to its spiritual possibilities, one is dealing with a depression in the ordinary clinical sense of the word. By contrast, during a dark night, while many features of depression may be present, a major concern of the person is that he or she feels spiritually impoverished or desolate, disconnected from the transpersonal realm, and is unable to pray or find meaning in his or her usual spiritual practices. There seems to be no light available, and death may feel like an appealing option. Unlike the situation in a straightforward depression, the individual going through a dark night is often able to maintain an outward appearance of effectiveness at work and in relationships with others—in fact, empathy for others is increased. One can even retain a degree of humor. One senses that there is a purpose behind the painful feelings, one wants to know what it all means, what is being demanded, and one is prepared to wait and see. One does not struggle against the despair but surrenders to the imperative of the Self and tries to get one's ego concerns out of the way. If one realizes that one is in a dark night, one is more inclined to think that one's mental state is part of a developmental process. That is, the Self is not absent or hidden, but is present *as* the painful mood. This is a possible depth psychological response to the notion of the *deus absconditus*, the hidden or absent God.[2] This phrase refers to a biblical and theological tradition which suggests that the divine may deliberately withdraw in a mysterious way. Rather than seeing this withdrawal as a punishment for disobedience, the psychological approach regards such painful affective states as a call to increased consciousness. In order not to be a Pollyanna, it is important to acknowledge here that many people suffer a prolonged dark night and never attain the light that is said to be at the end of it.

The understanding that the individual is undergoing a dark night of the soul leads to a different atmosphere in the therapy room than we experience in the case of a straightforward depression.[3] If the therapist is not aware of the distinction between these states of mind, it is easy to reduce the individual's unhappiness to an existential crisis, to factors in the unconscious, or to a biologically based major depressive disorder. To do so would be to ignore the spiritual significance of such episodes. Even as we work on those contributory factors that can be discerned, it is important to remember that a true dark night of the soul is mediated by the Self, apparently using difficult life situations so that one can discover one's own meaning in life or one's own experience of the sacred, for these are the times during which we contact the mysteries of existence. That is, the dark night has its own purpose for the *telos* of the personality. The therapist therefore works with this material with a different sensibility than one would if the situation were to be seen as an ordinary depression. The usual approaches to depression are not sufficiently helpful if the fundamental problem is a spiritual crisis. The dark night is an initiation into a new level of spiritual awareness, archetypally expressed in myths of descent into the underworld such as that of Inanna, described in chapter 9. The therapist does not need to metaphorically light candles to explore this darkness. He or she can remain in the dark—a place of not knowing what is happening—acting as a container, helping the birth of new understanding, acting as a witness, a reflecting consciousness, or a companion while the process runs its course, not directed by any theory of psychotherapy or treatment but allowing the darkness to reveal itself.

Parenthetically, St. John of the Cross composed his poem while being tortured and imprisoned because of a theological dispute. In spite of his terrible circumstances, he was able to embrace his situation and write about his experience of divine love. Before his imprisonment he practiced physical mortification as a path to spiritual purification, a practice that always leads to the suspicion of masochism in the guise of spirituality. But there is a ring of truth in his poetry, and it would be an untoward reduction to point to his character structure as a way of discounting his discovery of divine love as a result of his experience.

The mystics have charted some of the features of the dark night in a way that can be helpful to the contemporary therapist working with an individual going through such a phase. The mystics tell us that during the dark night it feels as if grace is suspended, but in fact God has illumined the soul with divine light, which is referred to as a ray of darkness because it cannot be perceived by the ordinary mind. This divine light shuts down one's ordinary faculties so that one can develop a new way of seeing that is spiritual in nature. In the purgative way, one has been reading and thinking with the ordinary mind, but now we are required to go deeper than that, so all ordinary light is taken away. We then no longer have

confidence in the ego and the intellect, so that we have to be totally dependent on God. We have left behind everything we know,
without knowing what will happen. We might try the traditional
practices of prayer and meditation, but they don't work. We might
try a practice we have not tried before, but that is also a mistake.
Or, we might give in to despair, feeling that we are abandoned by
God. The individual feels completely alienated from God, totally
desolate and disoriented. However, this period is not an abandonment but the prelude to a deeper revelation. The traditional advice
is that, if one cannot read and think, one should not try to do so,
but just be peaceful in the knowledge that the divine is there. One
can ask for what is needed, in humility and trust. It is important
to maintain inner quiet, realizing one cannot do anything without
God. One has to give up the idea that what one has done so far is
due to one's own efforts. There is no need to be judgmental about
oneself or others. A desire for the divine grows, but with no self-
interest. Eventually one can only say yes, one can only surrender
and accept. This is the beginning of the stage of union with the
divine, in which the river simply flows into the ocean.

The final stage of this process, the stage of union or unity, is
rarely seen. According to the literature, this stage allows a stable
sense of direct contact with, or absorption into, the Absolute, as
well as the realization of the unity of oneself with others and with
the earth. Not much can be said about this experience because it
transcends verbal description and involves a loss of the sense of
a separate, personal self, although such individuals function normally in consensual reality.[4] Having arrived at this stage, the developed mystic participates in ordinary social life with a renewed
consciousness, often teaching or involved in socially useful movements and often a critic of the status quo. Other such individuals
may be highly evolved yet living in total obscurity, simply because
they feel no need to do anything else.

However one views the spiritual journey, there are fundamentally only two outcomes. One leads to the nondual experience of
union with the divine, such that there remains no concern with individual uniqueness, just as a drop of water is lost in a glass of wine.
The everyday personality persists but is not particularly important.

Alternatively, the goal may be one of relationship to the divine, experienced as a lover or a friend. This requires the full development of the authentic personality in a conscious relation to the sacred.

DEVELOPMENT OF A GOD IMAGE: SYMBOLS OF THE SELF

The development of a personal connection to the divine is one aspect of spiritual development. Here, I find Jung's approach helpful, although it has been controversial and often unacceptable to theologians.[5] For Jung, human beings have an innate or a priori capacity to experience the divine. This archetypal potential in the psyche, which Jung calls the Self, is projected onto particular figures such as Christ or whatever local image of divinity is present in a given culture. Jung says that he has to speak of the God-image rather than God, because "it is quite beyond me to say anything about God at all" (1973–1975, p. 260). In Jung's words,

> We find numberless images of God, but we cannot produce the original. There is no doubt in my mind that there is an original behind our images, but it is inaccessible. We could not even be aware of the original since its translation into psychic terms is necessary in order to make it perceptible at all. (1956–1957, par. 1589)

The transpersonal Self is often said to be the "God within," but rather we are contained within it, since it "acts like a circumambient atmosphere to which no definite limits can be set, either in space or in time" (Jung 1951a, par. 257). The Self is not simply an image; it is an active force (ibid., par. 411), a power in the soul that directs the evolution of the personality and also expresses itself symbolically in numinous imagery.

We do not know the relationship of the Self to the transcendent level of the divine. There seems to be a consistent psychological relationship between them, but we do not know if they are identical. To insist on equating them would be to practice metaphysics and not psychology. All we know is that the presence of such a potential is suggested by the ubiquity of God-images historically, geographically, and in the individual's experience. The Self is a psychological fact, but we do not know its nature or how it originates.

One's God-image may be highly personal and is often private and difficult to talk about. The God-image that we experience may not correspond to the images or metaphors of traditional theology. Images of God as a heavenly father, king, mother, judge, and so on may leave us cold if we do not experience the divine in those ways. One of the reasons for the decline in belief in mainstream religious organizations is that for many people traditional God-images are no longer living symbols—they do not work to connect us to the sacred. This is one meaning of Nietzsche's announcement that "God is dead." Some important attempts have been made to reinterpret traditional biblical God-images in more acceptable ways. For example, as an alternative to the power-drenched images of a God who is a ruler or king, the theologian Sally McFague, in *Models of God*, suggested that we may think of the divine in terms such as lover and friend of the world (1987, p. 20). For her, the world can be understood as the body of God. These metaphors are a big improvement over the old imperialist imagery because they stress relationship, a holistic, ecological sensitivity, the interdependence of all beings, an ethic of justice and care, and the acceptance of human responsibility for the fate of the earth. McFague's models are healthy alternatives to those traditional models of God that oscillate between the extremes of saying that God is so almighty that we have no power, and saying that God will take total care of us because we are helpless children, the traditional domination or escapism models of God. But the depth psychotherapist regularly sees people for whom none of these metaphors apply. Many people experience the divine in very personal and novel ways.

When the individual outgrows the traditional images, a spiritual vacuum ensues with a concomitant need for a new way of describing our experience of the divine. This is the situation for many contemporary people, and a depth psychological approach to spirituality may help in the discovery of a new God-image. New God-images are not created by the ego, and we cannot determine the form they will take; they arise spontaneously from the autonomous levels of the psyche (Edinger, Cordic and Yates 1996).

One of the ways we come to experience our personal God-images is by means of dreams. This opens up a controversial area within depth psychology. Traditional personalistic theorists of the unconscious only see its human levels, while the Jungian tradition describes a transpersonal level of the unconscious. For Jung, the Self is the maker of dreams, which must therefore be taken seriously as the voice of a greater wisdom—a notion in keeping with the old tradition of dreams sent by God (Sanford 1951). James Hall (1993) points out that when our authentic spirituality is repressed, perhaps because it is too unusual or idiosyncratic, it may emerge in dream imagery in a form that is radically different from our expectations. Dreams may produce numinous imagery that depicts an experience of the sacred, or they may directly tell us what we worship.

Ulanov reports that a man dreamed "it was dark and smoky, and there was a hissing sound. He saw himself (and yet he was also the self he saw) ardently, sincerely, deeply engaged in an act of worship, but the worship was of a giant pig. He awoke frightened, even more, stunned" (1986, p. 164). Ulanov does not mention the dreamer's associations to this image, but perhaps he worships greed. As well as the personal level of the dream, the Jungian therapist would also take into account an objective view of the image; the pig was an ancient mythological symbol of the Great Mother or the goddess in various cultures of antiquity. In the psychotherapeutic setting, this dream would give the therapist a clue about what is really sacred to the dreamer. These images are given to us from a source beyond the ego, often intruding into our complacency.

The unconscious refuses to be Christianized and insists on producing its own manifestations of the Self. If these are not recognized, one's internal connection to the Self is then ignored. This happens when the manifestations of the objective psyche are thought to be demonic or pagan, for instance, when the numinosum appears in the form of a magnificent animal, which happens because the Self has nonhuman aspects—as the totality it is all natural things. It was common in early religions for the divine to appear in the form of an animal, and traces of this idea are found in the Christian image of Jesus as the Lamb of God or in medieval depictions of the Holy Spirit impregnating Mary in the form of a dove. The Self still appears in modern dreams in animal form, apparently to stress the prehuman or instinctual level of the psyche, perhaps to remind the dreamer to rely on nature or instinct rather than the ego. Usually a dream animal is considered to be a Self-image when the animal is numinous or unusual in some striking way, for example, by virtue of its huge size or its golden color. For example, a woman dreamed of an immense leopard and tiger, each about three times as big as an elephant. Within this woman's personality lie undeveloped qualities of these animals that have not yet been humanized, and these potentials require attention. We associate sacred animals with pre–Judeo-Christian societies, but numinous imagery still takes this form in the psyches of modern people. Unlike her pagan ancestors, this woman will not *worship* these dream images—she will pay careful attention to them and try to listen to their meaning for her. From the psyche-centered point of view, attention to this kind of dream imagery is a religious practice, since the images reveal an aspect of the transpersonal psyche that speaks to the dreamer.

The Bible is full of references to the power of the divine manifested at the site of natural phenomena such as trees, rocks, mountains, rivers, and seas. In modern dreams the Self still expresses itself in these natural forms, each stressing a different aspect of the divine in nature. For example, the Self stresses its vegetative aspect when it appears in a dream in the form of a spectacular tree, which reminds the dreamer that the Self is expressed in the endless cycle of growth, decay, and regeneration in nature. It is not an accident that trees were considered to be sacred in many ancient cultures, for whom the tree seemed to be a receptacle for the divine essence. The tree manifests a life principle that is expressed in its recurrent leafing and blossoming. Because of its three levels—its underground roots, its trunk at the human level, and its upward pointing branches—the tree reminded the ancients, and still symbolizes for us, the connection between different dimensions of being. Similarly, mountains in dreams have their own links with the sacred. Because they suggest ascent and toil, the top of a mountain is often a symbol of the goal of a spiritual quest. The mountain seems to link heaven and earth, which is why there are many sacred mountains, such as Mt. Sinai or Mt.

Olympus, in world mythology. These are often places where the gods meet humanity.

Within any personality, there is conflict produced by tendencies and desires that pull the individual in opposite directions. Jung thought that the tensions between opposing aspects of the self are resolved into a higher synthesis within the Self. Consequently, dream symbols that show the uniting of apparent opposites are often Self symbols. Examples are images of a labyrinth with a way out, a snake with wings, the Taoist yin-yang symbol, a rose that is both white and red, or a figure that is both male and female or young and old. These symbols suggest that qualities that were previously felt to be in opposition to each other can actually be understood as complementary.

Another important type of Self image occurs in the form of mandala imagery. The word *mandala* is Sanskrit for circle. Mandalas are highly symmetrical geometrical figures, usually consisting of some combination of squares, circles, crosses, or triangles. They are always highly orderly and concentric, and in Eastern religious traditions they are used to focus the mind as an aid to meditation. Mandalas often have a fourfold symmetry; the number four is an ancient symbol of wholeness, stability, and organization. In dreams, mandala imagery may take the form of a symmetrical city with streets radiating from a central plaza, a garden with four rivers flowing from the center, or temples, wheels, spirals, flowers, labyrinths, or clocks. Jung noted that these images tend to occur in dreams during times of disorder and chaos, because the psyche has an innate tendency to correct itself if things get out of balance. He believed that the Self produces symbols of order in an attempt to compensate for the disorder that the ego feels, as if to remind the ego that, although things feel chaotic, an unrecognized pattern is at work that includes all the apparent contradictions. This tendency of the Self to produce symbols of order has led to its description as the archetype of order, but it must be remembered that the Self is also responsible for periods of disorder and crisis in life, usually in an attempt to stir things up in order to superimpose a new type of order.

According to Jung, the psyche has an innate religious function which operates either consciously or unconsciously (1944, par. 14).[6] This religious function is not concerned with whether the imagery it produces in dreams corresponds to the religious tradition of the dreamer—it produces whatever material is necessary. It is not unusual for dream imagery to originate in a religious tradition other than the one in which the dreamer was raised. Obviously such images are not the divine itself; they are symbolic expressions of a transcendent reality. We do not know what relationship they may have to the divine itself. A traditional Jewish or Christian theologian would strenuously object to this possibility—worshiping a dream pig sounds impossibly pagan. But these images tell us a great deal about our own psychology and about what we really value. Dream imagery such as the following tells us about a woman's projections onto her God-image, which is obviously colored by traditional patriarchal assumptions and her father complex:

> I am suspended in the sky by a hook through my chest. On the ground below me is an old man with a white beard, wearing a white robe. He is firing softballs at me from a cannon.

Such imagery tells us what we can let go of, what we have to see through if we are to approach the reality that is beyond any specific image.

Rizzuto (1979) tells us that the quality of our God-image is formed out of the experience of early object relations. Over time, the God-image formed as a result of early family experiences is combined with and influenced by the particular creedal formulations to which the individual is exposed, resulting in an adult God-image that is conditioned by the individual's personal history. A God-image that is punitive and demanding may represent the projection of these traits that belonged to a parent, or a God-image that is unconditionally loving and forgiving may indicate a need for these qualities because they were not present in one's parents.

Rizzuto (1979) found that the child's God-image is made up of a combination of the child's experiences of parents and the way the child sees people behaving in the extended family, documenting the suggestion of earlier researchers who had pointed out the close relationship between the structures of religion and those of the family (Vergote 1969). Much of these early family dynamics are unconscious; a woman I worked with used to get indigestion after taking communion every Sunday, a problem that turned out to be connected with envy of Jesus because he was especially close to God.

Illustrating the importance of early God-images, May describes how he held onto an image of God-as-Father for many years after his father died when May was nine years old (1992, p. 81). Clinging to this image provided him with an ongoing sense of connection to his father. When he finally let go of his paternalistic God-image, May reexperienced some of the grief he had felt at the death of his father. By holding onto an image of God-as-Father, he had refused to let his father die psychologically, but this froze his relationship to God. This is an instance in which the individual's personal dynamics were radically intertwined with his God-image. Similarly, especially if one's personal father was a difficult person, the Judeo-Christian's Father-God imagery may contribute to the rejection of (or at least ambivalence toward) that tradition. Realizing that we project our parental imagoes onto our God-image helps us to understand why people develop such ambivalent God-images. Some families discipline children by threatening them with punitive God imagery which instills a fear of God. For many fundamentalists, in a curiously compartmentalized way, God is not only loving but also willing to punish certain behaviors for all eternity. Even for traditional believers who are not fundamentalists, the notion of God as a heavenly parent is deeply ingrained in the monotheistic traditions, although most would agree this is an anthropomorphic image.

Personal and family attitudes are not the only source of a God-image; the child is also exposed to culturally prevalent God-images. In households where religion is important, the child hears preconceived notions about God that he or she is expected to believe. Sometimes, rejection of religion is based on rage at parents who tried to impose it on the child. When this rage is worked out in therapy, an individual spirituality may emerge.

Rizzuto (1979) builds on Winnicott's explanation for religion, which is related to his notion of the transitional object. From a very early age, the child invests a toy or blanket with a soothing capacity; this object stands in for the presence of mother. Winnicott (1971a) believed that the toddler has lost the sense of omnipotent control he or she had as a baby, which was illusory, and to aid in the movement from illusory omnipotence to objective reality the child uses objects in the outer world over which the child can exercise some control.[7] The transitional object is a kind of proto-symbol; it is given meaning by the child's imagination, so transitional objects exist in a "space" midway between the infant's subjective world and the reality-based world. The object therefore exists in an intermediate area of experiencing to which both the child's inner life and the outer world contribute—it is not fully inner yet not quite outer, not quite a hallucination but not quite objectively real. This is initially the area of the child's play, but then cultural experiences and creative products such as art, literature, theater, religion, and the God-image develop in this space. For Rizzuto, the God-representation is a kind of transitional object (1979, p. 179). Throughout life, this representation is continuously reimagined as it is affected by the official God-image of the individual's religious tradition and by life experiences, but it remains a transitional object. One's image of God is therefore very private, consisting of a mixture of sophisticated theology and infantile residues, some of which are unconscious. However it forms, the child's God-image begins as a rudimentary mental representation and continues to be elaborated throughout life.

There are significant differences between the theories of Rizzuto and Jung and also ways in which their ideas complement each other. While Rizzuto believes that the adult God-image begins as a transitional object of infancy, for Jung the transpersonal Self is present at birth; it is an innate or a priori *imago dei* that has nothing to do with the God of dogmatic theology and its claims to truth. The Self is an original, autonomous object, an archetypal potential for the experience of the divine that is filled in by life experiences, as described by Rizzuto. While Rizzuto does not deal with spontaneously arising numinous experiences of the Self, Jung pays little attention to the influence of childhood developmental factors on our experience of the Self. Instead, he pays a great deal of attention to the Self in the form of symbols and to the Self as the superordinate organizing principle of the personality. Clearly, both of their approaches are important. It is worth pointing out that while Rizzuto has described the influence of early relationships on one's

God-representation, this tells us nothing about the divine itself; as Jung pointed out, we cannot know the relationship between the representation and the reality.

One psychoanalyst (Stein 1981) who reviewed Rizzuto's book disliked it because it seemed to be a brief for religion and to be "crypto-Jungian" (which it is not), both great sins in the psychoanalytic tradition of that time. According to the review, Rizzuto ignores Freud's idea of maturity as the relinquishing of all illusions in favor of postoedipal love and work. The reviewer implies that Rizzuto is incompletely analyzed. Rizzuto has also been criticized for making God nothing but the sum of early object relations without leaving room for the reality of the divine itself as a contributor to the representational process (Leavy 1990). However, her approach is valuable because it allows us to study the psychological origins of the individual's God-image. When we see the ways in which early object relations affect our God-image, we see our projections onto that image. None of these can reflect reality. As we withdraw our parental projections from our God-image, we can develop a more mature spirituality, less contaminated by early object relations. Jung refers to this process as the transformation of God.[8]

Research suggests that one's God-image is also related to self-esteem. A loving and kindly God-image tends to be associated with high self-esteem (Benson and Spilka 1973), presumably because one then feels worthy of God's blessing. The image we have of ourselves radically affects the way we relate to others and to the divine. People who despise themselves are more likely to imagine that they are unacceptable to God, and they may be very preoccupied with the need for divine forgiveness and reconciliation. Not surprisingly therefore, therapy that improves the way one thinks about oneself also modifies one's God-image. Here we have to remember that our self-concept is an intrapsychic image or representation and not our true nature, which is ultimately a mystery. Similarly, one's God-image is only that, and so cannot reflect the divine itself, although it may have some useful symbolic or metaphorical value. An encounter with the sacred may take the form of an image, but the experience points beyond the image itself.

Cornett (1998) describes various typical projections onto our God-image. The narcissistic God-image (perhaps expressed in the commandment to "have no other gods before me") arises from the projection of narcissistic parents who demand a great deal from their children; the child is expected to meet the parents' needs for affirmation. The resulting God-image demands perfection from, and is constantly displeased with, his adherents. He is never satisfied and must have absolute obedience. He inspires fear and wants his supplicants to constantly acknowledge their unworthiness of his love. The punitive God-image, based on the experience of punitive parents whose love is highly conditional, makes the subject believe that he or she will be punished or rewarded for certain behaviors or will go to heaven or hell. Needless to say, one's sense of self is radically affected by such God-representations—one is either matching up to the desired God-image or not, and guilt or shame follow failure to do so. As we mature psychologically, or as the intensity of our emotional difficulties softens, so our God-images also mature. We are then less prone to color our understanding of the divine with personal psychodynamic factors such as the search for a heavenly protector as a solution to chronic anxiety. This development is often an unintended side effect of psychotherapy.

Incidentally, we should not assume that a person's God-image will be based on the tradition in which he or she was raised; the individual's God-image is unpredictable. People in conservative traditions may have a very benevolent God-image, and people from liberal traditions may have a punitive God-image. Incidentally, orthodox Jews are forbidden to have pictorial images of God, so there is no point in asking them about their notion of God in a way that presupposes some kind of visual image. Nonetheless, their liturgy and their individual psychology contain many metaphorical images of the divine as father, king, and the like.

Although these developmental explanations for the origin of our God-image are convincing, they are probably not complete. As Bowker pointed out, our sense of God may come from God as well as from social and psychological factors (1973, p. 131). In Jungian parlance, this would mean that we are archetypally or innately disposed to experience the Self in particular ways, and the environment in which we develop provides the necessary influences. It is thus the case that one's spirituality, or the way one is predisposed to experience the sacred, is neither based solely on relationships with parents nor solely on innate factors; one's childhood environment and one's archetypal disposition synchronistically correspond to each other. One's relationship with the Self is not modeled solely on interpersonal dynamics; this relationship is quite different from other object relations and has its own unique logic and its own organizing principles.

People are attracted to traditional God-images and theology that correspond to their psychological makeup, so that a person suffering from guilt and shame for developmental reasons is likely to be concerned with traditional notions of divine judgment. Belief in a day of judgment may be related to a judgmental parent. Belief in an afterlife may arise from death anxiety. That is, one can use a belief system for defensive purposes. A materialistic psychologist may feel that all such belief systems are based on personal psychodynamics, but that remains a matter of opinion. There is no way to verify or refute such claims, which are a matter of faith or belief, and they are unintelligible from a positivistic viewpoint.

When people use religious belief for pathological purposes, as we have seen in the massacres of opposing sects throughout history, we can reasonably assume that religion has been co-opted in the service of pathological narcissism and narcissistic rage. But even that is our assumption, based on our own values. Perhaps the people who flew into the World Trade Center thought they were doing the will of God and would not be considered pathological within their own subculture. However, one cannot simply use sociocultural norms to evaluate mental health, because an entire society may hold pathological beliefs or superstitions such as belief in witches. This is obviously a gray area.[9] What one can suggest is that when a religious belief system is held very dogmatically or rigidly, it is likely that it is being used narcissistically or defensively. The therapist also has to distinguish between a paranoid delusion and a religious belief that is held by an entire group. In the latter case, the belief is shared by many other people and is part of a long-standing traditional institution, while the former is highly idiosyncratic and accompanied by other signs of impaired reality testing.

Just as in therapy one's self and object representations change, so one's God-image may also change, along with unconscious beliefs about transcendent realities. In the context of the relationship with the therapist, a new spiritual narrative may emerge that helps to sustain the individual. At the appropriate time, the therapist can tactfully point out the ways in which the person's parental imagoes are affecting his or her God-image. Here the therapist has to be aware of the ways in which his or her personal God-image affects his or her ability to respond to this issue as it emerges in therapy.

Spiritually oriented psychotherapy is only concerned with the God-images of traditional religion to the extent that these images affect people's attitudes, behavior, and feelings. Contemplative psychotherapy is mainly concerned with spontaneously occurring personal experience of the sacred. This emphasis, and the notion that truth is found within oneself, is a long-standing part of the Western esoteric tradition, albeit the approach of a minority. Mainstream religion is much more collective, so that the individual who looks for internal sources of truth often feels isolated. The risk of working in a solitary way is that one may become disconnected from the restraints and collective wisdom that would normally be applied by a community.

THE ORIGINS OF HUMAN SPIRITUALITY

The question of the individual's spiritual development is closely tied to the larger problem of the origin of human spirituality in general. Our profession's view of this issue has evolved in the last few decades. For many years, mainstream psychiatry and psychology were dominated by a hard-core materialistic worldview. Religion was an unpopular topic of research because it was considered impossible to study spiritual phenomena using the approaches of empirical science (Slife, Hope and Nebeker 1999). The assumption was that if something exists, we should be able to measure it and ultimately explain its mechanisms in physical, naturalistic terms, without reference to supernatural agencies. Psychologists felt obliged to use classical physics as a paradigm for studying the psyche and so stressed quantitative and statistical methods. This led to machine metaphors of the mind and a "cult of empiricism" (Ash 1992). Recently, this attitude has begun to soften, and the unrelenting reductionism and determinism that used to dominate the profession have given way to a new interest in spirituality.[10] This may have happened because scientific positivism has become less fashionable in intellectual circles.[11] It is now understood that our method of approach limits what we may discover, that different approaches are applicable to different types of problems, and that creative and intuitive insights contribute to scientific discovery, although they must then be subject to proper scrutiny. Even in the face of empirical data, we tend to accept or reject theories based on whether or not they correspond to our own prejudices. Theories seem particularly compelling to us when they correspond to our own worldview and our own needs and feelings. It is now understood that empirical assertions must be seen in the context of the particular observer (Hesse 1980).

Given these limitations, there is no specific, objective method that would tell us the origin of human spirituality and religion, which mean so many things to so many people. To me, it seems that there is no adequate explanation for the sense of God or for human spiritual seeking, other than to say they are a built-in aspect of human nature that corresponds to a reality. Of course, there are many other approaches to this question, which has given rise to a good deal of controversy in the scientific community. For many scientists, spirituality and religion seem to be at odds with rationality, so there are attempts to reduce spirituality psychologically, sociologically, and biologically.

Materialistic biologists insist that religion evolved with the evolution of brain structure, although there is disagreement about whether religion was directly adaptive for our evolution or whether religion is just a byproduct of our evolution. Biologists who are believers simply point out that to lack a scientific explanation for a phenomenon does not mean it isn't real.

Some social scientists believe that religion is a way of legitimating and maintaining social order and institutions. Earthly roles and institutions such as kings are assumed to be copies of divine patterns, so that the ruler speaks for the gods or is a god himself. For Berger (1990), the sacred is a cosmos, a source of order, a canopy or shield against what would otherwise be terrifying chaos. For Durkheim, "God" is society worshiping itself, and the primary role of religion is to unite individuals into a common society (Pickering

1975). Other cultural theorists believe that religion arises because
human beings need to find meaning in the face of problems such
as suffering and injustice (Geertz 1966). Religion meets our needs
for intimacy and self-actualization. Or, the function of religion is
to allow one to transcend oneself and feel part of the larger order
of the universe.

PSYCHOLOGICAL THEORIES

As a general rule, reductionist psychological theories suggest that
spirituality is based on our need to reduce anxiety, give us a sense of
order and meaning rather than chaos, and help us with our death
anxiety. Psychologists who are believers argue that our spirituality
corresponds to a real spiritual dimension, to which we are drawn
because it is a deep level of our being, just as thirst would not have
evolved if we did not need water.

Reductionist views have arisen within all schools of psychology.
Early in the twentieth century, Leuba (1925) wrote that mystical
experience is due to pathological factors such as epilepsy, hysteria,
or intoxication. Many classical behaviorists reduced religion to socially reinforced, learned behavior, or they considered religion to
be superstitious behavior produced by random reinforcement and
the threat of punishment. There is a long psychoanalytic tradition
of seeing religion as a defense against harsh reality, a view that is
not surprising given that religion tends to become important during times of crisis. Freud interpreted religion in terms of infantile
longings. He thought that religion represents a refusal to become
fully adult because of the need for a heavenly father, and so is regressive. For Freud, the illusory aspect of religion is based on the
fact that it is derived from a wish; he does not clearly say that religious beliefs are false, but that they are wish fulfillments derived
from feeling helpless, so religion is a defense against facing painful
reality. However, this attitude radically oversimplifies the functions
of religion. The self-sacrifice, insistence on standards of behavior,
compassion, asceticism, and humility demanded by religions are
hardly good evidence of wishful thinking or adherence to the pleasure principle. Furthermore, even if we project human hopes, fears,

and needs into our spirituality, that does not prove there is no such thing as spiritual reality; these projections only mean that personality factors will color our relationship to it.[12] Incidentally, later research discovered that Freud's stress on God as a representation of a heavenly father is not always accurate; the preferred parent colors one's image of the divine (Vergote and Tamayo 1981), and more often than not this means mother. Many Hindu traditions stress the divine as mother rather than father. In any case, there is no reason to assume that we are dealing with projections; one might simply value the same attributes in a parent that one values in one's God-image.

Because religious rituals have to be carried out with attention to detail and stress purity and cleanliness, Freud also noted that religious rituals and obsessive-compulsive behavior share some characteristics, as if this disorder was a caricature of a private religion. In his mind therefore, neurosis is a form of individual religiosity and religion is a "universal obsessive neurosis" (1907, p. 119). Greenberg and Witztum (1991) report the case of a man who spent nine hours a day saying his prayers because he was so concerned about not making a mistake. However, Freud did not point out the differences between religious practice and obsessional states, which these authors make clear. Compulsive behavior goes far beyond what is required; it is focused on one area of religious practice and ignores others. Typically it is concerned with cleanliness and thoughts of blasphemy. Freud also ignores the fact that most people who perform religious rituals do so willingly and are not driven to the ritual by unbearable anxiety (Lewis 1994, p. 189).

I believe that Freud's real argument is with the anthropomorphic Judeo-Christian God-image. As various writers have suggested, it seems that he had his own spirituality. For instance, in *The Interpretation of Dreams* he says that there is a fundamental mystery underlying every dream, one spot at which it cannot be plumbed, its point of contact with the unknown (1900, p. 111, note 1). Here he reveals a spiritual sensibility—his sense of mystery.[13] Bettelheim (1982) pointed out that when Freud spoke about the psyche he used the German word *Seele*, which properly means soul, although it is often mistranslated as ego. According to Bettelheim, Freud viewed the soul as the seat of human identity and uniqueness, and he was aware of the spiritual nature of his work, but this awareness was suppressed by his translators and students in the interest of making his work more acceptable. Acceptance in the scientific community was a major concern for Freud, especially given his early immersion in empirical, positivistic science at a time when it seemed that Newtonian physics would completely explain reality. Adding to Freud's concern to make his work scientific, he did not want psychoanalysis to be thought of as a particularly Jewish process (Gay 1988). Given these conflicting feelings, and because in his day religion and science were thought to be irreconcilable, he may have suppressed or repressed the spiritual aspect of his work. Nevertheless, as Fromm (1950) pointed out, Freud's interest in the gods and goddesses of antiquity is evidence of his respect for the spiritual dimension. Various authors have commented on Freud's superstitions and his interest in the occult, parapsychology, and spiritualism.[14] Jung believed that sexuality was numinous for Freud, implying that sexuality was a private form of spirituality for him. Overall, as Kaiser (1988) suggested, Freud may have been protesting about manifest religion while adhering to latent religion. Perhaps Masson (1990) was pointing out an ironic truth when he noted that psychoanalysis itself became a kind of religion for its followers, with its own notion of salvation, its own dogma, priesthood, and rejection of other traditions.

Most of Freud's early followers joined in his view of religion as evidence of immaturity or neurosis. Some early psychoanalysts believed that the persistence of religious belief in an analysand indicated an incomplete analysis. Cornett (1998) suggested that some of this disapprobation may have been motivated by economic factors; it was important to keep psychoanalysis within rationalistic medical science for reimbursement purposes. In contrast, most contemporary psychoanalysts are open-minded about religion, or at least they treat it tactfully when it emerges in their analysands, because their discipline cannot comment on the veracity of religious beliefs.

In contrast to Freud, others in the early psychoanalytic tradition were sympathetic to religion. Most of these writers understood religion in terms of the residual effects of developmental experiences. Erikson (1950) found the roots of religion in the individual's early relationship with mother, whom he believed to be the source of religious images of nurture and care.[15] For him, the importance of religion is that it confirms the universal importance of trust and hope, which develop with the resolution of the first infantile stage of development. Religion also offers social support for the development of wisdom and integrity, which are the products of the final stage of development in old age—the sense of cosmic order and spiritual meaning, the acceptance of one's life as it has been, and the inevitability of death. Overall, Erikson thought that religion was important for the attainment of maturity.

Suttie (1935) pointed out that neurotic individuals are particularly attracted to religion because religion is concerned with relationships with others and with caring and so acts as a system of psychotherapy. However, he notes that when religion does not work for people with neurotic difficulties they use the tradition more and more defensively, which is why he believes that the Christian tradition was deflected away from love and social justice toward schism and intolerance. Guntripp (1956) also noted the relationship between problematic early relationships and distortions of religion. He pointed out that schizoid individuals may deny religion altogether, precisely because it is about emotional needs and relationships, or they may reduce it to an affectless philosophy of life. Or, if there was early loss leading to depression, the individual may feel sinful and guilty and need salvation through repentance. By contrast, more mature people will use religion for communion with others and with the ultimate. Guntripp believed that religion can produce a type of security and a context for self-realization not available anywhere else.

Typically, psychoanalytic self psychologists see religious belief and practice in terms of the search for a selfobject experience that was missing in childhood.[16] Normally, the infantile experience of merger with an idealized, powerful adult allows the experience of soothing and the regulation of internal tension—abilities that the infant cannot achieve itself. When such a figure was not sufficiently available, there develops a lifelong need to find a wise, strong figure that one can idealize and with whom one can merge psychologically. If one has never experienced a parental figure with goals and values that one can idealize, these are provided by an idealized God-image. One then attributes to one's God-image qualities of strength, love, and perfection. Similarly, the child needs to be mirrored, seen, and valued. For the self psychologist, to have a relationship with God is to be special, to be affirmed and cared for in ways that may have been missing in childhood. As well, to belong to a community of believers allows one to satisfy the selfobject need for twinship, the feeling that one is like other people, which also strengthens one's sense of self.

Some evidence for these aspects of religious affiliation is found in the fact that, as Ullman pointed out in his study of religious converts, prior to their conversion experience many people struggle with feelings of unhappiness, unworthiness, and low self-esteem (1989, p. 191). Most of them had been looking for love, protection, and unconditional acceptance rather than ideological truth. However, the self psychological point of view, while plausible, can only be a partial explanation for the need for spirituality; it does not explain why others who grow up with deficits along these developmental lines do not become religious, and it does not address the religious yearnings of people who had no such developmental difficulty. I believe that this kind of theory only explains the type of spirituality that develops, not the need for spirituality itself.

According to the self psychologists, the need to merge with a perfect figure explains why "the object of mystical experience is often described with reference to power and perfection" (Rector 2001, p. 182). God is an unfailing, idealized selfobject with whom the mystic merges. The experience of union with the divine common to all mystical traditions is then a way of coping with the mystic's narcissistic vulnerability, originating in his or her childhood failure to find a suitably idealizable figure. In this view, mystical experience is at least partially regressive or defensive, although not necessarily pathological, and helps to maintain the integrity of the self. However, even if the self psychological view explains the mystic's search for an idealized selfobject, this does not gainsay the reality of the divine itself or the experience of union with the divine. Perhaps such a state of union actually reflects a higher reality, in which case our usual sense of separateness is illusory. The experience of union with the divine, rather than being a regressive return to a state of blissful merger with mother, may actually represent a high level of spiritual attainment.

Overall, the resistance to spirituality in the psychoanalytic community is now much less than it used to be. It is even recognized that this resistance can be a defense against spirituality and that psychoanalytic theory may actually be used to repress religious material (Kung 1990).

There are also attempts to explain religion in terms of attachment theory, which is based on the notion that there is a built-in behavioral system in babies that evolved to maintain the proximity of infants to caretakers, to protect the baby from predators and other dangers. The baby emits signals such as crying, to which the mother is more or less responsive, leading to different degrees of attachment, either secure or less secure. From this viewpoint, God or Jesus or the saints are attachment figures, felt to be available for protection in the event of danger (Kirkpatrick 1997). Or, the knowledge of the presence of God allows the person to face life with more confidence because God is a perfectly reliable attachment figure. God imagined as a distant figure in the sky would correspond to insecure or avoidant attachment—here the child shows no preference for a parent or a stranger. There is empirical evidence (Kirkpatrick and Shaver 1990) to support the idea that children with insecure attachment relationships to their parents may compensate in adulthood by turning to a "loving, personal, available God" as a substitute. Understandably, adults who describe their mothers as cold, distant, and unresponsive in childhood are more likely to be attracted to a loving image of God. Many of the people in this group who have a religious conversion experience believe it was triggered by a relationship crisis.

Research suggests that children with secure attachment to parents are more likely to be influenced by their parents' religious beliefs than children with insecure attachments, because the securely attached child is more receptive to parental standards (Kirkpatrick 1997). It seems plausible that if one does not develop secure attachment to a parent, one may try to find it by connecting to God. Conversely, an avoidant attachment pattern may be one of the factors leading to atheism. Obviously, there is more to religion than attachment—religion also provides meaning, purpose, answers to existential questions, and values.

Attachment theory implies that religion is rooted in a lack of safety, or in fear, which takes us back to Freud and to the notion that religious experience is marked by feelings of dependence. The idea that religion is only about defense and protection is a deficit model of religion, which implies that religion is immature, although attachment models make religion an evolutionary necessity and tend to normalize our need for a divine figure. For attachment theorists, it is not surprising that people turn to God under stressful conditions. Faith and the sense of the presence of God provide emotional security, which attachment theory refers to as a secure base, a place of safety during difficult times.

Humanistic psychologists are generally well disposed to religion. Fromm (1950) thought that religion arose as human beings tried to cope with isolation and the fear of death, for which purpose we need a frame of orientation and an object of devotion. Maslow (1964), influenced by Fromm, found that it was not unusual for self-actualized people to have peak experiences characterized by wholeness, integration, self-forgetting, and a feeling of being fully alive in a satisfying way. Maslow realized that these experiences get lost in the verbal formulas, rituals, and organizations of institutional religion, which can be a defense against direct spiritual experience. He believed that self-actualization is actually hindered by orthodox religious belief and practice. Maslow is a good example of someone who rejected his (orthodox Jewish) childhood tradition but was deeply moved by art, music, and nature.

JUNG'S THEORY

Jung's contribution to this debate is to postulate the existence in the psyche of an a priori element of the divine, an original object that is not an introject and not the result of developmental factors. Because Jung locates this spiritual dimension within the psyche rather than in a transcendent realm beyond the person, spirituality has important implications for the therapist.[17] This idea is often not acceptable to the theologian who wants the divine to be more Other, or who is concerned that the divine not be reduced to something "merely" psychological. In his response to this critique, Jung pointed out that the psyche is real, so that whatever is psychological actually exists, and no less so than something physical. The God-image is a psychological fact. Another concern raised by theologians is that if the divine somehow exists within the psyche, God would be dependent on the psyche and so not absolute. Jung's position here is that human beings and God must exist in relation to each other or God would be of no consequence at all. A totally absolute or detached God would be meaningless to us, while a God that exists in the psyche is real to us (Jung 1928b, par. 394, note 6).[18] Here we see the relevance of Eckhart's distinction between the Godhead and God. The Godhead, or the Absolute, cannot be experienced, whereas we can experience God as a function of the Godhead within the psyche.

Jung is never definite about whether the transpersonal levels of the psyche (the objective or autonomous levels of the unconscious) are the primary source of our experience of God or whether they mediate the experience of a transcendent level of divinity. Although we find God-images in the psyche, Jung does not commit himself on the question of whether there is a divinity independent of these God-images. He feels that would be a metaphysical and not a psychological question.

Not only the theologians but also many psychologists object to Jung's approach. Fromm (1950) argues that Jung elevates the unconscious to the status of a religious phenomenon and reduces religion to a psychological phenomenon. My own view is that Jung is not reductive, since he makes no ontological claims about the nature of the divine. Rather, he leaves open the question of the source of religious experience and simply concentrates on our experience of the sacred, which is inextricably psychological.

Jung's view that the psyche has an intrinsic religious function means that rather than being a defense against anxiety, spirituality is built into our structure. Both Jung and William James (1958) recognize that religion carries out a function that no other aspect of human nature can perform. Rather than being pathological or infantile, spirituality is important for mental health. Rather than assuming that we need to be cured of religion, for Jung the experience of the psyche's religious function has a healing effect. Perhaps this is why, however we formulate it, a connection to the sacred is associated with mental health benefits.

Historically, whatever their private opinion, mainstream psychiatrists and psychologists tended to ignore their patients' spirituality unless it became a factor within their psychopathology. In recent years, this attitude has changed, perhaps because it has become clear that religion is important to most people in this country (Gallup 1995; Hoge 1996). Accordingly, in the current edition of the *Diagnostic and Statistical Manual* (2000) of the American Psychiatric Association, religious or spiritual problems have been given a diagnostic category (V62.89) applicable for cases in which the individual loses or questions his or her religious belief or converts to a new faith. As well, it is now clear that involvement in religion helps people cope in the face of adversity and is protective during times of stress, leading to reduced risk of suicide, drug use, violence, delinquency, and depression. Religious practice is also said to help heart disease and high blood pressure (Larson and Larson 1994). However, religion is also misused in the service of individual psychopathology, to rationalize misogyny, violence, and intolerance. Parental abuse of children, either physical or emotional, is sometimes supported by biblical quotations (Meissner 1992; Pruyser 1997; Josephson 1993).

PSYCHODYNAMICS INTERTWINED WITH RELIGIOUS BELIEFS

The therapist occasionally meets chronically unhappy people whose unhappiness is compounded by belief in religious teachings and standards of behavior which they cannot meet. These individuals suffer from a punitive superego, an internal critic or judge that makes them suffer in a variety of ways.[19] It typically accuses them of being bad and immoral. They suffer from guilt around sexuality because of childhood indoctrination about the evils of the body, or they have been told that anger is sinful. Other people are chronically unhappy not because of guilt but because of pervasive emptiness and shame. For example, a woman feels intense shame because she regularly has sex with a man she does not really care for, but otherwise she feels deprived, lonely, and unattractive. She feels there is something wrong with her because this behavior contravenes her early religious education. Psychoanalytic self psychology understands her compulsive sexuality in terms of a desperate attempt to obtain preoedipal needs for affirmation and mirroring, a way in which she enlivens herself and wards off intolerable emptiness. The drive for sexuality also reflects the yearning for union with the other, who is also an expression of the divine Other, and so expresses an unconscious spiritual yearning. Sexuality then becomes a vehicle for processes beyond genital sexuality itself, so that the therapist may listen to this woman's difficulties at both the psychodynamic and spiritual levels simultaneously. Whereas the tradition in which she grew up sees her sexual expression as sinful or immoral, the therapist sees it both as a way of dealing with the radical failure of mirroring she experienced in her childhood and also as purposeful, driven by the Self, pointing forward to an attempted redemption of her childhood by allowing her to give and receive love in the only way possible at present. Arguments about whether this is "real" love or not are irrelevant and patronizing. No one knows what love really is, and whatever it is we cannot qualify it by dictating where, how, and to whom it should be expressed.

Some people use religious doctrine and dogma to try to contain an emotional difficulty; the typical example is the moralistic, fundamentalist preacher thundering about sin in an attempt to control and project his own fear, greed, or sexuality. Members of fundamentalist traditions often have tremendous difficulty with the body, which cannot be trusted lest it begin to make forbidden sexual demands. They therefore try to impose a set of rules that regulate sexual expression. These rules, which have been internalized in childhood, become a therapeutic problem when the individual is trying to escape from fundamentalism. Even though he or she no longer believes in the dogmas of the tradition, persistent somatic tension and unconscious guilt or shame may prevent the person from enjoying the body.

People who grew up in homes that stressed the Puritan or Calvinist work ethic (the duty to work for the benefit of society and the salvation of the individual) may have a harsh superego that drives them to work excessively.[20] This often produces a fear of failure and a need to prove their worth to introjected, critical parents. They may also use overworking to distract themselves from painful internal emptiness. Others have been conditioned to believe that relaxation is vaguely sinful, or they feel they must justify their existence because they were unwanted children or that only accomplishments allow them to feel loved. The body then becomes chronically rigid, the individual is in a constant state of overarousal, and it is impossible to find internal peace. Needless to say, it is common for such people to turn to substances or other compulsive activity in an attempt to obtain temporary release from these pressures.

Some people in this situation suffer from the tension between exhortations to work and religious teachings not to control things and trust a benevolent providence. They have been told to remember that the "Lord is my Shepherd," or we can be like the lilies of the field or the birds of the air which do not need to work. They have been told to "turn it over to God," a teaching that, when authentic and not just the result of denial or avoidance, has a powerfully calming effect. However, for some people an attitude of spiritual surrender is too reminiscent of the subjugation to authority they experienced in childhood. Others cannot let go of a driven need to work because of identification with an overworked parent. At the other extreme, what is rationalized as spiritual surrender can become an excuse for passivity, resignation, or an avoidance of ordinary responsibility. In its mature form, the faith or knowledge that things are the way they are supposed to be allows a letting go of control that is based on trust rather than a regressive dependence. William James called true letting go "regeneration by relaxing. . . . It is but giving your little private convulsive self a rest, and finding that a greater Self is there" (1958, p. 107). He accurately described self-surrender as "the vital turning point of religious life" (ibid., p. 195). Otherwise, people feel that "everything is up to me," which produces an attitude of chronic tension and reveals a deep lack of faith. However, self-surrender, the letting go that is such a valuable teaching of traditional spirituality, is not an easy task because of our need to control what happens to us, which is based on fragmentation anxiety, the need for mastery, and the need to maintain self-esteem.[21] When the self is strengthened in psychotherapy, letting go becomes more possible. With this in mind, the therapist cannot distinguish between the person's psychological and spiritual needs, and the process of psychotherapy simultaneously involves both.

Many people who were emotionally or physically abused in childhood have a profound sense of being "un-chosen"; such is their level of self-hatred that they feel as if the universe made a mistake because they were not supposed to be here. Typical therapeutic tasks in these situations are to soften the superego, reduce painful emptiness, enhance self-esteem, and strengthen an enfeebled sense of self. There is also an important spiritual dimension of such situations. For the spiritually oriented therapist, the individual has a divine right to be on the planet. Whether or not this is articulated is a matter of judgment, but it is implicit in our responses to the person.

Needless to say, the therapist may not be spared the necessity for personal development in this area. This is particularly true among psychotherapists who were the "parentified" oldest child of many siblings. These therapists feel overly responsible for (rather than responsible to) the people with whom they work in therapy. To work with a spiritual sensibility means that we loosen the grip of such internal injunctions so that our work can arise from more authentic compassion.

SPIRITUALITY AS A MOTIVATIONAL FORCE

All theories of psychotherapy include some idea of what motivates human behavior. For Freud, sexuality and aggression were most important, while contemporary theory has added more types of motivation (Lichtenberg, Lachmann and Fosshage 1992) based on our understanding of fundamental needs such as the need to regulate our physiology, the needs for attachment and affiliation, to explore and assert ourselves, and for sensual and sexual pleasure. Some authors think in terms of a hierarchy of motivations and needs, going from the more basic, such as the need for food, shelter, safety, and a firm sense of self, to higher needs such as meaningful work, love, and the fulfillment of one's potentials. I suggest that the spiritual search can be added to the list of motivating factors which are important in self-regulation, self-organization, and relationships with others. I do not believe that we progress from the psychological to the spiritual levels, with the implication that the spiritual is somehow higher, because the spiritual dimension is present at all levels of the psyche.

All these motivational needs are operating all the time, but at different times in the therapy different motivational systems are operating, and the therapist has to sense empathically which is uppermost at any given moment. When a spiritual question has arisen and is motivating the person, if the therapist does not think spirituality is important, the person may sense this lack of interest and stop talking about it in order to stay connected to the therapist. Or, this situation may produce a clash of values in the therapy. This is true especially if the therapist sees talk of spirituality as a defense against dependency and helplessness, or if the therapist simply thinks that such talk is a waste of time and is waiting for something "more important" to emerge. In that case, the therapist is actually guiding the person's associations to fit the therapist's theory of what should be happening. However, we don't know what *should* be happening to the soul, so faith in a larger process is essential for the spiritually oriented therapist. It is worth reiterating that the etymology of the word *therapist* comes from the Greek word for servant or attendant, so the psychotherapist attends or serves the soul. Here, the psychological sense of the word *soul* does not carry theological implications. The word *soul* is a metaphorical way of indicating the spiritual dimension of the personality or the deepest and most important level of the individual's subjectivity. (For a fuller discussion of soul in psychotherapy, see chapter 5.)

I do not think of the psyche as "opening into the realm of spirit" as if they are somehow different dimensions of reality, because I believe that psyche cannot be separate from spirit. When we work with psychologically important material, we are doing spiritual work. Another way of saying this is that the personal and the transpersonal dimensions of consciousness are inextricably woven together. For example, for Jung, a complex consists of an archetypal or transpersonal core surrounded by personal material; we cannot have one without the other. This means that object relations theory, psychoanalytic self psychology, or cognitive behavioral paradigms describe the personal level of the complex, but there is always a transpersonal core to our psychopathology. Therefore, it is surely a mistake to say that negative feelings such as rage and hatred are purely psychological, while positive feelings such as love and compassion are spiritual. Any feeling stimulated by a complex has a spiritual component to it, and since our emotions are embodied they indicate the presence of spirit incarnate in the body. Unless this is true, we would have to say that the sacred is only sweetness and light, but if Jung is correct that the Self has a dark side, which fits with our experience, painful emotions are also manifestations of the Self.

NOTES

1. There are people who, like William James's "once-born" souls, do not experience dark nights but rather a more joy-filled spirituality. I think they are less likely to be in psychotherapy than those who go through periods of spiritual darkness.

2. Isaiah (45:15) talks of God as hidden. The Hebrew Bible often depicts God as hiding himself or withdrawing when people disobey his commandments. Psalm 86 and especially Psalm 88 are good examples of the experience of divine absence. For a review of the biblical origins and theological development of this idea in Luther and Barth, see Hanna Hadon's (1995) discussion.

3. May makes a radical distinction between spiritual direction and psychotherapy that I do not think is entirely valid. He feels that a different atmosphere obtains when he carries out spiritual direction than the atmosphere in the room when he is engaged in psychotherapy. In the former case, the atmosphere is spacious, peaceful, open, and receptive; a "kind of quiet clarity in which it is easier to allow and let be" (1992, p. 113). However, I do not think that one has to call oneself a spiritual director for this atmosphere to prevail. It tends to occur spontaneously whenever one is dealing with overtly spiritual material, whether in psychotherapy or in any other setting.

4. This stage has been well described by Bernadette Roberts (1984).

5. Theologians have various objections to the idea of the Self as an intrapsychic God-image. They accuse Jung of reducing the transcendent divine to something that is purely intrapsychic, which makes the divine something only subjective and too immanent, located within the human personality

rather than in a realm beyond human beings. Yet there is no reason that a transcendent divinity should not express itself psychologically or that the psyche should not contain a supraindividual quality. The psyche is real, so that to say that the Self is experienced psychologically makes the Self a living reality.

6. I believe this religious function exists so that we may experience the sacred dimension of existence. Obviously this belief is not amenable to a positivistic form of verification.

7. An example of the baby's illusory omnipotence is that the hungry baby feels as if it has made the breast appear. What the baby needs internally is provided by mother's attunement, so the inner and outer worlds come together.

8. For a full discussion, see Edinger (1992).

9. For a review, see Meissner (1996, p. 241).

10. For a scholarly summary of these developments, see chapters 2 and 3 of Richards and Bergin (2005).

11. Positivism is a philosophy of science that rejects metaphysics and believes that in order to be taken seriously, statements about reality must be observable, testable, subject to empirical verification, shown to be true on the basis of evidence, and not dependent on the bias of the observer. Many early behaviorists and some psychoanalysts adopted this attitude, which suggests that psychotherapy can be carried out by an objective, impartial therapist. For them, values have no place in psychotherapy. Part of the irony of this situation was that these therapists had metaphysical beliefs about the nature of the universe, such as atheism, materialism, and scientific naturalism, beliefs which were themselves nonempirical. Meanwhile, physics has moved away from simplistic notions of objectivity independent of the observer's consciousness.

12. In a letter of 26 November 1927 to pastor Oskar Pfister, Freud acknowledged that his theory of religion was only his personal opinion, and one could use psychoanalytic theory to argue the opposite view. See Meng and Freud (1963).

13. Einstein (1949) expressed a similar spirituality when he stood in awe at the complexity, order, and mystery of the universe.

14. For a review of this aspect of Freud, and a discussion of the psychodynamic origins of Freud's attitude to religion, see chapter 2 of Meissner (1984).

15. For a review of Erikson's approach to religion, see Zock (1990).

16. The term *selfobject* was coined by Kohut to describe another person who is experienced intrapsychically as a part of oneself. The selfobject supports or enhances one's sense of self by carrying out functions such as mirroring and validating, emotional attunement, or soothing and providing a sense of direction, goals, and values.

17. Various texts describe Jung's approach to religion. See, for example, Heisig (1979) or Schaer (1950).

SPIRITUAL DEVELOPMENT153Saturday

18. To find support for this idea, Jung quotes Meister Eckhart: "By this kingdom of God we understand the soul, for the soul is of like nature with the Godhead" (Jung 1923, par. 418). For Eckhart, there is a sense in which God is dependent on the soul, or God is a function of the soul, and the soul is a function of the Godhead, where the Godhead is total reality.

19. It is important for the depth psychology–oriented therapist not to group all forms of depression into the same DSM category of "mood disorders." The DSM mixes different types of depressive problems into the same category, ignores the very important depressive character structure, and does not distinguish between guilty or introjective depressions and empty depressions of the kind found in narcissistic and borderline personalities. See, for example, Blatt (1998). In this context, for the dynamically oriented therapist, the recent *Psychodynamic Diagnostic Manual* (PDM Task Force 2006) is much more helpful than the DSM.

20. Christian fundamentalists often believe that suffering and hard work redeem sin. Their hard work is motivated by guilt. Many of them have an antipleasure attitude to life, because of biblical verses that suggest that joy is not good for the soul, such as Luke 6:25 and Gal. 5:21.

21. For a fuller discussion of letting go, see Corbett (1996, pp. 35–36).

CHAPTER 5

Psychotherapy as Care of the Soul

THE MEANING OF SOUL IN PSYCHOTHERAPY

This chapter suggests that psychotherapy is a contemporary form of care of the soul, with the understanding that the psychotherapeutic approach to the soul differs radically from the traditional religious connotations of that word.[1] Depth psychologists have used the word *soul* a great deal in recent years—in fact it is in danger of being overused—so it is worth clarifying the variety of ways in which they use the term. Although it has become very fashionable to speak of the soul, there is no uniformity of meaning in the psychological literature. In fact, there is so much variation in the use of the word that one can only grasp its meaning by the particular context in which it is used.

The traditional use of the word *soul* refers to a suprasensory reality, an ultimate principle or a divine quality in the individual. Depth psychologists have appropriated the word as a way of distinguishing themselves from other schools of psychology. Some depth psychologists use the notion of soul to deliberately imply an overlap between psychology and spirituality or to suggest a particular depth of experience or a romantic sensibility. For the psychotherapist, the main importance of this word is that it distinguishes between everyday ego concerns and deeper levels of meaning. The word *soul* is also a useful term for that mysterious, often uncanny sense of presence, familiar to all therapists, that occasionally pervades the therapy room.

Part of the attraction of Jung's psychology is that it is a psychology of the soul rather than the mind or the brain. In 1933, while many psychologists were trying to extirpate words with a religious connotation from the field of psychology, Jung suggested that the recovery of the soul is an essential task for us. He insisted on the reality of the soul as a principle in its own right, but he uses the term in more than one way. Jung sometimes uses the word *soul* as if it were synonymous with the psyche. This usage has the advantage of not separating the human being into compartments that belong to two disciplines, one the province of spirituality and the other of psychology. For Jung, the psyche is a primary realm in its own right, and the psyche creates the reality in which we live. His ontological position is therefore what he calls *esse in anima*, or being in soul, meaning that the way we experience the world is a combination of the way the world is in some objective sense and the way the psyche or the soul imagines or fantasizes about it (Jung 1923, par. 77). This is a third position between a purely materialistic perspective (*esse in re*) and a purely mental one (*esse in intellectu*).

At other times, Jung uses the term *soul* as if it were a functional complex within the psyche, a kind of psychological organ which produces images and symbols, such as dream images, that act as a bridge or translator between consciousness and the unconscious. When we dream or have a numinous experience, transpersonal levels of the psyche interact with human levels of consciousness. In this sense, the soul is that which allows us to link with spirit and perceive the sacred—what we know about the spirit comes to us by means of the soul. In this capacity, the soul is a bridge that casts the experience of spirit into emotions and images which are transmitted into personal awareness and into the body.

Unknown dream figures of the opposite sex are sometimes referred to as "soul figures." Jung believed that a female figure in a man's dream or a male figure in a woman's dream describe parts of the psyche that are particularly unconscious to the dreamer. He thought that opposite-sex figures in a dream bridge to deeper levels of the psyche than same-sex figures because contrasexual figures are more unknown to us. The soul is therefore a link to the unconscious.

Hillman wrote of the soul as "a perspective rather than a substance, a viewpoint toward things rather than a thing itself" (1975, p. xvi). For him, the soul is the capacity for imagination, reflection, fantasy, and "that unknown human factor which makes meaning possible, which turns events into experiences, which is communicated in love and which has a religious concern" (Hillman 1972, p. 23).[2] Hillman is fond of Keats's notion that the world is a "vale of soul-making."[3] Many depth psychologists understand this phrase to mean the work of processing our experience psychologically, casting our experience of a situation into words and images, seeing the situation metaphorically, even mythically, and developing interiority. However, to call this soul-making can be seen as a reversal of the natural order, a backward perspective, because it is the soul itself that allows us to do these things. If we think of the soul as a primary principle, we cannot "make" soul; to do so would imply something beyond the soul that is doing the making. It is more likely that the soul makes us, or makes us human. Our problem is to experience everyday life soulfully. Our daily activities are then a bridge to the soul, which makes the world and the body necessary.

Hillman makes much of the distinction between soul and spirit, suggesting that the soul is feminine, deep, moist, and dark while the spirit is masculine, fiery, light, impersonal, and ascending. Yet the soul, which is surely not gendered, can also soar and feel dry, and there are forms of spirituality that are based in the earth and stress descent rather than ascent. Hillman is therefore describing different aspects of the soul itself, rather than distinguishing between soul and spirit. For Hillman, spirit is active, making form, order, and distinction, whereas soul is about experiencing life metaphorically, about natural urges, memories, the imagination, fantasies, and suffering. He makes this distinction so that we do not confuse (soul-centered) psychotherapy with spiritual disciplines such as yoga and meditation. He believes that only the soul but not the spirit suffers psychopathology, so that the soul is the proper province and the root metaphor of psychotherapy (Hillman 1989). Hillman points out that it is important to distinguish soul and spirit when we are trying to understand the soul's own logic, its suffering, fantasies, and fears, which is a different project than a metaphysical approach to spirit and its ultimates (1975, p. 68). Nevertheless, it seems overly dualistic to separate soul and spirit so rigidly; traditionally, the spirit includes the soul.

Other writers use the term *soul* when referring to the deepest subjectivity of the individual, especially to emotionally important experiences. Very often, experiences are referred to as soulful precisely because they provoke intense feelings, especially among therapists with a strong thinking function for whom feelings are numinous. This is a useful sense of the word; soulful emotions such as love, hatred, terror, sadness, and joy—the bread-and-butter of psychotherapy—become sanctified if we approach them spiritually.[4]

Some therapists think of the soul operationally as an ontologically a priori, spiritual essence or even a subtle substance within the person, which is close to the traditional meaning of soul. This attitude reminds us of the connotation of the soul as transcendent and that people are more than biological machines. As Jung puts it, one can think of the psyche as containing a divine power or that the psyche is a metaphysical principle in its own right (1954c, par. 836). The problem of dualism arises here, how this essence interacts with the body or how the body acts as an instrument of the soul. Perhaps to avoid this issue, William Blake suggested that what we call body "is a portion of the soul discerned by the five senses" (1975, p. xvi). This attitude is preferable to the idea that the soul is trapped in the body. In psychotherapy, one can think of soul and body as two aspects of the same reality, experienced differently because of the limitations of our perceptual apparatus. One can use a personally appealing model or metaphor to avoid thinking in terms of soul-body dualism. For example, we could think of psyche and body as existing on a gradient of different densities of emanation from a unitary source. The physical body is at one end of this spectrum, while the psyche is situated at a more subtle level of the same continuum.

For the therapist to recognize the reality of the soul and its continuity with the transpersonal dimension of consciousness is to practice with a spiritual sensibility. Other contemporary depth psychologists express their spiritual orientation by means of the emerging field of ecopsychology. They sense that the individual soul is actually continuous with the soul of the world, known since antiquity as the *anima mundi*. This is nature's consciousness, or psyche as indistinguishable from nature itself. What we divide into the workings of ego, soul, spirit, and body are different processes or manifestations of this larger consciousness.

In his seminal work on the soul, Christou (1976) points out that the proper field of psychotherapy is subjective experience, which is not the same as the brain, the body, or the mind. The soul is the experiencing subject, not the mind or the body that is experienced. Just as there is a difference between a physical object and our sense data about it, for Christou there is a distinction between states of mind, such as willing, perceiving, thinking, and feeling, and our *experience* of these states of mind, what we do with them, what they mean to us subjectively. The soul is that which experiences all these.

Christou points out that there is a difference between ordinary states of mind and deeply meaningful experiences, which are the province of the soul. Mind is the name we give to ideas and thought, but soul is the name we give to our ability to transform these ideas in our imagination. We use our imagination to elaborate our bodily states and our feelings, and the result is much more than simple conceptual understanding of an original experience. "Soul" therefore implies not just intellectual or aesthetic understanding of an experience, but our gut-level relationship to it, its effects on our sense of self, and the ethical demands of the experience on the personality. When an experience is soulful we participate in it, we do not just impartially observe it.

According to Christou, the mind, the body, and our emotions are *sources* of psychological experience, but they are not the experience itself—to fail to make this distinction is to confuse different levels. Behavior and ideas are of a different order than the order of the soul. There is a distinction between a science of the mind and the reality of the soul. The realm of soul is the realm of meaning that is discovered when we look into ourselves, when we are inspired or deeply affected by music, art, ritual, a person, the natural world, by love or beauty. The soul is about what we do with our mental and physical states in our imagination and our fantasies, what they mean to us subjectively. The soul is about what matters to us.

"The soul remains the great unknowable . . . . We know that the soul is an everyday experience, yet we have no language to talk of it which is not vitiated by abuses of the language of reason or sense perception" (Christou 1976, p. 25). The soul is a reality of its own, not simply transcendental or biological; "it is about life, about how people think, feel, behave, their problems and their ways . . . it is also about spirit and the meaning of life to people" (ibid., p. 30). Just as the body and mind develop in their own ways, so "the soul has its own developmental processes leading to psychic maturity and psychic plenitude" (ibid., p. 37). These are the proper concern of psychotherapy, which is not just about the "mind" or "behavior."

Until the nineteenth century, psychology (then known as moral philosophy) was considered to be the study of the soul, but by the end of that century psychology was thought of as a science of the mind (Reed 1997). In its original theological sense, the soul is impossible to study using empirical approaches that are valuable in the physical sciences, and even in the psychological sense described above, the soul needs its own methods of study. Many dreams and spiritual experiences have no rational explanation, or they have their own rationale—they defy the inductive scientific approach because they always produce something totally new, unexpected, and impossible to replicate, so they are anathema to positivistic approaches. A materialistic orientation may try to force the soul into the Procrustean bed of its own approaches to reality by calling it mind, but if Christou is correct, these are not synonymous terms.

The quantum physicist recognizes that to observe certain experiments is to affect their outcome; how equally true that is for the situation in psychotherapy, when the soul observes itself. The notion of an objective therapist is a thing of the past. The attitude with which the therapist sits in the room is crucial. As Christou puts it, "We can never arrive at spirit if we do not put spirit in from the beginning" (1976, p. 6). If we are aware of a transcendent presence in the therapy room, we will approach the work with reverence and with respect for the mystery involved, whether we call this a soulful or a spiritual sensibility. For the spiritually inclined therapist, this attitude cannot be dismissed as a projection; it is the perception of a reality. Jung suggests that the spiritual appears in the psyche as an instinct, "indeed as a real passion, a 'consuming fire'" (1948a, par. 108), and just as hunger needs a real meal, so "spiritual hunger needs a numinous content" (1958, par. 652). For psychotherapy to ignore our spiritual instinct would be to ignore one of the main motivational factors within the personality.

Depth psychologists stress the perspective of the soul because this approach frees us from the sense that life consists simply of day-to-day material reality with no other meaning to it. We do not want to register events mechanically; we want to allow ourselves to deepen into our world as much as possible. Jung notes that many of his patients were unhappy in spite of their material success because they were ignoring soulful concerns such as the discovery of meaning and purpose and their unlived life. Their success remained at the level of the ego, while an important distinction between ego and soul is that, while the ego is the voice of consciousness, the soul has many voices, not all of which are conscious. The perspective of the soul is therefore not the same as that of the ego. The ego is concerned with reality orientation and everyday practical matters that may not be of great emotional significance or depth of meaning. The soul may address a question of meaning to the ego, but the ego's preoccupations may obscure the soul's concerns. Sometimes the ego is afraid to respond to the soul's questions, even when we realize what they are. Then the call to awareness that can be produced by suffering falls on deaf ears. Ideally, however, the ego takes up the soul's preoccupation and the gap between their concerns narrows.

An approach to psychopathology based only on the relief of symptoms may help people cope better with their environment without concern for the meaning of their suffering, but Christou pointed out that such a cure may be achieved at the price of ignoring the values of the soul. Therefore he suggests that the "proof of psychotherapeutic cures takes the form of 'testimony,' a 'witness,' rather than that of logical conclusions or empirical observations of an objective event" (1976, p. 3). This is a radically different view of psychotherapy than one oriented toward symptom relief, but in the following section I hope to show that it is nonetheless effective.

PSYCHOTHERAPEUTIC CARE OF THE SOUL

As well as its technical aspects, psychotherapy involves compassion, attention, and mindfulness, which are qualities stressed by all the spiritual traditions (Germer, Siegel and Fulton 2005).[5] Careful attention to the person can be transformative without invoking any metapsychological theory, perhaps because such attention requires interest, caring, and valuing of the person. These factors, along with empathic listening without judgment, are some of the key ingredients common to all schools of psychotherapy. By caring for another person, the therapist opens herself or himself to the suffering of the other, which can be done authentically only out of love or compassion. These factors are not a function of technical training, yet without them no amount of training will enable someone to become a good therapist. Therefore, one of the functions of technical training in psychotherapy is to allow the practitioner to deploy love or compassion in a helpful way. Without a good grasp of the necessary skills of psychotherapy, the therapist's love would remain too unfocused to be of value to most of the people who come to therapy.

True empathy requires that one puts oneself aside as much as possible in order to be present for the other—a spiritual practice by any definition. For the therapist to see the divine essence in the other—the spiritual level of mirroring—is not only helpful psychologically but is also a profound form of spiritual connection. To recognize that at the deepest level there is no separation between me and the other, or that we both participate in the same transpersonal field of consciousness, is a further form of spiritual realization. These aspects of the work do not need to be articulated by the therapist; they are implicit in his or her behavior, and such awareness affects the quality of the therapeutic field.

All therapists pay attention to the person's life story, with special interest in his or her developmental difficulties. Jungians add the notion that the person's symptoms also have teleological importance for the future course of the personality. At the same time as we listen from these points of view, the therapist can hear the person's story as a spiritual biography. From this perspective, the transpersonal Self, which is present at birth, provides a blueprint (what Kohut (1984) refers to as the self's nuclear program) for the development of the personality, which therefore has a deeper source than the interaction of genes and the environment. Because the Self is an aspect of the divine within the personality, the personality is spiritually determined. For the purposes of a spiritual approach to psychotherapy, development includes the incarnation of the spiritual potentials of the individual. These potentials include the development of psychopathology, or emotionally painful complexes. Jungian thought describes an archetypal core to our complexes and considers the archetypes to be spiritual principles in the psyche.[6] Our complexes are emotionally toned, and emotion is felt in the body. Therefore, to pay attention to a person's emotions is to attend to the embodiment of spirit, or the soul. Important complexes act as a kind of spiritual axis in our lives, for example, when an abusive childhood leads to a lifelong struggle with hatred, rage, and the need for forgiveness.

To foster the process of personality development is a practice of care of the soul, especially when the therapy encourages the incarnation of archetypal or spiritual potentials that would otherwise remain dormant. Furthermore, psychotherapy deals with relationships, which are of profound spiritual importance, and this includes our relationship to the sacred dimension and its effects on our lives.

If spiritual questions such as the meaning and purpose of the individual's life are directly addressed in therapy, is the therapist then acting as a spiritual teacher or guide? These are different roles than the traditional role of the therapist, but such is the spiritual vacuum in our culture that a combination of these roles may be necessary at times. However, questions remain. Is it justified for the therapist to address spiritual questions? Would this tend to promote artificially or even exploit an idealizing transference? Is the therapist assuming a role for which he or she is not qualified, and does he or she risk imposing his or her own spirituality onto the patient? As well as these quandaries, various authors have warned of the ethical and legal issues that may arise if the therapist works spiritually as well as therapeutically.[7] In spite of these potential hazards, there are therapists who believe that their role is to directly help the person identify his or her spirituality, because to do so helps healing (Gersten 1997). For example, Matthews suggests a combination of "prayer and Prozac" (Matthews and Clark 1998, p. 88). However, we cannot assume that the therapist is more spiritually advanced than the patient.

The therapist's personal values and beliefs are usually implicit and not discussed with the person unless he or she raises the issue of spirituality. A religious therapist's implicit use of spirituality might include a silent prayer on behalf of the person. Some therapists have a sense of profound spiritual communion with the person and a sense that what is being said is truly sacred. They feel a sense of a spiritual presence in the room or an intuition of spiritual guidance (West 2000). These typically remain private experiences. But should the therapist explicitly suggest practices such as meditation, prayer, or scriptural reading? If so, at which point in the therapy should this be done, and how would doing so affect the transference? Especially in the throes of an idealizing transference, some people would comply with the therapist's suggestion as a way of staying connected to the therapist. Would such a suggestion imply that the therapist feels the situation is otherwise hopeless, and that the therapeutic relationship is not enough to be helpful? Or would it enhance the process if the person feels that God is helping? One might think that suggesting prayer to a religious person would be helpful, whereas in fact the person might be struggling with doubt and loss of faith or anger at God, so at times the suggestion to pray can be quite the wrong thing to do. Furthermore, the outcome of prayer is unpredictable, and if the therapist explicitly recommends it, its apparent failure may adversely affect the therapeutic relationship. The therapist might be identified as part of the religious establishment, thus contaminating the transference situation.[8]

A case can be made for the idea that some of the approaches depth psychologists use to contact and activate the unconscious are analogous to prayer. Examples are visualization, active imagination (*vide infra*), sand tray, and expressive or body therapies of all kinds. All these modalities have the potential to release unconscious material, and the same is true of prayer. When we pray, we express what is most important to us, and in the process of doing so material may spontaneously arise from the unconscious, so that prayer is in a way the opposite of repression.

If spiritual problems loom large and the therapist feels unqualified to deal with them, he or she could suggest a referral to a minister, priest, or rabbi. However, referral may be resisted if the person is unable to discuss his or her problem with a minister because of a fear of judgment. Clergy are often unaware of the connection between a particular God-image and the psychodynamics and developmental history of the individual. In such a case, they take the person's spiritual questions too much at face value, as if these questions were purely matters of faith or doctrine, without realizing that spiritual problems are inextricably connected to the individual's psychological structures. Furthermore, the therapist may be working with a person whose difficulty was triggered by contact with clergy.

It may be helpful for the therapist to suggest a particular spiritual intervention if he or she works within the client's belief system as long as the therapist is not imposing his or her personal beliefs onto the person. For example, some pastoral therapists working with a Christian individual suggest guided imagery in which Jesus appears and heals trauma—but the type of imagery used has to be chosen very carefully or it may exacerbate the problem, just as any failure of a spiritual practice may make the person feel like a failure. Richards and Bergin have listed several spiritual interventions used by contemporary theistic psychotherapists, such as prayer, reference to scripture, and encouragement to forgive (2005, p. 281ff.). Transpersonal therapists may suggest meditation or techniques that alter consciousness such as shamanic journeying, holotropic breath work, the use of entheogens or past life regressions. Typically, these practices are recommended for people who are relatively psychologically healthy because of the concern that transpersonal practices may be too dangerous for vulnerable people, although Boorstein (1996) has reported that meditation may be helpful even for very fragile personalities. These practices sometimes allow the emergence of material into consciousness that may otherwise remain inaccessible to ordinary psychotherapy. This material can subsequently be processed with the help of a therapist.

In spite of the benefits of spiritual practice, many depth psychotherapists feel that actively encouraging spiritual techniques is too similar to introducing an institutional form of spirituality into therapy, rather than waiting to see what happens organically within the therapeutic relationship. The recommendation of specific techniques may imply that the therapist knows what is best for the individual in a given situation and may reflect the therapist's agenda or an untoward use of power, thus distorting the therapeutic relationship. Apart from the obvious issues of compatibility with the person's belief system and temperament, perhaps the main problem with suggesting a spiritual practice is that to do so may be a way of avoiding a transference-countertransference issue or a therapeutic impasse. Such a recommendation may be a way of fostering an idealizing transference in an artificial manner. We must also be aware that spiritual practices can be used defensively, as a way of avoiding personal material.[9]

During a personal crisis, one purpose of traditional spiritual interventions such as prayer is to obtain guidance from the transpersonal realm. We may also accomplish this by attending to dreams and other spontaneous manifestations of the psyche. When one works with dreams one is seeking the view of the unconscious on a situation, and this may lead to an entirely new perspective. Similarly, the practice of active imagination is like a waking dream in which one allows spontaneous images to emerge from the unconscious, as if one were watching an internal screen (Hannah 2001). This process is not the same as the use of visualization, guided imagery, or daydreaming; active imagination is a process that first receives imagery and then actively responds to it. We allow the images to arise without interfering; what arises is involuntary and not produced by the ego. In this work, the imagination is not understood in its colloquial sense as fantasy, a purely subjective creation of the mind that may have nothing to do with objective reality. The imagination is considered to be a form of perception, so that as Corbin (1972) points out, the *mundus imaginalis* or the imaginal world gives us information that is as real as that provided through the senses and the intellect. Because such imagery arises from the autonomous psyche, active imagination is in accord with the view of romantic poets who saw the imagination as a divine faculty within the person. In William Blake's words: "The Eternal Body of Man is the Imagination, that is, God himself" (as cited in Frye 1990, p. 30).

The therapist is operating spiritually when he or she helps people find meaning in their life story, especially in their suffering. Suffering may be the result of the activation of material in the unconscious, such as a fear of abandonment that has been lying dormant since childhood and is now released by a current experience of abandonment. Jung points out that once the unconscious opens up, spiritual suffering results, and we hope that "from the psychic depths which cast up the powers of destruction the rescuing forces will also come" (1932, par. 532). For example, motifs appear in dreams that are healing and act as a revelation. This psychological approach contrasts with traditional religious approaches to suffering, but today therapists are often called upon to help people with problems that used to be the province of the priest. In Jung's essay on this cultural development, aptly titled "Psychotherapists or the Clergy," he suggests that an emotional problem can be understood as the suffering of a soul that has not discovered its meaning (ibid., par. 497). Suffering may result from spiritual stagnation or psychic sterility. Then the therapeutic problem is to find the "meaning that quickens," something that will give meaning and form to our confusion when we have no hope, no love, no faith, and no understanding of our own existence. These qualities are gifts of grace that cannot be taught or learned. They cannot be given by any method; they can only be based on experience. Jung points out that ideally people who suffer spiritually would consult a clergyman, but many people in this situation refuse to do so because the tenets of Christianity have lost their authority for them. Admonitions to believe do not work. In the last resort, he found that what works is finding a religious outlook on life, although not "religious" in the sense of a belief in a particular creed.

The therapist has to bear the tension between the suffering and pain that he or she hears and an awareness of its spiritual possibilities. To mention these too soon is a potential therapeutic disaster, because to spiritualize the problem prematurely runs the risk that the person will feel the therapist has not really registered the severity of the pain or that the therapist is minimizing it by suggesting it's somehow "good for you." A spiritual attitude can be used defensively by either person to avoid suffering in the guise of "transcendence." One therefore must go through the usual thera-

peutic work with the person's difficulty as well as—and usually well
before—discussing its spiritual implications.

When we ask whether it is legitimate for the therapist to deal
with spiritual questions, we remember the historical link between
priest and healer. From antiquity until the rise of psychotherapy as
a separate discipline, advice about existential dilemmas was typically the province of priests.[10] But now the psychological approach
to these questions and the approach of the religious traditions are
based on entirely different assumptions about human nature. The
spiritual traditions tell us we are a spiritual being, while mainstream
psychology tells us we are a personal self. A spiritually oriented
approach to psychotherapy sees both of these as true at different
levels. Developmental psychology and our psychodynamics only
describe a part of our nature, because the ground of our being is
beyond all that. The therapist with a spiritual sensibility sits in the
room with a particular attitude of openness to this ground, seeing
it in operation in every area of the person's life, even if the therapist
does not articulate this attitude, which is usually the case. This
attitude informs our practice—it is a background assumption for
the therapist. If the therapy is conducted with a spiritual sensibility, faith in the ground acts as a container for the work, which has
a spiritual quality if the psychological problem is seen as a call
from the Self to increase consciousness. With this attitude, psychotherapy is a confessional activity—a contemporary version of
the ancient tradition of the cure of souls, part of the tradition of the
listening healer whose origin is lost in time (Jackson 1992). Parenthetically, it is worth noting Frankl's (1986) distinction between
the attempt of psychotherapy to *heal* the soul and that of religion
to *save* the soul. These are very different projects; therapeutic work
does not require adherence to a particular theology of salvation.

In his essay debating the respective roles of clergy and psychotherapists, Jung asks what would have happened if Saul had been
talked out of his trip to Damascus, as described in the book of
Acts.[11] Jung implies here that Saul had to take the road to Damascus because it was his destiny to do so. The question of destiny, or
the notion that the personality has a specific telos or goal, is a controversial one. If the idea is correct, it means that our suffering is
somehow necessary, and we should be careful to try to understand

its intention even as we try to alleviate it. In this view, the unfolding of the personality has a definite purpose, and life provides the experiences we need for our individuation process, even though these may be painful.

Classical Jungians such as Whitmont (2007) believe that painful events are manifestations of the individual's destiny and that suffering steers us in a particular direction that we would otherwise not have taken. Whitmont invokes the notion of *amor fati*, or the love of one's fate, playing one's assigned part, realizing that we do not control the outcome. For him, the cooperation of the ego is necessary for the realization of the individual's destiny, within the limits of the ego's capacity, and we must embrace what happens to us because it is part of our archetypal purpose. He uses the analogy of using the wind while sailing. The wind, like the pressure of the spirit, is impersonal; it moves the boat, but the sailor must align with it properly. Using this metaphor, one way the therapist can assist in the discovery of meaning is to ask where a particular situation is taking the person, how it is changing the course of his or her life. At times, the therapist must go along with what may be a "daring misadventure" (Jung 1932, par. 530), with no fixed idea of what is right for the person.

The notion that suffering is necessary to move the personality toward a particular goal is problematic for many reasons, not the least of which is the problem of free will versus determinism that it implies, not to mention the fact that one cannot necessarily accept the reality of terrible trauma. To see child abuse as "necessary" for the development of the personality in a particular direction raises difficult ethical—not to mention metaphysical—questions. The idea that the personality has a specific destiny or goal implies that not only are we pushed from the past by developmental factors, it is as if we are also pulled toward a future that has not yet happened but which exists as a potential, perhaps at some other level of reality. This would mean that ordinary cause-and-effect is not the only process at work in our lives. Whitmont points to the problem of temporality at the quantum level to justify this argument. While it is true that there is a debate among quantum physicists about the possibility of backward causation, and it is possible that at the non-local level events in the past, present, and future are correlated with each other, it is a conceptual mistake, as Hogenson (2007) points out, to assume that descriptions of such quantum phenomena can be applied to events at the macro level.[12] Nevertheless, depth psychology has not yet come to terms with Bell's theorem in quantum physics, which states that there are no local causes in the universe, so that the linear, cause-and-effect theorizing of traditional developmental psychology may need to be revised. Meanwhile, the notion that the individual has an essential destiny operates as a belief that some therapists hold, a kind of personal myth that helps the therapist deal with suffering by assuming that it must be the way it is. One's unique opportunity then lies in the way one bears the burden. It makes a difference if we look back at a difficult childhood with the sense that it had to be that way in order that the rest of one's life would evolve as it did.

The depth psychologist can sometimes discern connections between emotional difficulties and the individual's spiritual life, because early developmental experiences are formative not only of one's personality but also of one's spirituality. Capps (1997) has suggested a possible relationship between childhood experiences, psychopathology, and spirituality in the case of the chronic depression that afflicted William James, Carl Jung, Rudolph Otto, and Erik Erikson. Capps notes that in childhood each of these men experienced the loss of a close relationship to his mother, or at least the loss of her unconditional love and the loss of the sense that he was her beloved son. This led to melancholia, which provided an impetus that contributed to their turn to religion in the search for reassurance and comfort. For example, because of an early separation from his mother, Jung says that he always felt mistrustful when the word *love* was spoken, and women for a long time felt unreliable (1961, p. 8). Capps believes that such early loss, which predisposes a person to become melancholic, leads to a religious disposition, as if one spends the rest of one's life looking for the original lost object. The mother is a lost object in Freud's original (*Mourning and Melancholia*) sense, and the religious person searches for the lost object in the form of God. Capps suggests that the experience of being forsaken by God, what used to be called religious melancholia, originates in the feeling of separation from mother, especially when this happens in a cruel or unfeeling manner. Capps suggests that morality develops as a way of winning back one's mother by being good. Because of mother's abandonment, one feels a deep internal sense of badness, and hence much of the religious emphasis on sin. The problem with this argument is that many people experience such early loss without becoming religious, and some religious people had normal maternal relationships. One could also argue that the baby's connection with the divine exists prior to the connection to mother, because the Self is an original internal object. Mother then is a stand-in for the Self; the loss of the connection to mother reactivates the loss of connection to the Self, which is what we are really looking for.

Capps goes on to say that the numinous adult experience of the *mysterium tremendum* is actually due to the experience of being terrorized by mother as a child. For him, this explains the dread and trembling within religious experience, the feeling of being overpowered, the sense of the annihilation of the self, and the sense of unfamiliarity and astonishment produced by the numinosum. According to Capps, it is not surprising that we proclaim the love of God, given the fact that children often love the adult who also fills them with terror (1997, p. 110). In other words, the experience of the numinosum is the return of a repressed childhood complex; it is not *sui generis* but the result of childhood trauma. Capps denies that this is a reductive approach because he does not challenge claims for the existence of God. Nevertheless, his attempt to link the search for the divine with the search for the lost object of infancy ignores the fact that the experience of the sacred may be an entirely new object relationship, teleologically oriented and not necessarily predicated on early loss.

When looking at the connections between psychopathology and spirituality, Jung's approach to the structure of the complex is useful, because it depicts an archetypal or transpersonal core surrounded by a shell of developmental experiences, memories, and images. Since the archetypal level is, according to Jung, an "organ (or tool) of God" in the psyche, the implication is that a transpersonal element participates in our emotional lives (1973–1975, p. 130). One's psychopathology seems to channel one's spirituality into a particular direction, for example, when a serious mother problem correlates with an interest in the goddess or the feminine aspects of the divine. We cannot *reduce* our spirituality to psychopathology, but it is clear that our psychopathology colors our spirituality and contributes to its particular content. Just as we do not choose our complexes, so we do not choose our spirituality; they both arise from the unconscious, which has an objective aspect.

PERSONAL HISTORY AS A SACRED TEXT

Each theory of psychotherapy has its own ideas about the important influences on the development of a sense of self. In the Jungian tradition, the development of the personality, or individuation, is thought of as an incarnation—the gradual embodiment over a lifetime of a set of spiritual potentials given by the Self. Therefore the personality has a spiritual basis; its destiny is determined by the Self, which incarnates to form an empirical personality that has a particular trajectory. This means that the life story of the individual can be thought of as a sacred text. For the spiritually oriented psychotherapist, the individual's story is analogous to the stories told by the spiritual traditions in their sacred texts, which are said to give life meaning and to reveal the intentions of the divine for humanity.

Most psychotherapeutic schools of thought suggest that by scrutinizing our developmental history we can develop a coherent narrative about what otherwise seem to be meaningless symptoms. Yet the discovery of such a story (what Hillman referred to as a "healing fiction") is not sufficient to deal with lifelong problematic character traits.[13] More important is the development of tolerance for painful affective states such as fragmentation anxiety, narcissistic vulnerability, and so on. The self is strengthened and new psychological structures are built in the context of the therapeutic relationship. Only with this as a container does the discovery of meaning in one's life story become a valuable effect of psychotherapy. This meaning cannot be imposed; it has to be discovered. The therapist's theoretical orientation is just one way of explaining and ordering what happened to the person. Ideally, therapists would avoid formulating their explanations in terms of a particular ideological account of human psychology, but we cannot achieve such objectivity. Neither can we avoid influencing the material that emerges in psychotherapy, since it is well known that the therapist's nonverbal cues affect what the person talks about. To avoid becoming a source of doctrine, the therapist must be aware that a person may feel pressure to understand the meaning of his or her life story in a particular way, in order to stay connected to the therapist.

SPIRITUAL ADVICE AND CHARACTER STRUCTURE

Our religious traditions give a good deal of useful spiritual advice, but sometimes this advice is not usable because of the dynamics of the individual personality. The development of a spiritual practice that arises organically within the individual is then needed. For example, a nun was referred for psychotherapy because of her explosive temper, which made it hard for her to live in community. She had been advised to deal with her persistent anger by remembering Christ crucified as an example of loving forgiveness, whereupon she would try to suppress her anger, but to no avail. She could not use a spiritual approach to her anger because of her particular psychodynamics. Because her family had constantly humiliated and attacked her, she grew up full of shame and narcissistic rage. She was easily hurt and intensely vulnerable to any comment that seemed even remotely critical. To ask her to forgive those who offended her was to ask her to ignore an enormous reservoir of pain. Forgiveness was good spiritual advice in principle, but not usable because of her character structure.

This problem was reproduced during the therapy. After each angry interaction, the resulting disruption in the relationship would be discussed and understood until she and the therapist could forgive each other. Gradually her vulnerable sense of self strengthened and she became less sensitive to the perception of attack. Forgiveness arose organically as a development within her personality. No matter how enlightened the advice given by her spiritual advisors, forgiveness could not be imposed. She had to become conscious enough to reduce the emotional intensity of her complex, and this work was her spiritual practice.

This situation is an example of the way in which religious traditions do not take into account the person's unconscious or the autonomous nature of the individual's complexes, thus separating the person's psychology from her official spirituality. The teachings of such a tradition run the risk of being too difficult to implement, and so become either a source of guilt or emotionally irrelevant. By contrast, if our spirituality takes into account our emotional difficulties by acknowledging the archetypal core of the complex, we discover how the numinosum plays a part within our suffering. We may then speak of the transpersonal dimension playing a part within both normal and abnormal psychology.

HEALING PRACTICES AND THE SACRED: PSYCHOTHERAPY AS RITUAL PROCESS

There seems to be an archetypal pattern to healing that is reflected in the healing practices of pre-technological societies. This pattern is also at work as a deep structure nested within our systems of psychotherapy. Perhaps we can clarify some of its essential elements.

In many cultures, health is associated with order and disease with chaos or destruction. Living in a sacred cosmos, traditional tribal cultures maintain health by proper relation to the sacred, by observing taboos and ritual. This means attention to the world of spirits, demons, or the gods as defined by the mythology of the culture, just as any therapy must fit the patient's worldview (Ellenberger 1970). Traditional myths are sacred stories, a revelation of sacred reality. Thus, shamanic healing practices take place within a particular mythic orientation, a cosmology, a view of reality that is shared by the tribe; life is saturated with meaning when life is lived according to a myth. In shamanic healing rituals, the cosmogonic or creation myth, or the myth of the origins of disease and healing, is often chanted over the sick person. This places the patient in a mythic context, establishes meaning and order, and is thus comforting, giving the hope of transcendent help and expectancy that assists healing. Notice how similar is our own healing ritual; we believe in the myth of psychotherapy, especially in the particular tradition in which we have trained. We have our own ritual practices and techniques that we believe will restore order in the person's life, and we work within a shared cultural myth and belief system.[14] It is not clear to what extent the helpful effects of psychotherapy are based on specific therapeutic techniques, and how much the operative elements are the intention to help, the provision of a tangible intervention, and the sense that something is being done by an attentive, caring person (Shapiro 1978). Some shamanic traditions describe the shaman entering the spirit world to do battle with spiritual forces on behalf of the patient, to retrieve his lost soul, or to search for the curative element (Eliade 1951; Sandner and Wong 1997, pp. 63–69). When the therapist works to recover memories or integrate split-off aspects of the personality, we are practicing a form of soul retrieval. When the therapist struggles with a complex and its archetypal underpinning, we have one foot in the human realm and the other in the spiritual realm. In other words, the psychotherapeutic approach has its own sacred aspects, which in our age have become obscured by a morass of technical training, credentials, and regulations.

Claude Lévi-Strauss, the structural anthropologist, noted that as long as the myth recited by the shaman was believed by the patient and his society, it had some therapeutic value; it did not matter whether the myth corresponded to objective reality (1963, p. 167). He assumed that shamanic healing is effective because of the psychological relationship between the disease and what was thought to be the demon causing it. As well, the shaman gives the person language to express otherwise inexpressible states of mind. The person can then understand what would otherwise be a chaotic situation in an orderly way, and this induces a process of reorganization of the person's psychology. We do the same things in psychotherapy.

According to Eliade (1951), the shaman has various important qualities: the intensity of his or her experiences of spiritual ecstasy; the ability to enter these states at will; and skill at guiding the soul. The therapeutic process also involves guiding the soul, and the therapist, while not necessarily a practitioner of ecstatic states, may have had the experience of contact with transpersonal reality. The future shaman is called to his or her vocation whether he or she likes it or not, and tradition has it that it was mortally dangerous to ignore the call. The work of psychotherapy is also a vocation, and like the shaman the therapist has often suffered a prolonged illness that acts as a form of initiation into the work. For both therapist and shaman, the work of healing oneself becomes the core of the training to help others. That is why dreams of dismemberment or torture, usually followed by renewal of the body, occur to both shamans and psychotherapists, implying that an initial sacrifice is necessary before we are made whole (Jung 1954b, par. 448). Eliade suggests that the shaman's ability to heal is proportionate to the severity and duration of his or her initiatory illness (1951, p. 36). It is important to understand that this is an impersonal, archetypal process, which means that traditional views of suffering as punishment for sin can be replaced by the notion that suffering is necessary for the transformation and maturation of the personality.

In traditional cultures, the ritual elder knows how to locate, utilize, and maintain the sacred space in which healing occurs (Eliade 1958). If one sees psychotherapy as a spiritual practice, the therapy room becomes sacred space. For this reason, it feels like a violation, sacrilege even, to expose the soulful material that emerges during psychotherapy to third parties. This space must be protected, and it is a great pity that the profession has not taken a firmer stand on this issue. Gibson (2000) makes a good case for viewing pastoral psychotherapy as a confessional sacrament, but there is an element of this in all forms of therapy. Jung suggested that confession is the first stage of psychotherapy; its purpose is to relieve the person of the burden of painful material that has made him or her feel alienated from others (1931, par. 134). Whenever intense emotion is revealed, when private fantasies, long-held secrets, or painful memories are brought to light, we are engaged in the ancient practice of the "cure of souls." This means the discovery of personal meaning, connection to the transpersonal, and, with grace, a sense of the renewal of life. As Gibson points out in his discussion of this issue, such confession should function as an activity sanctioned by the community, but at present our licensing bodies and codes of ethics are "too thin and too frail to provide the kind of consumer and practitioner protection required by deep confessional practice" (2000, p. 179). The obvious example is the need to reveal personal information to third parties.

ARCHETYPAL ELEMENTS OF PSYCHOTHERAPY

The gripping power of archetypal forces is so intense that in antiquity they were personified as gods and goddesses. At times in psychotherapy, a particular archetypal process is constellated (activated) so strongly that the therapist feels a compulsive urge to behave in accord with a particular archetypal image. When the Great Mother is constellated, the therapist (whether a man or a woman) is possessed by a powerful need to be nurturing.[15] When the archetype of the Healer takes over, the therapist feels an urgent need to suggest healing practices. When such an archetypal process is constellated, both participants are gripped by an impersonal psychological force; one can no longer think of "the therapist's" material or "the patient's" material—we are in a common soup of emotion and tendency to action. The ancients would say that a god or goddess has visited the room and made a certain demand. Needless to say, in such a situation it is important not to act out unconsciously and not to identify with the archetypal demand as if the therapist *is* the Healer or the Great Mother, but to become conscious of and try to understand what is affecting the field in which we are working.

Apart from the specific demands made by any particular person, therapists tend to work in a way that is strongly influenced by the particular archetypal processes that are dominant in their soul, such as the archetypal Mother, Father, Sage, Healer, or Priest/Priestess. These forces radically affect the therapist's style of practice, and like all archetypal processes they are ambivalent, with light and dark aspects to them. For many therapists, the archetypal image of the Wounded Healer is particularly important.

THERAPIST AS WOUNDED HEALER

The vocation to become a therapist has various sources. It partly results from developmental factors, such as the childhood need to care for an emotionally wounded parent. If one believes that the individual has a particular destiny to live out, one's family of origin is not an accident; it corresponds to the archetypal disposition of the child's soul. Often, the therapist-to-be has to become a therapist because his or her childhood wounding initiates him or her into a career of helping others. When the Wounded Healer archetype is dominant in the soul, one's own suffering enables one to help others. Our wounds affect the way we work with others, and the way we work with others affects our own wounds. Without one's own wound, one's understanding of the suffering of others would be superficial.

It is useful to use myth as an analogy for these processes by contrasting two images of healing from Greek mythology: Chiron, the archetypal Wounded Healer, and Apollo, the god of healing. Chiron was the wisest of the centaurs, an immortal, half human and half horse; he combines in one symbol the divine, the human, and the instinctual or creaturely levels of the body. Although a great healer and teacher of medicine, he suffered from an incurable and chronically painful wound that made him lame. In other words, the healer also needs healing. A Chironic approach to healing makes the therapist profoundly sensitive to the suffering of the other and opens up the therapist's own vulnerability. One knows the person's suffering empathically, deeply within oneself rather than objectively or in terms of psychological testing. Because of our wound, we know we are limited. At this archetypal level the wound is a numinous power, part of our destiny, a wound "in which the healer forever participates" (Kerenyi 1959, p. 99). Adler (1951) suggests that the purpose of the therapist's wound is to make the therapist aware of his or her healing ability; otherwise, he or she might not discover it.

When a person seeks psychotherapy, an inner healer is activated which stimulates the person's intrinsic, self-healing ability. As Guggenbühl-Craig (1971) puts it, the patient has a physician within himself, just as there is a patient within the physician. The therapist's wound is activated by contact with the distressed person. Unless this is conscious, the therapist may project his or her own wound onto the person. The therapist is then trying to stay at a safe distance, hoping that he or she will not be affected by the problem. However, it commonly happens that the therapist is "infected" with the person's wound, for example, by means of projective identification or some form of unconscious-to-unconscious communication.[16] We then feel both the person's wound and the need to acknowledge our own material. Often, this is what it takes to be helpful. The therapist's own participation in the healing process then becomes paramount, sometimes to the extent that we cannot be sure whether we are dealing with ourselves or the other person. As Meier puts it, a third quantity, the archetypal image of the Wounded Healer, has then entered the picture, and this affects both people (1959, p. 30).

The therapist cannot predict the outcome of the therapy because healing is a transpersonal and ultimately mysterious process. The therapist has to be deeply involved in the work but not identified with the image of the Healer. A "cure" in the sense of symptom relief may or may not happen, but the spiritual importance of the work is that the person's suffering becomes meaningful rather than random torment. At times, the best we can do is mourn an unalterable fact, a childhood pain or trauma that caused a "basic fault" in one's sense of self, as Balint put it, which "has cast a shadow over one's whole life, and the unfortunate effects of which can never fully be made good. Though the fault may heal off, its scar may remain for ever" (1968, p. 183).

AN APPROACH TO THE SHADOW OF THE HELPER

The Chironic Wounded Healer is affected at a deep level of his or her being by the work she or he does, whereas the god Apollo, an archetypal image of technical medicine, was described as "mortally clean" (Balint 1968, p. 39). Apollo was a remote divinity who was not affected by his healing work, so Apollonic medicine is objective, rational, wears a white coat, thinks in terms of cause and effect rather than synchronicity and acausality, and radically splits the healer from the patient.[17] When this form of healing is used in psychotherapy, the psyche loses its mystery and becomes an object of empirical investigation, quantification, and brain research. The therapist's own wound is repressed and projected onto the patient, who becomes the only sick one. If one is overidentified with the Healer, one needs to cure to maintain one's self-esteem and one has to have somebody in the sick role to work with; one is then using the other to meet a need of one's own. This split means that the therapist must maintain a distance from the patient and an illusion of invulnerability, which leads to a power position that reduces the capacity for empathy (Guggenbühl-Craig 1970; 1971). We then also ignore what Searles (1979) demonstrated: that the patient suffers on behalf of the therapist to try to heal the therapist.

An Apollonic stance is understandable; suffering is frightening. Very often, we find it difficult to help others because consciously or unconsciously we identify with the suffering person. We imagine empathically what he or she feels, and we project what we think the person needs based on what we would need in that situation. What the person actually feels may be quite surprising. Because of our fear, we may not allow ourselves to be fully present to the person. We are afraid when we do not know what to do, and we hate to feel incompetent. The suffering of the individual before us may feel like it is too much to let in, sometimes because we have difficulty setting limits or because unbearable suffering may lead to a compulsive need to help, demanding too much personal sacrifice. Or we feel that the sheer amount of human suffering is so overwhelming that we despair of making any difference. An important place for supervision occurs when the therapist becomes so immersed in the other's suffering that the therapist cannot get out of it because it stirs up personal difficulties. We may find it difficult to establish a balance between giving to others and taking care of ourselves, so that burnout is a constant danger for many in the helping professions. These situations are made more difficult if we identify with our professional persona, relying on theory or technique rather than using them as a way of accurately focusing our humanity.

When the therapist has experienced suffering of similar quality or intensity to that which the patient is experiencing, a mutual recognition occurs that is deeper than words. Both people realize that this recognition has happened, and in a mysterious way this is helpful even when nothing more can be done. One's own suffering makes one more receptive to the suffering of others, and at this level of our common suffering the technical aspects of psychotherapy are far less important than the ability to be present in the right way. Instead of a particular technique, one needs a mind that is quiet, receptive, attentive, and alert, not loaded with concepts. Within that mind, without evaluation or the desire for change, new insights or intuitions may arise. It is then as if the heart and gut have their own eyes and ears to which we must pay attention.

When we are able to help, we have to strike a balance between reasonable satisfaction at a job well done and a subtle inflation at the expense of the person we are helping, in which case helping others is a way of bolstering the therapist's sense of self or feeling important and needed. We may become overidentified with the Healer archetype, as if healing were an ego function. It is important to remember that whatever psychotherapeutic skill we have allows us to implement a transpersonal healing potential that is autonomous. It is not up to the therapist to decide whether or when healing will occur or the form it will take. If we are identified with the ego, so that we think that what happens in the therapy is purely a matter of our own ability or the correct technique, we are more easily overwhelmed and more afraid of suffering. It is then as if only the two of us are in the room; we are unaware of the presence of the Self.

The human capacity for empathy suggests that we have evolved to share our suffering. While one can think of empathy in terms of limbic system resonance and the countertransference, these approaches do not take into account the spiritual importance of affective attunement.[18] Shared affective states are important because they remind us that we are not separate entities—we participate in the same field of consciousness. If one is aware that there is a transpersonal ground within which we are working, one can trust that an objective process is arising that is somehow necessary for the soul. To assist with a painful affective state then becomes a spiritual practice and an act of faith in the ground. As long as the therapist can tolerate the painful affect, there is no need to resist it—to do so usually makes things worse. Instead, one can allow oneself to suffer with the person by connecting with the emotion that has been induced in one's body and focusing on it, as if the body were a sounding board. When projective identification occurs, the traditional advice is to pass the experience through one's own psychological structures and say something that will help the person "metabolize" and assimilate the emotion. This is not always done verbally; without saying anything, one can open the heart and allow the emotion to move as it will in the body. Usually, having

risen to a crescendo, the distress gradually dissipates. The technical
aspects of this process are of background importance only while
the experience is going on. The therapist can later reflect on the
contribution of his or her personal psychology and the countertransference implications of the experience, but to do so during the
experience itself tends to interfere with the process. In the presence of profound suffering, trying to think of technical ways to be
helpful, for example, by making an interpretation in the traditional
sense, is like trying to kick a ball while simultaneously thinking
about the physics of motion.

An awareness of the presence of the Self helps the therapist
to let go of his or her personal agenda, for example, the need to
feel helpful or to be a "healer." This presence means there is an
unseen background to even the bleakest situation that may provide
unexpected help, illumination, or inspiration, so that we may find
ourselves saying or doing something that seems to come from no-
where. In desperate situations, while we do what we can to help,
what eventually happens is directed by the Self, not by the ego.
Unless the therapist has consciously experienced the Self it may be
impossible to trust that it exists. But once one knows it exists, one
can relax to some extent in the realization that the ultimate outcome of psychotherapy is not in our hands but is part of the destiny
of the individual. To state this is potentially dangerous, because it
could lead to a facile rationalization for not making enough effort
to help or to the superficial dismissal of suffering as "karmic" or
unimportant in the larger view of things. But even when we are
powerless to help, it is always important to be a witness or a companion with an open heart.

Sometimes, just to be fully present and open to the other's pain
is enough, although one's inability to change the situation challenges the therapist's need to be effective and activates his or her
inner critic. But helping is then the therapist's agenda, and having
an agenda makes a demand on the other person and makes the
atmosphere tense, when what is needed is surrender or spontaneity.
If the therapist's ego thinks it has to do all the heavy lifting, burnout is a likely consequence. However, healing is not something we
do, it is something that happens. I cannot put this more eloquently
than Virginia Satir: "The whole therapeutic process must be aimed

at opening up the healing potential within the patient or client. Nothing really changes until that healing potential is opened. The way is through the meeting of the deepest self of the therapist with the deepest self of the person, patient or client" (1987, p. 19). We cannot answer the question of "how" this is to be done, because it is not an ego function. It may or may not happen; at best, we can set the stage by being as conscious, as technically competent, and as open as possible. Perhaps, if the wounded healer paradigm is correct, the key to allowing this process to occur is for the therapist to be constantly aware of his or her personal vulnerability, because at that level the therapist's ego is at its most tenuous, which may be a precondition for true contact between people. Otherwise, the therapist's ego becomes a castle, and we observe the other through a window in the wall.

One way to say this is to suggest that the work of therapy is to liberate the soul's capacity to heal. We sense that this is happening when we feel something powerful but incomprehensible going on in the therapy room. Something happens through the work that has a life of its own; when the Self speaks through us, the result is unexpected. The ancients would have said that a god is visiting. It is an everyday experience to see people benefit from therapy even though the therapist has no clear idea of what is helpful. Some aspects of psychological change are so subtle, or so unconscious, that we cannot detect them as they are happening; we only know them by their effects.

SACRIFICE

Sacrifice of the therapist's need to understand what is happening and sacrifice of any need to use the work for self-enhancement are important aspects of the therapist's spiritual practice. It requires self-sacrifice to stay in a therapeutic relationship that has become painful for both parties because of a negative transference. There is a degree of self-sacrifice involved in staying in the therapy room, hour after hour, while being hated, feeling rage directed at oneself, without retaliating or collapsing, accepting that this is necessary. The other side of the coin is also true; when the therapeutic relationship is pleasant, with mutual affection, for the sake of the therapy the therapist has to sacrifice what he or she realizes could have been an enjoyable social or sexual or professional relationship. These sacrifices are made, day after day, because we realize that there is some deeper meaning, some other level of reality expressing itself, and this is more important than our own needs. We cannot express exactly what this reality is because we sense it at a level of soul-to-soul connection, for which words are an inadequate medium, but we feel its presence and we surrender to it.

William James makes clear the connection between surrender and sacrifice, noting that within the religious life "that personal attitude which the individual finds himself impelled to take up towards what he apprehends to be divine . . . will prove to be both a helpless and sacrificial attitude" (1958, p. 54). According to Jung, when we truly sacrifice something that we value greatly, the object must be given away as completely as if it had been destroyed (1954b, par. 390). This is important because it is possible to give to others in a way that looks like a sacrifice but is actually a manipulation, a way of inducing indebtedness in another person. We are then not really giving but getting something for ourselves. By contrast, true sacrifice is an act of love and an expression of our values. Jung suggests that when we give up an emotionally important object, to some extent the sacrifice becomes a sacrifice of oneself (ibid., pars. 397–398). He uses the example of God's demand that Abraham sacrifice his son Isaac (Gen. 22:1–14). We can imagine that a father in the position of having to kill his son would feel as if he were killing a part of himself; he would then be at the same time both the one who sacrifices and the sacrificed. Analogously, when the Self calls me to sacrifice myself, the Self, which is my deepest essence, is also sacrificing itself. Jung believes that the Self wants the ego to allow this process to happen, which, as Edinger points out, requires the ego's conscious sacrifice of itself (1986, p. 35). If the ego accepts this need for sacrifice it may prevent the unconscious from manifesting itself destructively.

To sacrifice to a god with a particular purpose in mind, such as self-enhancement or gain, implies a particular God-image and a corresponding theology. Human and animal sacrifice occurred throughout the ancient world, and there are many ways to understand its origin. In some traditions, the divine is thought to need gifts, or reciprocity is expected so that we have to give to the god in order to receive. Sometimes sacrifice is a form of communication with the divine. Sacrifice can be a form of placation which allows expiation for sin, or it reenacts a mythic event. The God of the Hebrew Bible was imagined to need the blood of animals, while God sacrificed himself and his only son in Jesus. For Christians, the sacrifice of Jesus is a sin-offering that offers atonement and redemption. This archetypal and mythic background helps the therapist understand religious believers who are distressed because their lifelong good behavior, which involved considerable self-sacrifice, was intended to prevent suffering but did not do so. Their disappointment is often the result of a reward-punishment psychology, an anthropomorphic projection in which the divine is imagined to be a record keeper who tracks our merits and failings and gives or takes away in kind.

Like all spiritual practice, sacrifice can be used defensively. There are occasions on which the personal self must be sacrificed for a higher purpose—even, as some traditions would have it, for the maintenance of cosmic order. How then can the therapist discern whether what looks like a courageous sacrifice is the result of devotion or is a masochistic exercise in disguise? If the person is staying in an unhappy marriage and tells the therapist that he or she is "making a sacrifice for the children," how do we know whether this is a rationalization of dependency and a fear of change? Even more difficult: what would the therapist say to a modern-day Abraham who declares that God tells him to sacrifice his son? Kierkegaard (1843) saw Abraham's action as an example of absolute faith, so that Abraham could take the leap of totally trusting the goodness of God. But we are now suspicious of people who say that God tells them to do things, since this can rationalize all kinds of mayhem from personal vendettas to all-out holy war. History shows us how, in following what they believe to be God's will, true believers are able to split off empathy for their victims and commit terrible acts with a clear conscience. The problem for the spiritually oriented therapist is therefore one of discernment; how do we know what comes from the Self and what comes from social conditioning, from a narcissistic need or a pathological complex?

It is easy to solemnly intone "thy will be done," but who knows the nature of that will?

It is worth remembering that, when working therapeutically with people who are steeped in the biblical tradition, Bible stories have important if unconscious psychological influences. The story of the binding of Isaac is part of the mythic background that influences the Western tradition. Chilton (2008) has clearly documented the ways in which this story has been used to rationalize martyrdom and other forms of religious violence in Judaism, Christianity, and Islam, even though Abraham descended from Mt. Moriah without having killed Isaac. The background to the story of Abraham is that in spite of being promised descendants "as many as the stars in the sky," Abraham remains childless during an age when progeny were particularly important. Isaac is born late in Abraham's life, making Isaac particularly precious, so the command to sacrifice him is unbelievably terrible. Accordingly, Abraham is usually represented as an archetypal image of total obedience to God. The Bible says that Abraham is being tested by God (Gen. 22:1), and the story is traditionally understood to represent the Hebrews' repudiation of the pagan practice of child sacrifice. As Edinger pointed out, the story also represents the development of a more humane God-image, since Isaac is saved at the last moment (1984, pp. 97f). All myths have multiple levels of meaning, and today we can add a depth psychological hermeneutic to the traditional understanding. If the therapist were to view a contemporary Abraham with a psychodynamic eye, he or she would wonder how the impulse to kill Isaac arose in Abraham, and how he really felt about Isaac. We would also be concerned with what it would be like for Isaac to grow up in the knowledge that his father came very close to killing him. Nothing is said in the Bible about the effect that this traumatic episode had on Isaac, although various commentators see him as consciously offering himself as a willing sacrifice (see, for example, Kugel 1998, p. 322ff.). Perhaps the knowledge that his father had murderous intentions toward him explains why he follows closely in his father's footsteps and remains a virtuous but rather powerless character during his life.

NOTES

1. In traditional Christianity, the *cura animarum*, the cure or care of the soul, referred to the exercise of the priest's office. The notion that psychotherapists are continuing this ancient practice is not an original idea; in 1978, Thomas Szasz pointed out that psychotherapy is a modern version of this tradition. One can agree with this point without subscribing to his overall iconoclasm.

2. Hillman has summarized his writing on soul in Gibson, Lathrop and Stern (1986, pp. 29–35).

3. The context of this phrase is a letter Keats wrote in 1819: "The common cognomen of this world among the misguided and superstitious is 'a vale of tears' from which we are to be redeemed by a certain arbitrary interposition of God and taken to Heaven—What a little circumscribed straightened notion! Call the world if you Please 'The vale of Soul-making.'" As an alternative to traditional Christian thinking, Keats suggests that we come into the world as pure potentiality, containing sparks of the divine which he calls "Intelligence." What he means by soul is individuality, which he calls a "sense of Identity," that is acquired through suffering, which he calls "Circumstances" (Keats 1958).

4. In Jungian psychology, complexes are emotionally toned. The core of the complex is an archetypal process, and the archetype is a spiritual principle. Consequently, emotion produced by a complex can be thought of as the experience of the embodiment of spirit.

5. See also Rubin (1996), especially chapter 6, "Meditation and Psychoanalytic Listening." In this context, the spiritually oriented therapist might consider the idea found in yoga philosophy that attention does not arise within the ordinary mind or the ego; attention happens through the mind, which is an instrument; it is Purusha, the Self, or pure spirit that attends.

6. For a fuller discussion, see Corbett (2007).

7. For discussions of the ethical issues involved, see Tan (2003) and Richards and Bergin (2005).

8. The issue of the explicit integration of spiritual practice such as prayer into therapy is discussed by Tan, (in Shafranske 1996, p. 365); see also Benner (1988).

9. For a discussion of these issues, see Richards and Bergin (2005, pp. 229–257).

10. The book of Leviticus contains laws that are both priestly and healing; in ancient Greece, the priests of the temple of Aesclepius combined both functions; and the apostles both healed and preached.

11. Saul was on his way to persecute Jesus' followers. He was blinded by a bright light and heard Jesus' voice asking, "Why do you persecute me?" As

a result of this experience, Saul became an apostle, and his ministry radically affected the course of Western civilization.

12. Backward causation is one way to understand an experiment known as the delayed-choice experiment, described by Wheeler (1983).

13. In *Healing Fiction* (1991), Hillman suggests that to heal the person we must heal the story in which the person finds himself. However, the sense of self is more than a story—it is an embodied set of experiences consisting of innumerable affectively toned relational transactions which are largely unconscious.

14. Various authors have described the similarities between psychotherapy and ritual practice; see, for example, Moore (2001) and Usandivaras (1985).

15. For example, Winnicott's (1971a) emphasis on the good-enough mother, or psychotherapy as two people playing together, or the idea that the therapy provides a facilitating and nourishing environment for the patient, suggests to me that he worked out of the Mother archetype.

16. Jung suggests that "psychic infections" are the "predestined concomitants" of this work, part of the instinctive disposition of the therapist's life (1946, par. 365).

17. Michael Kearney (2000) has drawn an important distinction between Apollonic and Asculapian healing; Chiron was the teacher of Asclepius, and presumably in the same tradition.

18. For a discussion of limbic resonance, see Lewis, Amini and Lannon (2000).

CHAPTER 6

Psychodynamics and Spirituality

In this chapter I would like to illustrate some of the relationships between developmental factors, psychodynamics, and the individual's spirituality. For this purpose I will look at the lives of two important philosophers with opposite attitudes to religion: Søren Kierkegaard, a religious existentialist, and the atheist mathematician Bertrand Russell. I should add two preliminary caveats here. One is that we are dealing with the analysis of texts rather than the men themselves, and this has obvious limitations. Then, some philosophers dislike the attempt to relate a particular thinker's philosophy to psychodynamic factors because they believe that logic and conceptual thought are independent of the way a particular mind works.[1] Yet, although our approach to major philosophical problems may be partly independent of our psychology, it seems inconceivable that psychodynamic factors would not play some part in influencing a writer's interests and conclusions.

FAITH AND DESPAIR IN THE LIFE OF SØREN KIERKEGAARD

The problem of despair is paramount in Kierkegaard's life. Erikson's (1964) notion of the importance of basic trust is particularly relevant to this problem, which is a common theme among existentialists. According to Erikson, reliable care in the first eighteen

189

months of life provided by loving, trustworthy caretakers contributes to the development of basic trust, a hopeful sense that most situations in life will work out well. The infant then develops a healthy balance between trust and reasonable levels of mistrust, while a lack of basic trust in early life leads to the belief that life is not safe. There are degrees of success in this developmental stage, which affects the extent of one's confidence that life will provide what is necessary. Without this trust, one is prone to despair, a state of mind that tends to arise during periods of loss or stress, when hope is difficult to maintain. While despair is obviously a psychological crisis, it also leads to a crisis of faith and raises profound spiritual questions.

Kierkegaard believed that to exist as a self-conscious, reflective being is inevitably to despair as we feel our impermanence and insignificance. We must then either try to live in despair or take the leap into faith, since there are no rational reasons for religious belief. Even though he had a powerful thinking function, he knew this had to be sacrificed, so he spoke of the "crucifixion of the understanding" as a way to come to faith. Kierkegaard would try to use his intellect to ward off his unruly feelings, but without much success (Dru 1959, p. 128). From his journals, Kierkegaard sounds like a depressive character, a man who found life difficult. He notes that: "Since my earliest childhood a barb of sorrow has lodged in my heart . . . if it is pulled out I shall die" (Rhode 1990, p. 23). He is silent about his mother, but he describes his dominating father as melancholic, severe, brooding, and oppressively religious. His father's preoccupation with guilt and a dismal form of Christianity exerted a powerful influence on Kierkegaard. His father made him "as unhappy as possible in every way, made my youth a torment without peer" (ibid., p. 29). Kierkegaard described a "thorn in the flesh" which prevented his relating to life and subjected him to the consciousness of sin and guilt. In his journals, he writes that he was always "nailed fast to some suffering or other, bordering on madness" (Hong and Hong 1976, p. 105).

From the point of view of psychoanalytic self psychology, it seems that Kierkegaard's chronic melancholia was related to the constantly unhappy, devitalizing responses of his childhood self-objects. He identified with and internalized his depressed father,

PSYCHODYNAMICS AND SPIRITUALITY

whom he loved deeply, perhaps as a way of connecting with him. Kierkegaard's uncertainty about life wounded him severely; he tortured himself, just as he was emotionally tortured by his self-objects. He turned to the divine to provide an unfailing selfobject, or as a reliable attachment figure, presumably because his human selfobjects proved to be painfully unreliable. Why or how he made this turn remains a mystery, but without this turn his sense of disillusionment and despair at the world would have been over-whelming. Kierkegaard therefore dealt philosophically and spiritually with his sense that life could be futile or meaningless. In this way, he was able to affirm the value of life rather than surrender to despair. Whether we regard his turn to faith as defensive or as the result of a call from the divine itself is very much a matter of opinion.

Kierkegaard decided that the leap into faith also required a decision to renounce the world and break off all attachments, especially those most cherished. For him, only the isolated individual was the source of authentic choice. I suspect this somewhat schizoid attitude resulted from the sense that dependence on others was dangerous because it was potentially too hurtful. He also rejected the established Church, which he regarded as neither honest nor truly Christian. In order to feel safe, he had to turn to the inner world, which allowed him to focus on his subjective experience of the divine—the safety of an internal object that is absolutely trustworthy. For Kierkegaard, subjective truth is more important than objective truth. In his words: "the thing is to find a truth which is true for me, to find the idea for which I can live and die" (Dru 1959, p. 15).

If a modern-day Kierkegaard were to come for therapy, the therapist might see his spirituality and his personality dynamics as inextricably connected. As Guntripp (1969) pointed out, the schizoid problem involves a flight from life. Kierkegaard's attitude seems to have been "I don't need anyone, only God." The problem of developing a secure, trustworthy connection to the therapist would therefore be paramount, but to allow dependency on a human being would be difficult if not terrifying for this person. To do so would be both a psychological and a spiritual task, since a spirituality that does not include human relationships is only partial.

BERTRAND RUSSELL'S SPIRITUALITY

Can psychodynamic factors contribute to the development of atheism? Bertrand Russell believed that the existence of God, although not impossible, was so improbable that it was not worth considering in practice. Russell (1927) systematically examined and rejected all the standard arguments for the existence of God in the Christian sense. He concluded that people believe in religion because of a fear of death and of the mysterious. In spite of that, one can hardly say Russell had no spirituality; in the beginning of his autobiography, published at the age of 87, he spoke of the overwhelming passions that governed his life as "the longing for love, the search for knowledge, and unbearable pity for the suffering of mankind" (1971, vol. 1, p. 13). He wrote that his search was intended to bring ecstasy, relieve loneliness, and to prefigure the vision that saints and poets have had of heaven. He wanted to reveal the hearts of men, explain the light of the stars, and apprehend how number (mathematics) "holds sway above the flux" (ibid.). Here we see his superior thinking function trying to deal with his tumultuous emotional life. In an extraordinary grasp of the unity of humanity, pity arose in him because "echoes of pain reverberate in my being, children in famine, victims tortured . . . I long to alleviate the evil, but I cannot, and I too suffer" (ibid.). He believed in kindness as well as clear thinking and wanted to "do whatever might be possible towards creating a happier world" (1971, vol. 3, p. 220). He had "semi-mystical feelings about beauty . . . and with a desire almost as profound as that of Buddha to find some philosophy which should make human life endurable" (1971, vol. 1, p. 146). From a man who refused to accept the Christian God-image, these are deeply spiritual sentiments, which he lived to the full as a social critic and an activist in the nuclear disarmament movement.

Various developmental factors contributed to his social activism and his rejection of a benevolent God-image. Russell lost his mother at age two and his father eighteen months later. He did not remember his parents but discovered that they had been radical freethinkers and ardent social reformers, which was also true of Russell himself. Apparently he identified with what he was told about his parents. He was raised by his grandparents and also identified strongly with their values. His grandfather, who died when Russell was six, believed in human progress and an end to war. Russell's grandmother, his most important caretaker, was public-spirited and indifferent to social opinions, although in spite of her affection for her grandson she was a difficult person—austere, caustic, and Puritanical, with a humor that was "full of animus" (Russell 1971, vol. 1, p. 20). He recalls that she made him unusually prone to a sense of sin, so that "many of my most vivid early memories are of humiliation" (ibid., p. 26). He was a solitary child, spending many hours in the garden of his grandparents' house:

> the most vivid part of my existence was solitary ....Throughout my childhood I had an increasing sense of loneliness, and of despair of meeting anyone with whom I could talk. Nature and books and (later) mathematics saved me from complete despondency. (ibid., p. 30)

Particularly in adolescence, the pain of solitude plagued him, and he could not assuage his emotional emptiness and pining. Russell was a profoundly depressed individual, presumably due to his early losses compounded by an unresponsive selfobject milieu. He often contemplated suicide and was saved only by his passion for mathematics. He was also fearful and subject to violent nightmares in which he was being murdered, "usually by a lunatic" (ibid., p. 85). Presumably these dreams reflect the pathogenic quality of his early relationships. One can only speculate to what extent this harsh childhood environment contributed to his lifelong preoccupation with social justice. It was as if he projected his internal sorrow onto the world and worked to alleviate it there—an example of how one's psychological structures can radically influence one's philosophy of life. Russell's grief for himself was not different than his grief for the world—in this he exhibited a powerful spiritual sense that the individual is not separate from the world. Yet his spirituality was not one of passively accepting suffering; rather, he turned his personal tragedy into the task of helping others. Just as we do not know the origin of Kierkegaard's turn to the divine, we do not know the origin of Russell's turn toward social activism—that is an irreducible mystery, part of the inscrutable destiny of the individual, but it is a deeply spiritual affirmation of the value of life.

Mathematics and logic were emotionally as well as intellectually important for Russell. Mathematics was an antidote to self-doubt and death. He wrote that the purpose of mathematics was to overcome his "terrible sense of impotence, of weakness, of exile amidst hostile powers" (1959, p. 211). He even hoped that mathematics would help to solve various human problems as it was applied to other sciences. I think he sensed, perhaps unconsciously, that what he had lost in childhood was irretrievable and could never be regained; he therefore had to find an alternative to strengthen himself. In the absence of adequate human relationships, he used mathematics, logic, and his superb thinking to soothe and comfort himself, maintain his self-esteem, and give his life meaning. Logic was a way of dealing with his chaotic feelings, a way of arriving at certainty in an uncertain world. Since personal relationships had failed him at such a vulnerable age, Russell searched for an impersonal truth that would anchor him, with no risk that he would be betrayed by loss or abandonment – hence his impersonal spirituality. For example, he believed that the best way to overcome the fear of death was "to make your interests gradually wider and more impersonal, until bit by bit the walls of the ego recede and your life becomes increasingly merged in the universal life" (Russell 1956, p. 52). Again, these are deeply spiritual sentiments.

Russell rejects the Christian God-image in part because it is too relational and too personal, perhaps too evocative of his inferior feeling function. In a profoundly disturbing passage of his autobiography, he says "I am conscious that human affection is to me at bottom an attempt to escape from the vain search for God" (1971, vol. 2, p. 38). This means that, for him, both human affection and the search for God were futile—presumably because it did not feel safe to depend on anyone. Given the unreliability of his early caretakers, he could hardly be expected to trust any kind of relationship, whether with a human being or with a personal God. Indeed, Russell's love affairs and marriages did not last long; for most of his life he could not find the love he needed to sustain him fully, although his fourth marriage at the age of eighty was happy, suggesting that his relational capacity had finally matured.

He could not turn to a personal God because he could not afford to believe in something for which he had no model of relationship, no personal experience, and no logical proof. Instead, he turned to the abstract safety of mathematics and philosophy.

Russell's long-standing aim was to discover whether, and to what extent, knowledge is possible. "There is one great question," he wrote to Lady Ottoline Morell in 1911: "Can human beings know anything, and if so, what and how? This question is really the most essentially philosophical of all questions" (quoted in Slater 1994, p. 67). Here one is reminded of Arieti's suggestion that some chronically depressed people are haunted by the life-long pursuit of a dominant goal that is omnipresent, determining the individual's actions. This transcendent purpose, which may be grandiose, may itself become a source of depression when the individual realizes it is unattainable. Arieti believed that this goal represents a search for love; unconsciously, the person feels that he will become worthy of love only if he succeeds in achieving the goal. "Often at a conscious level too, the search for the dominant goal coincides with the search for perfect love" (Arieti and Bemporad 1980, p. 141).

If an individual with Russell's dynamics were in psychotherapy, I doubt that the form of his spirituality would change, even if the intensity of his depressive dynamics could be alleviated. In principle, his painful internal emptiness could be improved by a therapeutic relationship that develops internal structure. However, his temperament—he was probably a thinking intuitive type—would dictate that he follow a path of *jnana yoga*, an approach to the divine through knowledge, skepticism, and inquiry.[2] Such individuals tend to have an impersonal God-image. It is unrealistic to imagine that someone with Russell's developmental history and temperament would be drawn to the Christian God-image. Apart from relieving his emotional suffering, psychotherapy might become spiritual direction as he discovered that his search for truth was a form of spiritual practice. The therapist could help Russell see that his spirituality was in accord with his nature. The therapist would validate his spirituality as it was expressed in his thought and his social activism, which were as surely an expression of love as any devotional practice. To my mind, Russell was a

deeply spiritual man who was so passionately concerned about the
fate of humanity in the face of the threat of nuclear war and social
injustice that he was willing to be imprisoned twice for expressing these beliefs, the second time at the age of eighty-nine. Such
behavior demonstrates that there is no (Cartesian) gap between
the soul and the world, between one's vocation and its realization
in action.

In view of his intense but individualized spiritual life, it is tragic
and ironic that because of the misunderstanding or frank bigotry
of some traditional believers Russell was often condemned for being "irreligious." For example, in the late 1930s, an offer to Russell
of a teaching appointment at New York's City College was revoked
following a large number of public protests. A 1940 judicial decision found him "morally unfit" to teach at the College. According
to the judgment, not only was he a pacifist, he was considered to be
an enemy of religion and morality. His opinions about the repres-
sive nature of contemporary sexuality (he believed in sexuality outside of marriage and the value of masturbation) were considered
to be too libertarian.[3] Such prejudice has often been the fate of
individuals with a unique spirituality that did not conform to traditional expectations. Sometimes the larger society could not accept that that these individuals' spirituality was different but valid,
and sometimes they were the victims of true believers who could
not tolerate any questioning of their beliefs. In such a situation, the
validating responses of an attuned therapist would affirm the person's experience of his or her personal spiritual vision. Whether one
calls this psychotherapy or spiritual direction is merely a semantic
difference. In either case, psychotherapy would only be useful if the
therapist lays aside all personal spiritual preferences. The therapist
is at most a catalyst for a natural process. One senses this is happening when the person discovers a spirituality that expresses his
or her capacity for love and relationship, which may take many
forms. In Russell, love was expressed as a passionate sense of social
justice and a delight in analytical philosophy. The therapist who
has found this love in himself or herself expresses it by helping the
person find and express love in that person's own way, not necessarily in accordance with any preexisting creed.

THE SPIRITUAL IMPORTANCE OF MIRRORING

The importance of mirroring the child's affective state is now well recognized. However, the spiritual importance of this need is less well acknowledged. To mirror a child means to respond to the child in a way that is attuned to his or her emotional life and to respond to his or her sense of value and self-worth. Ideally, the child feels delight in his or her aliveness and contact with the world, pleasure in the experience of the body, and a sense of pride in achievement. These life-affirming emotions must be responded to appropriately for the child to be able to claim them as legitimate. To own these feelings, Kohut believes that the child needs to be the "gleam in mother's eye," to feel significant in the eyes of others, and to be seen for who he or she really is. For Kohut (1984), this need arises from the grandiose self of the child. From an archetypal or spiritual perspective, the source of the child's grandiose self—his or her sense of value and importance—is the Self, the divine child, the child of God within the psyche. That level is an internal, numinous presence. When the child's mirror needs are not met, the result is an emotionally deprived individual with a lifelong urgency to find a responsive selfobject. When the divine child was not seen in childhood, the individual was deprived of connection with the Self as an internal presence; the divine is somewhere else. From a human point of view, the mirror-hungry personality needs a continuous source of external support for his or her self-esteem, which is fragile. From a spiritual point of view, when we mirror such a person we are actually recognizing the Self, the divine essence within the personality.

Needless to say, for many people, the divine is thought of as an unfailing, mirroring selfobject—a Being who is aware of one's existence. As the psalmist says, "the Lord hears when I call to him" (Psalm 4:3). The spiritual dimension of the therapist's task is to witness the divinity in the individual with whom he or she works as well as the human level. Mirroring is usually understood to involve only the personal levels of the mind, but the spiritually oriented therapist can at the same time maintain an awareness that the Self is also being mirrored when the individual's inner life is taken seriously and treated respectfully. Here lies a deep level of the importance of empathy. I suspect that one variety of atheism arises from early failure of this process, leading to the bitter feeling that there is no one who really cares.

Religious institutions take advantage of the human need to be mirrored in a variety of ways. They reassure their adherents that they are seen and valued by God and that they will be rewarded for good behavior, at the same time as the institution defines the nature of good behavior. The need to be mirrored therefore provides an impetus for compliance with the rules of the institution. Some of the people who regularly attend churches and synagogues are not simply motivated by the urge to worship; they need the affirming responses of the rest of the congregation and the twinship experience of being like others. Confession and repentance not only allow some alleviation of guilt, but also a sense of acceptance by the divine; these processes are said to affirm the individual's basic worth in the eyes of God. If one cannot value and accept oneself, it is a relief to feel that good behavior makes one acceptable to God. It is a relief to believers burdened by guilt to hear that "he who hears my word . . . does not come into judgment" (John 5:24). The problem is that to read this in a text may not have the power of the experience of being valued and accepted by a human being.

A further important function of the therapist is to mirror the individual's true vocation. A well-known component of the midlife period is sadness as a result of lifelong dedication to a useful career rather than the discovery of a vocation. At first this sounds like a purely secular problem. But although they may overlap, a calling is not the same as a career. One may train for a career without much passion. A true vocation can be seen as part of the destiny of the individual. Jung suggests that the personality "always has a vocation, which acts like the law of God from which there is no escape" (Jung 1934, par. 300). This inner voice is often muffled and hard to hear because of layers of social and family insistence on following a conventional path in life. Living out this vocation is based on faith that arises from the subjective perception of a truth that one knows one has to follow—what Jung called the "law of one's own being" (ibid., par. 295). This can be thought of as part of a spiritual blueprint for the development of the personality, and not merely a result of the chance interaction of genes and the environment. In Jung's words: "Personality is Tao," that is, there is an "undiscovered vein within us" that is like "a flow of water that moves irresistibly to its goal" (ibid., par. 323).

It is an important spiritual task to assist in the discovery of this level of the soul. Of course, the therapist has to be conscious of the possibility of inflation; vocation is found in characters like Hitler as well as like Gandhi, and it is a common feature of paranoid delusional states. However, it is possible to distinguish between a narcissistic need to be dominant and an authentic following of the prompting of the Self. The former is a defense, an attempt at restitution of an enfeebled sense of self driven by feelings of vulnerability and shame and does not take into account social responsibilities and the needs of others. A true vocation feels like an internal lodestar, a devotional task that acts as an internal source of creativity and passion. It does not lead to messianic feelings of special election and privilege.

THE SPIRITUAL DIMENSIONS OF IDEALIZATION

According to Kohut, the need to idealize arises because the child needs an adult who seems to be strong and wise, able to sooth the child when he or she is distressed. A psychological merger with this adult is calming. Such a figure, usually but not necessarily a parent, also provides a sense of direction, goals, and values. When no such figure is available in childhood, when no one seems to be a source of the requisite perfection, the individual grows up hungry to find such a person and may enter psychotherapy predisposed to view the therapist in an idealized light. The therapist's response to an idealizing transference depends on his or her therapeutic orientation. For some schools of thought, idealization of the therapist is a defense against envy or hostility, while for others idealization is a regressive avoidance of an Oedipal transference. Kohut's position is that idealization is an early and primary developmental need. When no idealizable figure is available in childhood, throughout life the individual is likely to attach to anyone who seems to provide the necessary strength, calm, and sense of order. The idealized

figure is revered and seen as larger than life, while his or her faults
are not seen.

The result may be the idealization of an unworthy figure such
as a gang leader or a dictator such as Hitler. Politicians and other
celebrities are commonly idealized in our culture. From an archetypal point of view, the need to idealize is a search for the Self
projected onto the idealized person; he or she becomes a God-
figure who is all-powerful and utterly dependable. For the theist,
God is the ultimate idealizable figure. As the psalmist says: "I am
not afraid of ten thousands of people / who have set themselves
against me" (Psalm 3:6). To feel a part of that greatness is soothing
and affirming of one's own importance, especially if one feels that
one has a special relationship to God or a special understanding
of God's wishes, which is apparently the case for some preachers.
In that frame of mind, one can justify all kinds of beastly behavior
with a clear conscience as long as one has the illusion that one
is doing God's will. Such fantasies are dangerous among people
whose violence becomes incorporated into their spirituality.

Fundamentalists of all religious traditions often lack the internal structures that would provide them with personal goals and
values. Consequently, to avoid psychological turmoil, they need an
external set of clear rules and regulations such as those provided
by a sacred text or its theological superstructure. One version of
this problem is found in those individuals who try to control other
people's behavior in an attempt to control vicariously their own
impulses. Compliance with a set of preordained standards and
rules that are said to be divinely ordained diminishes the need for
personal decision making and gives an illusion of certainty. Such
compliance requires some narrowing of one's perception of reality
and oversimplifies one's understanding of human nature and the
complexity of human relationships.

When working therapeutically with a religious fundamentalist,
one has to bear in mind a variety of constraints on the individual.
He or she is not supposed to think independently, if doing so would
challenge the beliefs of his or her tradition. Belonging to a rigid
system requires submission to a set of doctrines and to authoritarian leadership, so that resentment is almost inevitable but is usually
considered to be sinful. The God-image of the fundamentalist is

usually demanding, punitive, or sadistic and often seeks to restrict pleasure (especially sexual pleasure) within prescribed limits. This God-image hates the shadow aspects of the individual's personality, such as greed or violence, so these problems tend to be projected onto other groups.

Typically, people who join cults with charismatic leaders are searching for an idealizable figure who seems to offer a sense of direction and purpose in life. Cultic religious groups are attractive to adolescents looking for an identity, to people at a major turning point in their lives, or to those seeking to re-create the experience of a family structure, perhaps in an attempt to obtain the emotional supplies that were not present in their families of origin (Jacobs 1989). However, the demands of most cults become excessive, so their members become torn between loyalty to the group and outside relationships. Because of disappointment with the group and its leader, more than 90 percent of those who join new religious groups leave within two years (Levine 1986). Some cultic groups are dangerous and lead to psychological damage when the ex-cult member experiences rage and shame at being duped, a sense of betrayal by the cult leader, and guilt at the time and money they invested in the cult. For a while, ex-cult members may doubt their own judgment and may become mistrustful of other people and cynical about spirituality in general. In spite of all this, many individuals who leave destructive groups say that the experience produced a maturational benefit by forcing them to meet the challenge (Vaughan 1987). Deikman (1996) provides a useful review of the psychotherapeutic treatment of ex-cult members.

While the individual is emotionally contained by the group, the idealized cult leader gives "answers" and direction and seems to be a source of strength and inspiration. The leader becomes a replacement for the wished-for parent, offering love, discipline, and spiritual guidance. In return for these provisions, unquestioning subordination to the leader is required. Many religious communities promise their followers a transformative effect on their sense of self, while others also promise world transformation. Kakar (2003) has pointed out that many devotees of religious gurus idealize these teachers because the followers are seeking some kind of emotional healing, not simply spiritual development. Rajneesh, for example, explicitly promised his followers, "I will be part of your healing process" (1979, p. 238).[4] Although obviously eccentric and flamboyant, he was seen as an enlightened leader who was creating a new world order. His devotees believed that they could move closer to enlightenment by a form of heart-to-heart, silent communication with him (Clarke 1985). Complete surrender to Rajneesh was required for this purpose. This movement was purportedly psychotherapeutic, leading to self-transformation, with the deliberate intention of facilitating a psychological merger between Rajneesh and his devotees (Rajneesh 1985). Therapists and other leaders within the community fostered a massively idealized transference to Rajneesh, who was seen as omnipotent and a perfect master. His devotees were encouraged to become a part of his perfection. However, the relationship was completely one-sided. Unlike the situation in psychotherapy, the devotee does not have the opportunity to resolve an idealizing relationship with the guru and so is prone to traumatic de-idealization when he or she discovers the guru's shadow. By contrast, in psychotherapy, the therapist is gradually de-idealized as a result of disruptions and failures in the relationship that are repaired and explained. Such de-idealization prevents the relationship from becoming addictive. However, if the guru never allows himself or herself to appear imperfect and is never humanized, the follower's idealization can never be understood or interpreted and so becomes interminable. This phenomenon is not confined to Eastern gurus; it is also seen in the devotion of evangelical Christians to their preachers.

There are many dangers to the aspirant who idealizes an unscrupulous or undeveloped spiritual teacher. The devotee gives up the capacity for personal discrimination and may lose touch with an internal sense of the divine, which is then projected onto the teacher. The devotee becomes vulnerable to manipulation by the shadow of the teacher or preacher. However, there are benefits; at the cost of personal autonomy, total devotion to a revered guru allows freedom from concern and a sense of deliverance. By belonging to a special group and having a relationship with a special figure, the individual feels important, perhaps (secretly) spiritually superior or special, thus enhancing his or her self-esteem. It is not unusual for the devotee to be abused in such groups, but this is usually rationalized as necessary for spiritual development. So powerful is an idealizing transference that even outrageous behavior by the leader is rationalized and assumed to arise from his or her superior spiritual awareness.

At the same time as the cult leader is idealized, strong ties develop to other members of the group, who provide support and mirroring. Being part of a close-knit group allows a twinship experience, the sense that one is like others and not an alien. To belong to a group of like-minded people sustains the sense of self. However, members of a religious community with a charismatic leader usually feel that he or she is too far above ordinary mortals for them to be anything like the leader.

Jung (1928b) referred to charismatic individuals such as priests, medicine men or gurus, as *mana*-personalities, individuals apparently possessed of a bewitching quality, magical knowledge, or spiritual power who appear in all cultures. *Mana* is a Polynesian term for a supernatural force, which is actually the power of the unconscious projected onto a heroic figure or godlike being who identifies with this power and so feels special. A charismatic individual, according to Kohut (1978), idealizes himself. He does so, for example, when his mother, who initially worshiped and idealized him as a child, withdraws her empathy, interest, and support. The child then has to assert his own perfection, using the admiration of others to maintain his self-esteem. Subjectively, he views the world as an extension of his own grandiose self. He feels that the world revolves around him, and he demands control over his followers without regard for their independence. Because charismatic individuals often lack empathy, they have no sense of the vulnerability of others and they cannot acknowledge their own vulnerability or any need to reach out to others. They are only interested in their own ideals. Some of them realize that they derive their self-esteem from a position of high status or authority, but at the same time they feel phony inside. Such an impostor fills his empty inner world with outer achievements. If is he is a guru, he is supposed to be one with God, so he must appear to be a perfect leader for those looking for a new life or for those in a crisis of faith.

An individual who was deprived of love in childhood might be powerfully attracted to a charismatic spiritual teacher who promises unconditional love. An intense, idealizing transference is fostered when the aspirant is encouraged to meditate on the teacher as a form of the divine or as one who can transmit spiritual energy. The guru asks for the individual's devotion, which the guru claims to deserve because of his special level of attainment. In return he offers his followers the promise of spiritual fulfillment. In the process, his followers support the leader's intense infantile need to feel special, while they draw strength from their merger with his apparent greatness. If the leader is a politician, the same idealizing dynamic obtains in the minds of his or her admirers, for whom the politician seems to have the answers to various social problems. Because the charismatic individual and the group who follows him are not fully psychologically differentiated from each other, the followers pay a high price for the idealization of a charismatic individual—they risk sacrificing their own individuation process and their capacity for discrimination and creativity.

It is important to add however that we cannot dismiss the guru phenomenon as nothing but an idealizing transference; for the fortunate seeker, the discovery of a true teacher may be what Babb (1986) refers to as a "redemptive encounter" that makes life worth living again. The word *guru* is a Sanskrit term with various etymological origins, but in general it means one who removes the student's darkness or one who is heavy with spiritual knowledge. The authentic spiritual teacher is a person of integrity and high spiritual attainment who is not motivated by a narcissistic need for self-enhancement and the exploitation of his followers. He or she can awaken the student to a personal sense of the divine or to the inner teacher and offers guidance that saves time and enables the student to avoid known pitfalls. In some traditions, the guru is the embodiment of divine love, and the experience of this love in human form may awaken a connection to the Self within the student. The teacher's capacity for inspiring and mediating divine love can have a powerful healing effect. Then the individual's psychopathology—a negative mother or father complex with low self-esteem or self-hatred—could be the trigger for important spiritual development. However the need for such love can easily be exploited, which is why, in some traditional Eastern cultures, the student is encouraged to doubt the teacher and if necessary spend years testing the teacher. The student is asked to confirm the authenticity of the teaching with personal experience rather than blind trust. In such a case, disappointment is much less likely.

In the therapeutic setting, idealization of the therapist arises organically when the individual needs to make up for a thwarted developmental process. At such a time, it is important for the therapist to allow the idealization for as long as necessary, while remaining conscious of the need for an experience of the divine as the true source of idealization and that the therapist is only a placeholder or way station for this experience. It is important that the therapist not become inflated by the idealized projection since it does not belong to the therapist. One might, for example, imagine the idealization being sent "up" to where it does belong, while being careful not to reject it. Gradually, as the therapist's flaws and limitations become evident, the person will be able to re-collect his or her idealized projection and the therapist will be seen in a more ordinary light. This enables the person to develop a connection to the divine in a way that is not centered on a particular human being.

Idealization typically makes the therapist feel special, so most therapists enjoy working in the presence of such transferences. Exceptions occur when the therapist was forbidden to feel special in childhood, or if he or she was envied or attacked when he or she expressed self-importance, in which case it feels uncomfortable to be idealized. Conversely, a therapist who needs to be idealized to support his or her sense of self may try to foster an idealizing transference, which is a form of exploitation analogous to the abuse by gurus described above. This risk is reduced by understanding the psychology of idealization and by the therapist's personal work on his or her narcissistic vulnerabilities.

The development of an idealizing transference is likely to predispose the person to see the therapist as a source of spiritual authority. Here it is worth remembering Freud's salutary contribution to this area. In several of his later works, we see his concern to demystify or deconstruct any form of absolute or oppressive authority, realizing that the need for authority makes people susceptible to tyrants. Freud saw the human need for authority as the result of the wish to find someone who will control our desires. For him, this need became one of the sources of the religious impulse. Freud realized that at the height of the transference his patients saw him as an absolute authority because they craved perfect love and unassailable truth. Freud (1927) suggested that the notion of divine providence or a perfect Father provides just such an illusion. However, Freud also realized that we are ambivalent about authority; we like the reassurance the authority provides but we resent its restriction of our freedom, and we realize that its pure truth is too simplistic to be sustained. This attitude is applicable not only to social authorities but also is a warning about pretensions to spiritual authority.

ENCOUNTERING EVIL IN PSYCHOTHERAPY

The therapist's sense that he or she is in the presence of evil becomes a considerable challenge to the therapist's spirituality.[5] If the therapist is committed to the Jewish or Christian tradition, he or she may have a clear idea of the nature of evil based on traditional values and biblical commandments. However, many therapists not committed to these traditions find the Bible's absolutes too rigid to be helpful in the individual situation. The Bible's forbidden behaviors are not sufficiently nuanced and are very much a part of the attitudes of the times in which the Bible was written. The psychotherapist who is not committed to a specific religious tradition does not think of evil behavior in terms of an absolute moral code that dictates the exact nature of good and evil. Such a therapist, faced with a complex human situation, has no objective, absolute knowledge about what is right. The therapist's assessment of any behavior is always tempered by understanding that unconscious factors drive behavior, and these are not under conscious control.

For many therapists, deciding that something is evil is a human judgment based on what we believe should not be happening. The therapist is therefore on the horns of a dilemma when material that feels evil arises in the therapy room, since it is well known that judgment is antithetical to good therapy. Judgment is also problematic because it is affected by factors in the therapist's own psychology; we are subject to the eternal problem of condemning in others what we cannot tolerate in ourselves. The therapist's judgment arises almost involuntarily when we hear expressions of unbridled hatred and violence, gratuitous cruelty, ruthless competitiveness, and malignant narcissism or sociopathy which produce a gross lack of concern for others. These are the types of behavior to which the word *evil* refers here. These all have psychodynamic, developmental, and societal origins, which may lead to radical evil. Nevertheless, I believe that Rumi is correct when he denies the existence of absolute or metaphysical evil or evil that is primary rather than secondary to frustration, fear, unmet needs, pain, and the like (quoted in Nicholson 1950 p. 152).

As therapists, our response to evil behavior partly depends on our ability to tolerate it, which often depends on the degree to which we were exposed to evil in our own development. For example, many therapists are sensitive to hearing reports of child abuse, particularly when they were affected by such violation in their own childhoods. In such a case, it is inevitable that the therapist's reservoir of pain and rage will be activated, leading to such intense countertransference revulsion that it may be difficult or impossible to understand a child abuser empathically.

The therapist's response to evil also depends on his or her beliefs about whether or not we can accept the presence of evil as an integral part of ultimate reality. Some spiritually oriented therapists may concur with Meister Eckhart's belief that if God is truly infinite everything that exists, including evil, exists within God. This is a statement of the underlying unity of the world that can be found in all mystical traditions. To accept that things are the way they must be is to avoid making judgments about reality in the knowledge that there is a larger intelligence at work in spite of the condition of the world. Whether or not we agree with Eckhart, we somehow have to reconcile our perception of evil with the existence of this intelligence. We cannot insist that the experience of evil is illusory, but we can have faith that there is a subtle, spiritual dimension that holds the entire system together in some way that we can intuit but not articulate. Dante called this level of reality the "love that moves the stars," while others believe it is impersonal. In either case, the spiritually oriented therapist feels that reality is ordered and not random. Alternatively, the atheistic therapist, perhaps with an existentialist bent, may deny any such spiritual basis to reality but still insist that life must be affirmed in spite of the presence of evil, which must simply be faced and dealt with.

The therapist's notion of the origin of evil behavior is important to the way he or she will respond to it. Some therapists believe that evil is innate and inevitable—a bad seed or *Rosemary's Baby* approach. Others believe that while we might be born with the potential for evil, environmental factors are necessary to evoke it. In that case, evil behavior is the result of developmental disasters in the perpetrator's childhood. It is arguable that to suggest that evil behavior is the result of cruelty and abuse in childhood makes evil derivative, the corruption of something that was potentially good. Miller (1990), for example, believes that cruelty to others represents revenge for cruelty done to oneself in childhood. Such writers believe that evil people were usually massively abused in their childhood, leading to chronic rage and hatred. These feelings cannot be contained; they must be evacuated onto others who are forced to feel the way the evil person was made to feel as a child. By having absolute power over others, by being predator rather than prey, by identifying with those who tormented him, the evil person prevents himself ever having to reexperience the terror and helplessness with which he grew up.

The therapist occasionally hears dreams that reinforce the view that evil is rooted in suffering, such as the following:

> I was standing in my bathroom when suddenly I had a terrible feeling of dread. I was paralyzed by what was behind me, because I knew it was evil. I also knew I had to turn round and look it in the eye. I was afraid to move and couldn't breathe. I finally turned and saw a dark-haired man. When I looked into his eyes I saw total sadness. My fear dissipated. The heavy weight on my body lifted. I was enveloped by a deep sense of peace.

This dream clearly indicates that evil contains sadness within it, although it is arguable that this sadness is secondary to a primary level of evil and is not the cause of evil. This issue cannot be proved either way and so remains a matter of personal commitment. It is, however, difficult to work therapeutically with evil behavior if we believe it to be innate. It is easier to be empathic with evil that we believe to be the result of developmental difficulties that make it impossible for the person to control his or her actions. There is then hope that the therapy may modify the situation. For this purpose, it is essential to understand the person as deeply as possible.

Through a psychodynamic lens, we can think of evil behavior as the result of distorted development that leads to intrapsychic structures, or complexes, that cause suffering. Here I use the term *complex* in Jung's sense, as a kind of subsystem in the psyche consisting of a cluster of memories, thoughts, images, fantasies, and emotions that form something like a subsidiary center of consciousness, even a subpersonality. The complex always has its own agenda and its own way of meeting its needs. When the complex is negative, dominated by painful feelings, it leads to behavior that may be totally at variance with the behavior of the larger personality. Most important, we see the world and other people through the lens of our complexes, which affect our belief system. We are drawn to religious (and political) doctrines that are consistent with these internal mental structures.

Using Jungian language, when a person is overwhelmed by intense feelings, a complex has been constellated (Jung 1948c). The person in the grip of a negative complex behaves in an evil way because he or she is "possessed," or temporarily overwhelmed, and later exclaims, "What came over me?" Under ordinary circumstances the complex may be isolated from the rest of the psyche, as if it exists in its own compartment, but when triggered it may take over and become autonomous, for example, producing an outburst of rage. When a complex produces problems such as envy, hatred, and destructiveness, it forms part of the shadow side of the personality, that part of us that we wish were not so. Depth psychology therefore does not view evil in terms of a metaphysical entity such as the devil; to do so is the province of theology. It is more psychologically manageable to think of evil in terms of complexes, anger dysregulation, a bad internal object, or the effects of a pathogenic selfobject.

Very often, people who come to therapy have been unsuccessfully struggling with a complex but cannot fully control it. The complex is often totally or partially unconscious and is thereby inaccessible to good advice, good intentions, and spiritual teaching, which is why these often fail to be helpful. For example, as darkness falls, a man who feels lonely and afraid finds it intolerable to be alone. Desperate to try to control his mounting panic, he visits a bar, trying to find someone who will comfort him, but every time this happens he ends up having an impersonal sexual encounter. He has been told by his minister that this behavior is sinful, but the therapist does not make this kind of judgment. We see this individual as possessed by a complex that produces uncontrollable anxiety. He has no conscious idea of the developmental origin of this problem, which was formed by repeated childhood abandonment. There are many similar sources of uncontrollable behavior. It is well known that a person abused in childhood may identify with the aggressor and become a child abuser. We are also subject to the displaced, intolerable experiences of our parents, which children internalize. These experiences may transmit trauma from generation to generation, producing cumulative effects within the children of such families in whom the trauma lives on as a kind of psychological foreign body. Such problems compel uncontrollable and poorly understood behavior whose origins are split off from consciousness.

For the spiritually oriented therapist, the notion of the complex is important because in Jung's model the complex consists of both personal and transpersonal material.[6] The human level of the complex is well described by personalistic theories such as object relations theory, psychoanalytic self-psychology, and cognitive-behavioral theory. Depending on one's preferred theory, one could say that the human shell of the complex consists of childhood deprivation, conflict, early trauma, attachment problems, our unlived life, our unmet selfobject needs, or pathogenic internal objects. At the core of the complex is an archetypal process, so that the personal and archetypal dimensions are always inextricably intertwined.

To put the archetypal and the human levels together, consider a man with a powerful father complex. He experienced his father as domineering, controlling, authoritarian, arbitrary, and punitive. At the archetypal level, we could use mythological imagery to describe the situation; the father was a Zeus-like figure who demanded to be worshiped and obeyed. It is as if the father has identified with this archetype, so that he acts as if he is the law itself, a tyrannical ultimate authority who punishes his son severely if he was disobedient, just as Zeus punished mortals. Because of this father complex, this son grew up in terror of authority. Another father was an Apollo type, preoccupied with truth, rationality, logic, and clarity. He inspired his son to be compulsively clean and a perfectionist, from which his son could only escape when he lived out his father's unlived Dionysian shadow—intoxication and addiction. The personal levels of these complexes can be explained in terms of traditional psychoanalytic theories. At the same time, it is important to see the archetypal level, because this allows us to understand the extraordinary gripping power of the complex and its spiritual importance. The archetypal Father is a spiritual principle in the psyche, reflected in many mythologies as a sky-father deity such as the biblical Yahweh. The therapist realizes that the person with such a father complex is essentially struggling with transpersonal energies, what the ancients would have called a god, before which the ego is fragile. This puts his struggle in a larger perspective than would be possible if we were to describe it in purely personalistic terms.

To illustrate the power of an unconscious complex as a source of religious experience, Jung uses the biblical story of Hosea, a pious Hebrew prophet who was commanded by God to marry a harlot (1940, par. 32). The story is usually seen as a metaphor for the relationship between Israel and God, but Jung makes the point that what felt like a divine command to the prophets of old, we would consider to be the result of the prompting of a complex. In other words, when we work with a person's emotional life, we are at the same time working with a spiritually important dimension of the psyche. The archetypal dimension is also important because renewal may arise from this level and not only by means of the therapeutic relationship.

What would be the therapist's reaction if called upon to work with a woman who had killed her children, or who was thinking of doing so? Euripides' drama *Medea* tells this story, describing one of the most terrible crimes imaginable. Medea, the daughter of Aeetes, the king of Colchis, is a witch who can work magic for good or evil. She is in love with Jason, to whom she has been married for ten years. She and Jason live in Corinth, where the people are afraid of her magical powers and her ruthlessness. Jason wishes to divorce Medea in order to marry the daughter of Creon, the king of Corinth, for the sake of power and wealth. Jason is an opportunist, with no capacity for understanding the feelings of others. He rationalizes his behavior by telling Medea that he wishes to leave her for the good of their children, since they are the sons of a barbarian (non-Greek) mother and so by law are not Greek citizens. In truth, it is obvious that he has no further use for Medea, and to add insult to injury he views her outrage at his betrayal as an indication of her poor judgment. He has no sense of gratitude; not only did Medea betray her father by helping Jason capture the golden fleece, she has already killed Jason's uncle and gruesomely dismembered her own brother to help Jason, and she has suffered exile from her own country. But Jason has no guilt and merely assumes that this is what happens when women like Medea fall in love with men as great as he is. After all, he did let her share in his success, and he introduced her to the glories of Greek civilization. By our standards, a contemporary Jason would be considered to be a severely narcissistic personality.[7] As a result of Jason's rejection of her, Medea becomes severely depressed, weeps constantly, and wishes she were dead. Not only is she abandoned by Jason, she has lost her security, she feels ashamed and rejected, and she fears that people will laugh at her plight unless she takes revenge. Although she is aware that she is doing something evil, she first poisons Jason's bride-to-be and Creon. Then, to our horror, Medea stabs her sons to death.

At the archetypal level of the complex, Medea represents the type of mythic female demon who murders children; she is the death-dealing, devouring, negative Mother archetype. Neumann (1949) suggested that the fear of being killed by one's mother, a theme found in many mythologies, produces a deeper level of anxiety than the fears Freud described in the Oedipus complex. Perhaps that is one reason this story has given rise to so many versions since the dawn of European civilization. According to Claus and Johnston, Medea's story was already old and popular by the eighth century B.C.E. (1997, p. 3). Since then, Medea has been the subject of countless poets, philosophers, artists, plays, ballets, and operas. Interestingly, as Claus and Johnson point out, Sophocles and Seneca portray Medea in two ways. She is a witch, adept at herbal poisons and surrounded by snakes, a priestess of the underworld goddess Hecate, who ruled magic and the uncanny. Yet she also has a positive side; she is a helper-maiden and the founder of cities. According to one version of the myth, after her death she marries Achilles in the blessed Elysian Plains, which is the abode of privileged souls. She is therefore a complex figure, not a simple type, and her mixture of traits contributes to our interest in her. We know instinctively that something of Medea lurks in the human soul, not just in her capacity to do anything for love, in her murderous rage and need for revenge, but also in our fear of strangers among us.

That still leaves us with the issue of infanticide. Why does she kill her children as well as her rival? This surely has a calculated aspect to it; she realizes that Jason does not really love Creon's daughter and will not be too hurt by her loss. Indeed, Jason expresses no grief at her death, but the death of his children will really hurt him, so if Medea wants revenge she has to kill them. By doing so, she will make Jason experience the intensity of pain that she feels. At the same time, Medea herself is hurt by the death of her children, so she punishes herself for her crime as she punishes Jason. At least now she does not feel herself to be a passive victim. I would also point to her narcissistic vulnerability; she says that she can endure guilt, however horrible, but she cannot endure "the laughter of my enemies" (Vellacott 1963, p. 41).

A further motive is suggested by Euripides' feminist sensibility. Even before Jason's betrayal, Euripides portrays Medea as acutely conscious of the second-class status of women in Greek society. She is angry that men control everything and furious at her dependency on men. Medea complains that she would rather fight battles than have a child. She would rather be a man so she can be a soldier. Accordingly, Jacobs (1998) suggests that her hatred of the favoritism shown to men allowed her to kill her brother, and by killing her sons she once again kills males who are more beloved to a man than she is. Medea tells us, "I understand the horror of what I am going to do; but anger, / The spring of all life's horror, masters my resolve" (Vellacott 1963, p. 50). Her rage overpowers her conscience.

Presumably, faced with a contemporary Medea, the therapist could empathically understand her rage even though nothing could justify what she proposes to do. At the human level, we would say that Jason was an essential selfobject for Medea, and the loss of him is excruciatingly painful, so that her rage is a fragmentation product of a disintegrating sense of self. But the story also gives us the archetypal basis of the problem that forms the core of the complex with which she is struggling. According to the myth, Medea's love for Jason was imposed on her by the goddess Hera with the help of Aphrodite.[8] That is to say, Medea was in thrall to archetypal forces over which she had no control. In antiquity, these forces were personified as gods and goddesses. They describe particular spiritual qualities within the soul and also aspects of the personality that express them. It is important to understand their numinous, gripping power, so that we may grasp the intensity of the forces at the core of the complex that possessed Medea.

The Hera archetype produces an intense need to be a wife. Hera depicts a powerful marital bond that wants loyalty and fidelity above all else. Jason had promised Medea eternal commitment, a characteristic most important to the Hera aspect of Medea's psychology. In Hera's mythology, she is constantly humiliated and enraged by Zeus's affairs and is vengeful toward his paramours, because for her marriage is not just a legal contract; marriage is sacred, and to damage it is sacrilege—she needs the same devotion that she gives. Making matters worse, Zeus does not seem to need Hera—he even gives birth to Athena without Hera's assistance, just as Jason does not seem to need Medea after he has used her for his own purposes.

In the myth, Medea fell in love with Jason at the instigation of Aphrodite, the irresistible goddess of love, who works by "enchantment"—a mythological term that we would understand to indicate unconscious processes. Because of her love for Jason, Medea could not resist his pleas to help him steal the golden fleece. Euripides has the chorus pray that they never suffer from the "inescapable arrow" of Aphrodite, whom they dread because she may "[c]raze my heart to leave old love for new" (Vellacott 1963, p. 36).

Apparently, the loss of a passionate, divinely inspired love made Medea behave in a bestial manner. This is why Jung says "the gods have become diseases" (1957, par. 54).

What would a therapist say to a contemporary Medea who came to therapy with this intention? Could we empathically grasp her state of mind? (Of course, the Tarasoff rule would apply, but for the purposes of discussion I would like to consider the situation purely from a therapeutic standpoint.)[9] We might initially wonder if she is a psychopathic serial killer except that unlike the true psychopath she feels guilt and remorse. The typical psychopath has no capacity for love or commitment, but these are the very qualities in Medea that cause the problem. She suffers from love, which she describes as an "evil power in people's lives" (Vellacott 1963, p. 27). All the evil actions she performs are carried out because of love for Jason, love she cannot control. She has been made unstable by the intensity of her love, not by the lack of it, reminding us that love often stirs up the darkest corners of the personality. However, Medea assumes that Jason is the whole problem, and it would be the therapist's task to point out that she must also deal with what he has made her face in herself—her capacity for murderous rage, which in the myth is particularly dangerous because of her magical power. This story therefore makes the point that uncontrolled power over others tends to lead to evil.

It would help the therapist to be empathic with Medea's pain, hatred, and rage if we realize that without her fantasies of revenge she would feel weak and helpless, which would be unbearable. She uses her rage and hatred to hold herself together, as an alternative to feeling like a passive victim. There would be no point in simply condemning her intention to kill her children if she were to announce it in therapy; she knows full well how wrong her action would be. The therapist would be no use to her as a moral judge. One has to understand that her love was divinely inspired, that she was in the grip of forces beyond human control. Archetypal forces such as love are impersonal; they have no interest in human moral standards, and the problem for the ego is to take a stand in relation to them. Medea cannot stand up to the affective intensity of the forces within her. The therapist's task is to assist Medea with containing her rage and pain within the therapeutic relationship, by providing the necessary selfobject function so that she expresses her feelings and works through them but does not act on them. This is possible since the therapist can see both the human and the archetypal forces at work, but the therapist is not at their mercy to the same extent as Medea.

We expect a transference repeat of her difficulty within the therapeutic relationship, so it is entirely likely that Medea will become enraged at the therapist from time to time, perhaps when she senses actual or imagined betrayal by the therapist. Given her capacity for murder, the therapist's countertransference is likely to be one of terror. This dynamic must be understood and explained if the therapist is to help her, but there is another level to consider. In therapy, our contemporary Medea might realize that because of the archetypal pressure of Hera in her soul, she had been seeing Jason in an idealized light. She has to see him as he really is and let go of wishing he would come back to her. Perhaps with the therapist's help she can diminish the intensity of her belief that being a wife is the only way for her to be fulfilled. She might discover and express other aspects of her personality, especially those parts of herself that she had ignored or suppressed for the sake of the marriage. For example, in one version of the myth, Hera rejects her son Hephaestus because he was born with deformed feet, which embarrassed her. However, Hephaestus is an enormously gifted craftsman and passionately creative. This mythologem or psychological structure suggests that Hera rejects her creative product because she judges it to be inadequate. If Medea could learn to value what she has produced, she might be able to channel or sublimate her rage into creative work. If she could see that she was in thrall to a mythic pattern, she could develop some distance from it and even stop repeating it. She would then not identify with these archetypal forces and not be so possessed by them.

Are we justified in saying that the archetypal forces that possessed Medea are truly spiritual? Is this not tantamount to saying that they are elements of the divine even though they have caused such disastrous behavior? To acknowledge this, we must expand our notion of the spiritual dimension to include the fact that we may experience it in painful ways. All archetypal processes have both a light and a dark side, which is why Jung believed that for the

Self to be truly a totality, it must contain both light and dark aspects.[10] Like all archetypal processes, Hera is an aspect of the Self. The dark side of the Hera archetype is illustrated by her vindictive jealousy and rage directed at Zeus's paramours. Therefore when Medea struggles with her overwhelming need for revenge, she is struggling with a complex on two levels: a human level that consists of her narcissistic vulnerability and a transpersonal element that consists of the dark side of the Self. This puts her struggle in a larger perspective than a purely personal one. Therapy that helps her with her evil intentions is a process of the redemption of evil.

Part of the power of the shadow arises because the archetypal core of the complex is an energetic force within the personality. This force "causes or compels definite modes of behavior or impulses; that is, they may under certain circumstances have a possessive, numinous, or obsessive force (Jung 1961, p. 347). These forces are daimones, a reference to the ancient Greek notion of an autonomous, primal force. Jung calls one's daimon a "determining power," although he believes that the ethical decision about how to respond to it is left to the individual (1951a, par. 51). When we relate to it successfully, the energy of the individual's daimon becomes available as a valuable resource. The daimon can be a muse for the artist or a motivating force for the social reformer. Or, the daimon can appear as a process such as sexuality or rage (von Franz 1981). These forces can be integrated to varying degrees, depending on the individual's tolerance for intense affective states. One of the tasks of psychotherapy is to help the individual develop the capacity to withstand the pressure of these archetypal forces. Sometimes this pressure is so intense that the most one can hope for is containment of the shadow without acting on it or projecting it onto others.

The spiritual journey sooner or later leads to a confrontation with the shadow side of the personality. May regards "the discernment of good and evil" as an authentically spiritual task, implying that this would not be a part of psychotherapy (1992, p. 16). In fact, much psychotherapy is about becoming conscious of the shadow, without which it cannot be changed. Psychotherapeutic work on the shadow is an important spiritual discipline; it is soul work par excellence.

For the therapist, evil can be thought of as the result of emotional disorder rather than solely a moral problem. At the human level of the complex, evil behavior is produced by thwarted development, a damaged sense of self, or a self in the process of fragmentation, trying to hold itself together. A degree of empathy is therefore necessary when dealing with the shadow, since it results from childhood abuse, neglect, or because some aspect of the child was not allowed expression in the family. Therefore the shadow is important for the continuing development of the personality; it is the area in which new consciousness may arise.

The more we try to suppress the shadow, the more energetic it becomes. Accordingly there is no point in fighting the shadow, which merely increases the intensity of an intrapsychic split and produces more internal conflict, which may be acted out as social conflict as the shadow is projected onto other people. As Neumann puts it, we need the moral courage "not to want to be either worse or better" than we actually are (1960, p. 111). He suggests that we enter into an agreement with the shadow, meaning that at times we may allow it some expression rather than try to get rid of it entirely. If we befriend it within reason, it is less likely to become hostile to consciousness.

As well as its origins in our developmental vicissitudes, our shadow is partly formed by unconsciously internalizing the shadow of the society in which we live. The social and personal levels of evil then interpenetrate each other—racism is an example. Most of us have to negotiate a way to live with the dark side of society without totally succumbing to it. For this purpose, we have to be conscious of the lure of cultural propaganda and collective opinions.

When dealing with the shadow, the therapeutic approach differs from the traditional religious approach, which attempts to deal with evil using rituals of purification, such as the sacrament of confession or various forms of penance. As a rule, these only have a temporary effect because they do not change the intrapsychic structures that led to the behavior; they are an external fix. The psychotherapeutic approach to evil behavior requires consciousness and the repair of damaged psychological structures by reworking them within the therapeutic relationship.

NOTES

1. For a discussion of this issue, see Sharfstein (1980). A useful discussion of Jung's typology in relation to various philosophers is that of King (1999).

2. The Myers-Briggs Type Indicator would refer to Russell's temperament as INTJ.

3. Russell's *Marriage and Morals* (1929) was a central focus of this decision.

4. However, the degree of manipulation of his followers eventually became clear. The group deteriorated into violence, drug abuse, and paranoid fantasies until it was dissolved by the United States government. The story is told in FitzGerald (1986).

5. For a general discussion of evil from a depth psychological point of view, see Corbett (2007, chap. 5) and Corbett (1996, chap. 9).

6. In Jung's model, the archetype is "humanized" by one's parents, and depending on their behavior one may experience the light or the dark side of the archetype. Since the archetype is a spiritual principle in the soul, this model leads to the conclusion that evil behavior may have spiritual underpinnings, what Jung refers to as the dark side of the Self. Some people object to this notion since it seems to put good and evil on the same footing. The concern is that if both are aspects of the Self, there is a risk that evil may somehow be justified.

7. Here arises the problem of judging another culture by the standards of our own. In his discussion of Euripides' *Medea*, Vellacott warns us not to prejudge Jason, who had "entirely respectable ambitions" by contemporary standards (1963, p. 8). Jason upheld the principles that the Greeks valued most: a controlled, orderly, proportionate life in opposition to what they considered to be barbarism. Nevertheless, one has to wonder what initially drew Medea to Jason. Perhaps we can understand his appeal to her in terms of her father complex, which made her attracted to ruthless, powerful men. Her father Aeetes was the brutal king of a barbarian race that was hostile to strangers. When Jason demanded the golden fleece, Aeetes set him impossible tasks because an oracle had told him he would die if the fleece were stolen. He promised Jason the fleece if Jason could harness fire-breathing bulls to a plow, sow a field with dragon's teeth, and kill the armed men that sprang from this seed. Medea's sorcery allowed Jason to succeed in these tasks, but Aeetes did not fulfill his promise.

8. The problem that arises here is that the Greek myths arose in a heavily patriarchal culture, so the stories are written through that lens.

9. The Tarasoff rule originated in a decision of the California Supreme Court in the case of Tarasoff v. Regents of the University of California (17 Cal.3d 425 [1976]). A patient told his therapist that he intended to kill a particular woman and subsequently did so. Her parents sued the therapist

for failing to warn them or their daughter about the danger. The California
Supreme Court held that if a therapist believes "that a patient poses a serious danger of violence to others, he bears a duty to exercise reasonable care
to protect the foreseeable victim of that danger." In 1985, the California
legislature codified the Tarasoff rule. A psychotherapist has a duty to warn
a third party if the therapist believes that a patient poses a serious risk of
inflicting serious bodily injury upon a reasonably identifiable victim.

10. To suggest that the Self has a dark side is a different God-image
than that of traditional Christianity, which prefers to see the divine as only
loving and light, an attitude that, carried to an extreme, suggests defensive
splitting. Yet the shadow of the divine is present in that mythology too; the
avenging angels of the book of Revelation are bloodthirsty.

Psychotherapy as a Form of Spiritual Direction

When suffering is seen as a spiritual as well as a psychological problem, psychotherapy becomes service to the soul, consonant with the etymological sense of the word *psychotherapy*. At these times, psychotherapy provides a contemporary form of the traditional practice of spiritual direction. The word *direction* is an unfortunate term when it implies that the individual is expected to submit to authority or surrender personal responsibility, neither of which suits the therapeutic attitude. However, direction in its basic sense simply means an indication of possible paths. The individual may discover a sense of direction with the guidance of someone who knows a certain territory, or by temporarily identifying with someone one admires, or during the course of an idealizing transference. For the therapist, words such as *witness, companion*, or *attendant* would be preferable to the word *direction*, but this word is now deeply rooted in our spiritual traditions. Even the word *spiritual* is problematic when it implies excessive otherworldliness leading to detachment from material necessities or indifference to the body and social reality. More appropriately, to be spiritual means to be sensitive to the subtle or sacred dimension of existence that is always present in daily life.

Various clinicians have become interested in the integration of spiritual direction into psychotherapy (Tan 2003), but the word *integration* implies that these are different disciplines. Indeed, psy-

chotherapy is often contrasted with spiritual direction, because
from a traditional theistic perspective the focus of these practices
is different (West 2000). However, I take the position that by its
very nature psychotherapy includes an element of spiritual direction, at least potentially, for various reasons. The psyche reveals or
manifests the sacred, for example, as numinous experience and as
a vehicle of relationship to the sacred. As well, the psyche contains
an image, or possibly an element, of the divine in the form of the
transpersonal Self. The Self can also be thought of as the totality of
the psyche, and it acts as the spiritual blueprint for the evolution of
the personality. For these reasons there can be no firm distinction
between our psychology and our spirituality. No problem is purely
psychological or purely spiritual; only convention and language
separate them. Our psychological lives can only be differentiated
from our spirituality if we define spirituality narrowly, in terms of
the dictates of one particular tradition. When the therapist is aware
that he or she is in service to the soul—and this attitude does not
need to be spoken—the therapy room becomes sacred space, the
hour becomes sacred time, and the process becomes a ritual in the
best sense of that word.

There is no need to tie the psychotherapeutic notion of spiritual direction to the dictates of any particular tradition. For example, theistic writers define this practice as helping a person to
develop a deeper personal relationship with God, to increase his
or her awareness of God, or to facilitate surrender to God's will,
usually in terms of the theology of a particular tradition (Benner
2002).[1] In the Christian tradition, it is assumed that the Holy
Spirit acts by means of the relationship between director and directed. This approach is valuable when both participants share this
theology. However, it may not be helpful if the director is committed to a theology that does not reflect the individual's personal
experience of the sacred. The nature of the transference, especially
an idealizing transference to a charismatic director, is such that
the director's opinions may influence the individual's approach to
the sacred. This does not necessarily lead to an authentic personal
spirituality. To avoid this difficulty, the therapist must be receptive
to whatever form of spirituality seems to emerge organically. To
help a person discover a sense of meaning and purpose in life or to

PSYCHOTHERAPY AS SPIRITUAL DIRECTION

assist a person in understanding the spontaneous manifestations of the transpersonal psyche are forms of spiritual assistance that require no prior theistic commitment.

For the Jungian tradition, the connection between the personal and transpersonal levels of the psyche is known as the ego-Self axis. For the purposes of psychotherapy, it is assumed that this is a relationship or a dialogue rather than a one-way system. We experience relationship with the Self by means of dreams, synchronicities, symptoms, and important life experiences—the Self therefore plays an important part in the psychotherapeutic process. The therapist's task is to help the person understand these experiences, draw attention to what is being ignored, and sometimes help discover an appropriate response. If the Self is truly a spiritual principle in the psyche, this work is no different than traditional spiritual direction, which helps the individual pay attention and respond to the manifestations of God in his or her life (Barry and Connolly 1982). What is different is that the contemplative psychotherapist is not committed to a background dogma or doctrine, such as the idea that we are sinful creatures in need of redemption. In the context of spiritual direction between two people who belong to the Christian tradition, such ideas may tilt the work of spiritual direction in a particular direction, but they do not play a part in psychotherapy unless the person is concerned with them. It must be admitted that the therapist's theory of psychotherapy influences the course of the work, but the therapist makes psychological rather than theological or metaphysical assumptions.

Spiritual direction is usually distinguished from psychotherapy in that it is not intended to deal with complex emotional problems. Some writers argue that spiritual direction and psychotherapy are fundamentally different enterprises and that it is unwise to risk "psychologizing" the process of spiritual direction (McNamara 1975). Somehow, psychological material seems more tangible than the discernment of our spiritual life. The concern seems to be that the spiritual director will become distracted by psychological difficulties and not pay attention to "purely" spiritual material. The director's tradition decides what is truly spiritual and what is psychological or secular. In other words, to keep the two fields separate is an attempt to legislate what is spiritual, and this attitude betrays an unwarranted split between the psychological and the spiritual. The doctrines and dogmas of a particular tradition dictate the way in which we "should" experience our spirituality. The theistic spiritual director believes that he or she helps the individual toward understanding or deepening his or her relationship to God, while the spiritual approach to psychotherapy sees the symptom or the dream as a call from the Self. In both cases we acknowledge the presence of a transpersonal process, but for the spiritually oriented therapist this does not necessarily mean the divine is as imagined by a specific tradition. It means that we pay attention to the manifestations of the sacred in whatever form they arise. Sacred experience may or may not take a recognizable Judeo-Christian form; the transpersonal levels of the psyche are autonomous, or as the New Testament has it (John 3:8): "The wind blows where it wills." The spirit does what it wants to do—presumably, without regard to any theology.

In a typical attempt to keep spiritual direction and psychotherapy separate, May (1992) argues that while psychotherapy focuses on thoughts and feelings, spiritual direction focuses on one's prayer life, religious experience, and a sense of relationship to God. He objects to labeling emotional life and relationships spiritual because, although he recognizes that in the broad sense all human experience is spiritual, for the purposes of spiritual direction he is concerned that we not broaden our definition of spirituality excessively. However, our emotional lives and relationships are colored by our affectively toned complexes, which in the Jungian tradition are considered to have both a human level and an archetypal or transpersonal core. During psychotherapy, we may not only look into the psychodynamics of emotional suffering but also discern its archetypal underpinnings and its larger meaning for the person's life. We are then trying to clarify the person's connection with the transpersonal dimension. Whether we call this treatment or spiritual direction is only a semantic difference. It is often our emotional distress that opens us to our spirituality, which may be why we sometimes see emotionally fragile people who have deep faith and a profound personal spirituality. If we separate spiritual direction and psychotherapy, we imply a degree of separation between psyche and spirit that does not exist, except in our language and our cultural attitudes. For example, dreams, which are quintessentially psychological, may contain both personal and transpersonal material and can be an important source of spiritual experience.[2] Attention to dreams is therefore a spiritual practice in its own right, in the absence of any particular emotional distress.

May points out that the spiritual director may lose sight of the fact that the divine works through the director, just as the secular psychotherapist may believe that he or she is the instrument of healing. However, when psychotherapy is practiced with a spiritual sensibility, we realize that the Self produces any healing that occurs, not the egos of the participants. May also suggests that psychotherapy is mostly intended to help one live well, whereas spiritual direction is more about liberation from attachments and surrender to the will of God and so is often opposed to the cultural standards that psychotherapy tries to encourage. However, these distinctions are not entirely valid. If we pay attention to dreams in psychotherapy, we realize that we live in relation to the larger consciousness of the Self, and during times of suffering this relationship often requires surrender of the ego's position. Furthermore, ethical psychotherapy is not an instrument of social control. On the contrary, psychotherapy fosters the individuation process, which may lead to attitudes that contradict cultural norms. In spite of May's attempts to separate the two disciplines, he eventually acknowledges that, as psychotherapy becomes increasingly holistic, it becomes more clearly ministry and less and less of a technical process.

Both psychotherapy and spiritual direction allow people to learn more about their authentic spirituality by discovering what is sacred to the individual and the ways in which the person deals with spiritual questions. Here I would disagree with Victor Frankl's (1986) opinion that the psychotherapeutic "cure of souls" can only lead the patient to the point where he develops a religious disposition, at which point the therapist has no further role. One does not have to develop this disposition *de novo* as much as discover it, because the psyche has an innate religious function. The therapist facilitates the emergence of this function by trying to discern ways in which the transcendent dimension is operating in the person's life. For some people this may mean a return to their original spiritual tradition. For others, it may mean the discovery of an entirely personal approach to the sacred, expressed for example by numinous experiences or the experience of novel symbolic material in dreams. If one tries to force a person to adopt a spirituality that is not in accord with his or her temperament and personality structures, one does violence to the soul and prevents the person from following the impulse of the heart. This attitude may offend those who believe it ignores the absolute truth of the revelation at Sinai or the story of Christ, since these are said to apply to everyone.

The psychological approach is predicated on the notion that revelation is continuous, producing symbolic manifestations of the sacred whose form is not confined to the Judeo-Christian tradition. Both religious traditions and depth psychology stress the importance of symbols, although they understand the symbol differently. Traditional cataphatic spirituality (the notion that we can say something affirmative about the divine) uses imagery such as religious icons as vehicles of connection to the sacred. We find this approach in many traditions. Millions of people may find the same symbol, such as the cross, sacred. For the depth psychologist, at least in the Jungian tradition, novel symbols may arise from the soul spontaneously, typically in a dream, as we saw in chapter 2. We have no control over this process, and the symbol may take a unique form that is only relevant to the individual.

By contrast, the apophatic approach considers the sacred to be beyond all representations. This form of spirituality is found in the mystical traditions and during those image-less, silent, but mysteriously powerful moments that are not uncommon in psychotherapy. It is important that we recognize such moments for what they are—an experience of the presence of the Self. Both the way of images and the way of silence are of value. Symbolic experience of the sacred grounds the experience in memory and allows us to talk about it, but even the way of symbols ultimately requires an apophatic approach, because the source of sacred symbols is beyond symbols.

Both the psychotherapist and the traditional spiritual director are much less concerned with diagnosis than with discernment. May makes a useful distinction between these two processes. Diagnosis refers to a distinction made by means of knowledge or judgment, based on the logical classification of signs and symptoms using reason. Diagnosis accentuates a subject-object distinction, in which the doctor makes an apparently objective assessment of a patient. The word *discernment* also refers to the act of separating but does not carry the logos quality of the word *diagnosis*.[3] For May, discernment is therefore "a graced charism [a divine gift] that happens *through the relationship*" (1992, p. 151–2; emphasis in original). Here, intuition is important and intimacy is necessary; too much subject-object distinction or too many attempts at objectivity ruin the process of discernment, although knowledge has its place in this process. Discernment allows insight into the nature of things but sometimes cannot be put into words because its results are too subtle. May believes that whereas diagnosis seeks solutions to mystery in order to destroy it, discernment seeks a discriminating appreciation of mystery.

As a part of his distinction between psychotherapy and spiritual direction, May believes that psychotherapy is a profession for which one can be trained, but spiritual direction requires both a spiritual aptitude and a vocation. I believe he overdraws this distinction, because psychotherapy also requires a vocation and a particular gift— a combination of empathy and therapeutic intelligence—that can only be trained if it exists as a potential within the personality. The therapist's aptitude for psychotherapy seems to have little relationship to his or her academic background. Although technical training is essential in order to practice psychotherapy, technical training alone is not sufficient, which is why our process of awarding degrees, licenses, and other credentials does not guarantee that a person will become a good therapist. Among the most important developments we can expect from formal training are that it will enhance the expression of the trainee's natural ability. In supervision, one sees trainees who obviously had a natural therapeutic gift damaged by professional training that forced them to work in a manner totally at odds with their temperament. Certain types of training produce the ability to manage people in a way that prevents authentic contact. Similarly, some trainees with a natural aptitude for working with spiritually important material are told to ignore this subject or treat it as if it were defensive.

The traditional minister of religion is charged with interpreting the will of God to his or her congregation within the framework of a particular set of theological assumptions. The therapist, however, may be working with a suffering person who has no emotional or intellectual connection to any tradition, and then there is no such framework on which the therapist can depend. One only has recourse to the therapeutic relationship and the individual's personal experience of the sacred. This situation has the disadvantage of being unpredictable but the advantage of being specific to the individual.

Besides its unpredictability, there are at least two other problems with a depth psychological approach. The first is that even when the overt symptom, such as chronic pain, seems to be understood and seems to have served its purpose psychologically, it may not disappear. Gerhard Adler suggests, correctly I believe, that in such cases the symptom acts as a constant source of stimulation "lacking which the newly won level of consciousness would get lost again" (1979, p. 70). Or, the person's destiny is to be a perpetually wounded healer. Another puzzle is that some people feel better as a result of psychotherapy without our having understood the meaning of their symptom or why they recovered. Presumably something essential has then been provided at an unconscious level of contact between the two people, but we were not sensitive enough to discern it, or we do not have the theoretical language to describe it. Or, we might just admit that the transpersonal dimension has its own dynamics that cannot be understood by the ego.

THE TRANSPERSONAL LEVEL OF THE THERAPEUTIC RELATIONSHIP

Traditional schools of psychotherapy describe the therapeutic relationship in terms of personal dynamics. From the point of view of contemplative psychotherapy, this relationship is also a form of spiritual connection. Jung pointed out that the transference-countertransference has a transpersonal as well as a personal level because it has a numinous archetypal core that contributes to its power. According to Jung, the fundamental archetypal process that underpins the transference is the *coniunctio*, Latin for "union," a sacred marriage that is an image of wholeness and the union of opposites (1946, par. 355; 1955–1956, par. 1). This intrapsychic spiritual union is the soul's attempt to unite with the other to find what is missing, to achieve peace and rest. Kohut's notion of the selfobject, an intrapsychic experience of the other as part of oneself, describes the human level of this process, but whenever we are strongly drawn to another person, for example, when a powerful transference process is operating, we are dealing not only with personal material. We have been gripped by the numinous power of the *coniunctio*. This term was used by medieval alchemists to depict the union of different substances, which is Jung's metaphor for the process of psychotherapy in which both participants are changed, as if a chemical reaction has occurred. The ego has no choice in this matter, according to Jung, because "you have become the victim of a decision made over your head or in defiance of the heart . . . the experience of the Self is always a defeat for the ego" (Jung 1955–1956, par. 778). The therapist participates in but does not control this level of the work, and only its personal levels can be analyzed in terms of childhood. There is also a dimension that points forward, toward the future development of the personality, whose final goal is unknown.

The two people in the therapy room feel separate but in fact are part of an underlying unitary process, which in medieval times was referred to as the *unus mundus*, or "one world." Our conscious level of apparent separateness, and the unconscious level of an undivided continuum, which is the level of the Self, are linked in subtle ways that are difficult to discern. We see the link between apparently separate events most clearly in the phenomenon of synchronicity, when an event in the material world corresponds to the subject's psychological predisposition in a way that is acausal but meaningful.

The therapist feels as though he or she operates at the level of separateness, using knowledge, theory, skills, and previous experience. At times during psychotherapy all these play a part, but at times change occurs in ways we do not understand. It is a commonplace in psychotherapy that intuitions, wisdom, precognitive awareness, and unexpected insights arise from an unknown source, which can be thought of as eruptions from the unitary continuum. These experiences feel more like acts of grace than something explicable in terms of developmental psychology or psychodynamic theory. To understand this mysterious aspect of the therapeutic relationship requires a radical change in our usual viewpoint, which is heavily conditioned by the notion that we are separate entities and by the kind of thought that traditional Western science considers to be rational. To be sensitive to the presence of the unitary continuum, one has to stop thinking in terms of cause and effect, give up determinism as the sole explanation for phenomena, and stop seeing a radical division between ourselves and the world and between psyche and nature. Instead, we can think in terms of synchronicity, acausality, nonlocality, and invisible patterns of relationship which may be analogous to the quantum entanglement described by particle physicists.[4] This subject is discussed further in chapter 8.

CONNECTION TO THE TRANSCENDENT DIMENSION IN PSYCHOTHERAPY

The need for a connection to the transcendent dimension often intensifies in the midst of a life crisis. Religious traditions offer teachings and practices for this purpose, but if such a preexisting framework is lacking, it may be difficult to articulate one's experience of the transcendent level. Often one can only say that it feels like a presence, an inner knowing, an intuition or a feeling, which may satisfy the therapist with a spiritual sensibility but would not be an appealing approach to therapists committed to positivism or strict empiricism. Nevertheless, during the process of psychotherapy, a suffering person who is not committed to any particular religious tradition may raise the issue of his or her relationship to the transpersonal realm.

The person can often sense whether the therapist is willing to consider the spiritual as well as the psychological dimensions of his or her situation. The therapist is faced with the need for the psychotherapeutic dimension of spiritual direction whenever the person asks about the meaning of his or her suffering or questions whether it is random or the result of a larger intelligence. In this situation, if the therapist is not committed to a particular tradition, there is no absolute spiritual authority or sacred text on which he or she can depend. Each human situation demands its own unique resolution, although the sages of the wisdom traditions offer teachings that may be helpful.

In this context, the therapist may be asked about the value of prayer. An important function of prayer is to open oneself to the transcendent realm, but prayer may be impossible for a variety of psychodynamic reasons that can be addressed psychotherapeutically. There may be powerful emotional barriers to love, trust, and gratitude, or there may be excessive hatred within the personality, all of which militate against the possibility of prayer. A dismissive attitude to prayer may correlate with an unresponsive childhood milieu in which asking for help was invariably fruitless. Or, the person may have difficulty expressing feelings in prayer because of shame. A person may tell the therapist that he or she prays for help but is not sure whether there is a response, or whether what seems to be an internal, felt response is coming from the Other or from his or her own mind. An apparent lack of response to prayer may mean that the response does not occur in a form that the person understands or expects. The therapist therefore has to be aware of the possible ways in which the response may occur. In the Jungian tradition, it is axiomatic that a response may occur in the form of dreams, synchronistic events, numinous experiences, and spontaneous waking imagery. Because these do not arise from the ego, they are always surprising.

Unless one takes into account these manifestations of the unconscious, the person may feel that there is no response to his or her prayer, so that a synchronistic event, for instance, may be dismissed as mere coincidence. In fact, a dream may comment on an important life situation, or one may feel a response to a prayer when a crisis situation turns in an unexpected direction. Depending on one's metaphysical commitments, such a turn may be felt to be due to chance, coincidence, the result of the individual's own actions, or the result of synchronicity or divine intervention, and these are not easy to tease apart. In situations of doubt, it is not uncommon for people to use some form of divination—an attempt to discern the divine intention—using oracular methods such as the *I Ching*, tarot cards, or astrology, all of which depend on synchronicity. The therapist may be asked to comment on the result, which is a comfortable question if he or she is at home with these approaches but otherwise requires therapeutic tact. When there seems to be no response to prayer, the most one can do is to hold the question and wait. In this situation it is important to suspend disbelief and skepticism; if one is truly in a relationship with the Other, one accepts that whatever happens *is* the response.

When working with an individual who is suffering intensely, the therapist's spirituality will inevitably come to the fore, whether or not it is articulated. In these situations I have often been asked directly about my own beliefs. Even for analytically oriented practitioners, this is probably not the right occasion to withhold a straightforward answer in favor of exploring the meaning of the question in terms of the transference. To do so would seem evasive, especially if the therapist has something helpful to offer. At the same time, one has to be aware of the effects on the transference-countertransference of a response based on the therapist's own convictions or confession of uncertainty. The person may go along with the therapist's spiritual attitude because of identification with the therapist, or to maintain the relationship, or as part of an idealizing transference. Just as agreement with the therapist may be problematic, the person may disagree as part of a larger pattern of resistance or a negative transference.

Some people are particularly interested in the way in which the therapist copes with his or her personal suffering and the way in which this relates to the therapist's spirituality. This question arises if the person knows that the therapist is going through, or has been through, a difficult personal crisis such as illness or loss. It can be a source of comfort if a person is suffering intensely but senses that the therapist's spirituality was of value when the therapist went through a similar situation. It helps the therapist to be present with the suffering of others if he or she has been through his or her own periods of darkness and can fall back on faith based on personal experience of the sacred. In some mysterious way this faith may be communicated to the person, perhaps nonverbally.

NOTES

1. An excellent historical overview of the practice of spiritual direction is given by Kurtz (1999).

2. In both Judaism and Christianity, it is accepted that the divine may use dreams as a means of communication, since there is ample biblical reference to dreams sent by God. The Talmud makes many references to dreams, and St. John Chrysostom, St. Augustine, and St. Jerome were all influenced by dreams. But later Christians such as Martin Luther saw dreams as the work of the devil; they believed that the Church was the sole interpreter of God's word, so that anything given in a dream must be demonic. The Church's disapproval of dreams seems to have been due to St. Jerome's mistranslation of the Hebrew word for witchcraft, confusing it with the practice of observing dreams. When he translated the Bible into Latin in 382 c.e., he translated the phrase "you shall not practice augury or witchcraft" (Lev. 19:26) as "you shall not practice augury nor observe dreams" (in van de Castle 1994).

3. Discernment arises from the Greek roots *dis/dia,* meaning "apart," and *cernere/krisis,* meaning "to separate."

4. Quantum entanglement refers to the connection between two particles whose quantum states, such as their direction of spin, are linked together. One particle cannot be described without taking into account its counterpart, even though the objects are widely separated in space. This connection leads to nonlocal correlations between them.

CHAPTER 8

The Nondual Perspective in Psychotherapy

The nondual approach to psychotherapy, which is just beginning to appear in our literature (Blackstone 2007; Prendergast and Bradford 2007; Prendergast, Fenner and Krystal 2003), is based on an ancient spiritual philosophy found in Advaita Vedanta, Taoism, Sufism, Buddhism, and some Christian mystics (Loy 1997). The contemporary emergence of the nondual perspective into psychotherapy may be related to the affinity between nondual philosophy and the quantum mechanical view of reality.

In the nondual model of reality the separateness that seems to exist between people is true only at a relative level. At the absolute level, all of us and everything that happens are aspects of an underlying unity.[1] Both participants in psychotherapy are enclosed within a larger, undivided, superordinate field of consciousness. The notion of a field in which the therapeutic couple is deeply connected has become popular among various authors (Smith and Smith 1996; Mansfield and Spiegleman 1996). For Jungian writers, this field is not simply the product of the two people in the room; the consciousness of the transpersonal Self is an overarching presence.[2] Jung's notion of the Self is a psychological way of talking about the Atman-Brahman of the Indian tradition or of nonlocal consciousness, within which there are no boundaries and no separate selves. This approach is broader than the notion that psychotherapy occurs within an intersubjective field produced between two separate individuals.

At the most fundamental level of reality, the nondual model sees no separation between therapist and patient, who are both expressions of a larger totality. Obviously we are separate at the level of the body, the ego, and conventional reality, but the nondual tradition argues that we both participate in an underlying level of transpersonal consciousness, where we are not separate. The therapist and the other person are both expressions of the Self, which is the same in both of them. (This is perhaps one meaning of Jesus' saying, "As you did it to one of the least of these my brethren, you did it to me" [Matt: 25:4].)

At first glance, it seems counterintuitive or slightly absurd to say that at the level of consciousness we are not separate individuals or that there are no others; this sounds like an outrageous claim that belies common sense. I will first describe some of the evidence for this claim, and then indicate the implications of the nondual model for the practice of psychotherapy.

THE EVIDENCE FOR OUR CONNECTEDNESS

SUBTLE SYNCHRONISTIC CONNECTIONS

There is evidence from clinical practice that we are deeply connected. It is an axiom in Jungian circles that the people with whom we work reflect aspects of ourselves and bring material that the therapist also needs to deal with. When the therapist is getting divorced, several people who come for therapy have marital problems, and so on. I believe this phenomenon reflects a deep level of symmetry in nature in which psyche and world—which are not separate—reflect each other. Two examples point out the subtlety of these synchronistic connections within the therapeutic couple, which may take some time to become evident.

In the first example, a woman has been working with me for two years in weekly therapy. We have established a good relationship, and things seem to be going well, but it is clear to both of us that more work needs to be done. Her family discord is increasing, so that her husband and daughter need therapy as well. As a result, finances become strained, and she feels that she can no longer afford to see me regularly. I feel it would be harmful to stop at this point, and very infrequent visits will not be helpful. I offer to see her at a reduced fee. She is taken aback by this offer, and I am surprised at how startled and upset she becomes.

She has always been a giver and a helper, and she is uncomfortable with the idea that anyone might give to her. As a child, her caretakers were insatiably demanding and she was constantly made to work and take care of younger siblings and her mother. If she did not work, she was abused and criticized, so she developed the pathogenic belief that her ticket to being on the planet was purchased by giving to others. Otherwise she feels useless and has no purpose. For me to give to her by lowering my fee puts her in a precarious position. She is afraid that I will be angry and resentful. She is also afraid that the situation would become too intimate, because as long as she is paying me we have a professional relationship, but if I do not charge her a full fee we have a much more personal relationship. Can she really allow herself to believe that I actually care about *her*, rather than the work she does and the money she gives me? If she exposes her need to be valued for her own sake, the risk of being disappointed and abandoned by me is great. She can take refuge in the fact that she is paying for my care, but to experience my care for her own sake is too much, overstimulating. I must have some other agenda. In any case, she feels that she does not deserve my doing something like that for her; she is not worthy enough. In her mind, she must pay in full to earn her way in life.

She dreams there is a crisis, perhaps a war. She needs refuge and she comes to my house for help. I tell her that she can stay. Then we are in bed together. We both wear flannel pajamas, buttoned all the way up. We lie next to each other, rather uncomfortable, careful to maintain a proper distance in the bed, careful to be very proper, anxious to maintain a boundary. There is no sexual feeling. Then we are in the therapy room, and a toddler comes in, about two years old. He has a huge, foot-long penis. He dances happily around the room.

Synchronistically, I have the same problem with receiving as she does. I too was brought up mainly to give to others, and I have always had a difficult time accepting that people would want to give to me. Until I became conscious of this, I felt much more comfortable giving than receiving, so she brings me my own problem. It is not an accident that I work with her; from the nondual perspective, she represents that part of me that prefers to give rather than receive.

The two-year-old dream child suggests the length of the relationship, which has given birth to a creative new potential. Her dream of our being in bed is certainly a transference dream that tells us something about the state of our relationship, but the dream also applies to me. I'm also uncomfortable being too close to that part of me that has trouble being given to by others. That aspect of me has been in a war, and also needs refuge. In other words, her dream is relevant to both of us, which is perhaps why Jung said that we dream of what lies between us.

The second example is another woman, a psychotherapist, who tries to get me to be more active in therapy. She says she wants me to say more, give her more of my opinions, more of what I am thinking about her, and she wants me to make more interpretations. Snared in this challenge to my narcissism, I duly start to make interpretations. In the next several sessions, I suggest that she's worried that I'm hiding the fact that I really don't like her or that I feel critical of her. Or she's worried that I'm not telling her I would like to get rid of her, or I really do know exactly what is going on but I am withholding information to maintain power over her. Or I am maintaining my superiority by being withholding, or I secretly disdain her ignorance and stupidity, and so on. None of these suggestions make any impression on her.

One day she says to me, "I just want you to be more *like* me. I want to know what's going on in you so I can see if it's the same as in me, so that I know that you are *like* me." She wants twinship, a feeling of sameness with me. As a child, she always felt she did not belong in her family, she did not fit in, she was an alien. This is still a pervasive feeling. She wants to know what I'm thinking because she needs to know if I feel the same way she does or if we are actually very different. She wants me to be like her so she can feel more human and not so alone in the world.

I grew up with the same problem; I too always felt as if I did not fit in. I dealt with this problem in a different way, which is partly why I could not initially see what she needed. She had kept alive the hope of being like other people, but as a child I gave up trying to fit in. By eventually becoming an analyst I found a mode of being that allowed me to remain somewhat detached, still an outsider, but at the same time related to others by understanding what they were feeling and thinking while keeping my own thoughts and feelings private. For both of us, understanding others in this way is a way to stay connected and helps us cope with the feeling that we do not belong. That seems to be a safe way to relate to people while remaining apart at the same time. Such meetings of the therapist with people suffering from similar difficulties are related synchronistically; they are linked by a common meaning rather than being causally connected.

THE SPIRITUAL IMPORTANCE OF EMPATHY

As Kohut described it, empathy is the capacity to "think and feel into the inner life of another person" (1984, p. 82). There are various levels at which an empathic connection may occur (Hart 1999). Most superficially, we recognize what the other is experiencing but we remain outside the experience, perhaps because we do not want to be too deeply affected by the other's pain. At a deeper level of empathy, we feel what it is like to be in the other's shoes but we retain our sense of personal identity. Finally, at least for moments in the therapy room, it is possible to enter so deeply into the world of the other person that we experience "becoming the other and forming one merged self" (ibid., p. 119). In a series of books and papers, Mahrer has suggested that we are then beyond empathy in the clinical sense of the word; instead we have actually abolished any subject-object dichotomy (Mahrer, Boulet and Fairweather 1994). At such moments, it is not unusual for one of us to say exactly what the other is thinking and feeling. It is as if the idea or the emotion is in the air, and one of us articulates it, but it does not necessarily originate in either person independently. Rather, it feels as if we are both being affected by an autonomous image or emotion that arises in the field surrounding us, and it is impossible to say where the experience originates. At the unitary level of consciousness, the problems that arise in therapy are individual; they are generally human. At such moments in the therapy room, there is no sense of separateness. It is not simply the case that we put ourself aside for the moment to feel ourselves into the inner life of the other person, nor do we infer our understanding of the other based on our understanding of ourselves. Rather, for the moment there is no longer any division between oneself and the other because we both participate in a shared ground of consciousness, what has been termed a *psychic unity*. Hart (1997) borrows Husserl's term *transcendental empathy* to describe this experience. Sprinkle refers to the psychological merger of the participants as "psychological resonance" (1985, p. 206). Empathy is a state of consciousness in which we are connected to each other within the larger field of the Self. Since we feel fragmented while the Self is a whole, we begin to see why empathy has a helpful effect.

States of profound empathic connection cannot be deliberately induced. They occur spontaneously when an archetypal process—the *coniunctio*, a state of psychological and spiritual union—determines the process of the work. The presence of such union is marked by mutually experienced body sensations, shared imagery and insight, a mutual sense of meaning or knowing, or the experience of love or timelessness during the therapy. Although brief, such experience of being part of a unitary level of consciousness may be closer to the truth of things than our ordinary, ego-bound state of separateness. Nevertheless, therapeutic skill and tact are necessary to work with such situations because a powerful experience of the loss of psychological boundaries has dangers well as therapeutic advantages.

The unitary level seems to be a dimension of reality that we do not access with our usual perceptual apparatus. Even though this level is always present, we may only become aware of it during those moments of intense meeting that have been called present moments, now moments, moments of meeting, or moments of implicit relational knowing, which are all brief experiences of the *coniunctio*.[3] These experiences of profound union in the therapy room can have healing importance. A mutual knowing then occurs that does not involve conscious processes. All therapists (retrospectively) recognize periods in which they are so totally absorbed in the work that the ego is suspended. The therapist is then in a state of nondual awareness, and responses emerge spontaneously as if spoken through the therapist. The therapist becomes distracted from this state when his or her personal material is activated or when he or she becomes anxious or bored. Then the concerns of ego-consciousness obscure the subtle level of consciousness that is present all the time.

Empathic connection with the other person is easy to talk about in terms such as vicarious introspection or projective identification, but it actually reflects a plunge into nonlocality (*vide infra*). The connection at this level occurs at the transcendent or nondual level of reality. We know we are at this level when the other person's words could just as well have come from oneself, as if there were no real difference between us. We let go of all private thoughts and inferences about what is going on, about how to say something and what the person means by something. We let go of all roles and identities, including the wish to help. This attitude requires submission to the situation, but it is not a defensive avoidance of the patient's suffering, and it is by no means the same as indifference, since the therapist remains deeply connected to the suffering person. There is awareness of a transpersonal dimension in the room but no otherworldly avoidance of the human level. There is no technique that allows us to induce this transpersonal level at will; we suddenly find ourselves in it as an act of grace. Because there is no separate sense of self within this field, one can only recognize it retrospectively; it is meaningless to say "you and I are now at that level," since at the level of the totality there is no separate you and I.

The skeptical therapist might attempt to reduce descriptions of states of union to regressive attempts to recapture a lost state of infantile merger with mother or to nothing but projective identification. Projective identification is usually described as a process in which the contents of one mind are projected into another mind. However, if both participate in a shared level of consciousness, there is no separation between the two people, so no projection across a boundary is involved.

THE ORIGIN OF THE SENSE OF SELF

THE QUESTION OF OUR TRUE NATURE

For the spiritually oriented therapist, the nature of the person is a central issue.[4] It makes a difference to the way we practice if we believe that human beings have an essentially spiritual nature and there is a transcendent level of our being that affects our destiny. This is especially true if we also believe that the transcendent level takes an interest in the therapeutic process and even guides it.

In what follows, for the sake of convenience and brevity I use the terms *ego* and *self* as if they were interchangeable, a usage which is not strictly correct. The meaning of the word *ego* depends on the literature one is reading; for Jung it means whatever is conscious, while for Freud the ego is not entirely conscious and is contrasted with id and superego. Because the word *ego* implies drive-defense psychology, which he was trying to avoid, Kohut used the term *self* to mean the person. I use the phrase "sense of self" to imply that the self is a subjective experience rather than an ontological entity.

Because the experience of a separate sense of self seems to deny the reality of a unitary level of connection between people, it is important to understand how the sense of self arises. In this section, I borrow heavily from the sages of the nondual spiritual traditions. These sages tell us that, at the deepest level of reality, which is a unity, there are no others. Yet this seems to be a meaningless claim, given the fact that we experience separateness. Furthermore, narcissistic disorders, which are pathologies of the ego or the personal self, cause tremendous suffering and destructiveness. For these reasons it is important that we understand the nature of the feeling of "me."

The "who am I?" question is an enormous one in the history of both Eastern and Western thought, where the nature of the self has been debated endlessly. Our sense of self is difficult to explore because it seems to be so fundamental. In a typical Western society, we grow up with the sense that we are self-contained individuals, and our consciousness seems to be private and personal. We feel like bounded creatures, contained within a skin, and there seems to be an inner world and an outer world. The body seems to be the container for the personality. The healthy ego can distinguish inner from outer reality and has the ability to differentiate itself from others. Without this ability we would be psychotic and unable to cope with our environment, which is why it is illusory to pretend that the ego is unimportant. The problem is to discover its true functions and its limitations. Our greatest spiritual teachers, such as the Buddha and Christ, could tolerate the enormous suffering they endured only because they had a firm ego.

The development of our sense of self is highly conditioned by a variety of factors. As well as our genetic constitution, in childhood our sense of self is built up by the accretion and internalization of experiences with our early caregivers. Interactions with others become building blocks for the development of personality; the development of self-esteem, for example, is largely dependent on the way in which selfobjects treat the child. Accordingly, the sense of self is largely made up of relationships. The baby is given a name, which becomes an early part of the baby's conscious identity—we gradually feel as though we are that name. The baby is treated as separate from others, and separateness is fostered as the child is told that certain objects are "yours" and others are "mine." In Western cultures, the child begins to use the word *me* or *mine* between eighteen months and three years of age, often as a result of competition for an object with other people. The development of a sense of self is also enhanced by an increasing sense of agency; the child realizes she can make things happen and control objects. The child also compares himself with others in terms of abilities and aptitudes and so develops a sense of uniqueness, the sense that his experiences are different from those of others. As we grow, the sense of who we are is also radically conditioned by our culture, our religious tradition, our mythology, opinions and ideas we are exposed to, likes, dislikes, preferences, relationships, memories, experiences, tribal attitudes, identification with nationality, and so on. Gradually, the child also realizes that he or she belongs within a set of social roles or categories, such as brother or sister, son or daughter, and realizes that he or she has a gender. The influence of gender is a good example of the way in which culture affects our sense of who we are. Feminist writers have pointed out the ways in which the female sense of self has been historically subordinated in our culture, such that the paradigm for self-development in the West has been derived from the experience of white, heterosexual, economically powerful males who did not take into account women's experience.

During development we find ways to sustain our sense of self in the face of environmental demands. We call this process character development, which is about the particular way we adapt, hold ourselves together, preserve self-esteem, and reduce anxiety. To protect and enhance our sense of self we strive for success, knowledge, and status. Because our early environment is never perfect, the self invariably feels incomplete in some ways, so we develop belief systems such as ideologies and religions which buttress the self and help us defend against fragmentation anxiety. A degree of anxiety about survival seems to be an inherent property of the self. The more the self feels vulnerable, the more it becomes defensive and combative. A further source of conditioning lies in the unconscious, which contains some material that is the result of repressed personal experience and some that is archetypal or innate. What we call the personality results from the interaction of all these factors.

Gradually we develop a mental image of who we are and we identify with this image, which seems to be "me." This image is continuous over time because of memory. We see the world from an empirical, consensual point of view, in which other selves seem separate. We have become totally identified with the contents of our minds, or as Krishnamurti puts it, the self is created by thought, or "there is no thinker separate from the thought" where *thought* is a general term that includes emotion and other mental contents (1975, p. 252). Our mental life and much of our behavior arise from this intense conditioning, which becomes a personal story about who we are. It is therefore not true to say that the ego is not real; it is real at its own level, which is the level of mental image. The separate sense of self is also an idea, a belief, a set of memories, and a felt sense; the illusion is to imagine that this is *all* we are. Stated briefly, my personal history tells me who I am based on my biography; it does not tell me my true nature or what I am spiritually. Various Eastern spiritual traditions point out that, as we look beyond our personal history, what we find is that our sense of self is like an onion, layer after layer, with nothing at the center. They point out that to say "I am" is not the same as saying "I am this or that particular person." To see that what we call the self or the "me" is a story, a conditioned image in the mind, helps to reduce our identification with this image, but this is not the kind of image that can be dissolved quickly.

The idea that the sense of self refers to a mental image rather than an independent entity seems odd to us because our political and psychological theories stress the individual, and society seems to be made up of individuals. The nondual traditions counter this notion of separateness by pointing out that there cannot be a "me" without a "you," so that we cannot be independent of each other, just as no one exists independently of the environment. We can no more be separate from the totality than the north and south poles of a magnet could exist independently. The apparent separateness of the body is an illusion, because the body can only be thought of in the context of its world, with which it constantly exchanges material. It takes the whole ocean to produce any given wave, just as it takes the whole universe to produce you or me. In fact, the "me" is just one particular place where the universe is expressing itself. Instead of seeing the skin as a boundary between the world and me, the skin can be seen as the place where they are connected. The fact that the body seems to be a solid entity is the result of the slow speed with which it changes. A whirlpool looks like an entity but is constantly moving; a candle flame is a stream of burning hot gas that only looks like a "thing." Similarly, the body is a process, not an isolated thing. Incidentally, there is no need to be concerned about any loss of individuality. Each snowflake has a different shape, but they are all made of the same material, so one can have differentiation without substantial difference.

In depth psychology, the ego is often treated as if were an entity because of a set of historical circumstances. Descartes began a tradition of thinking of the self as a thinking substance, a kind of nonspatial entity.[5] In Freud's early writing, the term *ego* was roughly synonymous with the (mental) self. In psychoanalytic thought after

1923, the ego was considered to be a set of functions, such as control of body movement, control of instinctual drives, perception, memory, the capacity to delay impulses, thought, defenses against anxiety, and reality testing. The ego was said to have a synthetic function that integrated all these processes. The ego was initially a hypothetical entity that Freud used to explain behavior. Gradually however, rather than remaining a postulate, the ego was assumed to be a causal agent. But we cannot prove the existence of a theoretical entity using the same observations the theory attempts to explain; that would be a circular argument and would assume the existence of what needs to be proved. To use the ego to explain behavior is to confuse postulation with explanation. The notion of ego as an agent is based on the presumption that if thinking is going on, there must be an entity that is thinking; in fact, the ego *is* its thoughts and feelings. Pace Descartes, there is no separate "I" doing the thinking and feeling. Again quoting Krishnamurti, at the level of the ego we *are* our sorrow, our worries, our loneliness, our pain, joy, fear, and pleasure.

To see that at the level of our common humanity there is no separate "me" and "you" requires a depth of feeling and understanding that does not come automatically, and it is of no use as a purely intellectual concept. It requires that we realize that conflict results from separateness, because we have all been conditioned differently and we all have different opinions and wants. When we feel separate we compare ourselves to others, we do not feel safe, and trouble begins (Krishnamurti 1984).

The notion of an insubstantial self is found not just in Eastern philosophy; it is also found in postmodern thinking, which suggests that the sense of self is the result of discourse—a particular version of events (Burr 1995). Or, the sense of self is built of culturally available language and narrative forms; our storytelling ability gives us our sense of identity. We develop these stories to make sense of our experience.

Different cultures construct the self differently, and cultural attitudes to the self vary widely (Burkitt 2008). Some Eastern societies frown on the individualism and self-expression that the West values; these attitudes are seen as uncivilized. Cultures such as Japan prefer the idea that we are interdependent. Similarly the Hindu Self, the Atman, is not the same as the personal self that has desires and thoughts. In traditional Indian culture, the personal self is not as important as it is in the West (Marsella 1989). In the West, we profess belief in independence and autonomy, although in reality our thoughts and behavior are radically affected and often homogenized by advertising, government propaganda, television, and popular mythology.

The ego is essential for material survival, for dealing with the environment, and for technological progress. It is also the basis for all kinds of oppressive ideas, both religious and political. We see the result of an overinvestment in the ego in our constant warfare. Millions of people have died because of the ego's grandiosity, its fears, its insistence on its own God-image, its favorite political system, its need for territory, and so on. In terms of these processes, all egos are alike—they just have different contents. After successful therapy, we end up with the ego or the self in a more comfortable state, but it still suffers, because it remains afraid of loss, deterioration, and pain. That is, the ego's happiness is always transient and subject to sudden change. We try power, drugs, status, and money to shore it up, but the ego is never satisfied for long.

The ego is dependent on the workings of the brain, which is the result of a long period of evolution. Our modern brain is largely the same as the brain of the earliest Homo sapiens, our ancestors who appeared about 100,000 years ago—a short period in our evolutionary history—except for the plastic effects of our culture on brain structure. Since then, our species has developed different skin colors, languages, and local customs, but at a deeper level all human egos have essentially the same problems; we all experience the same feelings of sorrow, confusion, grief, concern with survival, brutality, and violence. We all take the same pleasure in being special, important, and unique. The causes of human suffering and happiness may be different, but our subjective experience of these states is exactly the same. Krishnamurti titled his book *You Are the World* (1973), in which he points out that unless we see this sameness we build barriers around ourselves, whereupon division and conflict start. We build walls around us so that we can feel safe because we are afraid, and our fear is soothed by having power and prestige. There is no other reason to have power over others. Fear of others, which is based on factors such as predator anxiety, is reinforced by our sense of separateness, and this fear in turn produces aggression.[6]

Various depth psychologists have approached the notion that there is a level of reality in which we all participate. All these writers suggest an intrapsychic blurring of the edges between people that may take many forms. Balint is typical of the object relations tradition; he suggests that the therapist should not "insist on maintaining harsh boundaries, but must allow the development of a kind of mix-up between the patient and himself" (1968, p. 145). The concept of the selfobject within contemporary psychoanalytic self psychology comes the nearest to recognizing that without the other there is no me. This is the relevance of the selfobject experience to nonduality; the self is built up of relations with others and sustained by connection to others. Selfobject theory challenges the myth of individualism by insisting that we can never be radically independent of others. However, terms such as "affective attunement" or "mirroring" are abstractions, distant from the heartfelt connection that goes on in the course of psychotherapy.

CONSCIOUSNESS AS THE UNIFYING FACTOR OF HUMAN EXPERIENCE

Nothing is more familiar to us than our consciousness, yet we have no adequate theory of consciousness. Materialistic approaches see consciousness as a secretion of the brain. The alternative view is that consciousness is a superordinate, irreducible principle, the common ocean in which we all swim, the larger mind beyond the personal mind. For this view, the critical point is that consciousness cannot be divided, so that at the deepest level we all participate in the same consciousness.

There are various sources of evidence for this idea. One of them is the type of experience that could not be explained if consciousness were merely the result of brain function. So-called anomalous or nonordinary experiences such as synchronicities, telepathy, precognition, and clairvoyance, suggest that there are deep but invisible connections between people and between human beings and the material world.

THE EVIDENCE FROM QUANTUM PHYSICS

Depth psychology has to take into account that traditional materialism, positivism, mechanism, determinism, and realism have been challenged by advances in quantum physics, which makes many claims that are counterintuitive. Our assumptions about the basic nature of reality are being revised in the light of the new understanding that quantum theory has revealed. For example, to suggest that we are all deeply connected within a unitary field of consciousness is consonant with contemporary ideas that the universe is a unified whole, within which all the parts are connected.

One of the most difficult aspects of quantum theory is the notion of nonlocality, which challenges the commonsense idea that objects are isolated in space. Nonlocality means that objects that appear to be separate are actually connected in ways that transcend time and space. The physicist John Bell showed that a pair of quantum-connected particles that were once in contact remains connected no matter how far apart they are. Bell's theorem shows that individual phenomena seem local, but there is a deep reality beneath the phenomenal surface that is maintained by an invisible quantum connection whose influence is unmediated and immediate. Objects and people are visible manifestations that emerge from a hidden level of quantum reality, the level of the wave function, an underlying field of energy.

It is often argued that the effects of these quantum connections are so small that they can be ignored for practical purposes at the macro level of our reality. Therefore we can make no claims about a person by appealing to quantum-level phenomena. Here we have a dilemma; it may indeed be a mistake to try to ground psychological theory on the evidence from quantum physics, but it also seems a mistake for psychology to ignore what physics tells us about the deep structure of reality. After all, for practical and local purposes we can assume that the earth is flat. Whether that matters or not depends on how far we want to travel.

THE PROBLEM OF THEORY IN PSYCHOTHERAPY

Theory is elaborated by conceptual thought, and as Krishnamurti constantly pointed out, we cannot discover that which is *beyond* thought *using* thought. The problem for our theories of psychotherapy is that there is a transcendent level in us that cannot be put into words or concepts. Our theories will never be able to articulate it fully. Theory in psychotherapy is a mixed blessing; it is important to be rooted in an intellectual discipline, and it helps to have a unifying perspective so that we can teach various skills and know why we are doing what we do. Theory can be of value during periods of confusion. But when theory makes us view the other person through a screen of words and concepts, theory gets in the way of our experience of the spiritual essence of the person. Commitment to a theory may make us too confident that we understand what is going on. Theory then acts to *prevent* change. Anything that is fixed becomes mechanical, and there is a risk that the accumulation of theory and technique that we impose in our training may produce a restricted image of the person or a routine that may prevent the therapist from seeing what is actually happening. That is why Jung pointed out that each patient needs his or her own theory, and it is why Kohut warned that the therapist must resist the temptation to squeeze his or her understanding of the patient into the therapist's theoretical preconceptions (Kohut 1984, p. 67).

At the same time as we recognize its limitations, we have to acknowledge the paradox that theory is gradually helping us understand the empirical personality. Theory helps us articulate in what ways we have been conditioned and how our mind is working. But it is risky for the therapist try to change things in terms of a particular theory of mental health or development. We each have our favorite theory, but each theory is only one perspective on the person. A Freudian will discover the Oedipus complex, a Jungian will discover the archetypal level of the psyche, a Kleinian will discover infantile destructiveness, a psychoanalytic self psychologist will discover the selfobject transference, and so on. The move into any particular theory may be an escape from the overall reality of the person. When we search our memories for what to do, when we try to remember what the books say, we move away from what is before us. When we search our knowledge base to try to understand what is happening during therapy, the mind becomes agitated instead of still, but to have clarity of perception the mind must be still. It would be ideal to see the other without the interference of theory, but during difficult moments in the therapy room we have a tendency to fall back on theory instead of remaining completely involved in the situation.

It is often argued that there is no immaculate perception, and that to see anything at all requires a theory about what is important, about what to listen for. However, we can be in the position of the musician who has so embodied her knowledge that no music theory shows when she plays. Otherwise, to the extent that we deliberately apply theory, we are caught in conceptual thought, and we are not really free to see what is in front of us because we see the person through a preconceived image. This becomes an additional source of distortion beside the countertransference.

Even when images of the person or the person's situation emerge spontaneously from the unconscious, for example, in dreams, an overemphasis on these images prevents our seeing the whole of the person. Images are fragments, or they are like a fine beam of light in a dark room that allows us to see a tiny area very well but tends to ignore the rest of the room. An excessive focus on images fragments the personality. An image is inherently dualistic and divisive because it is so specific that it says "this and not that," so that to see the other by means of an image is not to relate to the totality of the person.

I doubt that advances in psychotherapeutic theory will completely solve this problem. The spiritual reality of a person cannot be organized, classified, or even articulated. Truth is always alive and changing, but theories are inert, they only look at parts of the person and they try to translate the problem into their own terms. That is why the limitations of all new theories of psychotherapy are gradually exposed. Psychotherapy based on theory becomes an ideology, and by their nature ideologies are always divisive. I've had the experience of treating therapists who had different theoretical orientations to my own, and our different expectations caused mutual dissatisfaction. In order to see a person clearly, we need to be inwardly free, and conceptual thought cannot be free because it is always a product of commitments to what is already known.

At the same time, paradoxically, it is also true that without a set of skills we could not practice; there are occasions when there is nothing more practical than a useful theory. In that context, I would like to describe a minimalist approach that includes the theory of nonduality combined with Krishnamurti's emphasis on total attention without judgment, evaluation, or comparison. I believe that Bion (1967) arrived at this point when he recommended that the therapist have no memory, desire, knowledge or understanding, because these try to change reality instead of accepting it. This attitude is predicated on the idea that these factors impair perception; only if I really see the other can I really understand the person, and only real understanding of the other brings about the necessary action and responses. Bion realized that memory is not an accurate record because it is distorted by unconscious forces. Desire, such as desire for the person to change, affects judgment. Memory gives us an impression of what we think has happened, while desire shows us what we would like to have happen; both interfere with our experience of what is actually happening in the moment. This may seem like a council of perfection, since we all have some kind of lens through which we view people, but Bion's point is that what is already known may be either obsolete or false. The important aspect of any session is the unknown. When the therapist compares what he or she hears with his or her yardstick of correctness, he or she is in the past, not with the other in the moment. In Bion's words: "In any session, evolution takes place. Out of the darkness and formlessness something evolves" (1967, p. 18).

To illustrate the importance of accurate perception, Krishnamurti uses the metaphor of what happens when we see a poisonous snake or a child about to step into the path of a car; we do not need to think about what to do. When action arises out of clear perception, there is no choice and no conflict; action and perception arise together.

How then can I look at another person without previous theory, knowledge, and memory interfering? Can the mind of the therapist be free of concepts? We must not *try* to use this approach; if we make an effort, we reinforce the ego, and distortion tends to happen whenever the ego gets involved. What is needed is full attention but no effort; this is a matter of allowing rather than doing. Full attention requires what Krishnamurti (2001) calls choiceless awareness, which is awareness with no preferences. Choiceless awareness allows the freedom to see the reality of what is present. Total attention uses the whole mind and body, one's whole being, without any motive and without resisting or preferring, without listening for anything in particular. When we fully attend, there is no "me." Then there is a larger consciousness operating, and real compassion can arise.

The necessary discipline is to experience the other without words or concepts, as we do when we look in silence, when we communicate nonverbally, and we understand with heart, body, and soul. For this to happen, we must see the person not as someone liked or disliked, but as the person is. For example, if I see hatred and immediately condemn it, my judgment prevents clear perception, without which there is no real understanding. Open awareness has no opinion; it listens out of silence, not out of thought.

To perceive the person clearly and to be totally involved in the situation can be more helpful than analysis based on theory. In most psychotherapy sessions we move between theory and total involvement. As soon as I say to myself "this is a transference reaction," my perception is conditioned by theory and I do not see the immediacy of the person. Without any such cognitive interference, the space between us disappears, or at least I am not conscious of it. There is no observer and observed, and we have the same hopes and fears, anger, pain, ambition, envy, and so on. When I move out of this state to think about the person, so that there is an observer and an observed, I am not totally involved. If I then move back into total attention, that space disappears and perception goes on that is not affected by the ego. It is important to pay attention with no particular expectation, in which case one may spontaneously experience an energetic sense of this contact, a bodily sense of the presence of the other person (Schwartz-Salant 1988; Reed 1996). Sometimes this takes the form of an embodied countertransference, the arousal of particular bodily sensations in the therapist (Field 1989). For example, during a session with a regressed woman, a therapist reports the sensation of "letting down" in her breasts, as if she was lactating. Of course, one can understand this kind of experience as the result of projective identification. However, this phrase tends to imply a defensive operation or a subtle communication between two separate participants. From another viewpoint, such deeply empathic phenomena actually reflect mutual participation on a nondual level of consciousness in which mothering is going on at an archetypal and personal level.

At such a level, I see something about the other that cannot be put into words but is so vital, so true, that I feel it strongly. This does not happen if I am caught in theory; if I'm working from theory, I know what *should be* rather than what actually is. This is a danger of analysis in its traditional sense; at the moment that I analyze another, a space opens between us, and authentic contact and relationship are inhibited. Analysis is the response of the past, of my knowledge and my accumulated learning and experience, all of which affect my response to what is in front of me. Consequently the notion of listening perspectives can be problematic; a perspective only allows us to listen to a part of the person rather than the whole person—one listens *for* something rather than simply listening *to* the person. I can then only discover what my perspective tells me is there, and psychotherapy is not a search for what is already known, but for what we do not know. All theories are partial, but people are complex and whole. Any psychological problem is a function of the whole person.

There is no point in asking what to do during the therapy if theoretical ideas come into one's mind. That would involve the search for another theory, another formula and another authority, which will perpetuate the problem. There is no "how to" for avoiding the interference of theory; at best we can be aware of the problem and notice it happening. Trying to stop thinking about theory is like trying not to think of pink elephants and leads to an internal struggle. When we see that we have drifted into theory, thinking stops naturally and the mind becomes quiet as we watch it. If we do anything other than be aware that conceptual thought is going on, we confuse the picture again. It is important to have no particular motive when we pay attention in this way, because motives are a part of self-centeredness. We simply realize that if we start thinking theoretically about the other, our thoughts open up a psychological gap between us. Only with bare awareness will our minds become quiet again. So it is important not to react *against* our conditioning and theories; that would just produce more conflict. Similarly, one has to be careful not to think "if I do this, I'll be a better therapist."

The therapist cannot be compassionate if he or she is ambitious, envious, greedy, competitive, inflated, afraid, or seeking personal power. Yet most of us suffer from some combination of these qualities. When they arise in the therapy room we want to distance ourselves from them and let them belong to the other person. Similarly it is difficult to be with the other's fear and despair, because somewhere these are also our own. When these feelings arise, we may be able to interpret them in the traditional way, or we may only be able to sustain a receptive silence, without judgment or comment. This kind of silence in the therapy room invokes a special quality of space in which there is no you and me, no division. Into that space may come that which is beyond thought. If we are truly open, a process may happen that Krishnamurti (1991) calls "insight into what-is." Here the word *insight* is not used in the traditional psychoanalytic sense, where it means understanding one's own dynamics. Insight in Krishnamurti's sense means a totally new perception of the way things actually are, not based on previous knowledge. This insight brings an instantaneous grasp and inward awareness that involves the whole body and mind. The presence of theory in the therapist's mind prevents the arising of this kind of insight because the mind can then only see what it already knows is there.

SURRENDER TO WHAT-IS: A NONDUAL APPROACH TO SUFFERING IN PSYCHOTHERAPY

All psychotherapists work with people who face painful situations such as chronic illness, losses, and other situations that cannot be changed. Especially at these times, the therapist cannot call on any theory; he or she faces the patient only with his or her humanity and personal worldview. The nondual perspective leads to a particular attitude to these life situations. This strategy is useful in the therapist's own life and also assists with his or her ability to sit with the suffering of others. Needless to say, this attitude does not need to be articulated in the therapy room.

The underlying assumption of the nondual approach is that the universe is in perfect order, and whatever is happening is part of the larger order and so must be the way it is, even though we do not like or understand a particular situation. The nondual approach to suffering therefore suggests surrendering to what-is, or what is traditionally called letting go. This means radical acceptance of whatever is the present reality. Radical acceptance does not imply passivity, inaction, grudging tolerance, submission, or resignation in which one simply feels like a helpless victim. Acceptance means that one sees the futility of trying to escape the situation and one embraces it, recognizing that a transcendent dimension is at work. One's suffering is not random; it is part of a larger process. Any necessary action arises out of this attitude rather than out of the rejection of what-is. Far from being passive, the act of surrender may actually improve one's ability to cope with a situation and allows a broader perspective to emerge. Having done whatever can be done, radical acceptance then allows the situation to unfold, realizing that the ego is not in control. Acceptance is therefore not heroic and is not a question of mastery. By contrast, if we act out of resistance to what-is, we may produce more difficulties. To the extent that we respond to suffering out of anger or fear, we are in danger of causing more suffering, whereas action that arises out of acceptance reduces friction and allows us to be peaceful internally, as if in the eye of the storm. Needless to say, as is true for all spiritual practices, it is possible to use the notion of surrender defensively, as a way of avoiding necessary action or of failing to take responsibility when it would be appropriate to do so. It is also important for the therapist to distinguish the process of transformative surrender from masochism. This produces unconsciously self-inflicted suffering such as a chain of financial losses, bad relationships, and recurrent accidents.[7]

Although the therapist might feel that a particular problem requires surrender, this is not something that the ego can decide to do even if we agree with the idea. For the ego to work at surrender would reinforce the ego itself, and at most it would lead to submission. Understanding the necessity for surrender may facilitate it, but authentic letting go can only happen spontaneously as an act of grace. To recognize this is itself a form of acceptance. Furthermore, one cannot radically accept a situation in order to change it—that would be self-contradictory, a form of trying to reestablish control. For example, after years of physical impairment, distress, and depression, a woman in chronic pain finds that she spontaneously lets go of wanting to get better, whereupon her distress diminishes even though her pain is the same. There is no conscious reason for this; it happens of its own accord, not out of egoic effort.

Surrender is particularly difficult for people who are fearful because they grew up in dangerous families, since these individuals often need to control their environment to feel safe—they lack basic trust. Surrender is also difficult or impossible for people who cannot tolerate painful affective states. Without preliminary psychotherapeutic work that strengthens affect tolerance, a nondual attitude would be built on sand, because transformative surrender would cause too much fragmentation anxiety. However, once affect tolerance has developed so that fragmentation is less likely, the nondual approach becomes a therapeutic possibility. It is sometimes said about such surrender that one can only give what one has, so that if the personality or the ego is fragile or undeveloped, it can never really surrender (Hidas 1981). However, I find that this is not necessarily true; one can give whatever one has to give of oneself. Many emotionally disturbed people have a profound spirituality and great faith.

I should acknowledge that the very idea of surrender is antithetical to our cultural attitude of autonomous self-determination and self-promotion. We pay lip service to the value of humility, but it is not widely encouraged. We are also taught that effort is required for success. However, for the nondual approach, in order to surrender, effort is counterproductive. To surrender, one does not *do* anything; one is receptive and allowing. One cannot master the practice of surrender, because the ego cannot let go of itself. Rather, surrender happens spontaneously as one understands the situation one is in. In any case, for a nondual approach, the separate self is illusory. Suffering therefore does not "belong" to anyone in particular—it is simply happening and does not need to be viewed as bad or as "mine" (Parsons 2002). This realization is said to be the ultimate medicine for suffering, but it is obviously out of reach of the majority of us.

Part of the value of therapeutic work on the empirical personality is that, by looking at the structures of the personality, by seeing how they developed, we become better able to let go of identification with our story. We see that prominent personality traits, such as an intense need for success and recognition, are often an attempt to connect with, mimic, or compensate for the qualities that were lost to us in development because of selfobject failure. It is not helpful to reject these aspects of our personality, since such judgment produces an internal conflict between parts of the self that disapprove of other parts of the self. It is helpful to understand that our story unfolded the way it did of necessity, but the empirical personality is not our essential nature.

Because it is difficult to tolerate another person's suffering, the therapist may want to see a particular outcome of the therapy or to relieve a particular problem. We may also need to be effective as a way of supporting our own self-esteem, and we enjoy legitimate gratification when we are helpful. However, the therapist's needs may interfere with a nondual approach to psychotherapy. For the therapist, surrender means that, having done as much as we can, we let go of any narcissistic investment in the outcome of the therapy. We do not determine the outcome of the work. The therapist wants the best for the person and would like to help, but these are ego concerns, and the therapist cannot know what is right for the person's soul. We do not know the telos of the individual personality. Therefore, from the viewpoint of the soul, the idea of a "treatment plan" derived from the ego is inflated if not absurd, not to mention the fact that it means that the person has to submit to the therapist's agenda, which may repeat a childhood situation of submission to a parent's agenda.

There are other spiritual paths that lead to a radical acceptance of suffering. People who are temperamentally devotional types, on a path of love and worship of the divine, may accept suffering as a necessary "invitation" from the divine.[8] The end result of this path may be the same as the nondual approach, because if we completely surrender to the divine, there is no one to surrender any more, just a total merger. In the words of Kabir, "the lane of love is too narrow; it cannot accommodate two." That is, the paths of nonduality, wisdom, and discrimination and the path of love are ultimately not different.

Writing about her experience of the unitary nature of reality, Bernadette Roberts says: "For me, this disclosure occurred in the simple empirical gesture of a smile whereby *the smile itself, that which smiled, and that at which it smiled were known as identical.* In the immediacy of this way of knowing, the three aspects of the One were clear" (1984, p. 152).

NOTES

1. For many mystics, not only is reality undivided, there is no essential division between the divine and the world. However, although mystics from different traditions tend to understand each other on many issues, they may differ in their perspective on this question, and the therapist may be more attracted to one or another of these views. Some mystics, particularly in the Judeo-Christian tradition, think of the divine as distinct from the universe itself. For them, the divine is truly Other, transcendent, communicating with the world by means of revelation but still outside it, although paradoxically also immanent within the world. One may experience union with it, but not absolute unity. Some mystics are relative dualists, believing that although there is an essential difference between the world and the divine, there is a mutual participation between them. In the doctrine of panentheism, the divine is wholly immanent as a presence in all beings, but beings are not the divine itself.

2. Jungians generally speak of the ego-Self axis, meaning that the ego is in relation to the transpersonal Self. However, in several places Jung also spoke of the Self as the totality of consciousness, in which case what we call ego can only be a part of the Self. There cannot be interaction between them if they are not different; there is only apparent interaction at the level of the ego. In the esoteric traditions it is postulated that the totality may have different levels, such as subtle, causal, and psychic levels, of which the latter interacts with the ego. But for psychological and especially for therapeutic purposes this is speculative metaphysics, of no value unless these levels are experienced.

3. In *The Present Moment in Psychotherapy and Everyday Life* (2004), Stern describes moments of deeply shared connection and intimacy in the consulting room between analyst and patient. Most personalistic authors do not consider the transpersonal level of these interactions.

4. The literature in this area is abundant; see, for instance, Levin (1992) or Glover (1988).

5. The origin of our mythology of individualism antedates Descartes. It may have begun as a reaction against the feudal system, in which there was a rigid hierarchy and one could not escape one's social position because it was said to be fixed at birth. Similarly, the advent of Protestantism allowed an individual relation to God that did not require Church mediation. In these ways the notion of individuality was fostered, and with it the idea of legal and political rights.

6. For millennia, our hominid ancestors were the prey of wild animals. Predator anxiety evolved to keep us safe but is now one of the sources of mistrust of strangers and of paranoid fears.

7. Freud coined the term *moral masochism* to describe the idea of allowing suffering for the sake of what seems to be a greater good. The term *masochism* in this psychodynamic sense is not an accusation that the individual enjoys pain, and it is not a way of blaming the victim as if he or she gets perverted pleasure out of the abuse. A battered wife does not like to be beaten. She stays in the marriage because in her mind there is a greater good involved; it seems that tolerating abuse will accomplish some other purpose that justifies the suffering, such as not being abandoned or keeping the family together. It may be that, from an outsider's point of view, her staying in the marriage is more destructive and dangerous than leaving would be, but she feels that her well-being is contingent on her putting up with abuse. Or, she has been trained from childhood to believe that abuse is the price she has to pay for a relationship. This pattern happens in families when children learn that the best or the only way to get attention is to get into trouble or to be in pain.

8. A good example is the poem titled "A Divine Invitation" by Hafiz (quote in Ladinsky 1996):

> You have been invited to
> meet
> The Friend.
> No one can resist a Divine
> Invitation.
> That narrows down all our
> choices
> To just two:
> We can come to God
> Dressed for Dancing,
> Or
> Be carried on a stretcher
> To God's Ward.

CHAPTER 9

Suffering and the Discovery of Meaning in Psychotherapy

MEANING AND SUFFERING

An important component of psychotherapy involves helping people deal with suffering. To this end, I would like to discuss the value of discovering meaning within suffering, a process which may be important to individuals with a spiritual sensibility. There is something uncomfortable about talking about the meaning of suffering, because when one is suffering intensely it may feel as if nothing helps, least of all a wordy approach. Nevertheless, it is useful to have a framework that allows us to be with suffering with a degree of equanimity, whether the suffering is our own or that of the people with whom we work.

It is important to acknowledge that there is a difference between the nondual approach to suffering discussed in chapter 8 and a search for the meaning of suffering. Nondual philosophy would not encourage this search, on the grounds that the spiritual essence of the person does not suffer; that transcendent level of the person is totally unconditioned and so no story can apply to it. Being, including suffering, can be experienced as it is, with no need for commentary. From this nondual point of view, the meaning that we derive from suffering is a purely mind-created set of concepts, a story among many other stories that has no absolute reality or intrinsic meaning. The search for meaning can become a way of avoiding the reality of an experience, or the story we develop can further condition the mind or keep us attached to our suffering. However, the experience of most people in psychotherapy is that they are far removed from realizing the unconditioned level of consciousness or formless awareness that is their true nature. They cannot benefit from a nondual approach which asks the traditional question "who is suffering?" in order to begin a process of inquiry into the nature of the self. This approach suggests that the person become one with the suffering without getting involved in thoughts about why it is happening. This attitude is often impractical and unhelpful because the person's suffering is too intense. One cannot abide in unconditioned awareness when one is in great pain. In these situations, the discovery of new and liberating meaning is helpful in freeing the person from stories that have caused pain.

Suffering is one of the great challenges to any type of spirituality. Suffering forces us to discover our real spirituality rather than accept what we have been told. If the therapist is working with an individual who is committed to a particular religious tradition, when that tradition's explanation for suffering is satisfying, the therapist need only acknowledge this, should the subject arise. The focus of the work is then on the process of psychotherapy in the usual sense, and the person's religious beliefs provide a helpful background. However, for people who do not find traditional explanations of suffering to be helpful, something else is needed. Many people feel there is simply too much suffering in the world, of too much intensity, to believe in the adequacy of traditional theological explanations for suffering. A traditional response is unhelpful when the sufferer feels that he or she is being offered platitudes or when traditional religious wisdom does not deal with the specificity of the situation. The traditional explanations may fail when the sufferer, like the biblical Job, feels that his or her suffering is disproportionate.

When we suffer, it may be hard to maintain the sense that we live in relation to a spiritual reality or that life has any meaning, let alone a transcendent background. Suffering produces a spiritual crisis that may shatter faith in the notion of a benevolent, protective God, because it is hard to believe that such a God would allow the terrible things that happen. Suffering may therefore lead to a rejection of the standard images of God found within the monotheistic traditions. In such a case, the therapeutic couple must discover an alternative frame of reference from which to view the person's suffering. When this is successful we understand why it is said that religion is for people who fear going to hell, but spirituality is for people who have been there.

It is helpful if the individual finds a personal approach to the suffering of the moment, but in the long run, suffering cannot be dealt with by explaining each of its individual instances, because even as one problem is solved, another sooner or later arises. We have to deal with the larger issue of suffering itself. Is there an attitude toward suffering that will be useful regardless of the type of suffering? Or do we need a different approach to physical as distinct from psychological suffering—the pain of bodily illness rather than problems such as loneliness, loss, and despair? Is there a way to prevent suffering from corrupting us, so that we do not allow it to make us bitter and angry? Can this be done without turning to palliatives such as belief in an afterlife in which all will be well? What do we do when all our distractions and attempts to avoid suffering eventually fail us? When we realize there is no escape by trying to deny suffering, rationalize it, or merely becoming resigned to it—then what? During any serious illness we tend to ask: Why is this happening to me? When this question arises during psychotherapy, we are concerned to arrive at a response that is in keeping with the character structure of the individual. To do so requires attention to the specificity of the situation without applying preconceived ideas. Sometimes we can discern a symbolic meaning to the suffering, while other times the suffering seems meaningless and only the therapeutic relationship sustains the person.

If a suffering person in psychotherapy has lost faith in traditional religion, a series of questions may arise. Is there any spiritual background or meaning to the universe, or is the cosmos merely the result of a series of impersonal events determined by the laws of physics? Is there objective meaning to our lives, given to us by a spiritual source, or is our sense that a painful experience is meaningful just wishful thinking, a defensive illusion, or at best only subjectively true? Is life just a "tale told by an idiot," because the events of our lives simply happen by chance?

The question of whether life is intrinsically meaningful or whether we invent meaning is controversial but is not uncommonly asked in the therapy room. As Frankl put it, we are "meaning-seeking" creatures (1975, p. 112). For the therapist, there are a variety of ways to help a person find the larger meaning of a painful situation. We may discover its connection with other aspects of the person's life, so that he or she can discern a recognizable pattern. The person may realize how childhood events and relationships have contributed to the present situation. The person's suffering may seem to be purposeful because it moves the person in a particular direction that he or she would not otherwise take. Or the situation allows the person to discover a personal goal that makes him or her feel there is something worth doing in life. However we arrive at it, we are looking for meaning which produces a state of mind in which one feels emotionally satisfied or deeply moved, so that one is able to affirm life in spite of its difficulties. The discovery of meaning allows us to feel related to life as a whole rather than being an isolated entity. We may be able to see our suffering in a larger context, so that we understand it as somehow necessary to our lives. This kind of meaning allows a subjective sense of significance and value. A meaningful life allows us to feel that we have some work or vocation that is important, some person who matters to us, some reason for being here beyond living a banal, day-to-day existence.

An issue that arises here is whether the meaning agreed upon by the therapeutic couple is truly arrived at by a process of mutual explanation, so that an authentic aspect of the person's destiny is revealed, or whether meaning is simply constructed by explaining an experience in terms of the therapist's theoretical orientation. Ideally of course a theoretical explanation accurately mirrors the person's reality, but there are so many theoretical approaches that we cannot be sure this is the case. By insisting on a particular model of therapy, therapists may inadvertently contribute to the meaning they think they are discovering, just as a theologian may explain the meaning of suffering in terms of preconceived theological assumptions such as the notion that suffering is a punishment for sin.

In spite of this potential pitfall, it is the thrust of this book that for many people psychotherapy fills a cultural void that used to be occupied by religion, because today people go to therapists for reasons such as a life crisis or malaise that traditionally would have sent them to visit priests. The meaning that arises within psychotherapy illustrates the fact that our spirituality does not need to depend on a traditional institution. A sense of meaning in life can arise from working with one's own psychology, as an individual experience of the sacred, or by means of new approaches such as 12-step programs in the treatment of addiction. Rather than being seen as meaningless, a problem such as addiction can be seen to have spiritual dimensions as well as being seen as a disorder. Jung pointed out that alcoholism could be thought of as a spiritual problem if the craving for alcohol was thought of as a "low level" form of spiritual thirst (1973–1975, p. 624). Grof (1993) has further developed the notion of addiction as a spiritual crisis. At one level, addiction to alcohol or narcotics can be seen to be a way of coping with intolerable emotional pain; at another, it can be seen as a primitive way of dissolving the ego and merging with the totality or as a search for ecstatic union with the divine. Realizing this gives another level of meaning to the treatment of addiction.

A painful sense of meaninglessness or alienation may or may not be helped by a particular religious tradition. Traditions typically provide spiritual teachings that are collectively meaningful, but even when one subscribes to such doctrines one may also have to find additional, personal meaning in life. Frankl calls this the right or true meaning for the individual's life, which he believes is "something found," something "discovered rather than invented," something that cannot be given by a therapist (1988, p. 62). Of course it is difficult to know whether one has found the authentic meaning of one's life, meaning that is given by a larger wisdom or by life itself, or whether one is merely projecting a personal fantasy of transcendent meaning onto one's situation. But the notion that meaning is discovered rather than invented is consonant with Jung's notion that the personality has its own telos, or goal, toward which life events move us. It also fits with Jung's suggestion that dreams and synchronistic experiences have their own intrinsic or a priori meaning, existing outside of the person (1952b, par. 942). It is not necessary to be in therapy to find such meaning; many people find it in their work, in religion, in relationships, creative pursuits, and the like. Others try to deal with the sense that their lives are meaningless by filling their time with desperate activity. The entertainment industry provides endless distractions from uncomfortable feelings of emptiness.

A persistent sense of meaninglessness is often associated with a disorder of the self, a chronic dysthymia or an empty depression (Tolpin and Tolpin 1996). According to Jung (1952b), such a sense of meaninglessness is a form of "spiritual stagnation," and the task of the therapist is to help the person find what Jung (1932) called the "meaning that quickens," an *individual* sense of meaning. As he put it: "Meaninglessness inhibits fullness of life and is therefore equivalent to illness. Meaning makes a great many things endurable—perhaps everything" (1961, p. 340). If one can find a spiritual home in one of the established religious traditions, meaning is a priori, a certainty, because each tradition claims to have absolute truth. However, many people today are unable to believe these large-scale truth claims and prefer to find a more personal meaning. Even in the absence of overt suffering, unless some kind of meaning in life is found, one lives in a spiritual vacuum.

It requires a high level of spiritual attainment and trust in the sacred dimension to let go of the need for meaning and stop asking "why" questions when one suffers. For many of us, the need for meaning becomes acute in the presence of a life crisis. Problems such as chronic pain, anxiety, or depression impair the quality of life and seem completely meaningless. The depth psychological tradition suggests that we can discover the meaning of these symptoms by studying the manifestations of the unconscious such as dreams, visions, synchronistic events, and the transference. So while it is true that people come to therapy to get rid of these symptoms, as though they were foreign bodies in the personality, they can also be seen as signals that something needs attention. There is a deeper level to the suffering than the overt symptom. We might find, for instance, that in midlife we have unconsciously identified with collective aims and values and we are now forced by our depression to discover more personal values. We might find that our relationships are dry, our career feels empty, or that a long-cherished life goal seems to be slipping away. In these situations, our suffering, according to Jung, is produced by the Self, which is a source of superior wisdom and knowledge. Suffering may therefore point forward; it has a meaning in terms of the development and fulfillment of the personality. It is no accident that the journey of mythic heroes often begins with a period of intense suffering which triggers the hero's journey of discovery to break through personal limitations (Campbell 1968). It is as though our life has been going in the wrong direction, or our consciousness has become too narrow, so that the Self produces symptoms because a course correction is necessary. Suffering forces us to open up to the unconscious and its intentions for us. Paradoxically, therefore, the source of the problem and the healing potential of the problem both lie in the unconscious.

To wonder about the meaning and purpose of suffering is a typical human response to it. Some stoic souls with an existentialist bent simply accept their suffering philosophically, as part of the difficult side of life.[1] Yet this is not just a philosophical debate; there is empirical evidence that for people suffering from serious illness, the discovery of meaning and enthusiasm for life benefits healing, while persistent despair adversely affects the prognosis.[2] Prolonged states of demoralization or other negative emotional states such as helplessness and resentment have been shown to activate the recurrence of illness. Conversely, states of hope, purpose, gratitude, and joy seem to protect against the recurrence of many illnesses, presumably because of their positive effects on the immune system.

We are impressed with the testimony of those who have suffered and discovered some meaning within their suffering. In *Man's Search for Meaning*, Frankl insists that, no matter how little control we have in a terrible situation, we do have some choice about how we will respond. In Nazi concentration camps, there was no freedom and the prisoners had no control over their lives. People were treated abominably. Yet, according to Frankl, choices were made: some people gave up, and some behaved badly toward other prisoners, but others shared what they could or sacrificed their own lives for the sake of others.[3] Some even managed a sense of humor. Frankl decided that the search for meaning was so important that the will to live depends on it. He even suggested that in some way "suffering ceases to be suffering at the moment it finds a meaning," because meaning has a therapeutic effect (2006, p. 135). He believed that we have a "will to meaning" that makes us constantly search for it, and the extent to which we find life meaningful is a reliable indicator of mental health.[4]

For Jung, too, "meaninglessness inhibits the fullness of life and is therefore equivalent to illness" (Jung 1961, p. 340). He found that about a third of the people who consulted him for psychotherapy were not suffering from a clinically definable disorder. Their main problem was that their lives felt meaningless or aimless. These individuals were often able and courageous, but they suffered from "the general neurosis of our time," a sense of futility, the lack of a spiritual connection, and the lack of a believable myth, a story by which one can live (ibid.). Many people are in such a state today. Some are unhappy because they feel that life is meaningless, while others become depressed for other reasons and are unable to discover meaning within their depression. Unfortunately, our culture does not allow us to view depression as a potentially productive reaction to a life crisis that points to the need for introspection, time away from one's routine, and a reevaluation of one's situation. Instead, depression has been turned into a medical problem for which antidepressants are the main line of treatment. It would be preferable to use antidepressants as adjunctive, to relieve unnecessary suffering at the same time as one is trying to understand the meaning of the depression. Used on their own, antidepressants allow the person to adapt to a situation that may be wrong for him or her, without changing anything.

Many people who seem to be well adjusted and successful in their lives reach a point where they begin to ask "is this all there is?" They wonder if their success really means anything. Jung felt that people arrive at this point because they have looked for meaning in the wrong way, or they have contented themselves with the wrong answers to life's questions. They seek status, money, and outward success, but they remain unhappy even when all that is attained because they are "confined within too narrow a spiritual horizon" (Jung 1961, p. 140). If they were to develop into "more spacious personalities," their difficulty would disappear (ibid.). For Jung, in accord with Frankl, "meaning makes a great many things endurable—perhaps everything" (ibid., p. 340). So important is this process that Jung believed that his patients in the second half of life could not be helped unless they found a religious outlook. By this he did not mean belief in a specific creed or faith tradition, but rather the discovery of a personal myth of meaning that may arise out of direct numinous experience and a connection to the Self. This kind of meaning allows a new perspective. According to Jaffé (1983), Jung elevated the importance of meaning to mythic status, suggesting that humanity's metaphysical task, which makes our lives meaningful, is the continuous expansion of consciousness. This answer satisfied him, but it is only one example; each of us needs our own approach.

The question of whether life is random or meaningful is especially difficult for people for whom collective religion has lost its power. In the West, institutional Christianity and Judaism used to provide belief systems that address all of life's problems, but this is no longer the case. Many of us must search for meaning individually. We no longer live in the paradise of a priori certainties, so the search for meaning often involves a crisis of faith. For some people this is too difficult and they become fundamentalists, clutching to a preformed set of answers to life's difficulties. However, some fundamentalist attitudes make things worse by virtue of the meaning they attribute to suffering. For example, one fundamentalist Christian critique of psychotherapy refers to psychology as "ungodly" (Bobgan and Bobgan 1987, p. 6). (This is especially ironic; since the psyche is a vehicle to experience the numinosum, to study the psyche can be a way to study a mode in which the divine presents itself.) These authors suggest that suffering is due to our separation from God because of our sinful condition and because of the presence of sin in the world after the fall of Adam (ibid., p. 207). For these writers, Jesus is the only way to reestablish a relationship with God. There is only one path to redemption and psychotherapy is potentially destructive, because the "gate of salvation" (a quote from Matt. 7:13–14) is narrow (ibid., p. 225). This attitude may cause considerable guilt which must be alleviated by belief in the traditional teaching, in which case the tradition produces the disease for which it alone has the cure. To be told that suffering is the result of sin may lead to the sense that the sufferer has been abandoned by God or that he or she is being punished for sin, which adds to the individual's burden. Overall, to suggest that one particular spiritual tradition is the exclusively correct approach to suffering simply flies in the face of the evidence. Such traditional attitudes are based on preexisting concepts about the relationship of the human and the divine, but we cannot free ourselves of suffering by riding on the back of doctrines; we have to stay with the suffering, attend to it, and see what emerges from it.

If the traditional responses fail us when we suffer, we may find authentic personal meaning in the situation as a result of a numinous experience, which is self-authenticating and needs no validation by a spiritual authority. Autonomous meaning of this type can arise in various ways. One source arises through a dream such as the following, which occurred to a psychotherapist who was going through a distressing period during which he wondered if his work was effective and he feared he was wasting his life.

> There has been a large-scale catastrophe, perhaps an earthquake or war. Many wounded people are lying on cots in a huge building that is being used as a makeshift hospital. An unknown woman is leading me around. She directs me to simply be with and touch various wounded people. I am surprised to find that this helps them.

This dream produced a radical change of attitude; it was obvious that he could be helpful without doing anything particularly complicated. In the dream, none of his technical knowledge is required. He allows himself to be led by a soul figure, and he helps with simple contact and witness.

Visionary encounters are also helpful. A woman dying of cancer had spent the last year of her life trying to understand her childhood, especially the bitter conflict between her parents that had cast a dark shadow on her family. Even though she was at the end of her life, it felt important for her to try finally to gain some perspective on this problem. Shortly before she died, she woke one morning with the strong sense that her long-dead parents were standing by her bed, although she could not see them physically. To her surprise and relief, they seemed to be together in a peaceful way. A small golden bowl then appeared on her bed. The bowl was full of oil, and golden sparks seem to be emanating from it. Her parents communicated to her this message: "You are to use this to bless others." The oil seemed to be sacred and healing, and she associated it with the biblical tradition of anointing with oil.[5] Meaning is given with such numinous experience because of its emotional power, especially when it reverberates with a theme that has played an important part in a person's life.

The discovery of authentic meaning helps to strengthen one's sense of self. However there are defensive responses to suffering which avoid the real issue. The therapist must be careful about solutions that masquerade as "transcending" the situation or as "going beyond" one's suffering, when in fact they simply deny its gravity. Real transcendence means that we have fully experienced the situation and digested it as much as possible. We have developed a mature attitude to the suffering and perhaps we have sensed its deeper meaning. Only then can we be said to have truly left it behind.

The therapist will be able to discern whether an attitude to suffering is defensive or authentic by its effects. An attitude that helps one deal realistically with suffering produces benefits such as a new sense of direction in life, a reorientation of values, deeper self-awareness, and more compassion for others. These beneficial effects may not happen if we attribute masochistic meaning to suffering, such as "I can only be connected to God if I suffer," or if we develop a delusional meaning such as "I am the new suffering servant of God." These kinds of quasi-solutions to suffering leave the personality brittle because they merely paper over the cracks. Neurotic solutions are attempts to shore up a fragile sense of self, while delusional solutions are attempts to make sense of unbearable pain and chaos. These attempts avoid dealing with the problem at the same time as they keep the personality mired in it.

The meaning that we discover cannot always be generalized to others; it may be purely personal, or it may be based on traditional ideas such as karma and reincarnation, or notions that the world is a school for the development of the soul.[6] Like any traditional idea, the doctrine of karma can be used defensively, for example, to support a masochistic character style. Ideally, the idea of karma is not used to avoid responsibility or in the service of denial, inaction, indifference to others, or selfishness. These reservations aside, this concept may help us deal with a difficult situation with some equanimity. For example, one traditional attitude to painful karma is that the ego is playing a role in a drama and must play its part, while the true Self is unaffected by suffering. The idea of karma is typical of those mythic notions that satisfy our spiritual curiosity but leave open the question of their literal truth, since they cannot be conclusively proved or disproved. It is important to be sure that when a suffering individual espouses it, such a concept resonates deeply at a feeling or intuitive level rather than as a rationalization. The discovery of such authentic meaning produces emotional resonance within the therapist, while attitudes to suffering that are purely intellectual have no emotional depth to them. Then, appeals to karma or the will of God simply disguise resignation and frustration. Even though the therapist can empathically sense the difference between a defensive and an authentic response to suffering, it may be necessary to collude with a defensive solution if there is little hope that the problem can be dealt with in any other way.

The presence of a helpful connection to another person can make a decisive difference in determining whether suffering is eventually beneficial or harmful. Even if there is no one to whom we can turn during a period of suffering, we can sometimes draw on the memory of childhood experiences in which we needed help and soothing, when the presence of the right person (or even a pet) made all the difference. It is then as if the experience of a loving parent, for instance, lives on inside us as an internal asset and a source of strength. Such an early experience makes it more likely that the person will be able to make use of the therapeutic relationship when he or she is suffering. The outcome of our childhood experiences with suffering results in a certain attitude toward it that tends to persist into adult life.

When we have recovered from a period of suffering, we may discover that our suffering has created a kind of space inside us that allows us to contain the suffering of others empathically. Sometimes the larger meaning of suffering arises with the discovery that we can help others as a result of our own suffering. This commonly happens in the case of the addict or the victim of child abuse who recovers and then realizes that he or she is called to work with others suffering from the same difficulty. For example, a woman suffering from an eating disorder suffers great pain and distress about her body. She realizes that her suffering is not hers alone; she has the burden of making conscious and resolving the pathology of generations of her forebears, parents and grandparents, which they passed on to her and which she is determined not to pass on to her daughters. A problem such as an eating disorder also reflects the historical ill-treatment of women, so that she is struggling with both a personal and a societal problem. The larger issues of mothering, food, and body-image are very powerful and meaningful for her. Since she is herself a therapist, she is a wounded healer; she can use her awareness of her own wound to help other people. That is to say, we all carry our share of the collective burden embedded within our own, and our own experience is meaningful when we use it for the benefit of the collective. This attitude involves a degree of transcendence of oneself, which requires the ability to put oneself aside in the service of others. This involves a temporary letting go of one's own needs, a sacrifice that can only be made without resentment if we have a firm sense of self.

VARIETIES OF SUFFERING

For Jung, symptoms such as anxiety and depression are the attempt of the Self to stimulate greater awareness of neglected aspects of the personality (1928b, par. 438). Science and common sense do not substitute for this discovery. Jung believed that neurosis is actually the Self's attempt at healing; anxiety and depression tell us that something needs attention. They are the psychological equivalent of physical pain, so it is important to know what they indicate—for example, we might be avoiding an important developmental task. This forward-looking approach contrasts with approaches that look only to the past for the origin of such symptoms.

To illustrate the way meaning can appear during a physical illness, I would like to use the example of a man who consulted me with depression and chronic pain following heart surgery. For months after the surgery, he had suffered severe and constant pain in his sternum (breastbone). This pain was initially misdiagnosed, and for months he was given the wrong treatment.[7] Eventually it was realized that the problem was due to failure of the sternum to heal, but further wiring of the sternum did not alleviate his pain and the nonunion of the bone persisted. A second rewiring of the sternum about nine months after the initial surgery did help, but a year later he was still suffering pain. For many months he had been unable to work, and he often despaired of ever regaining his health.

This man's father had died when the boy was ten years old. His mother was completely wrapped up in her own grief and was extremely insensitive to him. She made him feel responsible for her emotional well-being. He tried everything he could to make her feel better, but nothing he did seemed to help her. He was unable to protect himself from her attacks on him and constantly felt guilty and vulnerable to her criticism. Eventually, he went into a helping profession in which he was expected to be constantly available to others without regard for himself. Since he had little capacity to protect himself against the intrusion of other people's needs, he continued a pattern he had established early in life.

At the physical level, the sternum protects the heart. The bone's failure to heal correlated with his incapacity to protect his own emotional life, which he had never learned to do. Synchronistically, at the time of the surgery he was in a relationship with a woman who made demands on him similar to those his mother had made. Needless to say, he could not protect himself from her constant intrusions. He noticed that every time she attacked him, the pain in his sternum worsened. He felt guilty whenever she was unhappy and felt that he had to take care of this vulnerable but critical creature. As a result of the therapeutic work, he was able to extricate himself from this relationship and see its connections to his mother problem. At the same time as this happened, as he learned to say "no," protect his feelings and defend himself, he finally received definitive surgical treatment for his sternum, which began to heal. The situation expressed itself in the body as pain in the bone that protects the heart and in the psyche as an inability to ward off intrusion. The meaning of this chronic pain seemed to be a call for him to become conscious of all this.[8] His experience exemplifies the fact that the meaning that arises out of suffering is so uniquely related to the individual personality that it is only usable by the individual.

The fact that a successful surgical repair of this man's sternum coincided with an improvement in his mental state is a good example of synchronicity, in which an event in the material world corresponds to the person's state of mind. A level of meaning is then revealed that we realize was latent in the situation but not conscious. This meaning seems to be discovered rather than constructed by the subject. The synchronistic event seems to have a purpose, to be part of a larger pattern in one's life, with the caveat that the correct interpretation of the event is important for its true meaning to emerge (von Franz 1992).

THE EFFECTS OF SUFFERING ON THE PERSONALITY

Suffering may be either helpful or harmful to the development of the personality, and the therapist may be able to tilt the balance in a favorable direction. People who have been through intense pain and anguish, in the words of Albert Schweitzer, are never the same again; as he puts it, they belong to the "fellowship of those who bear the mark of pain" (quoted by Joy 1947, pp. 287–88). Suffering often changes priorities and makes us question our usual values and commitments. When we suffer, we lose any fantasies of invulnerability we may have had and we feel afraid. If we are open to change, we may be initiated into a new state of being, but because of our fear of change we may try to maintain our existing ways of coping. Suffering may radically change our view of the world and ourselves, or it may confirm that we were right all along about life. Suffering forces choices upon us that we would otherwise avoid and often radically changes the course of our lives.

Suffering may force us to develop a level of wisdom and understanding that may otherwise be unattainable. Suffering tends to reveal character structure, both the light and dark sides of human nature. Our capacity for sacrifice, courage, resilience, and compassion may come to the fore, but our selfishness, our willingness to sacrifice others, our resentment and cynicism may surface. Suffering may lead to new realizations about how we want to live our lives and about what really matters to us. For example, when a serious illness occurs, people who have been excessively driven may realize that they must slow down and reevaluate their lives, sometimes radically transforming them. It is not unusual for illness to make people change jobs they dislike, let go of partners who drain them, pay attention to what they have been neglecting, or discover parts of themselves that have not had a chance to live. In the process, they may discover grief and rage about missed opportunities and mistakes. The release of all this may lead to profound transformation.

I believe that we can say that suffering has been helpful when it results in developments such as the following:

- Increased empathy and compassion for the suffering of others
- An improved quality of relationships
- The dissolving of narcissistic problems such as arrogance and indifference to others
- New experiences of the transpersonal dimension
- Increased wisdom
- Increased capacity for humor
- A restructuring of values
- Deepened self-knowledge

Suffering may not allow us to remain as we are. As an example of its transformative effects, consider the individual who tries to control everything and everyone as a way of coping with the helplessness and vulnerability he felt in childhood. Suffering that renders such a person helpless does not allow him to feel in charge of everything. The more rigid the defense, the worse is the plunge downward, so that we typically see severe depression in such a person when he becomes ill and dependent. His underlying terror at weakness surfaces when control is no longer possible. His need to dominate others is not adaptive in coping with suffering; it feels humiliating to have to rely and depend on others who possess greater knowledge and power. Similarly, the narcissistic character has never been empathic with the suffering of others, because to be empathic requires that one put aside one's own self, which is impossible if one's sense of self is fragile and is being shored up by defenses such as grandiosity. Accordingly, some people are impermeable to others until the softening effect of suffering renders them more empathic.

THE EMOTIONS THAT CAUSE SUFFERING: THE ARCHETYPE IN THE BODY

In the last three hundred years of the Western tradition, we have typically thought of mind and body as if they were radically different.[9] This is not surprising, since we experience them differently. We feel affect in the body, where it produces effects such as sweating, dry mouth, dilated pupils, a pounding heart, muscle tension, blushing or pallor of the face, and goose bumps, produced by surges of hormones. In contrast, our thinking, fantasy, and memories seem to be purely mental. However, it is possible to understand mind and body as two perspectives on a unitary reality, or the same reality perceived through different channels. It is then misleading to say that mind affects body or body affects mind as if they were different entities.[10] Our language differentiates between body and mind because we need both terms to describe our experience. But, just as the physicist must sometimes describe light as a particle or a wave, depending on how it is observed, different descriptions do not necessarily imply different entities. An image or a thought in the mind, and the emotion that belongs to it, normally arise simultaneously unless some form of mind-body splitting exists.[11] Painful complexes produce feelings such as shame, guilt, anxiety, or depression, all of which express themselves as both bodily sensations and mental imagery. We tend to think of our complexes as psychological, for example, when we say that someone has an inferiority complex. However, when a complex is activated, emotion invariably flares up, and emotion is felt in the body. The presence of intense emotion automatically makes a situation meaningful.

When a complex is activated, so too is the archetype at its core. This means that the archetype is not only a psychological presence; it is felt in the body in the form of the emotions generated by the complex. Because the body-mind is a unit, Jung's metaphor for the archetype is that of the light spectrum, which we can divide into its colors even though light is just light (Jung 1954a, par. 414).

Red end of spectrum   **Blue end of spectrum**

emotions in the body ————————————— images, thoughts, fantasies

physical arousal: increased heart rate,

muscle tension, sweating

In this metaphor, the blue end of the spectrum is analogous to everything mental. The red end of the spectrum represents the body. Emotion, at the red end of the spectrum, is the effect of the archetype in the body, while images are the archetype's effect in the mind at the blue end. When a complex is negative, our imagery and dreams about it are unpleasant and its emotional tone is painful, so that the body feels distress.

The theory of complexes gives us a psychological way of describing what used to be thought of in terms of spirit possession. The Bible describes how King Saul was envious of David because of David's success in war. One day, while David was playing his lyre, "an evil spirit from God rushed upon Saul and he raved within his house" (1 Sam. 18:7). Gripped by an attack of envious rage, Saul tried to kill David with a spear. The psychologist would say that Saul's murderous impulse was due to possession by a destructive complex that overwhelmed his usual personality. The "evil spirit" is the archetype at the center of that negatively toned complex. When a complex is activated, like King Saul our behavior may be dominated by the demands of the complex. Later, as we look back at the way we behaved when the complex gripped us, we say, "I don't know what came over me."

The Old Testament prophets were often possessed by powerful emotions which they experienced as the presence of God urging them to speak or behave in particular ways. The injustices and failures that they saw around them provoked their outrage. It was then a short step for the prophets to project these feelings onto an external divinity, by saying that God is angry, without realizing that they were gripped by a numinous element within their own personalities. The emotional intensity of such experience gives it meaning and makes it important to the individual, but this emphasis on emotion does not mean that religious experience is irrational. Feeling is just as rational as thinking; feeling simply evaluates the world according to its own criteria.

When speaking of the archetype, some depth psychologists focus on the imagery it produces because they assume that images and symbols are the most fundamental products of the psyche, or that image is the primary language of the psyche. However, emotion is just as primary as image, and an exclusive focus on image at the expense of emotion may foster a type of mind-body splitting, perhaps unconsciously perpetuating a preference for mind over body. Jung himself was clear that image and affect are equally important effects of the archetype and that emotion is a bridge by which the archetype enters the body. The implication of this for psychotherapy is that the eruption of an intense emotion is as much a manifestation of the archetype as is the production of a vivid dream image.

It is worth reiterating here that the archetype is a spiritual principle that embodies itself in the form of emotionally important, soulful experience, which is a way that spirit enters the body. This process is crucially important in development, as the Self gradually incarnates a set of archetypal potentials to form a personal self. These potentials are analogous to the DNA in the seed of a plant, providing information for development. However, for the child's potentials to incarnate, he or she has to be helped with the intensity of the emotions associated with them. Ideally, the child is helped to deal with intense emotions by his or her caretakers, so that these emotions are not overwhelming. But sometimes the child's parents are not helpful in the integration of particular affect states, and the child's feelings are too strong to bear. Then the emotions have to be split off or put into cold storage, isolated from the rest of the personality because they feel too dangerous or terrifying, or too threatening to the relationship with a parent. As a result, some aspect of the child's soul cannot embody. It is then as if a piece of soul is lost, or remains in suspended animation. Psychotherapists try to help the person deal with these unbearable feelings so that more of his or her soul's potentials can be embodied.[12]

Sometimes the potentials of a child's soul simply never have a chance to incarnate because the environment does not provide an opportunity for them to do so. A person with the potential to become a musician may never be given music lessons or encouraged to play an instrument. A potential poet or artist may be forced by his or her parents to "do something practical." Some of that person's soul then cannot embody. Such a person would be somewhat spiritually impoverished, until the suffering produced by a midlife depression makes her realize that she has an unlived life, as if a piece of her soul needs to be reclaimed. Part of the task of development in later life, and part of the psychotherapeutic process, is to assist in the incarnation of such unused potentials.

THE SPIRITUAL RELEVANCE OF SUFFERING

Because of their numinosity, Jung referred to the archetypes as the "organs" or "tools" of God. Since the archetype incarnates or enters the body as emotion, which may be painful, Jung suggested that suffering can be thought of as our subjective experience of the Self trying to incarnate itself within us. That is, when we are gripped by the intense emotion of a complex, be it negative or positive, the numinosum is present. Therefore, emotions have a transpersonal or archetypal significance; in traditional language, they are a divine influx. Work on our painful complexes therefore deepens our connection to the numinosum at their center. This is important because during periods of suffering, people often ask where the divine is, without realizing that the painful emotions themselves are manifestations of the numinosum.

The embodiment of the numinosum by means of emotion enables us to understand a mechanism by which a numinous experience can be helpful. When the experience of the numinosum is positive, its emotional effect is so strong that it counteracts the negative feelings produced by the complex. When the numinosum directly addresses a particular complex, the emotional tone of the complex is altered. A powerful emotional experience gives new meaning to an old problem, and this is one of the ways that healing occurs. Afterward, reflection on the experience influences us at a more cognitive level and puts the problem in a new light.

When we pay attention to a complex, or to the emotions it causes, we are simultaneously attending to a psychological difficulty and a manifestation of the archetype. This means that a psychological problem is also a spiritual problem. Therefore, what is called psychopathology—a complex or a neurosis—is also one of the ways that we experience the spiritual forces that move us. Another way to say this is that the spirit addresses us by means of our suffering, so that attention to our emotional difficulties is a form of spiritual practice. In fact, these difficulties are a good place to begin the spiritual search. Otherwise, there is a tendency to try to suppress our emotional difficulties by imposing a list of rules about good conduct. This top-down approach may be impossible to implement in the individual case, especially when a spiritual teaching undermines an important character defense. For example, an individual who is desperately money-hungry because of a deprived childhood or someone who uses money to buttress an enfeebled sense of self will shudder at Jesus' teaching that he should sell all he has and give it to the poor because it is easier for a camel to pass through the eye of a needle than for a rich man to enter the kingdom of God (Luke 18:22–25).

MYTHIC DEPICTIONS OF SUFFERING

Mythology is important to the depth psychotherapist because mythic stories depict archetypal situations and their psychological and spiritual truths. We resonate with these stories because their themes still occur—we have all felt like Sisyphus. We can sometimes locate our own story in a myth, or locate mythic themes in our own life, and it may be helpful to link one's own situation to a generally human experience so that one does not feel so alone. The mythic theme of descent into the underworld is often used as a metaphor for entrance into a period of suffering or deep personal exploration.[13] These stories metaphorically depict the need of the conscious personality to go into unknown realms of the unconscious. When the process works well, the protagonist returns with some kind of treasure or knowledge, indicating that such descent, although dangerous, can result in a precious discovery. The descent can happen without warning; Persephone is an innocent young girl suddenly seized and dragged down to the realm of Hades, the lord of the underworld, which happens to anyone who is raped, mugged, or unexpectedly violated in any way. Metaphorically, the underworld represents a layer of the psyche that contains much that is undeveloped or unknown to us, including deep veins of meaning. If one is not able to negotiate the journey, one may not be able to return. But those who do return are radically transformed.

A very early myth of descent is that of Inanna, a story that was written on clay tablets about 3,000 B.C.E. Inanna (also known as Ishtar and later related to Venus) was the Sumerian queen of heaven and earth, a goddess of grain, war, love, fertility, and sexuality. The story begins as she listens to a call from the "Great Below," presumably a deeper level of herself. Such a call appears as the sense that something in us needs attention. Sometimes people in midlife who seem to be completely stable and successful hear this call when they realize that they are not living their true life. They then want to change things radically, go back to school or start a new career.

When Inanna hears the call, she announces that she will attend the funeral of her sister's husband. Ereshkigal, queen of the underworld, is Inanna's dark, shadow sister. Psychologically, Ereshkigal and Inanna could be thought of as two aspects of the same personality, one of which lives in the light and is a glorious queen, while the other is rejected and consigned to the dark. Ereshkigal has no relationships; she is lonely, unloving, unloved, abandoned, and full of rage, greed, and desperate loneliness. To compensate for this, she is sexually insatiable—one story tells of a male god with whom she has sex for six days and six nights. When he leaves the underworld on the seventh day she still has not had enough. That is, Inanna's shadow contains compulsive sexuality that tries to compensate for loneliness and abandonment fears. Apparently, Inanna senses the need to get to know this part of herself. When we descend to the underworld, we discover aspects of ourselves that have been repressed or ignored or that lie dormant.[14]

When Inanna arrives at the gates to the underworld, Ereshkigal is not happy to see her sister, who is described as "all white." Ereshkigal is full of rage at having been ignored, and she is envious of Inanna's glory and splendor while she has to live in a dark place, eating clay and drinking dirty water. As an internal object, Ereshkigal represents something in Inanna that is envious of her success. Inanna is the goddess of love, a bright star, and Ereshkigal wants her to know what it is like to be rejected. Accordingly, Ereshkigal insists that Inanna be treated according to the rules for anyone entering her domain, that she be "bowed low."

There are seven gates to the underworld, a traditional number to express cyclical processes, the end of one period and the beginning of another. Therefore, the number 7 is often associated with a process of initiation into a new status. At each gate, Inanna has to pay a price to enter by sacrificing one of her royal garments. Each time she is shocked and indignant, and she asks "what is this?" but she is told not to question the ways of the underworld. So she removes in turn her magnificent headdress, her lapis necklace, her strands of beads, her breastplate, her ring, and her measuring rod. At the last gate, her robe is taken from her so that she is totally naked. In other words, all her symbols of power and prestige are removed. Psychologically, this reminds us of how suffering makes us give up our persona, our usual way of appearing to the world. Ereshkigal orders Inanna to be left to die, hanging on a hook until her corpse turns into a piece of rotting meat, a vivid metaphor for intense suffering. At this point in the story, to our surprise, we discover that Ereshkigal is actually in labor, so one could think of her as a part of Inanna that wants to give birth to something new. This is a part of the pain that Inanna hears from above that induces her to descend.

Before Inanna descended, she had told her assistant, Ninshubur, to appeal to the father gods if she does not return in three days. The first of these gods, Enlil, is the director of rationality; he wants nothing to do with her in the underworld. The second father god, Nanna, also cannot understand why she made the journey; they are both angry with her and will not help. It is not uncommon for the establishment, the guardians of what passes for common sense, to have little sympathy for the need for radical change. But Enki, the god of wisdom and healing, values her journey and realizes its importance. From the dirt under his fingernails, he creates two asexual creatures who become professional mourners who empathically mirror Ereshkigal's pain. As she moans, they moan; they echo her pain and anguish, which touches her deeply, in a scene that is a profound testimony to the healing effect of empathy. Ereshkigal offers them gifts, but they only ask for her to release Inanna, although usually no one is ever allowed to leave the underworld. However, Inanna had not just visited, she had died and been reborn there, and so new rules are made. She is allowed to leave the underworld if she will provide someone to take her place. Accordingly the demons of the underworld return with her to the upper world to find someone to replace her. These demons are remorseless, willing to tear apart wives and husbands, children and parents. The demands of the unconscious are relentless.

On her return, Inanna found that her sons and her servants had mourned for her, but her husband Dumuzi hardly noticed that she was gone; he did not weep for her nor did he greet her return. It is as if he ignored her spiritual journey, refused to help her, and showed no compassion for her. Instead he made himself more powerful. Inanna cursed him and made the demons of the underworld seize him, thereby forcing him to meet her dark aspects. As a result of a dream, Dumuzi realized he would have to go down to the underworld, but his sister shared this fate so that they each had to be there half a year.

In the process of meeting the part of her that suffered, Inanna had to die to her old self, but she was eventually brought back to life and spiritually transformed in the process. She now knows the darkness, and she returns more powerful and assertive of her own rights, determined to survive. Inanna's story in some ways prefigures the story of Jesus, who is also humiliated, tortured, and hung to die; Inanna is therefore an early image of a dying and resurrected deity.

Ereshkigal, the queen of the underworld, is a metaphor for unconscious parts of ourselves that can only be approached with difficulty, and only by means of a descent. The myth says that she was angry and grieving at the same time as she was giving birth. There is often a good deal of grief in the unconscious that we can avoid until we suffer intolerably. We are then confronted with this grief in the form of regret and pain about missed opportunities, mistakes we have made, and necessary sacrifices. This story suggests that meeting all this may result in transformation. Innana's stay in the underworld transforms her, because now that she knows her shadow sister she can better integrate that aspect of herself.

The story of Inanna is a mythic representation of what happens to us when we suffer. Suffering produces loss of authority and personal power, and often a loss of dignity and persona as well. When our usual way of being in the world no longer works for us, we may be plunged into a depression, metaphorically represented as the mythological underworld. At that time, our favorite distractions—such as alcohol, religion, work, or entertainment—are no longer useful. But the underworld realm of the soul into which we descend is a part of us, an area that we have so far managed to avoid. Often, periods of intense suffering reveal other aspects of our lives that are not working, such as an unrewarding job or a marriage that needs attention. In the case of chronic illness, it may take years for the descent to the underworld to occur. The illness gradually changes our identity and appearance; think of the changes produced by radiation and chemotherapy.

The kind of descent that Inanna went through is an initiation into the deep mysteries of the soul. To reach these levels requires a sacrifice of our usual ego attitudes for the sake of retrieving certain values of which we were unaware. Suffering makes the ego face what it has been ignoring, strips the persona, and makes us pay attention to parts of ourselves that have never had a chance to live. During periods of suffering, the hegemony of the ego is reduced, so that it is common for suffering people to have numinous experiences of nonordinary reality.

As we have seen, suffering can sometimes be seen as a kind of wake-up call from the Self, urging us to pay attention to ignored or neglected parts of ourselves. Unfortunately, what the Self insists on is often contrary to the ego's preferences, and this tension leads to considerable suffering. From a strictly spiritual point of view, everything that happens has to happen the way it does, but this is *only* true from the perspective of the soul, which is not the same as the perspective of the empirical personality. Sometimes suffering occurs as the Self brings about change that is obviously overdue but which we have been avoiding. Resisting such change is like trying to hold on to the dock as the ship is leaving. In situations when a problem is truly beyond our control, it is preferable to let go of the dock and see where the ship is heading. We can only do this with a degree of trust if we sense that a transpersonal process is going on that is beyond our capacity to understand. For some people this happens through an intuitive sense of connection to the Self. For others, trust is based on an experience of the numinosum, while a happy few have the gift of faith. In whatever manner the necessary trust arises, in its presence we can allow ourselves to be affected by the experience of suffering as we try to discover its intention for the soul. This requires radical acceptance and receptivity, and the traditional "letting go" of the ego's dominance, which puts the ego into a terrible crucible. The ego has to let go of its judgments about what is good and bad and realize that its likes and dislikes are irrelevant.

Suffering occurs when painful events and losses radically challenge our notion of how things should be. We discover that we are not who we thought we were, and the world is not the way we would like it to be. Often the real wound is to a grandiose fantasy or image of ourselves that is difficult to relinquish. But in the end, if we are to go on living, we have to come to terms with the discrepancy between the conditioning produced by family and culture and what our suffering tells us needs to be changed.

MAKING THINGS WORSE

The therapist may notice particular attitudes that are not helpful when working with a suffering individual. It is important to become conscious of these dynamics. An attitude of passive resignation tends to be a hangover from a relationship with a domineering parent who made submission to his or her will the major condition for allowing the child to have any relationship with the parent. Or, the person may assume that he or she is suffering because he or she has been bad, and then assumes responsibility for things over which he or she has no control.

The person's reaction to suffering may add additional problems to the primary problem that is causing the person to suffer, thus making the situation worse. Typical of such reactions are those of excessive self-pity, disproportionate self-reproach, unreasonable blame of others, pointless complaints about the unfairness of the situation, prolonged "if only" ruminating, or fantasies of the worst possible outcome. We also add to our difficulty by making the people around us suffer, for instance by being so angry about a problem that the atmosphere around us becomes difficult for those trying to help. Often it seems that reactions such as rage, envy, and hatred act as protections for unbearable feelings of vulnerability. Sometimes these secondary problems are unconsciously used to distract the sufferer from the primary problem and its implications. Often, such reactions are automatic and unconscious because they have been learned in childhood. They may have been the only recourse in a home in which no one really cared how the child felt. In some families, to protect the parents' feelings the child is blamed for whatever goes wrong. The child develops unconscious internal dialogues such as: "I have to blame myself because I dare not blame Dad—that would be too dangerous" or "It's best to blame other people when things go wrong, because its too painful to feel responsible myself" or "I must be bad for these bad things to be happening to me" or "Maybe if I blame myself they won't hate me so much" or "It's better for me to be bad than to have a bad parent." These attitudes persist into adult life as a misplaced form of loyalty to parents. Another unconsciously held belief may be: "Nothing good ever happens anyway—it doesn't matter what I do—no one really cares what happens to me." These schemata or unconscious pathogenic beliefs may delay or prevent any possibility of alleviating painful situations.

Another common type of depressive reaction occurs when the

suffering makes us relinquish fantasies which we had been using to buttress our self-esteem. The origin of such fantasy is found in our early social conditioning about what is important and desirable in life. The loss of various props to our self-image, such as our achievements and position in life, adds to our suffering but also forces us to ask questions about who we really are and makes us examine our real values.

TRADITIONAL RELIGIOUS PUNISHMENT THEORIES SEEN IN PSYCHOTHERAPY

In psychotherapeutic practice, one often sees attitudes toward suffering that not only originate in the person's family of origin but also in the individual's early religious training. These ingrained attitudes are difficult to change because they seem to have the authority of God or the Church behind them. When working with an individual who suffers because of these attitudes, it is helpful for the therapist to understand their roots in the Judeo-Christian tradition.

Because suffering is so hard to reconcile with a benevolent God-image, the Bible has many explanations for the existence of suffering, which is often seen as brought about by God as an act of judgment or as a purification or punishment for sin (Ezekiel 7:3 and 14:21). In the words of the Psalmist, "Before I was afflicted I went astray; / but now I keep thy word" (119:67): God is said to test us and "didst lay affliction on our loins" (Ps. 66:10–11), but in the end God makes things well because God purifies us with suffering: "I will smelt away your dross as with lye / and remove your alloy . . . I have refined you . . . I have tried you in the furnace of affliction" (Isa. 1:25; 48:10). Similarly, the New Testament tells us that suffering produces endurance (Romans 5:3), makes the works of God manifest (John 9:3), and keeps us humble in the face of revelation (2 Cor. 12:7). James believes that suffering is a test of faith that "produces steadfastness" (1:3–4). St. Paul writes that suffering "produces endurance, and endurance produces character, and character produces hope" (Rom. 5:4). St. Paul is content to suffer for the sake of Christ, "for when I am weak, then I am strong"

(2 Cor. 12:10), and he tells us that God always works for the good (Rom. 8:28). If we suffer with Christ we will be glorified with him (Rom. 8:17). The Letter to the Hebrews tells us that painful discipline eventually "leads to the peaceful fruit of righteousness" (12:11), and Jesus himself says that if we suffer for the right reason we are blessed and will be rewarded with the kingdom of heaven (Matt. 5:10–11).

These attempts to make sense of the problem invariably involve the assumption that the divine works the way human beings do. We can therefore think of these notions as projections that try to explain the situation in human terms. For example, the common notion that suffering is a test of faith is a human fantasy that perpetuates a pedagogic projection onto the divine. The problem is that doctrinal concepts, such as the notion that suffering is a punishment for sin, have the potential to cause more suffering by inducing guilt. Nevertheless, explanations of this kind seem to be necessary for many believers to hold on to, in order to preserve a particular God-image. In all disciplines, intellectual maneuvers are sometimes used to support a theory in the face of findings that tend to deny the theory's validity. Like scientists, traditional religious believers have ways of preserving their favorite doctrines. The biblical authors proposed their explanations for why God allows evil and suffering in order to maintain their image of an all-good God who is totally just. They insisted on this God-image at all costs, even though the evidence demands that we modify it to acknowledge that, like Job, we may not experience the divine as all good. Sometimes our experience of the divine seems very dark because of the suffering it either allows or causes; Jung refers to this as the dark side of the Self. With suitable tact, this idea may be introduced into the therapy when it seems important for the person to modify his or her God-image.

SUFFERING AS LIMINALITY

Our spiritual and psychological response to suffering must be a complex, multilayered one, even though it must be acknowledged that any psychologically based response will also be a human projection onto a mystery. We need a perspective that is both large enough to help individuals and also able to guide our cultural response to suffering. It would be helpful to think of suffering as an essential life transition with important psychological effects and developmental consequences. We can view suffering as an initiation into a new level of awareness and a new state of being. The most difficult part of this process involves a temporary stage known to anthropologists as liminality, which is a characteristic of the middle stage of rites of passage seen within tribal cultures. In the liminal stage, the initiate or the suffering person is not completely out of the old state (of being happy and well) and not quite into the new one. He or she is betwixt and between, in a situation of radical change, so that liminal states produce uncertainty and anxiety about the future. During this period, we lose our usual sense of who we are but have no idea where we are heading. This stage involves ambiguity and confusion.

The anthropologist Victor Turner calls a person in such a state a "transition-being." Turner regards liminality as a state of "pure possibility, whence novel configurations of ideas and relations may arise" (1987, p. 7). He suggests that initiation may generate new thought, and this is surely important for those who suffer. In tribal cultures during the liminal period of initiation, initiates are encouraged to think about their society, their mythology, and the powers that sustain them. For the suffering person, too, liminality can become a stage of reflection about his or her life. Serious illness always has this potential; not only does it produce pain and disability, but our usual values and commitments, our methods of dealing with stress, our relationships with others, our hope for the future, our feeling of control over our lives, and our sense of purpose are all called into question. Such transitions are therefore times of both potential danger and opportunity for the development of the personality, and people need help with them. If we are fortunate, suffering helps us understand more of ourselves and acts as a bridge to a new orientation to life, to the person we might become. We may need to become an entirely new being. Eventually, if the initiation is successful, we develop a new sense of our destiny of which we had been unaware.

However, there are some formidable obstacles to this end, and once again we may learn from pretechnological cultures. Turner pointed out that tribal cultures tend to regard the person in the liminal state as somehow polluting, which is why the initiates are always secluded from the rest of the tribe or disguised in masks or costumes. Human beings do not like what is unclear and contradictory to their usual values. In tribal cultures, initiates in the liminal period are in a state of sacred poverty; they have no rights and no property—they are structurally invisible to their societies. In our culture, too, suffering people tend to be neglected or not given an adequate place, except in institutions like hospice, which can be regarded as sacred spaces.

We have a good deal to learn about the value of suffering, although our culture tends to want to get rid of it as soon as possible, as if it had no value and no purpose. This is partly due to a lack of empathy and partly the result of our fear of suffering. Because of these dynamics, people may avoid those who suffer, as though suffering were infectious, or because suffering people remind us of what may happen to us.[15] Because affliction may make one feel defective, those who are afflicted may devalue themselves. Afflicted people may also envy those who do not suffer, and this combined with their bitterness may make it uncomfortable to be around them. For these reasons we ignore or marginalize the suffering caused by poverty, mental illness, loneliness, hunger, homelessness, and old age, and we do not have adequate social structures for helping people who suffer. Psychotherapy is therefore one of our best social containers for souls in pain.

CODA

The search for meaning may be a difficult night sea journey. But when they suffer, even people who have always been excessively rational become open to transpersonal experiences that they might otherwise dismiss. Such a man dreamed that he was at the foot of the cross at the time of the crucifixion. He looked down and discovered he was wearing expensive shoes, which he likes to wear to display his status. As he looked, his shoes turned into the shoes of the Fool of the Tarot deck. He said to the figure on the cross:

"What a fool I've been to reject you." The archetypal image of the Fool represents spiritual potential, the beginning of a new journey which offers a choice to the individual to develop the undeveloped aspects of his personality. A dream such as this represents the wisdom of the psyche. Such contact with the transpersonal dimension seems automatically to give a sense of meaning. We then feel part of a larger order of reality, we sense that there is a supraordinate order going on, and we see that life has a pattern to it, that we are not an isolated consciousness.

The spiritually oriented therapist does not need to be concerned if the mainstream of the tradition insists on treating psychotherapy as a purely secular pursuit. The philosopher Henri Bergson pointed out that humanity has forever been surrounded by electricity, but it took millennia before it was recognized. Similarly, there are spiritual forces in the psyche that guide our lives, and Western psychology is only beginning to discover them. Once one realizes they are present, one practices psychotherapy with a spiritual sensibility.

NOTES

1. I refer to the philosophy of existential nihilism, which says that there is no ultimate meaning to suffering, no specific answer to it, and no metaphysically based solace. Meaning is just an arbitrary creation. The meaning of life is that it has no meaning. Other people take a position of limited meaning, suggesting that we can live as if there is meaning without believing that the meaning we reach is absolute or objective, even if this is only an illusion. Or we can simply choose to live meaningfully and enjoy it, since life is what you make it.

2. For example, LeShan (1994) suggests that those cancer patients who find meaning in life, a vocation that they are enthusiastic about, and a way of life that they enjoy do much better than patients who do not. To have a reason to live seems to mobilize healing. The potential problem with such arguments is guilt if one feels personally responsible for one's illness. This guilt is not really justified, since the ego cannot influence these situations—the problem is usually in the unconscious.

3. Note that this position is arguable. It could be that people felt they were choosing but in fact were simply responding according to their conditioning.

4. Frankl's heroic image has been roundly criticized on the grounds that he misleadingly gives the impression that he was in Auschwitz for

some time, when in fact he was only there for a few days. He has also been criticized for being grandiose, authoritarian, essentialist, and reductive, and that logotherapy cannot deal with people who find life meaningless (Pytell 2006).

5. In biblical times, anointing with oil was a sign of blessing. I mention this episode because she asked me if I would tell as many people as possible about the vision, since she would not be able to do so.

6. The ancient notion of karma suggests that the soul, or a stream of consciousness with a particular set of qualities, periodically appears in a new body in order to continue to develop. The specific problems we have in this life are the result of our need to encounter experiences created in the past. This idea suggests that because every action has a reaction, either in this lifetime or another we eventually reap what we sow. In any lifetime, we have to work in conformity with our basic karmic patterns.

7. The pain was erroneously thought to be due to an inflammation of the pericardium known as Dressler's syndrome.

8. Sontag (1977) argued forcefully that "illness is not a metaphor" and that illness is resistant to metaphoric thinking. She complains about psychological explanations for disease, suggesting that psychological approaches undermine the reality of disease and seem to blame the victim. She prefers a focus purely on the physical aspects of illness. Like the New Age approach that she critiques, and indeed like much psychosomatic medicine, Sontag has misunderstood the relationship between physical illness and the psychology of the sufferer. It is misleading to say that the mind causes the disease in the body, as if body and mind were different entities. Body and mind are a unity even though we experience them differently. Mind and body reflect each other. The case I cite is an example of how the psychological situation and the physical situation express the same problem in different ways. "Failure to protect the heart" is a possible metaphor to describe the situation, but this does not mean that the situation is not desperately real and does not imply that the psychological problem causes the physical problem; they correlate with each other.

9. This has been true since the seventeenth century, thanks to Descartes, who distinguished between mind and body on the grounds that, whereas matter or body occupies space, mind is pure thinking stuff that occupies no space, as if it were a mathematical point.

10. As the Zen tradition asks, "Where would you like to cut the cat?"— meaning that there is no place to divide something that is a whole.

11. Mind-body splitting may occur when, for instance, a child is not allowed to have feelings such as anger, which are then split off or disavowed, in which case the individual has mental imagery without the feelings that would normally be attached to it. The emotions that he or she were not allowed to feel exist in a walled-off sector of the personality that may be difficult to access. A person who suffers this split may discuss a very dis-

turbing memory from childhood with few conscious feelings about it. Or, the person may become anxious or depressed but have no idea why, because no imagery or thoughts come to mind that allow the person to understand the feeling.

12. This is a process of "soul retrieval," which is well known to shamanic cultures. The difference is that the shaman journeys to the spirit world where he or she sees the soul in the form of an actual being that must be brought back. The psychotherapist works with split-off emotions and behavior that must be reintegrated.

13. Ulysses descended to the underworld to consult Tiresias, Dante was led down by Virgil, and Faust by Mephistopheles. Out of his grief for his dead wife, Orpheus descended to try to persuade Hades to release Eurydice. Osiris, Adonis, Dionysus, and many other gods of antiquity, long before Christ, made this descent.

14. It is interesting that another name for Hades (or Pluto) was lord of riches—the one who knew the location of hidden jewels.

15. The indifference or hostility of some politicians toward people on welfare seems to be predicated on the unconscious notion that suffering is infectious or that by denying it in others, it will never happen to them.

REFERENCES

Adams, J. E. 1973. *The Christian Counselor's Manual.* Phillipsburg, N.J.: Presbyterian and Reformed Publishing.

Adler, G. 1951. Notes regarding the dynamics of the self. *British Journal of Medical Psychology* 24:97–106.

———. 1979. *Dynamics of the Self.* London: Coventure Ltd.

Agosin, T. 1992. Psychosis, dreams and mysticism in the clinical domain. In F. R. Halligan and J. J. Shea, eds., *The Fires of Desire* (pp. 41–65). New York: Crossroad.

Albaugh, J. A. 2003. Spirituality and life-threatening illness: A phenomenologic study. *Oncology Nursing Forum* 30(4):593–98.

Albee, G. W. 2000. The Boulder Model's fatal flaw. *American Psychologist* 55 (2):247–48.

Allman, L. S., DeLa Roche, O., Elkins, D. N., and Weathers, R. S. 1992. Psychotherapists' attitudes towards clients reporting mystical experiences. *Psychotherapy* 29:564–69.

Alston, W. P. 1991. *Perceiving God: The Epistemology of Religious Experience.* Ithaca, N.Y.: Cornell University Press.

American Psychiatric Association. 2000. *Diagnostic and Statistical Manual of Mental Disorders*, 4th ed. Washington, D.C.: Author.

Anandarajah, G., and Hight, E. 2001. Spirituality and medical practice: Using the HOPE questions as a practical tool for spiritual assessment. *American Family Physician* 63(1):81–89.

Arieti, S., and Bemporad, J. 1980. *Severe and Mild Depression: The Psychotherapeutic Approach.* London: Tavistock Publications.

Ash, M. G. 1992. Historicizing mind science: Discourse, practice, subjectivity. *Science in Context*, 5:193–197.

Aziz, R. 1990. *C. G. Jung's Psychology of Religion and Synchronicity.* Albany, N.Y.: SUNY Press.

Babb, L. A. 1986. *Redemptive Encounters.* Los Angeles: University of California Press.

Bach, S. 1966. Spontaneous paintings of severely ill patients. In *Acta Psychosomatica*, vol. 8. Basel: Documenta Geigy.

Bachelard, G. 1938. *The Psychoanalysis of Fire.* A. C. M. Ross, trans. Boston: Beacon Press, 1964.

Balint, M. 1968. *The Basic Fault: Therapeutic Aspects of Regression*. New York: Brunner/Mazel, 1979.

Barnhouse, R. T. 1986. How to evaluate patients' religious ideation. In L. Robinson, ed., *Psychiatry and Religion: Overlapping Concerns* (pp. 89–106). Washington, D.C.: American Psychiatric Press.

Barra, D., Carlson, E., Maize, M., Murphy, W., O'Neil, B., Sarver, R., and Zinner, E. 1993. The dark night of the spirit: Grief following a loss in religious identity. In K. Doka and J. Morgan, eds., *Death and spirituality* (pp. 291–308). Amityville, N.Y.: Baywood.

Barry, W. A., and Connolly, W. J. 1982. *The Practice of Spiritual Direction*. New York: HarperCollins, 2009.

Baumeister, R. F., Exline, J. J., and Sommer, K. L. 1998. The victim role, grudge theory, and two dimensions of forgiveness. In E. L. Worthington, ed., *Dimensions of Forgiveness: Psychological Research and Theological Perspectives*. Radnor, Pa.: Templeton Foundation Press.

Beardsworth, T. 1997. *A Sense of Presence*. Oxford: Religious Experience Research Unit.

Benner, D. G. 1988. *Psychotherapy and the Spiritual Quest*. Grand Rapids, Mich.: Baker Book House.

———. 2002. *Sacred Companions: The Gift of Spiritual Friendship and Direction*. Downers Grove, Ill.: InterVarsity Press.

Benson, P. L., and Spilka, B. P. 1973. God image as a function of self-esteem and locus of control. *Journal for the Scientific Study of Religion* 12:297–310.

Berenbaum, H., Kerns, J., and Raghavan, C. 2000. Anomalous experiences, peculiarity, and psychopathology. In E. Cardeña, S. J. Lynn, and S. C. Krippner, eds., *Varieties of Anomalous Experience* (pp. 25–46). Washington, D.C.: American Psychological Association.

Berger, P. L. 1990. *The Sacred Canopy*. New York: Anchor Books.

Bergin, A. E. 1991. Values and religious issues in psychotherapy and mental health. *American Psychologist* 46(4):394–403.

———. 1995. Proposed values for guiding and evaluating counseling and psychotherapy. *Counseling and Values* 29:99–116.

Bergin, A. E., and Jensen, J. P. 1990. Religiosity of psychotherapists: A national survey. *Psychotherapy* 27:3–7.

Bergin, A. E., and Payne, I. R. 1991. Proposed agenda for a spiritual strategy in personality and psychotherapy. *Journal of Psychology and Christianity* 10:197–210.

Bergin, A. E., Payne, I. R., and Richards, P. S. 1996. Values in psychotherapy. In E. P. Shafranske, ed., *Religion and the Clinical Practice of Psychotherapy* (pp. 297–325). Washington, D.C.: American Psychological Association.

Bettelheim, B. 1982. *Freud and Man's Soul*. New York: Vintage Books.

Betz, B. J. 1968. Passive expectations and infantile aims. *International Journal of Psychiatry* 5:396–397.

Bion, W. 1967. Notes on memory and desire. In E. Spillius, ed., *Melanie Klein Today,* vol. 2, *Mainly Practice: Developments in Theory and Practice.* London: Routledge, 1988.

———. 1979. *Attention and Interpretation.* New York: Jason Aronson.

Blackstone, J. 2007. *The Empathic Ground: Intersubjectivity and Nonduality in the Psychotherapeutic Process.* Buffalo: State University of New York Press.

Blake, W. 1975. *The Marriage of Heaven and Hell.* New York: Oxford University Press.

Blatt, S. J. 1998. Contributions of psychoanalysis to the understanding and treatment of depression. *Journal of the American Psychoanalytic Association* 46:722–752.

Bloom, H. 1996. *Omens of Millennium: The Gnosis of Angels, Dreams and Resurrection.* New York: Riverhead Books.

Bobgan, M., and Bobgan, D. 1987. *Psychoheresy: The Psychological Seduction of Christianity.* San Francisco: East Gate.

Bogart, G. 1997. *The Nine Stages of Spiritual Apprenticeship.* Berkeley, Calif.: Dawn Mountain Press.

Bollas, C. 1989. *The Forces of Destiny.* London: Free Association Press.

Boorstein, S. 1996. Transpersonal techniques and psychotherapy. In B. W. Scotton, A. B. Chinen, and J. R. Battista, eds., *Textbook of Transpersonal Psychiatry and Psychology* (pp. 282–292). New York: Basic Books.

Boris, H. 1976. On hope: Its nature and psychotherapy. *International Review of Psychoanalysis* 3:139–150.

Bowker, J. 1973. *The Sense of God: Sociological, Anthropological, and Psychological Approaches to the Origin of the Sense of God.* London: Oxford University Press.

Bradford, D. T. 1985. A therapy of religious imagery in paranoid schizophrenic psychosis. In M. H. Spero, ed., *Psychotherapy of the Religious Patient* (pp. 154–180). Springfield, Ill.: Thomas.

Bromberg, W. 1975. *From Shaman to Psychotherapist: A History of the Treatment of Mental Illness.* Chicago: Henry Regnery.

Bromiley, G. V. 1979. *An Introduction to the Theology of Karl Barth.* Edinburgh: T. and T. Clark.

Bronheim, H. 1998. *Body and Soul: The Role of Object Relations in Faith, Shame, and Healing.* Northvale, N.J.: Jason Aronson.

Buber, M. 1952. *Eclipse of God: Studies in the Relation between Religion and Philosophy.* New York: Harper and Row.

Burkitt, I. 2008. *Social Selves.* Thousand Oaks, Calif.: Sage Publications.

Burr, V. 1995. *Introduction to Social Constructivism.* London: Routledge.

Caird, D. 1987. Religion and personality: Are mystics introverted, neurotic, or psychotic? *British Journal of Social Psychology* 26:345–346.

Campbell, J. 1968. *The Hero with a Thousand Faces.* Princeton, N.J.: Princeton University Press.

Cannon, W. B. 1932. *The Wisdom of the Body.* New York: Norton.

Capps, D. 1997. *Men, Religion, and Melancholia: James, Otto, Jung, and Erikson.* New Haven, Conn.: Yale University Press.

Cardeña, E., Lynn, S. J., and Krippner, S. C. 2000. *Varieties of Anomalous Experience.* Washington, D.C.: American Psychological Association.

Casement, P. 1985. *On Learning from the Patient.* New York: Guilford Press.

Chalmers, D. J. 1996. *The Conscious Mind: In Search of a Fundamental Theory.* New York: Oxford University Press.

Chilton, B. 2008. *Abraham's Curse: The Roots of Violence in Judaism, Christianity, and Islam.* Garden City, N.Y.: Doubleday.

Christou, E. 1976. *The Logos of the Soul.* Zurich: Spring.

Clarke, R. O. 1985. The teachings of Bhagwan Shree Rajneesh. *Sweet Reason: A Journal of Ideas, History, and Culture* 4:27–44.

Claus, J. J., and Johnston, S. I., eds. 1997. *Medea.* Princeton, N.J.: Princeton University Press.

Cloninger, C. R. 2004. *Feeling Good: The Science of Well Being.* New York: Oxford University Press.

Cohen, J. M., and Phipps, J.-F. 1979. *The Common Experience.* Los Angeles: Jeremy Tarcher.

Corbett, L. 1996. *The Religious Function of the Psyche.* New York: Brunner-Routledge.

———. 2006. Varieties of numinous experience. In A. Casement, ed., *The Idea of the Numinous* (pp. 53–67). London: Brunner-Routledge.

———. 2007. *Psyche and the Sacred.* New Orleans: Spring.

Corbin, H. 1969. *Creative Imagination in the Sufism of Ibn al-'Arabi.* R. Manheim, trans. Princeton, N.J.: Princeton University Press.

———. 1972. *Mundus imaginalis* or the imaginary and the imaginal. *Spring* (pp. 1–9). Dallas: Spring.

Cornett, C. 1998. *The Soul of Psychotherapy: Recapturing the Spiritual Dimension in the Therapeutic Encounter.* New York: The Free Press.

Crick, F., and Mitchison, G. 1983. REM sleep and neural nets. *Nature* 304:111–114.

———. 1986. The function of dream sleep. *Journal of Mind and Behavior* 7(2–3):229–249.

Deikman, A. 1996. Treating former members of cults. In B. Scotton, A. B. Chinen, and J. R. Battista, eds., *Textbook of Transpersonal Psychiatry and Psychology.* New York: Basic Books.

deMause, L. 2002. *The Emotional Life of Nations.* London: Karnac Books.

Diamond, E. L. 1982. The role of anger in essential hypertension and coronary heart disease. *Psychological Bulletin* 96:410–433.

Dickinson, E. 1976. *The Complete Poems of Emily Dickinson.* Boston: Little, Brown.

Dourley, J. P. 1981. *Psyche as Sacrament: A Comparative Study of C. G. Jung and Paul Tillich.* Toronto: Inner City Books.

———. 1994. Jung's conversations with Buber and White. In J. Ryce-

Menuhin, ed., *Jung and the Monotheisms* (pp. 125–48). London: Routledge.

Downie, R. S. 1965. Forgiveness. *Philosophical Quarterly* 15:128–134.

Dru, A., ed. and trans. 1959. *The Journals of Kierkegaard, 1834–1854.* New York: Oxford University Press.

D'Souza, R. F., and Rodrigo, A. 2004. Spiritually augmented cognitive behavioral therapy. *Australasian Psychiatry* 12(2):148–152.

Edinger, E. F. 1984. *The Creation of Consciousness: Jung's Myth for Modern Man.* Toronto: Inner City Books.

———. 1986. *The Bible and the Psyche: Individuation Symbolism in the Old Testament.* Toronto: Inner City Books.

———. 1992. *Transformation of the God Image.* Toronto: Inner City Books.

Edinger, E. F., Cordic, D. D., and Yates, C. 1996. *The New God-Image: A Study of Jung's Key Letters Concerning the Evolution of the Western God-Image.* Wilmette, Ill.: Chiron.

Eigen, M. 1995. Stones in a stream. *Psychoanalytic Review* 82(3):371–390.

———. 1998. *The Psychoanalytic Mystic.* New York: Free Association Books.

———. 1999. The area of faith in Winnicott, Lacan, and Bion. In S. A. Mitchell and L. Aron, eds., *Relational Psychoanalysis* (pp. 1–37). Hillsdale, N.J.: Analytic Press.

Einstein, A. 1949. *The World as I See It.* New York: Citadel Press, 2001.

Eliade, M. 1951. *Shamanism: Archaic Techniques of Ecstasy.* W. R. Trask, trans. Princeton, N.J.: Princeton University Press, 2004.

———. 1958. *Rites and Symbols of Initiation.* W. R. Trask, trans. New Orleans: Spring, 1994.

Ellenberger, H. F. 1970. *The Discovery of the Unconscious: The History and Evolution of Dynamic Psychiatry.* New York: Basic Books.

Emmons, R. A., and McCullough, M. E. 2003. Counting blessings versus burdens: An experimental investigation of gratitude and subjective well-being in daily life. *Journal of Personality and Social Psychology* 84(2):377–389.

Engel, G. L. 1962. *Psychological Development in Health and Disease.* Philadelphia: W. B. Saunders.

Erikson, E. 1950. *Childhood and Society.* New York: W. W. Norton.

———. 1964. *Insight and Responsibility.* New York: W. W. Norton.

Fallot, R. D., and Heckman, J. P. 2005. Religious/spiritual coping among women trauma survivors with mental health and substance use disorders. *Journal of Behavioral Health Services and Research* 32(2):215–226.

Fava, G. A., Rafanelli, C., Cazzaro, M., Conti, S., and Grandi, S. 1998. Well-being therapy: A novel psychotherapeutic approach for residual symptoms of affective disorders. *Psychological Medicine* 28(2):475–480.

Fava, G. A., Rafanelli, C., Grandi, S., Conti, S., and Belluardo, P. 1998. Prevention of recurrent depression with cognitive behavioral therapy: Preliminary findings. *Archives of General Psychiatry* 55 (9):816–820.

Fava, G. A., Ruini, C., Rafanelli, C., Finos, L., Salmaso, L., Mangelli, L., and Sirigatti, S. 2005. Well-being therapy of generalized anxiety disorder. *Psychotherapy and Psychosomatics* 74(1):26–30.

Ferenczi, S. 1995. *The Clinical Diary of Sandor Ferenczi.* J. Dupont, ed. M. Balint and N. Z. Jackson, trans. Cambridge, Mass.: Harvard University Press.

———. 1926. *Further Contributions to the Theory and Technique of Psychoanalysis.* J. I. Suttie, trans. London: Karnac Books, 2000.

Field, N. 1989. Listening with the body: An exploration in the countertransference. *British Journal of Psychotherapy* 5(4):512–22.

FitzGerald, F. 1986. Rajneeshpuram. *New Yorker*, Sept. 22 and Sept. 29.

Fowler, J. W. 1981. *Stages of Faith: The Psychology of Human Development and the Quest for Meaning.* San Francisco: Harper and Row.

Frank, J. 1963. *Persuasion and Healing.* New York: Schocken Books.

———. 1968. The role of hope in psychotherapy. *International Journal of Psychotherapy* 5:383–95.

———. 1974. Psychotherapy: The restoration of morale. *American Journal of Psychiatry* 131:271–74.

———. 1982. Therapeutic components shared by all psychotherapies. In J. H. Harvey and M. M. Parks, eds., *The Master Lecture Series.* Vol. 1, *Psychotherapy Research and Behavior Change* (pp. 5–38). Washington, D.C.: American Psychological Association.

Frankl, V. E. 1975. *The Unconscious God.* New York: Simon and Schuster.

———. 1986. *The Doctor and the Soul: From Psychotherapy to Logotherapy.* New York: Random House Vintage Books.

———. 1988. *The Will to Meaning: Foundations and Applications of Logotherapy.* New York: New American Library.

———. 2006. *Man's Search for Meaning.* Boston: Beacon Press.

French, T. M. 1952. *The Integration of Behavior.* Chicago: University of Chicago Press.

Freud, S. 1900. *The Interpretation of Dreams.* A. A. Brill, trans. New York: Macmillan, 1913.

———. 1907. Obsessive actions and religious practices. In J. Strachey, ed. and trans., *The Standard Edition of the Complete Psychological Works of Sigmund Freud*, vol. 9 (pp. 115–127). London: Hogarth Press, 1959.

———. 1927. The future of an illusion. In J. Strachey, ed. and trans., *The Standard Edition of the Complete Psychological Works of Sigmund Freud*, vol. 21 (pp. 1–56). London: Hogarth Press, 1961.

Fromm, E. 1950. *Psychoanalysis and Religion.* New Haven, Conn.: Yale University Press.

———. 1956. *The Art of Loving*. New York: Harper and Row.

———. 1968. *The Revolution of Hope: Towards a Humanized Technology*. San Francisco: Harper and Row.

Frye, N. 1990. *Fearful Symmetry: A Study of William Blake*. Princeton, N.J.: Princeton University Press.

Gallese, V., Fadiga, L., Fogassi, L., & Rizzolatti, G. (1996). Action recognition in the premotor cortex. *Brain*, 119(2):593–609.

Gallup, G. 1995. *Fifty Years of Gallup Surveys on Religion (The Gallup Report No. 36)*. Princeton, N.J.: The Gallup Organization.

Garrison, V. 1977. The "Puerto Rican Syndrome" in psychiatry and *Espiritismo*. In V. Crapanzano and Vivian Garrison, eds., *Case Studies in Spirit Possession* (pp. 383–449). New York: John Wiley and Sons.

Gay, P. 1988. *Freud: A Life for Our Time*. New York: Norton.

Geertz, C. 1966. Religion as a cultural system. In M. P. Banton, ed., *Anthropological Approaches in the Study of Religion* (pp. 1–46). London: Tavistock.

Germer, C. K., Siegel, R. D., and Fulton, P. R., eds. 2005. *Mindfulness and Psychotherapy*. New York: Guilford Press.

Gersten, D. 1997. *Are You Getting Enlightened or Losing Your Mind?* New York: Harmony Books.

Gibson, K., Lathrop, D., and Stern, E. M. 1986. *Carl Jung and Soul Psychology*. New York: The Haworth Press.

Gibson, T. 2000. Wholeness and transcendence in the practice of pastoral psychotherapy from a Judeo-Christian perspective. In P. Young-Eisendrath and M. E. Miller, eds., *The Psychology of Mature Spirituality* (pp. 177–80). London: Brunner-Routledge.

Glickhauf-Hughes, C., and Wells, M. 1991. Current conceptualizations on masochism: Genesis and object relations. *American Journal of Psychotherapy* 45:53–68.

Glover, J. 1988. *I: The Philosophy and Psychology of Personal Identity*. London: Penguin Books.

Goldbrunner, J. 1966. *Individuation: A Study of the Depth Psychology of Carl Gustav Jung*. Notre Dame, Ind.: University of Notre Dame Press.

Gollwitzer, H., ed. 1956. *Dying We Live*. R. Kuhn, trans. New York: Pantheon Books.

Good, M. J. D. 1992. *Pain as a Human Experience*. Berkeley: University of California Press.

Gordon, R. 1973. Moral values and analytic insights. *British Journal of Medical Psychology* 46(1):1–11.

Greeley, A. 1975. *The Sociology of the Paranormal: A Reconnaissance*. Sage Research Papers in the Social Sciences, vol. 3, series no. 90-023. Beverly Hills, Calif.: Sage.

Greenberg, D., and Witztum, E. 1991. Problems in the treatment of religious patients. *American Journal of Psychotherapy* 45:554–65.

Greyson, B. 1997. The near death experience as a focus of clinical attention. *Journal of Nervous and Mental Diseases* 185(5):327–334.

———. 2000. Near-death experiences. In E. Cardeña, S. J. Lynn, and
S. C. Krippner, eds., *Varieties of Anomalous Experience* (pp. 315–52).
Washington, D.C.: American Psychological Association.

Griffin, D. R. 2000. *Religion and Scientific Naturalism: Overcoming the
Conflicts.* Albany, N.Y.: SUNY Press.

Griffith, J. L., and Griffith, M. E. 2002. *Encountering the Sacred in Psychotherapy.* New York: Guilford Press.

Griffiths, B. 1977. *Return to the Center.* Springfield, Ill.: Templegate.

Grof, C. 1993. *The Thirst for Wholeness: Addiction, Attachment, and the
Spiritual Path.* New York: HarperCollins.

Grof, S., and Grof, C. 1989. *Spiritual Emergency: When Personal Transformation Becomes a Crisis.* New York: Penguin Putnam.

Group for the Advancement of Psychiatry (GAP). 1976. *Mysticism:
Spiritual Quest or Mental Disorder?* Vol. 9, pub. 97. New York: Author.

Guggenbühl-Craig, A. 1970. Must analysis fail through its destructive
aspect? In *Spring* (pp. 133–45). Zurich: Spring.

———. 1971. *Power in the Helping Professions.* M. Gubitz, trans. New
York: Spring.

Guntripp, H. 1956. *Mental Pain and the Cure of Souls.* London: Independent Press.

———. 1969. *Schizoid Phenomena, Object Relations, and the Self.* New
York: International Universities Press.

Hadon, H. 1995. The hidden God. In J. M. Spiegleman, ed., *Protestantism and Jungian Psychology* (pp. 50–65). Tempe, Ariz.: New Falcon.

Hall, J. A. 1993. *The Unconscious Christian.* Mahwah, N.J.: Paulist Press.

Hannah, B. 2001. *Encounters with the Soul.* Wilmette, Ill.: Chiron Publications.

———. 2011. *The Animus: The Spirit of Inner Truth in Women.* 2 vols.
Wilmette, Ill.: Chiron Publications.

Hardy, A. 1979. *The Spiritual Nature of Man: A Study of Contemporary
Religious Experience.* Oxford: Clarendon Press.

Hart, T. 1997. Transcendental empathy in the therapeutic encounter.
Humanistic Psychologist 25(3):245–70.

———. 1999. The refinement of empathy. *Journal of Humanistic Psychology,* 39(4):111–25.

Hastings, A. 1983. A counseling approach to parapsychological experience. *Journal of Transpersonal Psychology,* 15(2):143–67.

Hauser, M. D. 2006. *Moral Minds: How Nature Designed Our Universal
Sense of Right and Wrong.* San Francisco: HarperCollins.

Heisig, J. W. 1979. *Imago Dei: A Study in C. G. Jung's Psychology of Religion.* London: Associated University Press.

Hesse, M. 1980. *Revolutions and Reconstruction in the Philosophy of Science.* Bloomington: Indiana University Press.

Hidas, A. 1981. Psychotherapy and surrender: A psychospiritual perspective. *Journal of Transpersonal Psychology*, 13(1):27–32.

Hillman, J. 1972. *The Myth of Analysis*. Evanston, Ill.: Northwestern University Press.

———. 1975. *Re-visioning Psychology*. New York: Harper and Row.

———. 1989. Peaks and vales. In T. Moore, ed., *A Blue Fire* (pp. 118–20). New York: HarperPerennial.

———. 1991. *Healing Fiction*. New York: HarperCollins.

Hoge, D. R. 1996. Religion in America: The demographics of belief and affiliation. In E. P. Shafranske, ed., *Religion and the Clinical Practice of Psychology* (pp. 21–41). Washington, D.C.: American Psychological Association Press.

Hogenson, G. E. 2007. Reply to Whitmont: "The destiny concept in psychoanalysis." *Journal of Jungian Theory and Practice*, 9(1):39–45.

Holmgren, M. R. 1993. Forgiveness and the intrinsic value of persons. *American Philosophical Quarterly*, 30:341–52.

Hong, H. V., and Hong, E. H. 1976. *Kierkegaard's Journals and Papers*, vol. 1. Bloomington: Indiana University Press.

Hood, R. W. 1974. Psychological strength and the report of intense religious experience. *Journal for the Scientific Study of Religion*, 13: 65–71.

Horney, K. 1942. *Self Analysis*. New York: W. W. Norton.

———. 1945. *Our Inner Conflicts*. New York: W. W. Norton.

Horsbrugh, H. J. 1974. Forgiveness. *Canadian Journal of Philosophy*, 4: 269–89.

Hunt, H. T. 1995. *On the Nature of Consciousness*. New Haven, Conn.: Yale University Press.

Huppert, F. A., and Whittington, J. E. 2003. Evidence for the independence of positive and negative well-being: Implications for quality of life assessment. *British Journal of Health Psychology*, 8 (1):107–22.

Huxley, A. 1945. *The Perennial Philosophy*. New York: Harper Colophon, 1970.

Jackson, S. W. 1992. The listening healer in the history of psychological healing. *American Journal of Psychiatry*, 149(12):1623–32.

Jacobs, J. L. 1989. *Divine Disenchantment*. Bloomington: University of Indiana Press.

Jacobs, J. W. 1998. "Euripides' Medea: A psychodynamic model of severe divorce pathology." *American Journal of Psychotherapy*, 2:308–19.

Jacoby, R. 1993. Some conceptual considerations on hope and stress. *Stress Medicine*, 9(1):61–69.

Jaffé, A. 1983. *The Myth of Meaning in the Work of C. G. Jung*. R. F. C Hull, trans. Zurichd: Daimon Verlag.

James, W. 1958. *The Varieties of Religious Experience*. New York: New American Library.

Jaspers, K. 1963. *General Psychopathology*. Chicago: University of Chicago Press.

Jaynes, J. 1990. *The Origin of Consciousness in the Breakdown of the Bicameral Mind.* New York: Mariner Books.

Jenkins, R. A., and Pargament, K. I. 1988. Cognitive appraisals in cancer patients. *Social Science and Medicine,* 26:625–33.

Jenson, J. P., and Bergin, A. E. 1988. Mental health values of professional therapists: A national interdisciplinary survey. *Professional Psychology: Research and Practice* 19:290–97. Washington, D.C.: American Psychological Association.

Jones, S. L. 1996. A constructive relationship for religion with the science and profession of psychology: Perhaps the boldest model yet. In E. P. Shafranske, ed., *Religion and the Clinical Practice of Psychology* (pp. 113–47). Washington, D.C.: American Psychological Association.

Josephson, A. M. 1993. The interactional problems of Christian families and their relationship to developmental psychopathology: Implications for treatment. *Journal of Psychology and Christianity,* 12:112–18.

Josephson, A. M., and Wiesner, I. S. 2004. Worldview in psychiatric assessment. In A. M. Josephson and J. R. Peteet, eds., *Handbook of Spirituality and Worldview in Clinical Practice* (pp. 15–30). Arlington, Va.: American Psychiatric Publishing.

Joy, C. R., ed. 1947. *Albert Schweitzer: An Anthology.* Boston: Beacon Press.

Jung, C. G. 1923. *Psychological Types. CW,* vol. 6. Princeton, N.J.: Princeton University Press, 1971.

———. 1928a. Psychoanalysis and the cure of souls. In *CW,* vol. 11. Princeton, N.J.: Princeton University Press, 1958, 1969.

———. 1928b. The relations between the ego and the unconscious. In *CW,* vol. 7. Princeton, N.J.: Princeton University Press, 1953.

———. 1931. Problems of modern psychotherapy. In *CW* 16. Princeton, N.J.: Princeton University Press, 1954, 1966.

———. 1932. Psychotherapists or the clergy. In *CW,* vol. 11. Princeton, N.J.: Princeton University Press, 1958, 1969.

———. 1933. *Modern Man in Search of a Soul.* W. S. Dell and C. F. Baynes, trans. New York: Harcourt, Brace and World.

———. 1934. The development of personality. In *CW,* vol. 17. Princeton, N.J.: Princeton University Press, 1954.

———. 1940. Psychology and religion. In *CW,* vol. 11. Princeton, N.J.: Princeton University Press, 1958, 1969.

———. 1944. *Psychology and Alchemy. CW,* vol. 12. Princeton, N.J.: Princeton University Press, 1968.

———. 1946. Psychology of the transference. In *CW* 16. Princeton, N.J.: Princeton University Press, 1954, 1966.

———. 1948a. On psychic energy. In *CW,* vol. 8. Princeton, N.J.: Princeton University Press, 1960, 1969.

———. 1948b. The spirit Mercurius. In *CW,* vol. 13. Princeton, N.J.: Princeton University Press, 1967.

———. 1948c. A review of the complex theory. In *CW,* vol. 8. Princeton, N.J.: Princeton University Press, 1960, 1969.

———. 1951a. *Aion. CW,* vol. 9ii. Princeton, N.J.: Princeton University Press, 1959.

———. 1951b. Fundamental questions of psychotherapy. In *CW* 16. Princeton, N.J.: Princeton University Press, 1954, 1966.

———. 1952a. Religion and psychology: A reply to Martin Buber. In *CW,* vol. 18. Princeton, N.J.: Princeton University Press, 1976.

———. 1952b. Synchronicity: An acausal connecting principle. In *CW,* vol. 8. Princeton, N.J.: Princeton University Press, 1960, 1969.

———. 1954a. On the nature of the psyche. In *CW,* vol. 8. Princeton, N.J.: Princeton University Press, 1960, 1969.

———. 1954b. Transformation symbolism in the Mass. In *CW,* vol. 11. Princeton, N.J.: Princeton University Press, 1958, 1969.

———. 1954c. Psychological commentary on *The Tibetan Book of the Dead.* In *CW,* vol. 11. Princeton, N.J.: Princeton University Press, 1958, 1969.

———. 1955–1956. *Mysterium coniunctionis. CW,* vol. 14. Princeton, N.J.: Princeton University Press, 1963.

———. 1956–1957. Jung and religious belief. In *CW,* vol. 18. Princeton, N.J.: Princeton University Press, 1976.

———. 1957. Commentary on "The Secret of the Golden Flower." In *CW,* vol. 13. Princeton, N.J.: Princeton University Press, 1967.

———. 1958. Flying saucers: A modern myth of things seen in the skies. In *CW,* vol. 10. Princeton, N.J.: Princeton University Press, 1964.

———. 1959. Good and evil in analytical psychology. In *CW,* vol. 10. Princeton, N.J.: Princeton University Press, 1964.

———. 1961. *Memories, Dreams, Reflections.* A. Jaffé, ed. New York: Random House, 1965.

———. 1970. *Analytical Psychology: Its Theory and Practice.* The Tavistock Lectures. New York: Vintage Books.

———. 1973–1975. *Letters, 2 vols.* G. Adler and A. Jaffé, eds., R. F. C. Hull, trans. Princeton, N.J.: Princeton University Press.

Kaiser, R. M. 1988. Postcritical religion and the latent Freud. *Zygon,* 25(4):433–47.

Kakar, S. 2003. Psychoanalysis and Eastern spiritual healing traditions. *Journal of Analytical Psychology,* 48(5):659–78.

Kandel, E. R., Schwartz, J. H., and Jessell, T. M. 2008. *Principles of Neural Science,* 5th edition. New York: McGraw-Hill.

Karcher, S. 2003. *Total I Ching: Myths for Change.* London: Time Warner Books.

Kast, V. 1991. *Joy, Inspiration, and Hope.* College Station: Texas A & M University Press.

Katz, S. T., ed. 1978. *Mysticism and Philosophical Analysis*. New York: Oxford University Press.

Kearney, M. 2000. *A Place of Healing*. New York: Oxford University Press.

Keats, J. 1958. *Selected Poems and Letters*. D. Bush, ed. Boston: Harcourt Brace.

Kelly, T. A., and Strupp, H. H. 1992. Patient and therapist values in psychotherapy. *Journal of Clinical and Consulting Psychology*, 60:34–40.

Kelsey, M. T. 1974. *God, Dreams, and Revelation*. Minneapolis: Augsburg.

Kerenyi, C. 1959. *Asklepios: Archetypal Image of the Physician's Existence*. New York: Pantheon Books.

Kernberg, O. 1995. *Love Relations: Normality and Pathology*. New Haven, Conn.: Yale University Press.

Kierkegaard, S. 1843. *Fear and Trembling*. W. Lowrie, trans. Garden City, N.Y.: Doubleday, 1954.

King, T. M. 1999. *Jung's Four and Some Philosophers*. Notre Dame: University of Indiana Press.

Kirkpatrick, L. A. 1997. An attachment-theory approach to the psychology of religion. In B. Spilka and D. N. McIntosh, eds., *The Psychology of Religion* (pp. 114–33). Boulder, Colo.: Westview Press.

Kirkpatrick, L. A., and Shaver, P. R. 1990. Attachment-theory and religion: Childhood attachments, religious beliefs and conversions. *Journal for the Scientific Study of Religion*, 29:315–34.

Koenig, H. G., McCullough, M. E., and Larson, D. B. 2001. *Handbook of Religion and Health*. New York: Oxford University Press.

Kohut, H. 1978. Creativeness, charisma, group psychology. In P. Ornstein, ed., *The Search for the Self*, vol. 2. New York: International Universities Press.

———. 1984. *How Does Analysis Cure?* Chicago: University of Chicago Press.

Krishnamurti, J. 1973. *You Are the World*. New York: HarperCollins.

———. 1975. *The First and Last Freedom*. San Francisco: Harper and Row.

———. 1984. *The Flame of Attention*. San Francisco: Harper San Francisco.

———. 1991. *Explorations into Insight*. London: Victor Gollancz Ltd.

———. 2001. *Choiceless Awareness*. Ojai, Calif.: Krishnamurti Publications of America.

Kübler-Ross, E. 1969. *On Death and Dying*. New York: Macmillan.

Kugel, J. 1998. *Traditions of the Bible*. Boston: Harvard University Press.

Kung, H. 1990. *Freud and the Problem of God*. New Haven, Conn.: Yale University Press.

Kurtz, E. 1999. The historical context. In W. R. Miller, ed., *Integrating Spirituality into Treatment*. Washington, D.C.: American Psychological Association Press.

Ladinsky, D. 1996. *I Heard God Laughing: Renderings of Hafiz*. Oakland, Calif.: Mobius Press.

Larson, D., and Larson, S. 1994. *The Forgotten Factor in Physical and Mental Health: What Does the Research Show?* Rockville, Md.: National Institute for Healthcare Research.

Larson, D. B., Pattison, M., Blazer, D. G., Omran, A., and Kaplan, B. 1986. Systematic analysis of research on religious variables in four major psychiatric journals, 1978–1982. *American Journal of Psychiatry*, 143:329–34.

Leavy, S. 1990. Reality in psychoanalysis and religion. In J. H. Smith and S. Handelman, eds., *Psychoanalysis and Religion: Psychiatry and the Humanities* (pp. 43–55). Baltimore: Johns Hopkins University Press.

LeShan, L. 1994. *Cancer as Turning Point*. New York: Penguin Books.

Leuba, J. H. 1925. *The Psychology of Religious Mysticism*. New York: Harcourt Brace.

Levin, J. D. 1992. *Theories of the Self*. Washington, D.C.: Hemisphere Publishing.

Levine, S. 1986. *Divine Disenchantment*. Bloomington: University of Indiana Press.

Lévi-Strauss, C. 1963. *Structural Anthropology*. C. Jacobson and B. Schoepf, trans. New York: Basic Books.

Lewin, R. A. 1996. *Compassion: The Core Value That Animates Psychotherapy*. Northvale, N.J.: Jason Aronson.

Lewis, C. A. 1994. Religiosity and obsessionality: The relationship between Freud's "religious practices." *The Journal of Psychology*, 128(2):189–96.

Lewis, C. S. 1940. *The Problem of Pain*. New York: HarperCollins, 1996.

Lewis, M. 1980. On forgiveness. *Philosophical Quarterly*, 30:236–45.

Lewis, T., Amini, F., and Lannon, R. 2000. *A General Theory of Love*. New York: Vintage Books.

Lichtenberg, J. D., Lachmann, F. M., and Fosshage, J. L. 1992. *Self and Motivational Systems*. New York: Routledge.

Lindberg, D. C., and Numbers, R. L., eds. 1986. *God and Nature: Historical Essays on the Encounter Between Christianity and Science*. Berkeley: University of California Press.

Linley, A. P., and Joseph, S., eds. 2004. *Positive Psychology in Practice*. Hoboken, N.J.: John Wiley and Sons.

London, P. 1985. *The Modes and Morals of Psychotherapy*. New York: Hemisphere Books.

Lovinger, R. J. 1984. *Working with Religious Issues in Therapy*. New York: Aronson.

Loy, D. 1997. *Nonduality: A Study in Comparative Philosophy*. Amherst, N.Y.: Humanity Books.

Lukoff, D. 1985. The diagnosis of mystical experience with psychotic features. *Journal of Transpersonal Psychology*, 17(2):155–81.

————. 1988. Transpersonal therapy with a manic-depressive artist. *Journal of Transpersonal Psychology*, 20(1):10–20.

Lynch, W. F. 1965. *Images of Hope: Imagination as Healer of the Hopeless.* Baltimore: Helicon.

Mahrer, A. R., Boulet, D. B., and Fairweather, D. R. 1994. Beyond empathy: Advances in the clinical theory and methods of empathy. *Clinical Psychology Review*, 14:183–9.

Mancia, M. 2006. *Psychoanalysis and Neuroscience.* New York: Springer.

Mansfield, V., and Spiegelman, J. 1996. On the physics and psychology of the transference as an interactive field. *Journal of Analytical Psychology*, 41:179–202.

Marcel, G. 1962. *Homo Viator: Introduction to a Metaphysic of Hope.* E. Craufurd, trans. San Francisco: Harper Torchbooks.

Marsella, A. J., ed. 1989. *Culture and Self: Asian and Western Perspectives.* London: Routledge.

Maslow, A. H. 1964. *Religions, Values, and Peak Experiences.* Columbus: Ohio State University Press.

————. 1970. Religious aspects of peak experiences. In W. A. Sadler, ed., *Personality and Religion* (pp. 168–79). New York: Harper and Row.

————. 1971. *The Farther Reaches of Human Nature.* New York: Viking Press.

Masson, J. 1990. *Final Analysis: The Making and Unmaking of a Psychoanalyst.* Reading, Mass.: Addison-Wesley.

Matthews, D. A., and Clark, C. 1998. *The Faith Factor.* New York: Penguin.

May, G. M. 1992. *Care of Mind, Care of Spirit.* New York: HarperCollins.

McCarley, R. W., and Hobson, J. A. 1977. The neurobiological origins of psychoanalytic dream theory. *American Journal of Psychiatry*, 134(11):1211–21.

McCullough, M. E., Pargament, K. I., and Thoreson, C. E. 2000. *Forgiveness: Theory, Research, and Practice.* New York: Guilford Press.

McCullough, M. E., Worthington, E. L., and Rachal, K. C. 1997. Interpersonal forgiving in close relationships. *Journal of Personality and Social Psychology*, 73:321–36.

McFague, S. 1987. *Models of God.* Philadelphia: Fortress Press.

McGrath, A. 2007. *The Dawkins Delusion.* London: SPCK.

McNamara, W. 1975. Psychology and the Christian mystical tradition. In C. Tart, ed., *Transpersonal Psychologies.* New York: Harper and Row.

Meier, C. A. 1959. Projection, transference, and the subject-object relation in psychology. *Journal of Analytical Psychology*, 4(1):21–34.

Meissner, W. W. 1984. *Psychoanalysis and Religious Experience.* New Haven, Conn.: Yale University Press.

————. 1987. *Life and Faith: Psychological Perspectives on Religious Experience.* Washington, D.C.: Georgetown University Press.

————. 1992. The pathology of belief systems. *Psychoanalysis and Contemporary Thought*, 15:99–128.

————. 1996. The pathology of beliefs and the beliefs of pathology. In E. P. Shafranske, ed., *Religion in the Clinical Practice of Psychology* (pp. 241–67). Washington, D.C.: American Psychological Association.

Meng, H., and Freud, E. L., eds. 1963. *Psychoanalysis and Faith: The Letters of Sigmund Freud and Oskar Pfister.* New York: Basic Books.

Menninger, K. 1959. Hope. *American Journal of Psychiatry*, 116:481–91.

Miller, A. 1990. *For Your Own Good.* New York: Farrar, Straus and Giroux.

Miller, D. L. 2005. *Three Faces of God.* New Orleans: Spring.

Miller, W. R., ed. 1999. *Integrating Spirituality into Treatment.* Washington, D.C.: American Psychological Association.

Mintz, E. E. 1983. *The Psychic Thread: Paranormal and Transpersonal Aspects of Psychotherapy.* New York: Human Sciences Press.

Mitchell, S. 1993. *Hope and Dread in Psychoanalysis.* New York: Basic Books.

Moore, R. L. 2001. *The Archetype of Initiation: Sacred Space, Ritual Process, and Personal Transformation.* M. J. Havlick, ed. Philadelphia: Xlibris Publishing.

Morris, T. V., ed. 1994. *God and the Philosophers: The Reconciliation of Faith and Reason.* New York: Oxford University Press.

Murphy, M., and Donovan, S. 1994. *The Physical and Psychological Effects of Meditation.* Petaluma, Calif.: Noetic Sciences Press.

Myers, D. G., and Diener, E. 1996. The pursuit of happiness. *Scientific American*, 274(5):70–72.

Natterson, D. L. 1996. Love in psychotherapy. *Psychoanalytic Psychology*, 20:509–21.

Neumann, E. 1949. *The Origins and History of Consciousness.* Princeton, N.J.: Princeton University Press.

————. 1960. *Depth Psychology and a New Ethic.* London: Hodder and Stoughton.

————. 1968. Mystical man. In J. Campbell, ed., *The Mystic Vision* (pp. 375–415). Princeton, N.J.: Princeton University Press.

Nicholson, R. A. 1950. *Rumi, Poet and Mystic.* London: Allen and Unwin.

Nietzsche, F. W. 1878. *Human, All Too Human: A Book for Free Spirits.* R. J. Hollingdale, trans. New York: Cambridge University Press, 1996.

Nobel, K. D. 1987. Psychological health and the experience of transcendence. *The Counseling Psychologist*, 15:601–14.

Ogden, T. 1979. On projective identification. *International Journal of Psychoanalysis*, 60:357–74.

Ornstein, A. 1991. The dread to repeat: Comments on the working-through process. *Journal of the American Psychoanalytic Association*, 39:377–98.

Otto, R. 1917. *The Idea of the Holy.* J. Harvery, trans. London: Oxford University Press.

Oxman, T. E., Freeman, D. H., and Manheimer, E. D. 1995. Lack of social participation or religious strength and comfort as risk factors for death after cardiac surgery in the elderly. *Psychosomatic Medicine,* 57(1):5–15.

Panikkar, R. 1979. *Myth, Faith, and Hermeneutics.* New York: Paulist Press.

Pargament, K. I. 1997. *The Psychology of Religion and Coping.* New York: The Guilford Press.

Parsons, T. 2002. *As It Is.* Carlsbad, Calif.: Inner Directions Publishing.

Perry, J. 1974. *The Far Side of Madness.* Englewood Cliffs, N.J.: Prentice-Hall.

Peteet, J. R. 1994. Approaching spiritual problems in psychotherapy. *Journal of Psychotherapy Practice and Research,* 3:237–45.

———. 2004. *Doing the Right Thing: An Approach to Moral Issues in Mental Health Treatment.* Washington, D.C.: American Psychiatric Association.

Pickering, W. S. F., ed. 1975. *Durkheim on Religion: A Selection of Readings with Bibliographies.* London: Routledge and Kegan Paul.

Pollner, M. 1989. Divine relations, social relations, and well-being. *Journal of Health and Social Behavior,* 30:92–104.

Prendergast, J. J., and Bradford, G. K., eds. 2007. *Listening from the Heart of Silence: Nondual Wisdom and Psychotherapy.* St. Paul, Minn.: Paragon House Publishers.

Prendergast, J. J., Fenner, P., and Krystal, S., eds. 2003. *Sacred Mirror: Nondual Wisdom and Psychotherapy.* New York: Omega Books.

Prinz, J. J. 2007. Is morality innate? In W. Sinnott-Armstrong, ed., *Moral Psychology. Volume 1: The Evolution of Morality: Adaptations and Innateness.* New York: Oxford University Press.

Pruyser, P. W. 1976. *A Dynamic Psychology of Religion.* San Francisco: HarperCollins.

———. 1997. The seamy side of current religious belief. *Bulletin of the Menninger Clinic,* 41:329–48.

Psychodynamic Diagnostic Manual (PDM) Task Force. 2006. *Psychodynamic Diagnostic Manual.* Silver Spring, Md.: Alliance of Psychoanalytic Organizations.

Pytell, T. 2006. Transcending the angel beast: Victor Frankl and humanistic psychology. *Psychoanalytic Psychology* 23(3):490–503.

Racker, H. 1968. *Transference and Countertransference.* New York: International Universities Press.

Radin, D. I. 1997. *The Conscious Universe.* San Francisco: Harper San Francisco.

Rajneesh, B. S. 1979. *The Buddha Disease: A Darshan Diary.* Poona, India: Rajneesh Foundation.

————. 1985. *Glimpses of a Golden Childhood*. Rajneeshpuram, Antelope, Ore.: Rajneesh Foundation International.

Ramachandran, V. S., Hirstein, W. S., Armel, K. C., Tecoma, E., and Iragul, V. 1997. Neural basis of religious experience. *Society for Neuroscience Conference Abstracts* (p. 1316). Washington, D.C.: Author.

Reading, A. 2004. *Hope and Despair: How Perceptions of the Future Shape Human Behavior*. Baltimore: Johns Hopkins University Press.

Rector, L. 2001. Mystical experience as an expression of the idealizing selfobject need. In A. Goldberg, ed., *Progress in Self Psychology*, vol. 17, *The Narcissistic Patient Revisited* (pp. 179–96). Hillsdale, N.J.: Analytic Press.

Reed, E. S. 1997. *From Soul to Mind*. New Haven, Conn.: Yale University Press.

Reed, H. 1996. Close encounters in the liminal zone: Experiments in imaginal communication. *Journal of Analytical Psychology*, 41:81–116.

Reymond, L. 1972. *To Live Within: A Woman's Spiritual Pilgrimage in a Himalayan Hermitage*. Portland, Ore.: Rudra Press.

Rhode, P. R. 1990. *The Diary of Søren Kierkegaard*. New York: Citadel Press.

Richards, P. S., and Bergin, A. E. 2005. *A Spiritual Strategy for Counseling and Psychotherapy*. Washington, D.C.: American Psychological Association.

Rizzuto, A.-M. 1979. *The Birth of the Living God: A Psychoanalytic Study*. Chicago: University of Chicago Press.

Roberts, B. 1984. *The Experience of No-Self*. Boston: Shambhala.

Rochlin, G. 1965. *Griefs and Discontents: The Forces of Change*. Boston: Little, Brown.

Rolls, E. T. 2005. *Emotions Explained*. Oxford: Oxford University Press.

Roseborough, D. J. 2006. Psychodynamic psychotherapy: An effectiveness study. *Research on Social Work Practice*, 16(2):166–75.

Rubin, J. B. 1996. *Psychotherapy and Buddhism*. New York: Plenum Press.

————. 2004. *The Good Life: Psychoanalytic Reflections on Love, Ethics, Creativity, and Spirituality*. Albany, N.Y.: SUNY Press.

Russell, B. 1927. *Why I Am Not a Christian*. New York: The Truth Seeker Company.

————. 1929. *Marriage and Morals*. New York: W. W. Norton, 1970.

————. 1956. *Portraits from Memory*. New York: Simon and Schuster.

————. 1959. *My Philosophical Development*. London: George Allen and Unwin.

————. 1971. *The Autobiography of Bertrand Russell*, 3 vols. London: George Allen and Unwin.

Samuels, A. 2001. *Politics on the Couch*. New York: Other Press.

Sandner, D. F., and Wong, S. H., eds. 1997. *The Sacred Heritage: The Influence of Shamanism on Analytical Psychology*. London: Routledge.

Sanella, L. 1987. *The Kundalini Experience.* Lower Lake, Calif.: Integral.

Sanford, J. A. 1951. *Dreams: God's Forgotten Language.* New York: Harper San Francisco, 1989.

Satir, V. 1987. The therapist story. *Journal of Psychotherapy and the Family,* 3(1):17–25.

Scarry, E. 1985. *The Body in Pain.* New York: Oxford University Press.

Schaer, H. 1950. *Religion and the Cure of Souls in Jung's Psychology.* New York: Pantheon Books.

Schott, G. D. 1993. Penfield's homunculus: A note on cerebral cartography. *Journal of Neurology, Neurosurgery, and Psychiatry* 56: 329–33.

Schwartz-Salant, N. 1988. Archetypal foundations of projective identification. *Journal of Analytical Psychology,* 33(1):39–64.

Searles, H. F. 1979. The patient as therapist to his therapist. In *Countertransference and Related Subjects* (pp. 380–459). New York: International Universities Press.

Seligman, M. 2002. *Authentic Happiness: Using the New Positive Psychology to Realize Your Potential for Lasting Fulfillment.* New York: Free Press.

Seligman, M., and Csikszentmihalyi, M. 2000. Positive psychology: An introduction. *American Psychologist,* 55:5–14.

Shafranske, E. P., ed. 1996. *Religion in the Clinical Practice of Psychology.* Washington, D.C.: American Psychological Association.

Shafranske, E. P., and Malony, H. 1990. Clinical psychologists' religious and spiritual orientations and their practice of psychotherapy. *Psychotherapy,* 27(1):72–78.

Shand, A. F. 1920. *Foundations of Character: Being a Study of the Tendencies of the Emotions and Sentiments.* London: Macmillan.

Shapiro, A. K. 1978. Placebo effects in medical and psychological therapies. In S. L. Garfield and A. E. Bergin, eds., *Handbook of Psychotherapy and Behavior Change: An Empirical Analysis* (pp. 439–73). New York: John Wiley.

Sharfstein, B.-A. 1980. *The Philosophers.* New York: Oxford University Press.

Shaw, D. 2003. On the therapeutic action of analytic love. *Contemporary Psychoanalysis,* 39:252–78.

Shideler, M. M. 1962. *The Theology of Romantic Love: A Study in the Writings of Charles Williams.* New York: Harper and Brothers.

Slater, J. G. 1994. *Bertrand Russell.* Bristol, U.K.: Thoemmes Press.

Slife, B. D., Hope, C., and Nebeker, R. S. 1999. Examining the relationship between religious spirituality and psychological science. *Journal of Humanistic Psychology,* 39:51–85.

Smith, C. M. 1995. *Psychotherapy and the Sacred.* Chicago: Center for the Scientific Study of Religion.

Smith, N. L., and Smith, L. L. 1996. Field theory in science: Its role as a necessary and sufficient condition in psychology. *Psychological Record*, 46:3–19.

Sontag, S. 1977. *Illness as Metaphor*. New York: Farrar, Straus and Giroux.

Spanos, N. P., and Moretti, P. 1998. Correlates of mystical and diabolical experiences in a sample of female university students. *Journal for the Scientific Study of Religion*, 27:105–16.

Spero, M. H. 1984. *Psychotherapy of the Religious Patient*. Springfield, Ill.: Charles C. Thomas.

———. 1985. The reality of the God image in psychotherapy. *American Journal of Psychotherapy*, 39:75–85.

———. 1987. Identity and individuality in the nouveau-religious patient: Theoretical and clinical aspects. *Psychiatry*, 50:55–71.

———. 1990. Parallel dimensions of experience in psychoanalytic psychotherapy of the religious patient. *Psychotherapy*, 27(1):53–71.

Sperry, L., and Shafranske, E. P., eds. 2005. *Spiritually Oriented Psychotherapy*. Washington, D.C.: American Psychological Association.

Sprinkle, R. L. 1985. Psychological resonance: A holographic model of counseling. *Journal of Counseling and Development*, 64:206–8.

Stace, W. 1960. *The Teachings of the Mystics*. New York: Mentor Books.

Stark, R. A. 1965. A taxonomy of religious experience. *Journal for the Scientific Study of Religion*, 5:97–116.

Stein, H. F. 1981. Review of A.-M. Rizzuto, *The Birth of the Living God: A Psychoanalytic Study*. *Psychoanalytic Quarterly*, 50:125–30.

Stephens, B. D. 2001. The Martin Buber-Carl Jung disputations: Protecting the sacred in the battle for the boundaries of analytical psychology. *Journal of Analytical Psychology* 46:455–91.

Stern, D. N. 2004. *The Present Moment in Psychotherapy and Everyday Life*. New York: Norton.

Sternberg, R. J., and Barnes, M. L., eds. 1988. *The Psychology of Love*. New Haven, Conn.: Yale University Press.

Sternberg, R. J., and Weis, K., eds. 2006. *The New Psychology of Love*. New Haven, Conn.: Yale University Press.

Stevens, A. 1993. *The Two-million-year-old Self*. College Station: Texas A & M Press.

Suttie, I. D. 1935. *The Origins of Love and Hate*. London: Free Association Books, 1999.

Szasz, T. 1978. *The Myth of Psychotherapy*. New York: Doubleday.

Tan, S-Y. 2003. Integrating spiritual direction into psychotherapy: Ethical issues and guidelines. *Journal of Psychology and Theology*, 31(1):14–23.

Tan, S.-Y., and Johnson, B. W. 2002. Spiritually oriented cognitive behavioral therapy. In L. Sperry and E. P. Shafranske, eds., *Spiritually Oriented Psychotherapy* (pp. 77–103). Washington, D.C.: American Psychological Association.

Targ, E., Schlitz, M., and Irwin, H. 2000. Psi-related experiences. In E. Cardeña, S. J. Lynn, and S. C. Krippner, eds., *Varieties of Anomalous Experience* (pp. 219–52). Washington, D.C.: American Psychological Association.

Thompson, C. 1943. The therapeutic technique of Sandor Ferenczi: A comment. *International Journal of Psychoanalysis*, 24:64–66.

Tjelveit, A. C. 1986. *Ethics and Values in Psychotherapy*. London: Routledge.

Tolpin, P., and Tolpin, M. 1996. *Heinz Kohut: The Chicago Institute lectures*. Hillsdale, N.J.: The Analytic Press.

Turner, V. 1987. The liminal period in rites of passage. In L. C. M. Mahdi, S. Foster, and M. Little, eds., *Betwixt and Between: Patterns of Masculine and Feminine Initiation*. La Salle, Ill.: Open Court Publishing.

Ulanov, A. B. 1986. *Picturing God*. Salt Lake City, Utah: Cowley.

Ullman, C. 1989. *The Transformed Self: The Psychology of Religious Conversion*. New York: Plenum.

Usandivaras, R. J. 1985. The therapeutic process as a ritual. *Group Analysis* 28:1–17.

van de Castle, R. 1994. *Our Dreaming Mind. Dartford, Kent: Aquarian Press.*

van Lommel, P., van Wees, R., Meyers V., and Elfferich, I. 2001. Near-death experience in survivors of cardiac arrest: A prospective study in the Netherlands. *Lancet*, 358(9298):2039–45.

Vaughan, F. 1987. A question of balance: Health and pathology in new religious movements. In D. Anthony, B. Ecker, and K. Wilber, eds., *Spiritual Choices: The Problem of Recognizing Authentic Paths to Inner Transformation*. New York: Paragon House.

Vellacott, P. 1963. *Euripides: Medea and Other Plays*. London: Penguin Books.

Vergote, A. 1969. *The Religious Man*. Dayton, Ohio: Pflaum.

Vergote, A., and Tamayo, A., eds. 1981. *The Parental Figures and the Representation of God: A Psychological and Cross-cultural Study*. New York: Mouton.

von Franz, M.-L. 1980. *Projection and Re-collection in Jungian Psychology: Reflections of the Soul.* Peru, Ill.: Open Court.

———. 1981. Daimons and the inner companions. *Parabola*, 6(4):36.

———. 1986. *Number and Time: Reflections Leading Towards a Unification of Depth Psychology and Physics*. Evanston, Ill.: Northwestern University Press.

———. 1992. *Psyche and Matter*. Boston: Shambhala.

Walsh, B. T., Seidman, S. N., Sysko, R., and Gould, M. 2002. Placebo response in studies of major depression: Variable, substantial, and growing. *Journal of the American Medical Association,* 287(14):1840–47.

Wapnick, K. 1969. Mysticism and schizophrenia. *Journal of Transpersonal Psychology,* 1(2):49–67.

Watts, A. 1964. *Beyond Theology.* New York: Pantheon Books.

Welwood, J. 2002. *Toward a Psychology of Awakening: Buddhism, Psychotherapy, and the Path of Personal and Spiritual Transformation.* Boston: Shambhala.

West, W. 2000. *Psychotherapy and Spirituality: Crossing the Line Between Therapy and Religion.* Thousand Oaks, Calif.: Sage.

Wheeler, J. A. 1983. Law without law. In J. Wheeler and W. Zureck, eds., *Quantum Theory and Measurement.* Princeton, N.J.: Princeton University Press.

White, W. A. 1916. *Mechanisms of Character Formation.* New York: Macmillan.

Whitmont, E. C. 2007. The destiny concept in psychotherapy. *Journal of Jungian Theory and Practice,* 9(1):23–37.

Williams, C. 1990. *Outlines of Romantic Theology.* A. M. Hadfield, ed. Grand Rapids, Mich.: William B. Eerdmans.

Winnicott, D. W. 1947. Hate in the countertransference. In *Collected papers: Through Pediatrics to Psychoanalysis* (pp. 194–203). New York: Basic Books, 1958.

———. 1955. The depressive position in normal emotional development. *British Journal of Medical Psychology,* 28:89–100.

———. 1971a. *Playing and Reality.* London: Routledge.

———. 1971b. *Therapeutic Consultations in Child Psychiatry.* London: Hogarth Press.

Winson, J. 1990. The meaning of dreams. *Scientific American,* 263(5):42–48.

Wong, P. T., and Fry, P. 1998. *The Human Quest for Meaning.* Mahwah, N.J.: Lawrence Erlbaum Associates.

Worthington, E. L., Jr., ed. 1998. *Dimensions of Forgiveness.* West Conshohocken, Pa.: Templeton Foundation Press.

Wulff, D. M. 2000. Mystical experience. In E. Cardeña, S. J. Lynn, and S. C. Krippner, eds., *Varieties of Anomalous Experience* (pp. 397–440). Washington, D.C.: American Psychological Association.

Yahine, C. E., and Miller, W. R. 2006. Evoking hope. In W. R. Miller, ed., *Integrating Spirituality into Treatment* (pp. 217–33). Washington, D.C.: American Psychological Association.

Zaehner, R. C. 1961. *Mysticism Sacred and Profane.* New York: Oxford University Press.

Zieger, A. 1946. *Plays of the Greek Dramatists.* Cheshire, Conn.: Biblo and Tannen.

Zinnbauer, B. J., Pargament, K. I., Cole, B., Rye, M., Butter, E. M., Belavich, T. G., Hipp, K. M., Scott, A. S., and Kadar, J. L. 1997. Religion and spirituality: Unfuzzying the fuzzy. *Journal for the Scientific Study of Religion*, 36(4):549–64.

Zock, H. 1990. *A Psychology of Ultimate Concern: Erik H. Erikson's Contribution to the Psychology of Religion*. Amsterdam: Rodopi.

INDEX

abortion, 26
Abraham, and Isaac,
184–86
abuse: memories of, 96; of
children, 146, 149, 207,
210, 273
active imagination, 164,
166
Adams, J. E., 40–41
addiction, 75, 265, 273
Adler, G., 178, 228
Advaita Vedanta, 235
Aeschylus, 105
affect, therapeutic
approaches to, 102
aging, 26
Agosin, T., 74
Albaugh, J. A., 20
Albee, G. W., 20
alchemy, 56–57
Allman, L. S., 76
Alston, W. P., 62–63, 68,
81n2
Amini, F., 22, 89, 188n18
Anandarajah, G., 48n3
anima mundi, 159
animals, divine and in
dreams, 127–28
Aphrodite, 214
Apollo, 178–80
Aquinas, 104
archetype, 219n6, 278–79,
281; in psychotherapy,
177–83
Arieti, S., 195
Aristotle, 12
Armel, K. C., 82n16

Ash, M. G., 136
atheism, 35, 48n6, 143,
192, 198
Atman-Brahman, 235, 247
attachment theory, and
religion, 143–44
authority, 205–6
Aziz, R., 81n8

Babb, L. A., 204
Bach, S., 104
Bachelard, G., 111
Balint, M., 179, 248
Barnes, M. L., 89
Barnhouse, R. T., 71
Barra, D., 117
Barry, W. A., 79, 223
Barth, Karl, 33, 60
Baumeister, R. F., 95
Beardsworth, T., 63
behaviorism, classical,
47n1
beliefs, 76
belief system, defensive,
135
Bell, John, theorem, 170,
249
Belluardo, P., 7
Bemporad, J., 195
Benner, D. G., 187n8, 222
Benson, P. L., 133
Berenbaum, H., 69
Berger, P. L., 137
Bergin, A. E., 4, 7, 26, 32,
36–38, 40, 48n7, 152n10,
165, 187n7, 187n9
Bergson, Henri, 292

Bettelheim, B., 139
Betz, B. J., 107
Bion, W., 1, 87–88, 252
Blackstone, J., 235
Blake, William, 158, 166
Blatt, S. J., 153n19
Blazer, D. G., 69
Bloch, Ernst, 104
Bloom, H., 63
Bobgan, M. and D., 41,
269
body, 245; spiritual
importance, connection
to the sacred, 58–59. *See
also* mind and body
Bogart, G., 44
Bollas, C., 106
Boorstein, S., 165
Boris, H., 110, 112
Boulet, D. B., 239
Bowker, J., 134
Bradford, D. T., 72
Bradford, G. K., 235
brain, 7, 9, 11, 37–38, 57–
58, 77, 82n16; plasticity,
247–48
Bromberg, W., 5
Bromiley, G. V., 33
Bronheim, H., 32
Buber, Martin, 66
Buddha, 24, 61, 98, 192,
243
Buddhism, 235
Burkitt, I., 246
Burr, V., 246

Caird, D., 70

317

Campbell, J., 267
Camus, Albert, 104
cancer, 24, 30, 292n2. *See also* illness
Cannon, W. B., 103
Capps, D., 170–71
Cardeña, E., 52, 69
Carlson, E., 117
case examples, 236–39, 274–75
Casement, P., 106
Cazzaro, M., 8
Chalmers, D. J., 9
character pathology, and forgiveness, 98–99
charismatic leaders, 201, 203–4
child abuse. *See* abuse, of children
Chilton, B., 48n6, 186
Chiron, 178
Christian Church, 58, 79
Christianity, 4, 56, 96, 167, 220n10, 233n2; institutional, 269; mainstream, 12–13; violence in, 186
Christou, E., 159–61
Clark, C., 164
Clarke, R. O., 202
Claus, J. J., 212–13
Cloninger, C. R., 8, 12
Cohen, J. M., 89, 91
complexes, 163, 277–78, 280–81; autonomous, 51; in the Jungian tradition, 47n1, 171–72, 187n4, 209–14, 217–18
concentration camps, 267–68
confession, 176, 198, 218
coniunctio, 228–29, 240
Connolly, W. J., 79, 223
consciousness, 11–12; of the transpersonal Self, 235; unifying factor in human experience, 248–49
contemplation, 120
Conti, S., 7–8
conversion, religious, 82n14, 142

Corbett, L., 12, 54, 73, 81n5, 153n21, 187n6, 219n5
Corbin, H., 63, 166
Cordic, D. D., 126
Cornett, C., 26, 133, 140
counseling, Christian, 40
countertransference, 39, 100, 181, 207, 216, 228, 232, 251
Crick, F., 57
Csikszentmihalyi, M., 8
cults, 201, 203

daimon, 217
Dante, 90, 207
dark night of the soul, 120–23
Dawkins, Richard, 48n6
death, 26, 103–4, 106
Deikman, A., 201
DeLa Roche, O., 76
deMause, L., 37
depression, 10, 102, 121–23, 153n19, 170, 195, 266–68, 273, 276, 280, 285; treatment results, 7, 27–28
depth psychology, and soul, 155, 157, 161, 164–65
Descartes, René, 245–46, 293n9
despair, 102–3, 110, 112, 189–91
determinism, 16, 46–47, 136, 169, 230, 249
deus absconditus, 122
Diagnostic and Statistical Manual (DSM), 146, 153n19
Diamond, E. L., 95
Dickinson, Emily, 105
Diener, E., 7
discernment, 70, 76; versus diagnosis, 226–27
disease. *See* illness
dissociative disorder, 70
divination, 231
divine child, 61, 197
divine, as the transpersonal Self, 67

dogma, 60–61
Donovan, S., 115
Dourley, J. P., 13, 94
Downie, R. S., 95
dreams, 52, 55–58, 127–30, 166, 208, 225–26, 238, 251; examples, 55–56, 208, 270, 291–92; Jungian approach, 56–57
dream figures, as soul figures, 156
dream work, 13
Dru, A., 190–91
D'Souza, R. F., 11
dualism, 158
Durkheim, Émile, 137

ecopsychology, 159
ecstatic experience, 50
Edinger, E. F., 126, 152n8, 184, 186
ego, 242–47
ego-Self axis, 223, 259n2
Eigen, M., 55, 79, 88
Einstein, A., 152n13
Elfferich, I., 70
Eliade, M., 5, 175–76
Elijah, 63
Elkins, D. N., 76
Ellenberger, H. F., 5, 174
Emmons, R. A., 8
emotion, 11, 113n5, 163, 277–81; and soul, 158; and spiritual experience, 22
emotional distress, 5, 7–8, 70, 224–25
empathy, 162, 181, 198, 218, 227, 239–41
Engel, George, 106
Enlightenment, 12, 34, 48
entheogens (psychedelic agents), 54, 165
Erikson, Erik, 86, 107, 170, 189; on religion, 141
ethical humanists, 37
ethical relativism, 36, 48n8
Euripides, *Medea,* 211–17
evil, in psychotherapy, 206–10, 215–18
evil behavior, 42, 206–7;

origins, 208–9, 218, 219n6
evolution, debates about, 11–13, 137, 247
existential nihilism, 292n1
Exline, J. J., 95

Fadiga, L., 17n4
Fairweather, D. R., 239
faith, 28, 42, 60–62, 67, 85–88, 190–91, 286; in the psychotherapeutic process, 85–87; and skepticism, 34
Fallot, R. D., 19
father complex, 130, 204, 210–11, 219n7
Fava, G. A., 7–8
Fenner, P., 235
Ferenczi, S., 92
Field, N., 253
FitzGerald, F., 219n4
Fogassi, L., 17n4
forgiveness: factors preventing, 97–98; for offenses against humanity, 100–1; in psychotherapy, 95–102
Fosshage, J. L., 149
Fowler, J. W., 86
Frank, J., 52, 103, 107
Frankl, V. E., 103, 168, 225, 264–65, 267–69
free will, 46; versus determinism, 169
freedom, personal, 46–47
Freeman, D. H., 20
French, T. M., 106
Freud, E. L., 152n12
Freud, S., 91, 105, 149, 170; on authority, 205–6; meaning of ego, 242, 245–46; moral masochism, 260n7; Oedipus complex, 212; on religion, 138–40; on the soul, 139
Fromm, E., 89, 92, 106, 140, 144–45
Fry, P., 7
Frye, N., 166
Fulton, P. R., 162

fundamentalism, 147
fundamentalists, 200, 269; and psychotherapy, 41–42

Gallese, V., 17n4
Gallup, G., 146
Gandhi, Mohandas, 35
Garrison, V., 51
Gay, P., 140
Geertz, C., 138
gender, 243
Germer, C. K., 162
Gersten, D., 164
Gibson, K., 187n2
Gibson, T., 176
Glickhauf-Hughes, C., 42
Glover, J., 260n4
God, 4, 16n2, 75, 125–26, 200, 222; existence of, 28, 192; knowledge of, 33; and the unconscious, 60
God hypothesis, 9
God module, 77
God-image, 125; child's, 130–32; Christian, 195; discrepancies, 27; as expression of the Self, 82n12; impersonal, 195; Judeo-Christian, 139; narcissistic, 133; personal, 126–27, 133–35, 139; projection of parental imagoes, 131, 133, 136; punitive, 22, 24, 130, 134, 200–1; traditional, 135–36; as a transitional object, 132
gods, triune, 56, 81n6
Goldbrunner, J., 60
Gollwitzer, H., 103
good and evil, 206, 217
Good, M. J. D., 48n4
Goodenough, Erwin R., 78
Gordon, R., 36
Gould, M., 7
Grandi, S., 7–8
Greeley, A., 75
Greenberg, D., 72, 139
Greyson, B., 70

Griffin, D. R., 68
Griffith, J. L. and M. E., 30
Griffiths, B., 58
Grof, C., 70, 73, 265
Grof, S., 70
Group for the Advancement of Psychiatry (GAP), 78–79
Guggenbüh-Craig, A., 178, 180
Guntripp, H., 191; on religion, 141
guru, 82n14, 201–5

Hades, 282, 294n14
Hadon, H., 151n2
Hafiz, 260n8
Hall, J. A., 127
Hannah, B., 81n3, 166
happiness, 8, 31, 247
Hardy, A., 76
Hart, T., 239–40
Hastings, A., 73
hatred, 36, 91, 95; self-, 149, 204
Hauser, M. D., 38
Heckman, J. P., 19
Heisig, J. W., 152n17
Hephaestus, 216
Hera archetype, 214, 216–17
Hesse, M., 137
Hidas, A., 257
Hight, E., 48n3
Hillman, J., 172; on the soul, 157–58
Hilton, Walter, 91
Hirstein, W. S., 82n16
Hobson, J. A., 58
Hoge, D. R., 146
Hogenson, G. E., 170
Holmgren, M. R., 100
holotropic breath work, 165
homosexuality, as a sin, 39
Hong, H. V. and E. H., 190
Hood, R. W., 70
Hope, C., 136
hope: in literature,

hope *(cont.)*
104–5; mature, 111; in
psychotherapy, 102–13;
vignette, 108–9
hopelessness, 102–3,
109–10
Horney, K., 106–7
Horsbrugh, H. J., 95
Hosea, 211
human behavior, 149;
brain-based model, 11
Hunt, H. T., 67
Huppert, F. A., 7
Husserl, Edmund, 240
Huxley, A., 4, 88
hysteria, 70, 78

idealization, 199–204; of
the therapist, 205
illness (disease), 28–30; as
metaphor, 293n8
illumination, 120
imagination, 111–12,
159–60
immanence, 66
Inanna, 123, 282–85
individualism, 246, 248,
260n5
individuation, 68, 81, 92,
121, 172, 225
infanticide, 213
inflation, 77
Iragul, V., 82n16
Irwin, H., 73

Jackson, S. W., 168
Jacobs, J. L., 201
Jacobs, J. W., 213
Jacoby, R., 103
Jaffé, A., 269
James, William, 14, 54–55,
62, 145, 148, 151n1,
170, 184
Jaspers, Karl, 34
Jaynes, J., 77
Jenkins, R. A., 24
Jensen, J. P., 32, 48n7
Jessell, T. M., 9
Jesus, 24
Johnson, B. W., 11
Johnston, S. I., 212–13

Jones, S. L., 48n5
Joseph, S., 8
Josephson, A. M., 6, 146
Joy, C. R., 275
judgment, antithetical to
good therapy, 206–7,
252–53, 255
Jung, C. G., 5, 10–13,
42, 65, 81n6, 170, 176;
accused of psychologism,
59–60; on alcoholism,
265; archetypes, 278,
280; and Buber, 66; on
complexes, 150–51, 211,
215; controversy with
theologians, 66–67;
on daydreaming and
creative imagination,
111; essay on
psychotherapists versus
the clergy, 167–69;
on love, 90; *mana-*
personalities, 203;
meaning of *ego,* 242;
on meaninglessness,
266, 268–69; numinous
experience of the Self,
78; on personality
development, 198–99,
265–66; on power, 94;
on psychic infections,
188n16; reality of the
psyche, 15; on religion,
144–46; religious
function of the psyche,
25, 129, 145–46, 158; on
sacrifice, 184; on soul,
23, 156; spiritual in the
psyche, 161; spiritual
suffering, 167; on theory
in psychotherapy, 250;
on transference, 228–29;
on transpersonal Self, 87,
125, 127, 129, 132, 151,
216–17, 235, 267, 273
Jungian psychology, 56; a
psychology of the soul,
156

Kabir, 259
Kaiser, R. M., 140

Kakar, S., 201
Kandel, E. R., 9
Kant, Emmanuel, 88
Kaplan, B., 69
karma, 19, 272
Kast, V., 104
Katz, S. T., 61
Kearney, Michael, 188n17
Keats, John, 157
Kelly, T. A., 35
Kelsey, M. T., 58
Kerenyi, C., 178
Kernberg, O., 92
Kerns, J., 69
Kierkegaard, Søren, 185,
189–91
King, Martin Luther,
Jr., 35
King, T. M., 219n1
Kirkpatrick, L. A., 143
Koenig, H. G., 5, 20
Kohut, H., 80, 152n16,
163, 197, 199, 203,
229, 239; meaning of
ego, 242; on theory in
psychotherapy, 250
Krippner, S. C., 52, 69
Krishnamurti, J., 88,
90, 244, 246–47, 250,
252–53, 255
Krystal, S., 235
Kübler-Ross, E., 104
Kugel, J., 186
kundalini energy, 73,
82n15
Kung, H., 143
Kurtz, E., 232n1

Lachmann, F. M., 149
Ladinsky, D., 260n8
Lannon, R., 22, 89,
188n18
Larson, D. and S., 146
Larson, D. B., 5, 20, 69
Lathrop, D., 187n2
Leavy, S., 133
LeShan, L., 292n2
letting go, 148–49, 256–
57, 286
Leuba, J. H., 138
Levin, J. D., 260n4

Levine, S., 201
Lévi-Strauss, Claude, 175
Lewin, R. A., 113n3
Lewis, C. A., 139
Lewis, C. S., 30
Lewis, M., 95
Lewis, T., 22, 89, 188n18
Lichtenberg, J. D., 149
life crisis, 6, 230. *See also*
   spiritual crisis
limbic system resonance,
   22, 181
liminality, 289–91
Lindberg, D. C., 34
Linley, A. P., 8
logotherapy, 293n4
London, P., 40
love, 195–96, 203–4, 215;
   analytic, 92; barriers to,
   94; definitions, 89–90;
   divine, 60, 123, 204; and
   power, 94; romantic,
   92–94; in the therapeutic
   relationship, 88–95;
   transpersonal, 90, 93
Lovinger, R. J., 46
Loy, D., 235
Lukoff, D., 5, 72, 74
Lynch, W. F., 107, 111
Lynn, S. J., 52, 69

Mahrer, A. R., 239
Maize, M., 117
Malony, H., 32
Mancia, M., 11
mandala, 129
Manheimer, E. D., 20
mania, 78
Mansfield, V., 235
Marcel, G., 107
marriage, 26, 39
Marsella, A. J., 247
Maslow, A. H., 1, 54, 144
masochism, 99, 123, 256
Masson, J., 140
materialism, in
   mainstream psychology
   and psychiatry, 6–7,
   9–11, 249
mathematics, 194
Matthews, D. A., 164

May, G. M., 116, 118, 131,
   151n3, 217, 224–27
McCarley, R. W., 58
McCullough, M. E., 5, 8,
   20, 95, 99
McFague, S., 126
McGrath, A., 48n6
McNamara, W., 223
meaninglessness, 266
medicine men and
   women, 5
meditation, 115, 118, 124,
   157, 164–65
Meier, C. A., 179
Meissner, W. W., 104–5,
   146, 152n9, 152n14
Meister Eckhart, 16n2,
   145, 153n18, 207
memory, 252
Meng, H., 152n12
Menninger, K., 106
Meyers, V., 70
Miller, A., 208
Miller, D. L., 81n6
Miller, W. R., 7, 105
Milton, John, 88
mind and body, 253,
   277–78
mind-body splitting, 277,
   279
Mintz, E. E., 81n4
mirror neurons, 17n4
mirroring, 197–98, 203
Mitchell, S., 110
Mitchison, G., 57
Mohammed, 24
Moore, R. L., 188n14
moral philosophy, 160
morality, 21; encoded in
   the brain, 37
Moretti, P., 70
Morris, T. V., 60
Moses, 24
mother, as lost object,
   170–71
Mother archetype,
   negative, 212
mountains, sacred, 128
Murphy, M., 115
Murphy, W., 117
Myers, D. G., 7

mystical experience, 54,
   79–80, 142
mystical perception, 63
mysticism, pathologized,
   78
mystics, 79, 259n1;
   Christian, 120–21,
   123–24, 235
myth, 60; Christian, 61
mythology, 61, 128, 174,
   178, 220n10, 243, 247,
   281, 290

narcissism, 44, 77, 99, 135,
   242; spiritual, 118
Natterson, D. L., 92
naturalism, 32
nature, as a manifestation
   of the divine, 58, 128
near-death experience,
   70, 73
Nebeker, R. S., 136
Neumann, E., 61, 212, 218
neurosis, 106–7, 139–40,
   273, 281
Nicholson, R. A., 207
Nietzsche, Friedrich, 105,
   126
Nobel, K. D., 79
nondual philosophy, 235;
   and suffering, 261–62
nonlocality, 11, 65, 230,
   241, 249
Numbers, R. L., 34
numinosum, 62–63,
   69–70, 75, 116, 171, 174,
   269, 280–81, 286
numinous experience,
   53–80, 226; of love,
   89; negative, 62; and
   psychosis, 69–72; and
   reality, 67

"O" (Bion's), 87–88
obsessive-compulsive
   behavior, and religious
   rituals, 139
Oedipus complex, 199,
   212, 250
Ogden, T., 110
Omran, A., 69

O'Neil, B., 117
Ornstein, A., 109
Otto, Rudolph, 53, 55, 62, 170
out-of-body experience, 73
Oxman, T. E., 20

pacifism, 48n6
pain, chronic, 28–30
panentheism, 259n1
Panikkar, R., 85
pantheism, 58
paranoia, 99
paranormal experience, 51–53
parapsychological phenomena, 52
Pargament, K. I., 2, 6, 24, 95
Parsons, T., 258
pastoral psychotherapists, 32, 165, 176
Pattison, M., 69
Payne, I. R., 36–37
Penfield, Wilder, 77
Perennial Philosophy, 4
Perry, J., 74–75
personal history, as sacred text, 172–73
personal mythology, 31, 35
personality, 244
Peteet, J. R., 26, 38
Phipps, J.-F., 89, 91
Pickering, W. S. F., 137
Plato, 88, 94
Pollner, M., 70
positivism, 31, 137, 249
possession, 50–51
prayer, 30, 120–21, 124, 164–66, 231–32
predator anxiety, 143, 208, 248
Prendergast, J. J., 235
priests and priestesses, 5; linked to healer, 168
Prinz, J. J., 48n9
professional codes, of behavior and ethics, 36
projective identification, 28, 52, 109, 112, 178, 181, 241, 254

Pruyser, P. W., 78, 146
psyche: Jungian model, 12; as a means of connection to the sacred, 66; sacramental, 13; and soul, 15; spiritual dimensions of, 4; transpersonal levels, 13
psychic unity, 240
psychoanalytic self psychology, 108, 147, 151, 190, 210, 248; and religious belief, 141–42
psychobiology, 12
psychologists, typically not religious, 31
psychology: distinct from spirituality, 15; reductionist views, 138; as a science, 160
psychopathology, 8, 74, 146, 151, 157, 161, 163, 170, 281; and spirituality, 171–72
psychopaths, 99, 215
psychosis, 69–75, 78
psychotherapy: in place of religion, 265; recognition of the spiritual dimension, 11–15; as a ritual, 174–76, 222; as a science, 33; and spirituality, 6–7; as spiritual direction, 221–22; different from spiritual direction, 223–24; technical training, 162, 227; use of spiritual techniques, 165–66
purgation, 119
Pytell, T., 293n4

quantum physics, 11, 64, 160, 169–70, 230, 249

Rachal, K. C., 99
racism, 218
Racker, H., 92
Radin, D. I., 52
Rafanelli, C., 7–8
rage, 95–97, 131, 215, 217

Raghavan, C., 69
Rajneesh, B. S., 201–2
Ramachandran, V. S., 82n16
Reading, A., 105
reality, 53, 67, 74; and love, 93–94; nondual model, 235; transcendent, 9, 15
Rector, L., 142
Reed, E. S., 160
Reed, H., 253
referrals, to clergy, 165
reincarnation, 272
religions, 13
religion: criticized, 21; and evolution, 137; incompatible with scientific naturalism and empiricism, 31; origins, 137–38; and science, 34, 140; as a social force, 16n1; as a source of violence, 48n6; and spirituality, 2–3, 21
religious conditioning, 3, 8
religious values, shared by patient and therapist, 35
resacralization, 1
Reymond, L., 47n2
Rhode, P. R., 190
Richards, P. S., 4, 7, 26, 36, 38, 40, 152n10, 165, 187n7, 187n9
ritual, traditional/religious, 61, 139
Rizzolatti, G., 17n4
Rizzuto, A.-M., 130–33
Roberts, B., 151n4, 259
Rochlin, G., 105
Rodrigo, A., 11
Rolls, E. T., 11
romantic theology, 94
Roseborough, D. J., 7
Rubin, J. B., 92, 115, 187n5
Rumi, 207
Russell, Bertrand, 189, 192–96
sacred experience, 9, 49–50, 116. See also spiritual

experience, numinous
experience
sacrifice, 183–86;
defensive, 185; human
and animal, 184–85
St. Ignatius of Loyola,
83n19
St. John of the Cross, 120,
123
St. Paul, 80, 89, 104
salvation, 42, 168
Samuels, A., 37
sand tray, 164
Sandner, D. F., 175
Sanella, L., 82n15
Sanford, J. A., 13, 58, 127
Sarver, R., 117
Satir, Virginia, 182
Saul, 168, 278
scandals, sexual and
financial among clergy,
21
Scarry, E., 48n4
Schaer, H., 152n17
schizophrenia, 65, 78–79
Schlitz, M., 73
Schott, G. D., 77
Schwartz, J. H., 9
Schwartz-Salant, N., 253
Schweitzer, Albert, 275
science: and religion, 34,
140; and spirituality, 34
scripture, 26, 96; reading,
12, 164–65
Searles, H. F., 180
Seidman, S. N., 7
Self, 67, 80, 122, 134,
163, 182–83, 197, 236;
dark side, 57, 62, 80,
151, 217, 219n6, 289;
mother as stand-in, 171;
relationship with, 135,
223; spiritual principle
in the psyche, 223
self: cultural differences,
246–47; insubstantial,
246; sense of, origins,
242–48
self-esteem, 133, 197,
202–3
Seligman, M., 8

Seneca, 213
sexual predators, 100
sexuality, 8, 26, 59, 140,
146–47, 149, 196, 217
shadow, 217–18
Shafranske, E. P., 26, 30,
32, 187n8
Shakespeare, William,
113n6
shamans, 5, 294n12
shamanic healing rituals,
174–76
shamanic journeying, 165
Shand, A. F., 105
Shapiro, A. K., 175
Sharfstein, B.-A., 219n1
Shaver, P. R., 143
Shaw, D., 92
Shelley, Percy Bysshe, 105
Shideler, M. M., 93
Siegel, R. D., 162
sin, 20, 41, 50, 82n14,
147, 153n20, 171, 185.
See also suffering, as a
punishment for sin
Sisyphus, 104, 281
Slater, J. G., 195
Slife, B. D., 136
Smith, C. M., 34, 82n13
Smith, N. L. and L. L.,
235
somatization, 30
Sommer, K. L., 95
Sontag, S., 293n8
Sophocles, 213
soul, 150; and body, 158;
and spirit, 157–58;
traditional meaning,
155
Spanos, N. P., 70
Spero, M. H., 35, 117
Sperry, L., 26, 30
Spiegleman, J., 235
Spilka, B. P., 133
spiritual abuse, 44
spiritual advice, and
character structure,
173–74
spiritual assessment,
formal, in therapy, 27–28
spiritual bypassing, 101

spiritual crisis, 5, 7. See also
life crisis
spiritual development,
stages, 118
spiritual emergency,
73–75; and spiritual
emergence, 73
spiritual escapism, 117
spiritual essence, names
for, 98
spiritual experience,
10–11, 14
spiritual maturation,
psychological correlates,
116
spirituality: forms of,
1–3; as a motivational
force, 149–51; origins,
136–38; as personal
myth, 20; personal
versus collective, 8–9;
and psychology, 15; in
psychotherapy literature,
26; and religion, 2–3,
21; and science, 34; and
sense of self, 3; talked
about in therapy, 45;
useful, 8
Sprinkle, R. L., 240
Sri Anirvan, 47n2
Stace, W., 59
Starbuck, Edwin, 82n14
Stark, R. A., 49
Stein, H. F., 133
Stephens, B. D., 82n11
Stern, D. N., 259n3
Stern, E. M., 187n2
Sternberg, R. J., 89
Stevens, A., 81n3
Strupp, H. H., 35
subtle body, 71; and
spirituality, 22–23
suffering, 5–7, 9, 19–20,
167–70, 180–81; as a
challenge to spirituality,
262–63; childhood
experiences, 272; and
development of the
personality, 275–77;
fear of, 291; healing
potential, 23; in the

suffering *(cont.)*
Judeo-Christian
tradition, 288; and
meaning, 261–73;
nondual approach,
255–59; as a punishment
for sin, 24–26, 176, 270,
288–89; reactions to,
287–88, 290; religious
traditions' response to,
24
Sufism, 63, 235
superego, 26
surrender, 256–58. *See also*
letting go
Suttie, I. D., 92; on
religion, 141
symbols, 226
synchronicity, 63–65, 73,
179, 229, 231
synchronistic connections,
within the therapeutic
couple, 236
Sysko, R., 7
Szasz, Thomas, 187n1

Tamayo, A., 139
Tan, S.-Y., 11, 187n7,
187n8, 221
Taoism, 129, 199, 235
Tarasoff rule, 215
Targ, E., 73
Tecoma, E., 82n16
theism, 4; traditional God-
image, 9
theory, in psychotherapy,
250–55
therapists: and archetype
of the Healer, 177–83;
atheist or agnostic,
31–32; capacity for love,
91, 162; as spiritual
directors, 44, 163; as
spiritual directors, ethical
and legal issues, 163; and
spiritual orientation, 23,
168; as wounded healer,
177–79
Thompson, C., 92

Thoreson, C. E., 95
Tillich, Paul, 86
Tjelveit, A. C., 36
Tolpin, P. and M., 266
transcendence, 23, 66,
167, 271
transference, 91–92, 164,
228, 232; idealizing, 40,
163–64, 166, 199, 203–5,
221–22, 232; negative,
100, 183, 232
transpersonal dimension,
9. *See also* psyche,
transpersonal levels
transpersonal Self, 4, 118–
19, 125–28, 162, 222. *See
also* Self
treatment plans, 37, 94,
258
trees, sacred, 128
tribalism, 80
trust, 189–90
truth, 88, 191, 251
Turner, Victor, 290–91
twinship, 80, 198, 203

Ulanov, A. B., 127
Ullman, C., 82n14, 142
unconscious, 9, 11, 13–14
underworld, descent into,
282–85
union with the divine, 59,
124–25, 142–43
unus mundus, 64, 229
Usandivaras, R. J., 188n14

values, 36–40; clash
between religious and
psychological, 39, 43,
150
van de Castle, R., 233n2
van Lommel, P., 70
van Wees, R., 70
Vaughan, F., 201
Vellacott, P., 213–15,
219n7
Vergote, A., 130, 139
violence, 10
violent beliefs, 43–44

visions, 25, 50, 53–54, 60,
71, 266, 270
visualization, 164
vocation, 198–99, 227
voices, 50, 71, 77
von Franz, M.-L., 51,
82n10, 217, 275
voodoo death, 103

Walsh, B. T., 7
Wapnick, K., 53, 72
Watts, A., 111
Weathers, R. S., 76
Weis, K., 89
Wells, M., 42
Welwood, J., 101
West, W., 164, 222
Wheeler, J. A., 188n12
White, William Alanson,
106
Whitehead, Alfred North,
67
Whitmont, E. C., 169
Whittington, J. E., 7
Wiesner, I. S., 6
Williams, Charles, 94
Winnicott, D. W., 91, 106,
131, 188n15
Winson, J., 58
Witztum, E., 72, 139
Wong, P. T., 7
Wong, S. H., 175
work ethic, Puritan or
Calvinist, 147–48
Worthington, E. L., Jr.,
95, 99
Wulff, D. M., 69, 76,
82n17

Yahine, C. E., 105
Yates, C., 126
yoga, 157, 187n5, 195

Zaehner, R. C., 58
Zeus, 210–11, 214, 217
Zieger, A., 105
Zinnbauer, B. J., 2
Zinner, E., 117
Zock, H., 152n15

CPSIA information can be obtained
at www.ICGtesting.com
Printed in the USA
LVOW04*0426150416

483750LV00005B/14/P